William Scott

The Florists' Manual

A Reference Book for Commerical Florists

William Scott

The Florists' Manual
A Reference Book for Commerical Florists

ISBN/EAN: 9783337107444

Printed in Europe, USA, Canada, Australia, Japan

Cover: Foto ©Andreas Hilbeck / pixelio.de

More available books at **www.hansebooks.com**

THE
FLORISTS' MANUAL

...BY...

WILLIAM SCOTT.

A

REFERENCE BOOK

FOR

COMMERCIAL FLORISTS.

ILLUSTRATED.

PRICE, FIVE DOLLARS.

CHICAGO:
FLORISTS' PUBLISHING COMPANY.
1899.

.....INTRODUCTION.....

HE author of the following pages would never have assumed to instruct his brother florists, however limited their experience might be, had not he received many flattering comments on his cultural notes which appeared in the American Florist, and later in the Florists' Review. These notes were well received, even by men who were able to teach the author, and brought to my busy desk hundreds of inquiries on a wide range of subjects, which I found were beginning to be a great tax on my time.

Being made with that disposition which gratifies itself when any favor can be bestowed, we determined in an unguarded moment to compile our knowledge of commercial plants into a volume, and if those who favor us with a perusal of its pages glean only one hint which may help them in their business they will have received value for their money and we shall feel highly gratified aside from any pecuniary reward. We are one of those who esteem the respect and approbation of our fellow men, and particularly those in our own calling, far above riches, but if a substantial reward is sent us for our labors we shall again be grateful.

A friend of venerable age, with some experience as a writer, a student of horticultural lore, told me last winter that a business man should not attempt to be a literary man. We scarcely even then realized the truth of his words as we have the past three months. We scarcely knew at the start what a task we had undertaken. The writing has been done at odd hours snatched from business cares, and no little midnight oil, or rather gas, has helped the book along.

It was difficult to determine the limit of the book, but as will be apparent few plants are noticed but those of commercial value, and those only in a strictly commercial way. Had we known of any work giving plain cultural directions for our leading plants this book would not have been begun. My own business embraces nearly every branch, from selling a bunch of violets over the counter to planting a tree or seeding a lawn or building a greenhouse, and therefore we have with confidence touched on several features of the business besides the growing.

This book was never intended for men who have made specialties of a few plants with great success. Being specialists they have reduced their business to a science and make no mistakes, but they are few compared to the great army of florists who grow and retail and have to handle a great variety of plants. Many of these are not graduates of horticultural establishments but have left some other calling to engage in floriculture. Another class is the young man who has been brought up in places where the rose or carnation, or perhaps palms, was the specialty and where the opportunity of observing the care or culture of other plants was limited. To such a one we believe this book will be of service.

Looking back over thirty years' experience in this country we are amazed and gratified at the enormous strides the business of floriculture has made, and why should the limit be yet reached? We believe with confidence that the use of flowers and plants is yet to grow tenfold. They are the handmaid of refinement, good taste and real gentility, all of which is blessing the mass of the people more and more. We believe that our florist shop keepers and their clerks could imbibe a little more knowledge of the plants they handle without any detriment to their health or prosperity.

We wish to acknowledge to Mr. W. H. Taplin the several valuable articles on choice palms, ferns and cycads which bear his initials. It must be acknowledged that there is no better authority than Mr. Taplin on those special plants. For the very practical chapter on commercial Orchids we are indebted to Mr. Wm. Hewson, who handles a cattleya with the freedom, quickness and success that some men do a geranium. To my good friend John F. Cowell, Director of our Botanic Gardens, I am indebted for access to and hints on his collection of Nepenthes, Bromeliads, etc. The remainder of the pages are my own experience and observation.

If you think there is sometimes a little extraneous matter that is not connected with the subject, and may be called frivolous, don't blame the author, he could not help it no matter however much he tried to suppress it; occasionally there had to be a slight relief from the dry monotony of the subject.

And last the author owes much to Mr. G. L. Grant, the publisher, who has so ably put the matter in form and finely illustrated many of the subjects.

With a fervent wish that with all its imperfections these pages will be appreciated by many, I remain, with some confidence and much hope,

Yours very sincerely,

WILLIAM SCOTT.

Whatever ability I may possess in the glorious field
of horticulture, although far less than my early oppor-
tunities afforded, I inherited from my beloved father,
who was a good man and a great gardener, and to whose
memory, with reverence, I dedicate these pages.

WILLIAM SCOTT.

CONTENTS.

THE
FLORISTS' MANUAL.

ILLUSTRATED.

A Reference Book for Commercial Florists.

ABUTILON.

Greenhouse shrubs with drooping, bell-shaped flowers, ranging in color from pure white to crimson and purple, mostly erect in growth. A few of the species will endure a few degrees of frost, but they are best treated as cool greenhouse plants during our winters. The hybrids now both in beauty of leaf and flower far surpass the true species. They are largely used in sub-tropical flower gardening, growing very freely in our warm summers and are fine ornamental plants for the conservatory, and can either be grown as specimen plants in pots or trained to pillars or rafters. As a commercial plant, except for flower gardening, they are not of great value, being strong growers and occupying too much room for their value.

They are easiest propagated from the young tender growths. If desirable to increase your stock in the fall, September is the best month, keeping the sand very moist and not allowing the cuttings to wilt from the heat or sun. The plants lift from the open ground perfectly in October and if cut back during the winter will give you lots of cuttings which root most easily in the ordinary propagating bed.

A. vexillarium is a drooping species and used largely in hanging baskets, veranda boxes and carpet bedding. For a drooping plant for a vase they should be propagated in September from the young shoots of plants growing outside. By spring these should be in 3-in. pots and are most useful for the purpose described.

Abutilons are troubled with few enemies. The hose will keep down mealy bug, and aphis seldom appear. Any soil that water passes freely through will grow abutilons, but much manure should be avoided, as most of the kinds are very free growers. The following varieties are fine decorative plants: Savitzii, green and white foliage; Mrs. J. Laing, strong grower, flowers bright rose; Souvenir de Bonn, variegated foliage, orange flowers; Infanta Eulalie, compact grower for pots, flowers pink; Boule de Niege,

pure white; Thompsoni plena, free blooming double orange.

ACACIA.

A very large genus of shrubs or trees. Those of most commercial value are from temperate regions, South Australia and New South Wales. Some of the species, armata, for instance, make neat, compact plants for pot culture, while pubescens, one of the most graceful of all, is splendidly adapted for training on a pillar or wall of a light, cool house. A temperature of 45 degrees in winter will suit the commercial species, but their flowering can be hastened several weeks by more heat and at all times an abundance of water. They are

most free flowering and the prevailing colors are lemon and yellow. In a temperature of 45 to 50 degrees most of the species flower from February to May. A good loam with a fourth of leaf-mould or in the absence of the latter, Jadoo, will grow any of the acacias, but the soil should always be in that condition from proper drainage that water passes freely through it.

They are propagated from the half ripened wood in May or June, that is, the shoots made the previous spring. Place the cuttings in pans of sand or leaf-mould and sand and place the pans in a cold-frame, which shade on hot days and keep close till growth begins. When rooted, pot off and grow

Acacia Pubescens.

1

on in a cold frame. During the following winter keep in a cool house and after danger of frost shift into larger pots and plunge outside, where they must be well supplied with water. They should be stopped as soon as they grow in the spring to induce a branching growth. Although their propagation is not difficult, it will be found by the majority of our florists more profitable to import those plants that are wanted for our spring sales, as the price of well grown, compact plants is very low and they endure the passage without the slightest injury. Any plants unsold after flowering

ACALYPHA.

A genus of tropical shrubs that are grown entirely for the attractiveness of the leaves excepting the very recent introduction, A. Sanderi, which has long, cylindrical, pendulous flowers and is very ornamental. The acalypha is grown largely in Europe as an ornamental stove plant, but with us its chief value is as a summer bedding plant for mixed borders or sub-tropical beds. As most all the species are from the tropical islands of the Pacific, their requirements can be judged accordingly.

Acanthophoenix Crinita.

should be cut back severely, shifted if needed, and plunged outside during summer. Few insects of any kind, attack the acacia; plenty of water at all times and syringing except when in flower is what they want.

A. pubescens is not adapted for pot culture, but is the most graceful of all the genus, and for cutting as sprays is most valuable. It should be planted out either as a standard or against a pillar or wall. The most valuable species for pot culture for the commercial florist is armata, small globular flowers which cover the whole plant; dealbata, strong grower with handsome yellow racemes; Drummondi, a fine compact plant with drooping, cylindrical lemon colored flowers. There are hundreds of species, most all worthy of a place in a conservatory, but the few species mentioned above are the best for commercial use.

The most economical way to produce plants for spring use is to lift a few old plants before any danger of frost. These could be used for decorating till January, then shorten back the shoots, and if the plants are in a strong heat they will soon give you a number of young growths, which root readily in the sand in a good bottom heat and by end of May, if kept warm, will be just what you want for planting out in spring. A well enriched loam is all they want.

There are half a dozen or more desirable species and varieties which give a variety of bronze, brown, green, red, orange and carmine, blotched and variegated, making them very ornamental for summer gardening.

ACANTHOPHOENIX.

A. crinita is a remarkably handsome warm house palm that has been in cultivation for the past thirty years,

but is still rather an uncommon species. It has much the habit of growth of an areca, the leaves being pinnate, the leaflets long and drooping, and the plant in general very graceful in appearance.

One of the characteristics that distinguish acanthophoenix from areca is very distinct in the species in question, namely, the fact that the former is abundantly supplied with long blackish spines all along the stems, while no true areca bears spines, and in addition to this the under side of the leaves of A. crinita is silvery white. The latter peculiarity doubtless accounted for an erroneous name under which this palm was once introduced, that is, Calamus dealbata.

Being a native of Seychelles, and probably of low moist land near the coast of that island, we find that this palm is best suited under stove culture, a night temperature of 70 degrees and plenty of water being among the chief essentials to its welfare, while a rather light and well drained soil seems to give the best results.

In common with palms in general that require warm treatment, there is the ever-present probability of finding some injurious insects on acanthophoenix, the most likely pests being scale and, unless well syringed, also red spider, but with proper attention these pests may be kept down, and so beautiful a palm is worthy of a little extra attention in the line of cleanliness.

Seeds are the only means of propagation for A. crinita, and as the seeds of this species sometimes take over two years to germinate, it is scarcely probable that this palm will become popular for trade purposes. W. H. T.

ACER JAPONICUM (JAPAN MAPLE.)

The Japan maples are now grown in pots for conservatory decoration, and many are sold and forced for Easter. They are largely imported, but can also be obtained from American nurseries. Being perfectly hardy they can be procured in the fall and stored away in a cold-pit till they are wanted to pot and force. Give them two months in the house from time of potting till they are wanted in full leaf. If forced rapidly they are more likely to wilt when exposed to cold wind or dryness.

While I have alluded to these in the article on "Trees and Shrubs" I will add here that they are most beautiful little ornamentals for the lawn, either in groups or singly. They proved during the last unusually long, cold winter to be entirely hardy, coming through the winter unhurt and without the slightest protection.

There are several varieties of A. Japonicum, the foliage shaded from yellow to blood red, and all are worth growing.

ACHILLEA.

This is a large genus of hardy perennials, many of them suitable for the

done gradually withhold water till the foliage is entirely gone, then store away under a warm, dry bench till the following spring. In starting them in the spring shake out of the old soil entirely. They are propagated by cuttings, pieces of the stem growing freely in the spring with bottom heat; also by seed, sown in early spring. The beginner had, however, better buy the roots from a seedsman.

Although not of commercial value the achimines is a splendid plant for a private greenhouse during the summer months. There is a score of species, nearly all from tropical America, and from these hundreds of hybrid varieties. And it is the hybrids that are cultivated.

ACHYRANTHES.

See Bedding Plants.

ACROPHYLLUM.

A small evergreen shrub that is valuable for the private conservatory, flowering freely during the spring months. It is at home in a cool greenhouse but must not be exposed to frost. In summer it can be plunged outside. They require shifting as they grow, which should be done before they flower in spring. They can be propagated from the half-ripened wood in May and June. Like most of the Australian plants they thrive in a good coarse loam. A. venosum is the only species, which bears dense spikes of pinkish white flowers.

ADIANTUM.

For the most useful commercial adiantums see the article on Ferns, in which all the most important commercial ferns are treated collectively. The following adiantum notes are by Mr. W. H. Taplin:

A. LEGRANDI. The maidenhair family includes a wonderful variety in both size and form, and a collection embracing all the distinct forms grown into specimens would occupy a very large house.

A. Legrandi belongs to the dwarf section, the stipes or stems being usually but a few inches in length and the fronds very compact and closely clothed with small pinnae. In fact the growth in small plants is so close and overlapping that the foliage is quite subject to damping off unless the house in which it is grown is kept well ventilated.

Regarding the origin of this fern but little is known, and it seems probable that it is a seedling variation from Adiantum Pecottii, which it very much resembles, the chief distinction apparently being found in the longer leaf stems of A. Legrandi, while both varieties present the same dark green color of the foliage. As a trade fern A. Legrandi has not become prominent, and as a matter of fact it is less frequently seen in trade collections now than it was a few years ago, the demand in this line being confined to

Vase of Achillea the Pearl.

border and many are very valuable for the rockwork, but of little use to the florist. The one most useful to the florist and deserving special notice is "The Pearl." This little plant will thrive in any soil, is absolutely hardy, and should be in every florist's garden. It flowers in July and August.

It is most useful as a cut flower, and we have found it of great service in design work when short of carnations. The plants spread rapidly and every third or fourth year they should be lifted, divided, and replanted in more compact rows in the garden. This can be done in early spring and you will not lose the following summer's crop of flowers.

The plant is remarkably free flowering, it being just a mass of the small heads of white blooms, but what makes it of more than ordinary value is the good stem you can cut with the flowers.

ACHIMINES.

Hot-house herbaceous perennial tuberous-rooted plants that are held in high esteem in the gardens of Eu-

rope but seldom seen here. They are usually grown in pans from 6 to 12 inches across and 4 inches deep. They should have drainage and the compost should be a good light loam to which has been added a fourth of leaf-mould and rotted manure. They like neither a stagnant moisture nor a heavy soil.

Although not at all likely to become popular as a commercial plant they are by no means difficult to grow. The small soft roots should be planted in the pans about one inch apart in February or March, pressing the roots into the soil half an inch below the surface, and started growing in a temperature of 60 degrees. Later on, as spring advances, any house will do for them. Shade from the hottest suns. As they grow they like an abundance of water, and being subject to greenfly and red spider they must be lightly but regularly fumigated, and up to flowering time give them a daily syringing.

They are, however well grown, entirely useless unless each stem is tied to a small stake. They last a long time in flower. When flowering is

bright pink in color, finally changing to deep green.

The pinnae of the fertile fronds are usually smaller, the spores being found in an almost continuous band around the margin. These spores germinate fairly well if carefully gathered and preserved, and the young plants thus secured are much better than those obtained from division of the old crowns, as they grow more freely and in better form.

No special difficulty is experienced in the culture of A. macrophyllum, the main features being a moderately light soil, good drainage, and the glass shaded throughout the greater portion of the year. In regard to temperature, the same may be given as to A. Farleyense, namely, from 65 to 70 degrees at night, and also like the latter variety it may be said that A. macrophyllum does not like a strong draught over the young foliage while unfolding, else it is likely to be crippled, though after the fronds of this species are fully hardened they will stand quite a good deal of exposure without injury.

A. macrophyllum is a native of the West Indies and tropical America, and has been in cultivation for a little more than a century, though yet uncommon in trade collections.

A. MUNDULUM. This is one of the many interesting and useful forms of Adiantum cuneatum, and is correctly termed Adiantum cuneatum mundu-

Adiantum Legrandi.

ferns that are more sturdy and less brittle.

The culture of A. Legrandi presents no special difficulty, apart from the liability to damping that has already been alluded to, and by keeping the water off the foliage and giving free ventilation, the trouble from this cause may be reduced greatly.

In getting up specimens of these small growing adiantums for exhibition purposes, it is a good plan to group several young plants in a pan about 10 inches in diameter, and a shapely plant may thus be formed in a few months by treating them in the same manner as one would A. cuneatum for a similar purpose.

A. MACROPHYLLUM. This is one of the most distinct of the large family of maidenhair ferns, and as a matter of fact to many persons to whom the idea of a maidenhair fern is associated with the light and airy fronds of A. cuneatum, the rather stiff and heavy looking leaves of this species would seem to belong to an entirely different genus.

The large pinnated species of adiantum, among which we find A. macrophyllum, A. peruvianum, A. Seemannii and A. Wilsonii, form a very interesting group, and one which adds greatly to the beauty and variety of a collection of ferns. Adiantum macrophyllum is a moderate growing species, the fronds being erect, from one to two feet high, simple pinnate, and having stiff black stems.

The pinnae of the barren fronds are very large, being frequently three to four inches long, by about two inches wide, and when first unfolding are

Adiantum Macrophyllum.

lum. The varietal name, which signifies neat, is well applied in this case, the plant being of dwarf and compact habit, and is better adapted for small ferneries than as an exhibition plant.

The fronds of A. c. mundulum are shorter and rather stiffer than those of the parent form, not often more than nine or ten inches long, very dark green, and closely furnished with narrow, wedge-shaped pinnae. In general outline the fronds are deltoid, and when well matured they possess sufficient substance to be useful in cut flower work, where a small frond is required.

A. c. mundulum comes true from spores, and also germinates freely, the spores being produced abundantly on old plants. and it flourishes under the same treatment as A. cuneatum, thus being by no means difficult to manage.

Nicely grown plants in 3-inch pots are very short and bushy, and may be used to advantage where A. cuneatum proves too tall, and if the plants are not soft when used, will possibly last a little longer than the last named fern, under the same conditions.

A. c. mundulum is of garden origin, and although in cultivation since 1879, is not frequently met with in the trade, in fact, seems scarcer now than it was ten years ago, no doubt owing to the greater demand for ferns of more endurance than is found among the maidenhairs in general.

A. TETRAPHYLLUM. Among the less common species of maidenhair ferns, Adiantum tetraphyllum is deserving of special mention, and some idea of its general outline may be had from the illustration which accompanies this note. But, unfortunately, an ordinary photograph fails to show us the fine distinctions of coloring that present themselves in the living plant, and in consequence we are compelled to fall back upon cold type for our descriptions.

The plant in question has been found in fern collections for many years past, and has produced an occasional variation in form from time to time, though it is not a notably prolific species, perhaps the best of these variations from the type being that known as A. tetraphyllum gracile, in which the pinnae are rather narrower than those of the original species and the

Adiantum Mundulum.

young fronds show a higher coloring than is found on the type.

A. tetraphyllum may be classed as a moderate grower, the fronds reaching a height of 12 to 15 inches, and are usually four times divided, or rather divided into four segments. While unfolding the young fronds are frequently bright pink, this color gradually fading as the frond develops, until the mature leaf becomes dark green.

This species prefers warm house treatment, is evergreen, and grows best in a rather loose and open compost. It requires plenty of water at the root, but during the winter especially should not be watered overhead frequently, or the fronds are liable to become rusty. Snails seem to have a special liking for the young foliage of A. tetraphyllum, and close watching is required to get the best of these pests.

A. WIEGANDII. A few years since a much greater variety of ferns seemed to be grown for florists' use than is now found among the large trade growers. It is evidently a case of the survival of the fittest, or rather of the species and varieties that may be produced in large quantities with a minimum expenditure of time and labor. Adiantum Wiegandii is one of those varieties that has almost disappeared within a few years, though it is not a particularly tender fern, or one that is difficult to reproduce.

Adiantum Tetraphyllum.

We mention it as a variety rather than a species, because it seems probable that this fern is a form of Adiantum capillus-veneris, or else a cross between that species and A. cuneatum, its origin being somewhat obscure. But be this as it may, the fern in question is a very attractive plant of dwarf and sturdy growth, the fronds being almost upright, having black stems and rather large pinnae that are inclined to be cristate.

A. Wiegandii is compact in habit and in a large plant reaches a height

Adiantum Wiegandii.

of 12 to 15 inches, and holds its foliage in good condition during the winter. This fern comes freely from spores, the latter being plentifully borne by plants a year old and upwards, and the seedlings soon become satisfactory plants in 3-inch pots if treated in the same manner as A. cuneatum, a night temperature of 60 degrees being a proper mark at which to carry these ferns.

But little trouble is experienced from "damping" of the foliage with A. Wiegandii during the winter, even when grown quite close together, the regular use of the hose having less effect upon this fern than is often found with adiantums of low and compact habit. Thoroughly matured fronds stand well when cut, and the small plants will last longer than those of A. cuneatum in a fern pan, providing they are not used in too soft a condition.

AECHMEA.

See Bromeliads.

AERIDES.

See Orchids.

AGAPANTHUS.

A genus of strong growing, handsome greenhouse plants which do well out of doors during summer, and when the winter where there is not more than 10 degrees of frost. In the south of England A. umbellatus does well planted out of doors, with us it requires large pots or tubs and thrives in a well enriched coarse loam. In summer you cannot well over water them. In winter they can be stored under a bench in a cool house and will then require very little water. But be careful after so keeping them all winter not to expose them to a late spring frost or they will suffer and their beauty be marred for the whole summer. They grow very fast and can be rapidly multiplied by division.

The varieties are all from A. umbellatus, introduced into Europe from South Africa two centuries ago. Its erect stem and showy umbel of bright blue flowers is familiar to all. The best known varieties are albidus, pure white; aureus, leaves striped; variegatus, smaller but finely variegated leaves; and maximus, a blue of the largest size, as its name denotes.

AGAVE.

This noble genus includes a great number of species, one of them at least being known to every one—the well known "Century Plant." All the species have one characteristic; when fully matured they send up a stately flower spike from the center of the crown of leaves and then die. This is the case with the great majority, although there are a few that continue to flower year after year. They are almost all from Mexico, and one or two from South America and one or two from our extreme southwestern states.

There is a widespread fallacy in connection with Agave Americana. It is popularly supposed that they live 100 years and then flower and die, hence the familiar name. They will not flower till they have made their full growth, but that may be 50 years or 75 years. We remember a pair of A. Americana that we had watched from infancy, one the plain green and one variegated. They were of immense weight, each weighing a ton or more with the large tub and soil. About 1856 they both flowered and sent their candelabra-like spikes 25 feet in the air. It was a remarkable co-incidence that both showed flower the same season as no one knew their ages and the one who had taken them as suckers from the parent plant was long gone from his field of labor.

Within 40 years there have been several distinct and beautiful species discovered in Mexico, some of which have not yet flowered and no knowledge of their flower is available. Most of the species are stemless, but not all, their fleshy leaves radiating symmetrically from near the base of the plant. Nicholson's Dictionary of Gardening enumerates nearly one hundred species and then states there are many more which it is not worth while to describe as there is only one specimen of each in cultivation. They vary in size from 18 inches in height and the same in width to the majestic species of 10 feet in diameter.

The smaller species make beautiful plants for the greenhouse or for outdoor decoration, and the large species are noble objects for the adornment of large grounds but get very heavy and awkward to handle when of any considerable size. Few plants will put up with the rough treatment that is often given the agave. Their thick, succulent leaves provide them with the means of resisting long periods of drought.

The same general treatment will suit all the species. A well drained pot or tub, with good turfy loam; add leaf-mould or sand if heavy. They will stand the strongest sun out of doors and should receive plenty of water. In winter, if you wish merely to store them for next season's growth they will do very well in any cool house or even shed, but must not freeze, and when the temperature is low they will do without water for weeks. They are easily propagated by suckers, which you have only to cut off and pot.

The rarer species are too expensive for the commercial florist and in too little demand, and the larger species require too much labor and room to be of any profit; they are best left in the hands of the private gardener.

AGERATUM.

Since the wane of the carpet bedding and the return of the popular flowering plants to flower garden favor the ageratum has been in constant demand. A. Mexicanum is the only species in which we are interested. By selection many improvements have been made, a more spreading and dwarf plant has been produced as well as a variation in color. It is well to try the new varieties as they are disseminated as they are very inexpensive and frequently great improvements on existing varieties.

I have found that when propagated by cuttings for a few years a variety will often lose its character and gradually revert back to the original type. If I were asked what was the easiest of all plants to propagate I would say that the ageratum was absolutely the one, and so it is. Nothing but the most willful neglect will cause a batch of cuttings to fail. New varieties are, of course, raised from seed, which can be sown in January and the seedlings will flower freely by the following June.

It is by cuttings that our varieties are perpetuated. Lift a few old plants and pot into 5 or 6-inch pots before frost. Keep them cool and light till after Christmas, when you can begin propagating. It is well, however, not to propagate too early as the plants get stunted when not shifted on and it does not by any means pay to have this cheap bedding plant in larger than 3-inch, or at most 4-inch pots. The cuttings root freely with or without bottom heat and the plants grow rapidly in a temperature of 50 degrees. Their only enemy is red spider, which must be kept down by frequent syringing and the weekly fumigation.

New varieties of both the blue and white are being constantly sent out. The dwarf, compact sorts are the most valuable. The variegated variety of Mexicanum is of little value.

ALLAMANDA.

Few plants bring back childhood's days more vividly than the showy allamanda. Though not a commercial florist's flower it hardly has a rival as a hot-house climber. The leaves are sharp-pointed, oblong, and come three or four in a whorl. The flowers are funnel shaped, 3 to 5 inches across and rich yellow. Allamandas are usually seen trained near the roof where they do well and add greatly to the beauty of the house. They are also grown as specimens trained to a balloon-shaped or flat wire frame 3 or 4 feet high. In a competition for a number of flowering stove and green-

house plants in any horticultural exhibition in Europe the allamanda would be sure to be one. The only use the florist could make of the flowers, rich and fine as they are, would be to take sprays of the vine covered with flowers for the decoration of mirrors or chandeliers. For an elaborate golden wedding they would be a glorious acquisition.

Plants covering a large roof space would need a tub, and I have seen them planted in the border at the end of the house. A turfy loam with a sixth of cow manure, adding a tenth of charcoal to the compost, suits them well. They are from Equatorial America, so you will know what they want in temperature. Most of the species one of the finest, flowers in August and September. They are little troubled by insects of any kind, syringing and fumigating keeping them clean without any trouble. In the spring and summer they want lots of water; in the darker winter months much less. In our hot summers they require shade from the brightest sun, but only

enough to keep them from burning. They like the light, which they get in abundance when trained to the roof. In the late winter months, before they begin to grow, they should be pruned back as we do our hot-house grape vines, cutting back the previous year's growth to two or three eyes. If you wish to propagate them the last foot

or so of the last year's growth will root easily in our ordinary propagating benches where there is a little bottom heat, making each cutting with two or three eyes. Remember they are from the tropics and should not be exposed to a lower temperature than 60 degrees at any time of the year.

Of the several species and hybrids the following can be selected as the best: A. Chelsonii, yellow, large, flowers in July; A. grandiflora, pale yellow, large, flowers in June; A. nobilis, bright yellow, large, flowers in July; A. Schottii, yellow, throat striped with brown, very free bloomer, the best known and best for all purposes.

ALOCASIA.

These beautiful stove plants are grown entirely for the beauty of their leaves. They delight in our hot summers under glass and must be allowed to go below 60 degrees in the winter months. They require shade in the bright days of spring and summer, and where the house is heavily shaded they will be greatly benefited

Alocasia Metallica.

by a little fire heat at night. In shaded houses during rainy weather and cold nights, even in summer, there is a dampness and stagnation that is very uncongenial to most plants, and exotics in particular should have a little fire heat.

The compost in which they delight is one-third fibrous peat or Jadoo, one-third turfy loam in coarse lumps and one-third chopped sphagnum, to which add some charcoal. Although the roots delight in moisture it must not be stagnant around them, and the pots should be filled within a few inches of the rim with broken crocks. Keep the roots and the potting material well above the edge of the pot and cover the surface of the compost with live sphagnum, in which the young roots thrive. They must be given an abundance of water in summer, but much less in winter. It is not only the water they receive on the surface that benefits them, but they require a humid, warm atmosphere.

The best time to increase your stock of alocasias is in the spring by dividing the stems or rhizomes, which when first taken off and started should have a close, moist and warm temperature and be away from all draughts of air. A Wardian case on the greenhouse bench with some bottom heat is the ideal place.

The leaves are large, from one to two feet in length. All are beautiful, varying in coloring and markings from the well known A. metallica or cuprea, a dark metallic bronze, to A. longiloba, green with silvery markings. Among the best species and hybrids are those above mentioned and A. hybrida, A. Jenningsii, A. Johnstonii, A. Sedenii, A. Thibautiana, A. variegata, and many others, all beautiful plants for the private collection.

ALOYSIA CITRIODORA.

This universally liked plant is commercially known the world over as Lemon Verbena. It is classed as a deciduous shrub and is the sole representative of the genus. Where hardy I doubt whether it is quite deciduous. It makes a fine plant when planted against the wall or pillar in the greenhouse, but it is as a sweet scented plant for our gardens that we most prize it, and every mixed border, and every garden large or small has one or more. The florist finds this a most useful plant for cutting in the summer time, for what can be more welcome in a bunch of flowers than a few sprays of the sweet Lemon Verbena.

Don't sell out clean in the spring. Save a dozen plants and shift them on, plunging them outside in pots in summer. At the approach of frost bring them in and stand them under your lightest and coolest bench and give them only water enough to keep the wood from shrivelling. In early February we shake them out, shorten back the unripened and weak wood and start them going again in fresh soil and pots, with us a 4-inch. Placed in a temperature of 55 degrees, in a few weeks they are covered with young growths which are just the thing for cuttings. They root easily but not nearly so surely as many of the soft-wooded plants. I prefer the sand to be a little warmer than the house. Keep the sand well soaked, twice a day is not too often, and never let the cuttings wilt from the sun or dryness.

In April we shift them from a 2-inch to a 3-inch pot and plunge in a mild hot-bed, where by the middle of May, with one pinching, they will have made fine, bushy plants. They want lots of syringing to prevent red spider, and if the proper fumigation is regularly given they will not be troubled with fly. A florist should always be supplied with them for they are usually difficult to procure when wanted.

ALTERNANTHERA.

It seems as though it would have been almost impossible to carry out the wonderful designs in carpet bedding had we not had these little plants to serve us. Carpet bedding came into its greatest popularity shortly after the introduction of the alternanthera, some 30 years ago. It may be that their great fitness for that style of bedding helped to make it popular. Certain it is that alternantheras owe their popularity to carpet bedding. Nothing troubles the alternanthera but cold weather. They are all tropical plants, growing freely in our warm summer months but only just existing in the greenhouse during winter in a temperature of 60 degrees.

They are propagated by divisions or cuttings. In the former method the plants are lifted from the beds after the first slight frost, and after their tops are shortened and trimmed up they are stored away in a few inches of soil in flats. After the first good watering they are best kept rather dry till the following April, when they can be torn to pieces and either potted singly or again planted in flats and started growing in a warm, light house, or what is better, a hot-bed. Where very large quantities are needed the old plants are generally depended upon. Where only a few thousand are needed I prefer the cuttings.

Prepare some flats two inches deep and any convenient size, in which have one inch of light soil and one inch of sand. About the middle of August take off the cuttings from the plants outside and put them thickly in the sand. In a few days in the greenhouse they will be rooted and can be kept on any bench or stood out of doors till cold weather arrives. In the flats they will winter well and are little trouble. Keep them rather dry during the dark days and away from cold and damp. When potted off in April and placed in a hot-bed they make splendid little plants by bedding out time. They root and thrive like the proverbial "weed" if kept warm.

There is no trouble in wintering any of them except the one that is the most valuable, which is known in many places as A. paronychioides major, but which I feel sure is A. paronychioides magnifica, which is much the highest colored of all. In elaborate bedding room is found for most of the cultivated varieties. If you cannot give them a temperature of 60 degrees during winter the next best thing is to give the flats a light, dry position and

be sparing of water till the warm days of spring arrive. The most useful are A. paronychioides magnifica, almost scarlet when well colored, but not such a robust grower as the others; A. versicolor, bright rosy pink and bronze green; A. spathulata, reddish pink and brown shaded with bronze and green; A. amabilis, rose color and orange; A. amoena, orange red and purple; A. tricolor, dark green edge, center of leaf rose striped with purple veins and orange; A. paronychioides aurea nana, the best of the yellow or golden leaved sorts.

In very warm rainy seasons they grow so fast that the beautiful markings of the leaves do not show at their best. They should never be planted in a very rich soil. Their great adaptability for bedding is because they can be sheared to any sharp line and can be kept very dwarf.

AMARANTHUS.

Strong growing tropical annuals having feathery spikes of flowers and highly colored leaves. They are very suitable for the mixed border or for large sub-tropical beds. It is on account of the showy markings of the leaves that they are mostly grown. They should not be planted out till settled warm weather, with us the 1st of June, but they grow very luxuriantly in the warm months. They require deep, rich soil to obtain the best results.

Sow the seed the latter part of March in pans in a warm house and transplant when large enough to handle into flats, placing them two or three inches apart. The moist heat of a hot-bed suits them finely. If extra good plants are required they can be shifted from the flats singly into 3-inch pots, and nowhere will they do so well as in a hot-bed.

A few of the handsomest are: bicolor, foliage green and yellow; hypochondriacus, large spikes of crimson flowers; salicifolius, narrow drooping leaves, orange, carmine and bronze; sanguineus, blood red leaves; tricolor, a very handsome species with carmine and yellow leaves.

AMARYLLIS.

The Belladona Lily is the true amaryllis and the fine plants generally known as amaryllis are really hippeastrums. Several other genera are closely allied and as their cultivation is the same the cultural directions here given will include hippeastrum, crinum and valiota. They are bulbous but not herbaceous although resting partially during winter.

They seed freely and if sown at once and the young plants grown on in a warm house and rested slightly during the winter, will flower the third year. They can also be increased by the offsets from the old bulbs.

If you obtain the dormant bulbs start them in a little bottom heat, keeping the bulb near the surface of the soil. They flower when making their first leaves but must not be put away and neglected or stood under the bench after the flower is faded for it is then that the plant makes its principal growth and stores up strength for future flowering. Keep them watered and growing till the winter months, but as they are not deciduous, or only partially so, they are best in a light, cool house and with an occasional watering. After they require a 7 or 8-inch pot they need not be shifted but can be resurfaced annually. They like a rich, rather heavy loam. Few, if any, of our greenhouse pests trouble them. Being all tropical, when growing they must have a light, warm house and plenty of moisture.

The amaryllis flowers in July and August, the hippeastrum in April and May. Though hardly a florist's plant they are gorgeous flowers for the conservatory.

AMPELOPSIS.

Although more of a nurseryman's than a florist's plant there is one species of this most useful genus of hardy climbers that enters largely into the plant man's trade. We all handle, and some of us largely, that unrivalled climber, A. tricuspidata, so universally known as A. Veitchii. It has many aliases among our patrons, being called "Japan ivy," "Boston ivy," etc. For the covering of unsightly walls, stone or brick barns, and on the most costly mansions if the owner chooses, it has no equal, needing no support of any kind. When first climbing in its early years it assumes most picturesque forms, but whether it is good taste to cover densely the whole front of a fine house is a matter that must be left to the taste of the owner.

Though making but a moderate growth the first two years it is, when well established, a most vigorous grower and it climbs to the roofs of our loftiest houses. There is a fallacy about its growing only on the south and east aspects, and in one city I heard it stated that it did best on the north side. It will grow on every side of a house, north or south, but should be given a bushel of good soil for a start, and in exposed places some litter over the roots the first year. Millions have been planted in the residence portions of our cities and millions more are yet to be planted as our cities spread out. It is not a suitable climber for a frame house for the house must be painted and that settles the vine unless you are content to cut it down and begin again from the ground.

Propagation is by cuttings or seed. The cuttings can be put into flats and should be made in September with two or three eyes of the current year's growth. A light loam is a good compost for the cuttings and a shaded bench in the greenhouse is the place. Or, the cuttings can be put at once into the ground in a cold-frame. They should be wintered—whether propa-

gated inside or out—in a cold-frame and planted out the following spring. We have raised them from seed for a number of years and think it the cheapest method. Sow the seed in March thickly in flats, covering a quarter inch deep. In May or June pot them off into 2-inch pots and when there are benches to spare shift into a 4-inch and grow them on all summer inside, giving them an 18-inch stake. In September stand them outside and let them get the fall frosts slowly. I mention this because I have seen them kept indoors till October, and then when put out get a severe frost that would kill them to the ground. A deep frame with the pots plunged is the best place to winter them, removing the glass covering

Variegated Pineapple.
(Ananas Sativa Variegata.)

in April so that they are in no way forced. These plants a year old from the seed will be most satisfactory to sell to your customers, and being from pots there is no risk of losing one. Some readers may say you can buy plants cheaper than you can raise them. By the above method you will find Ampelopsis Veitchii a more profitable plant than many others you grow. It seems to thrive in any soil when once established. When growing it young we use a heavy loam.

ANANAS.

The beautiful variegated pine-apple is the variegated form of the pine-apple that is grown for its fruit, Ananas sativa. When well grown there is no variegated ornamental plant surpassing it in beauty.

Pine-apples, when well grown, can be fruited in two years. They were once a great feature of British gardens. The writer has helped or watched the packing of tons of Black

Jamaica and Queen pine-apples, some 45 years ago, when fruits of either of those fine varieties were worth from $5.00 to $10.00 each. That was in the days when the foreign or tropical grown fruit was little larger than a base ball and about as tough. Since then the cultivation of the pine-apple has been skillfully and systematically carried up in several tropical countries, perhaps to the greatest perfection in the Azores, and the fruit being almost equal, both in appearance and flavor, to those grown under glass, the industry is no longer profitable and would be out of the province of this chapter if it were.

The propagation of the pine-apple is by suckers which start freely from the base of the stem. They should be cleaned off and a small portion cut

square off and put into sandy soil in 3-inch pots and plunged into a bed where the heat of the house is not less than 60 degrees and the sand or plunging material is 80 degrees. Keep only moderately moist till rooted. The suckers appear at the time the plant is fruiting, and the larger the suckers when severed from the old plant, the better.

The soil best suited for them is a good, loamy sod, not too finely broken up. If heavy add sand with a fifth or sixth of leaf mould and rotted cow manure in equal parts. They should at all times be firmly potted. To hasten their growth they should be plunged during summer in a light house and shaded only during the very hottest hours of the day. If the soil is pure and there is no danger of burning no shade is needed. Plenty of water should be given in summer but the plants should be kept rather on the dry side in winter. By all means avoid a stagnant, wet soil.

This plant is beautiful at all stages

of its growth, and is particularly attractive when in flower and fruit, the latter lasting on the plant several weeks.

To those growing them largely for the trade I might mention an item in their culture which may or may not be in practice. As it was an excellent plan to produce a plant of the green foliaged fruiting varieties it cannot but be good with the variegated variety. It was to plant out the young rooted suckers from the 3 or 4-inch pots into 6 inches of good compost under glass during summer and lift them in the fall or following spring. Where some bottom heat can be given to the

raking the surface a few times, stamping down with the rake.

The commercial man who wants rows of these annuals should always sow in drills. For small seeds the corner of the rake will make a drill ½ to ¾ of an inch deep. After sowing, hold the rake in a perpendicular position and as you walk along beat the surface of the drill; that will sufficiently cover the drill. If your ground does not bake after a watering you can water the drills. If it does bake, as is usually the case, it is better to trust to the spring rains. When any of these summer annuals

ANTHURIUM.

Remarkable plants that are grown for their curious flowers as well as their fine leaves. The flowers are often used in combination with orchids. Their cultivation is very similar to that of many of the orchids. Whoever grows a few of the latter should grow A. Scherzerianum. The flowers of this well known species last in perfection two or three months.

They are from the West Indies, Central and South America. A moist, hot atmosphere suits them and they require an abundance of water in spring and summer. In the dark, cold weather less water is needed but the temperature should not go below 65 degrees at any time. The compost for potting them should be about like that suited to our terrestrial orchids: equal parts of peat, turfy loam, fresh sphagnum, broken charcoal (not powdered) or broken crocks. Fill the pot one-third full of clean broken crocks and then distribute the roots carefully among the compost, keeping the crown of the plant two or three inches above the rim of the pot, and cover the surface with fresh sphagnum.

There are a great number of species, all beautiful and curious and worthy of a place in every collection of hothouse plants. A. Andreanum and A. Scherzerianum are grand sorts for cutting.

ANTIRRHINUM.

Some very useful strains of the common A. majus (the Snapdragon) are now used for forcing. To get them true to color they must be propagated by cuttings. Plants struck early in the spring and kept from flowering can be planted out in September on the bench in 5 or 6 inches of good soil. A temperature of 50 degrees at night will suit them very well. They continue to bloom throughout the winter, and as a novelty the flowers are valuable. The white and yellow colors are most in demand.

As a border plant, see Hardy Perennials.

Anthurium Flowers.   A. Crystallinum.

Anthuriums.

bed they will make as much growth in six months planted out as they will in twelve months grown in pots.

ANGRAECUM.

See Orchids.

ANNUALS.

The title "Hardy annual" as applied to many of our summer flowering plants is a misnomer, for those that can be sown out of doors and come to perfection before frost touches them are very few. Many plants that are perennials we treat as annuals, growing them but one year and finding it most profitable to raise a new crop from seed each year; primula, cineraria, etc.

The few annuals that can be sown out of doors, such as candytuft, mignonette, poppy, eschscholtzia, etc., should be sown as soon as possible after the ground is dry enough to work. For the ornamental garden these are best sown in small patches, say eighteen inches across. Level and make fine the surface of the soil, sow thinly and cover the seed by finely

are grown for cutting flowers from, always sow in drills 15 or 18 inches apart on the hand cultivator can be used, as it saves much labor.

For the cultivation of all annuals needing the help of the greenhouse or frame, see Aster.

ANTHERICUM.

The variegated species, A. variegatum, is a very useful plant, used largely for the margins of beds, also for veranda boxes and vases. It stands our hottest suns, and is as well a very desirable plant for the window.

Plants lifted from the ground and potted can during the winter be divided. Or a few plants lifted and allowed to send up their long flower spikes will supply any number of young plants which spring from the flower stalk and these can be taken off and put in the sand, soon rooting and making plants. It is a very easy plant to grow in any soil, but to have good, useful plants in spring it should have a light house, pot room and plenty of water.

APONOGETON DISTACHYON.

A few flowers of this beautiful plant occasionally appear as a novelty in the windows of some of the best flower stores. It is certainly a novelty, too, in the cut flower market, though far otherwise as a cultivated plant, having been in cultivation for more than 100 years. It was introduced to Europe from the Cape of Good Hope in the latter part of the last century and has become so completely naturalized upon some lakes and streams as to appear like a native so great is its luxuriance.

Doubtless much might be done with it in American waters in southern latitudes, but the present object of this note is to advise those who have the facilities to give it a little attention under glass for winter flowering, and small indeed are its cultural needs. Grown under glass it would be an

Aponogeton Distachon.

consequence. It is better for a start to treat them as ordinary plants, planting the tuber, with its crown just covered in a pot of soil. It will then absorb moisture gradually, swell normally and when top growth is visible and well under way the plants may be immersed with safety. When new plantations are being established with divisions from growing plants no such precautions are necessary; these can be planted direct into other tubs or tanks.

AQUATICS.

These beautiful plants that are grown in the water garden are receiving more attention every year. Those who have never seen the two or three acres of lily ponds at Riverton, N. J., on the banks of the Delaware, in the nurseries of the Henry A. Dreer Company, can have no idea of the beauty of the nymphaea. A few plants of different varieties give no idea of their beauty as compared with scores of little oblong ponds separated by fine walks of grass and each filled with one species or variety of nymphaea.

In a botanical garden or park or private grounds the pond of aquatics will always attract the visitors and receive general attention. Not, I believe, wholly on account of their rarity, but largely for their beauty. And what can be more beautiful and refreshing than the broad leaves so placidly resting on the surface and the pool lighted up with the exquisite forms and colors of the flowers? Nearly every shade is there, but in no gaudy or blending colors. The yellows and pinks and blues and whites are of the purest and most pleasing shades. When the day flowering species want to close their petals (we will suppose in sleep), the evening and night flowering ones take their place.

Nymphaea.

Where and when the nymphaeas can be used as cut flowers for a vase or table decoration nothing can surpass them in elegance. The day flowering species are, however, available for use only in the day time, unless some trouble is gone to. Prof. J. F. Cowell of our Buffalo Botanical Garden, informs me that he is aware of a method by which the beautiful day flowering N. zanzibarensis and its varieties can be utilized for evening decoration. It may not be generally known, but has been thoroughly tested. Cut the flowers in the morning, when at their very best, and put the stems at once in ice water. This seems to arrest their growth and prevent change either way. To use a rather awkward expression, it paralyzes them, and providing you keep the temperature close to the freezing point, the flowers will remain open throughout the night. The first experiment was made by scooping out a hole in a block of ice, within which the stems of the lilies were put with water, and there they remained till 12 o'clock at night, fully expanded.

To those who intend investing large-

ever-blooming plant as in outside waters it flowers persistently till forced to a reluctant rest by the freezing of the water.

I have gathered flowers of it in midwinter when that season has been unusually mild, so that no forcing conditions are necessary under glass to ensure flowers in abundance during winter months. Tanks, tubs, or any receptacle could be utilized for its cultivation, placing in the bottom of them about a foot of compost consisting of loam and well rotted cow manure in proportions of about 3 to 1. The temperatures at which rose and carnation houses are kept will suit admirably and like these the aponogeton will enjoy all the sun it can get. As far as my observation goes of the plant under natural conditions it always appeared to thrive best and flower most abundantly along the margins of running water or in lakes through which there was a constant flow. This would indicate that it likes a change of water more or less frequently, conditions that can be met under cultivation by turning the hose into its tank or tub occasionally. The plant has a fleshy tuberous root, broad and flat at its apex, narrowing to almost a point at its base and from the crown of this tuber it sends out long roots in the soil surrounding, whilst the leaves and flower stalks find their way to the surface, each stalk terminated by an oblong leaf that floats on the water.

The flowers are borne on a forked spike (hence the name distachyon, meaning two spiked), are small and inconspicuous in themselves, but they are disposed in clusters in the axils of large showy white bracts. These bracts give the spike its color attractiveness, but the flowers have also a welcome charm in that they possess a delightful fragrance so sweet as to have earned for the plant the name "Water Hawthorn." The Cape Pond weed is another popular name for it and it matters not which is used, either being greatly preferable to its botanical cognomen, and should be used by those who would popularize the plant and sell its flowers.

When once the plant is strongly established it spreads freely by root increase and also reproduces itself from its own self-sown seed. Dry roots are also obtainable at times, these being imported from the Cape. The beginner with dry roots, however, must exercise caution in starting his plants, otherwise he may lose the lot. When the dormant tubers are potted up they are dry and more or less shrivelled. If then introduced to aquatic conditions there is a risk of the root tissues swelling too rapidly and rotting in

ly in aquatics, especially nymphaeas, the handsome work by Mr. William Tricker, "The Water Garden," will be found of great assistance.

New hybrid nymphaeas are being constantly sent out, all of great beauty, but those described here will be found, both in variety of color and in freedom of bloom, to be among the best.

The same general treatment will suit all. The hardy species can be left out all winter and will take care of themselves. The tender ones, among which are some of the finest, must be lifted after the first frost and their roots removed to the greenhouse. The roots can be placed in boxes or pots and covered with loam, which should be kept continually moist; in fact, as near the consistency of mud as possible, as that would be their natural state. The roots of all the nymphaeas are tuberous and they do not easily perish, providing they are not frozen or allowed to get too dry.

The nymphaeas are easily raised from seed, which can be sown in January or February in 4-inch pots of loam, keeping the pots a few inches under water in a tank in the greenhouse.

The hardy species can be placed in the pond by the middle of May, the tender kinds two weeks later. Those who have not the conveniences for raising the young plants can obtain strong plants for the specialist at a moderate cost. If the pond or pool has a naturally good soil at the bottom, less preparation is needed; but if, as is often the case, the pool or tank is made of cement or puddled with clay, then eighteen inches of rich soil must be placed over the clay or cement. Three parts good loam and one part cow manure will be a good compost, and you even can with advantage add a pound of bone meal to every bushel of compost. They are sometimes grown in large boxes, which are placed in the tank, but this is not the way to get fine flowers. You would not think of growing cannas in pots to produce the finest foliage and flowers, and growing nymphaeas in tubs or boxes is as undesirable.

The water need not be over eighteen inches to two feet above the soil, but the hardy species which are to remain out all winter should be sufficiently below the surface so that the soil does not freeze. A foot or two of ice can be above the plant, but the soil should not freeze. You will find that many of the hardy kinds seed themselves, and you will have an abundance of stock. No trees or shade of any kind should be allowed, as the nymphaeas delight in the broad sun. Finally, the secret of growing fine plants with an abundance of fine flowers is a good depth of loam, to which has been added a liberal allowance of animal manure.

Those enumerated below are among the finest:

N. zanzibarensis: Purple, day flowering, ten inches in diameter.

N. zanzibarensis rosea: Rose color, day flowering, ten inches in diameter.

N. zanzibarensis gigantea: Blue, day flowering, twelve inches in diameter.

N. Devoniensis: Rosy red, night blooming, eight inches in diameter.

Of the hardy nymphaeas, among the most useful are:

N. alba candidissima: White.

N. Laydekeri rosea: Beautiful rose.

N. Marliacea chromatella: Yellow, very hardy and free flowering.

N. Marliacea rosea: Very fine pink.

N. odorata: White, slightly tinted, very fragrant.

N. odorata rosea: Beautiful rose; the Cape Cod pink water lily.

N. tuberosa: Our common western white water lily.

N. tuberosa rosea: A fine form; one of the best of all, and fragrant.

Nelumbium.

This stately aquatic is now generally known and largely grown. N. speciosum, often called the Egyptian Lotus, will do in any pond where the roots do not freeze and has taken possession of some of the smaller lakes of Indiana. The large peltate leaves rise above the surface of the water, and the beautiful rosy pink flowers are borne on long stalks above the leaves. They have the appearance of very large double tulips.

The plants need the same general treatment as the hardy nymphaeas, and the compost can not be made too rich. One authority says they like to root into a stiff clay. If the bottom of your tank or pond is out of reach of frost, leave them there all winter. If not, lift the roots and keep in moist soil till spring.

There are now several varieties of N. speciosum. N. luteum is a native of our southern states and has very large yellow flowers.

Other Aquatics.

To accompany the nymphaeas and nelumbiums in the artificial lake or water garden, and of smaller growth, you can have the following:

Eichhornia crassipes major: Often called the Water Hyacinth. They spread rapidly and float without the roots being in any soil. Some of them must be removed to tubs of water in the greenhouse during winter to furnish a supply for the following season. This curious little aquatic is also known as Pontederia.

Limnanthemum: In appearance a miniature water lily with a pretty white flower.

Limnocharis Humboldtii: Yellow, poppy-like flowers. Good for the margins of ponds, but inclined to become a weed.

Papyrus (or Cyperus) alternifolius: This is well known and much cultivated in our greenhouses. It also makes a good aquatic for small ponds.

Papyrus antiquorum: The papyrus of the ancients, from which they made their writing paper. It is sometimes called the Egyptian bulrush. It has long, straight stems growing seven or eight feet high and is very striking in

appearance. Both this and alternifolius must be removed to the greenhouse before danger of frost.

Acorus japonicus: The variegated sweet flag.

Pontederia peltandra virginica: Greenish, calla-like flowers; hardy.

Calla palustris: A native, hardy plant.

Perhaps none of the above is of commercial value, except the nymphaeas, but if asked to stock a lily pond those noted will be found to be among the best, easily obtainable and good, free growers.

ARAUCARIA.

Of this noble genus of conifers A. excelsa is the only one of commercial value to us. A. imbricata is a hardy tree in England and when 20 to 30 feet high, with branches sweeping the grass, its symmetry is matchless. It is not, however, hardy here and does not make a useful plant for the greenhouse.

A. excelsa is called the Norfolk Island Pine, being a native of that faraway island. It will endure a very cool temperature, but not freezing. The plants are imported in large quantities from Europe. When ordering see that you are promised plants from cuttings. They are readily raised from seed but never make as fine plants as those from cuttings, the lower branches being always shorter and weaker, spoiling the symmetry of the plant. They are propagated from the leading shoots of the tops and branches inserted in sand, kept moderately moist, and covered with a hand-glass or frame till rooted.

The plants usually arrive in this country in excellent order, soon recovering from the journey and starting to grow. I have had the best success importing in the spring, the plants reaching here in May. You can then grow them on during summer and have well established plants for winter trade. Any good, fresh loam lightened up with a fifth or sixth of leaf-mould or very rotten manure will suit the araucaria. They will thrive during summer out of doors in the broad sun, but will lose color, and are best under glass with a slight shade and all the ventilation that you can give them. They want a uniform and moderate amount of water the year around. In the winter months 50 degrees is sufficiently warm.

The araucaria is not only the most graceful small tree we have but is very satisfactory for house culture when given a light window. Your customers should be told to keep them as light and cool as possible.

The forms of A. excelsa known as glauca and compacta are more expensive but are improvements on the type.

ARDISIA.

Dwarf, hard-wooded trees that flower and fruit when quite small; the best of the berried plants, surpassing the solanums, being more com-

Araucaria Excelsa.

pact, with better colored leaves, and densely covered with their berries.

A. crenulata is the best known and most useful. They can be propagated by cuttings of the half-ripened wood in April and May, but are more easily raised from seed. Sow the seed as soon as ripe in a temperature of 60 degrees. Be careful in transplanting into pots not to let the plants wilt from drought or sun. Grow them on in a light house and shift as they require it. The following spring they can be given their flowering, or rather fruiting, pot, and plunge on a light bench in the greenhouse.

June is the flowering time. When the fruit is set they can be plunged out of doors in the summer months. A temperature of 50 degrees at night will suit them very well during winter and the berries will last longer than if kept in a warmer house. When growing they want a warm, moist heat. They are easily kept shapely by pruning before they make their growth in the spring.

They are particularly valuable as ornamental plants because the pretty red berries are at their best in the winter months and small plants from

one to two feet, are the most useful. Some growers put the young plants into the open ground from the 2-inch pots in June, and they make larger plants than those kept in pots.

ARISTOLOCHIA.

Nearly all hot-house climbers, several of them having most curious and remarkable flowers. They are best planted out in the houses where they grow freely. They are, however, of little value commercially, except the hardy species, A. Sipho, the familiar "Dutchman's Pipe," which is one of the handsomest of vines. For covering a veranda, summer house or trellis it is admirably suited. Its peculiarly formed little flower, from which it takes its familiar name, is inconspicuous, being overshadowed by its large leaves.

You are constantly asked for a good hardy vine. Few plants are better than Aristolochia Sipho. It needs some support to twine and twist around. It is easily propagated from cuttings but if you are not in the nursery business you had better leave that to the nurseryman, who will supply you with

strong plants at a price that will enable you to make a good profit. A. Sipho thrives in any good garden soil. As a curiosity A. gigas is the most remarkable but it is not handsome and has anything but a pleasing fragrance.

ASPARAGUS.

Of this genus there are three or four species that are very useful and ornamental plants. The one having the greatest commercial value is A. plumosus. There seems to be some confusion about the name of this species, or there are two varieties. English catalogues make a distinction and call one variety A. plumosus nanus. With us the one that was actually dwarf has been lost track of and the one that grows twenty feet high is still called nanus. This is evidently a misnomer.

Seed can be sown at any time. Sow in flats and cover with an eighth of an inch of leaf-mould or sifted Jadoo and keep on a bench where the heat is not less than 60 degrees at night. It is well to be particular as to the source from which you got the seed. Imported seed frequently germinates poorly, but the home grown seed comes freely. We pot the seedlings into 2-inch pots, and if intended to plant in a permanent bed we first shift again into a 4-inch. A good, warm house suits it when young, but not a close, heavily shaded one.

An asparagus bed for the production of long strings should be on the ground. My own experience has given me a lesson on this point, and to use the words of Mr. W. H. Elliott, Brighton, Mass., our largest grower of this asparagus, "It should never be divorced from mother earth." One foot of soil on the floor of a lofty house will grow it for many years. Like all its family it flourishes best in rich soil; a good, heavy loam with a fourth or fifth of cow manure is the best compost for it, and in addition put a good dressing on the surface of the bed every midsummer. Although the same bed will last indefinitely I think it more profitable to renew the bed every three or four years. The roof of the house should be at least ten feet above the surface of the bed or you will not get the full benefit of the growth. Specialists like Mr. Elliott have houses twice that height.

It is not only the long strings that are used. The short sprays are in great demand for mixing with cut flowers, particularly bunches of roses. While many short sprays can be cut from the planted beds, many plants are grown on side benches in six inches of soil or in 6 or 8-inch pots with the view of producing sprays only. The plants will, if vigorous, throw up the long running shoots, but by nipping off the tops of the shoots when 18 to 24 inches long the production of branchlets is stimulated.

We have found small plants of A. plumosus very useful for fern dishes, outlasting any of the ferns. For this purpose the plants are best kept in

3-inch pots, though for large arrangements of flowers and foliage bushy plants in 4-inch pots are most useful.

A. tenuissimus needs precisely the same treatment as A. plumosus, but it is not such a general favorite. Its very finely divided, graceful branchlets are, however, preferred by some above A. plumosus.

A. Sprengeri is a more recent introduction and comes from Abyssinia (the other species are from South Africa). It is a strong grower, form-

little of the grace and fineness of plumosus and tenuissimus it is for certain purposes their superior, and when the sprays are matured their lasting qualities are equal to the well known durability of plumosus. To grow good sprays (and it can be grown five or six feet, and perhaps longer) you should give it the middle of a house where the winter temperature is 55 to 60 degrees. Plant fifteen inches apart in boxes as long as the width of the house between walks. Let the boxes be twelve inches wide

is a handsome object. It thrives in the most sunny and exposed places, or in the shade. The flowers are curious but of no value and in many cases pass unobserved for they are close to the ground at the base of the leaf.

They are propagated entirely by division, or rather by the young plants that spring from the sides of the older plants. Any good loam with the addition of some rotten manure will grow them, and they should have plenty of water at all times.

Old and familiar as this plant is there is never an over supply of it for it is not rapidly increased. It is now largely imported from Belgium and the plants are sold by the hundred leaves.

ASPLENIUM.

The spleenworts, as the asplenium genus has been termed (from the supposed medicinal value that ancient practitioners believed them to possess), form one of the largest fern groups in cultivation, over 300 species having been described, though it is rather doubtful if this whole number is at the present time in cultivation.

As may be expected in so large a genus, the aspleniums are very widely distributed, and in consequence we find among them species requiring warm house treatment, others that need comparatively little heat, and a few that are quite hardy in our northern and eastern states, there being more than half a dozen species that are native here.

The subject of our illustration, A. bulbiferum, belongs to the second division, or those that require only moderate heat, and though in commerce for many years, is by no means so plentiful as its merits would justify. A. bulbiferum is an evergreen fern from New Zealand, the home of many of our finest ferns, and has finely divided fronds of nearly triangular outline, these fronds reaching a length of nearly two feet in a good specimen, and being nearly one foot in breadth at the widest part. The plant has a gracefully drooping habit, this being accentuated by the weight of the numerous tiny young plants that frequently form on the upper side of the fronds.

This proliferous habit is found in several of the aspleniums, but is perhaps most marked in the species under consideration, the fronds often being studded over with young plants that are just showing their first leaf. This peculiarity is often taken advantage of in the propagation of A. bulbiferum, a common method being to bend over these proliferous fronds and then peg them down on the surface of a flat filled with light sandy soil, and the latter being kept moist soon induces the young plants to form roots, after which they may be readily detached from the parent frond. This operation is, of course, carried out in a shaded fern house, where the atmospheric conditions are favorable for the establishment of these young plants.

Asparagus Plumosus.

ing a large clump of roots and crowns from which it sends out long, strong shoots covered on all sides with fine branchlets. In older plants there is an inclination to run up strong shoots which may climb, but the value and beauty of the plant is in the long, pendent growths. It is a strong feeder and requires an abundance of water and will grow and keep its color in the full sun; only from our hottest suns should it receive any artificial shading.

It is easily raised from seed which is best sown in early spring. By the following winter the plants will give fine sprays. For hanging baskets it has scarcely a rival, either for the conservatory, the veranda or parlor window. The magnificent baskets that remain in good condition while hanging for months in a florist's window are evidence of its great adaptability to unfavorable surroundings. Three small plants put in a 10-inch basket in July or August will make fine ornamental baskets for winter, most useful for decoration or to sell at a good profit. While the Sprengeri lacks a

and eight inches deep. Raise the boxes three feet from the ground by some convenient means and keep them three feet apart. This will allow the sprays plenty of room to develop without getting dirty from the sand or soil of a bench. Small, well grown plants in 4-inch pots should be always in stock; for mantel decorations they are invaluable.

None of our well known greenhouse pests trouble the asparagus if it is given plenty of syringing and water. A rather heavy loam with a liberal addition of animal manure is all it wants.

ASPIDISTRA.

The species lurida and its variegated form are known to every cultivator of plants. It will bear more gas, heat and dust than most any other plant we grow. They are invaluable for vases in the cities, not only on the streets in summer time but in the rooms in winter. No one can fail to grow an aspidistra, and a fine specimen of either the green or the striped, with its leaves occasionally sponged,

Asparagus Sprengeri.

carry the soil down half an inch below top of flat. Then with a fine rose or sprinkler on the watering pot (or, to save labor we have the sprinkler screwed on the end of a ¾-inch hose), give the soil in the flats a good watering, sufficient to wet the soil through to the bottom. In half an hour sow the seed. Why we wait is to give the soil time to dry on the surface so that the seed can be lightly pressed into the soil with the board without the soil sticking to it. After we press the seed down we sift over the covering of soil. Whatever soil you use for covering it should not be of a texture that will bake and form a crust. Loam and leaf-mould, half and half, will do for the majority of seeds. Sifted Jadoo is also excellent but for asters a covering of the same material that the seeds are sown in is good enough. It should be finely and evenly sifted on.

The question is often discussed as to how deep seeds should be covered. As a rule the covering may be about the thickness of the seed, but we are sure that many seeds sown outside are covered six times their depth. With the aster and similar seeds we sift the compost on till all the seeds are out of sight, and that is sufficient. Another pressing down of the covering and the least amount of watering will do as you now have only that thin surface covering to wet. The thickness of the seed in the flat or pan must be entirely a matter of judgment, and since it is poor economy to sow very thickly to save space, as the seeds occupy a comparatively small space. I would say that if with asters every seed had a little square of one-eighth of an inch to itself it would be about the ideal way of sowing it, but spacing that or any of our seeds is out of the question. You had better err, however, on the safe side and sow thinly, for if crowded at the start it is a poor beginning for the little plant.

Seed when first sown (contrary to plants, which it does not hurt to let get on the dry side and then copiously water) should be kept at an even degree of moisture with no extremes. The flats should be kept in a shady place till the seedlings are above ground when they should get the full light and not be allowed to draw up for want of light and ventilation. When well up less watchfulness is necessary. A temperature of 55 degrees at night brings up the seed nicely and keeps the young plants growing till time to transplant into flats or into the hot-bed or bench.

As soon as they have made the first character leaf they should be transplanted. This is an operation that should be done very quickly but should be well done, which is more essential. While the little plant is held by the tips of the leaves by one hand, a rather blunt stick, held in the other, makes a hole in the soil into which let the roots of the plant hang down straight, and then with the stick press the soil around the roots. The plant should be so far in the ground that its seed

The aspleniums in general produce spores quite freely, and A. bulbiferum is no exception to the rule, but as the spores are somewhat slow in germination, the process above described is probably more often used. No special treatment is called for in growing this fern, and young plants grow nicely in company with Adiantum cuneatum and Pteris serrulata, though possibly enjoying a little more shade than is absolutely necessary for those species.
　　　　　　　　　　　　W. H. T.

ASTER.

A large genus, mostly hardy perennials, widely spread throughout the world. Many of them belong to North America and are the flowers of our fields, and of these many are worthy a place in the hardy garden. It is in the annual, the chinensis, section that we are interested.

Of all our so-called hardy annuals the Aster takes the leading place. Most all of our customers want a few. They are planted in the mixed border, or occupy whole beds, and with the commercial florist who grows for cut flowers they are a leading article. To obtain a good strain and cultivate them well is a matter of great importance to many of us. From the middle of July till frost cuts them off they are a prominent feature in all our flower stores.

Twenty years ago the raising of aster seed was left largely to the Continental Europeans, but now-a-days as good a strain as exists can be obtained here, and any of us who has the time and industry can save his own aster seed. The finest flowers of the purest colors should be marked and tied and allowed to get thoroughly ripe, when the stalks can be cut and put away in a cool, dry place and the seeds separated at your leisure.

In the following directions for the raising of the young plants from the seed to planting time I have endeavored to be explicit, as the same rules will apply to the raising of other annuals, such as stocks, zinnias, phlox, etc., and to which in their order I shall refer the reader to asters for directions for raising the young plants.

The seed should be last year's crop; older seed may grow but it is not to be depended upon. Successive crops may be wanted, or some early flowers grown under glass, so sowing can be done from middle of February till middle of April and even later. Sow in pans, or, if large quantities are wanted, in flats two inches deep. Always sow in colors. Fill the flats about even full with a light soil to which has been added a fourth of very rotten stable manure or thoroughly rotted leaf-mould, then press down with a piece of board or a block, which will

leaves are only just above the surface. In pressing the soil around the plant don't make a point of squeezing the soil around the neck of the plant near the surface; that is not the particular place. Put the stick away down by the side so that the soil is firmly pressed around the roots; that is the most important operation. If watered at once, thoroughly watered, and shaded for a day or two from the brightest sun, the seedlings scarcely feel the transplanting.

In the flats for plants we intend to sell to our customers middle and end of June we put the plants about one

the best and deepest soil we have, and if it is inclined to keep moist so much the better. Plant 18 inches between rows and 8 to 12 inches apart in the rows according to variety. When first planted out the small black jumping fly, often called the turnip fly or flea, is very troublesome, eating holes in the leaves. A syringing with a solution of paris green and extract of tobacco will kill the fly.

Violet growers who do not lift their plants till September can make good use of their benches by devoting them to asters during the summer. If planted end of May they are out of the way

attention than any other method of propagation. Asters are by no means difficult to handle (quite the contrary) but all seeds need care. You can put cuttings into the sand very clumsily and if shaded you can trust most anyone to water the bed and count on success, but there are many things to watch in raising seedlings. They are often unevenly sown, or careless watering will wash most of the seed to one corner of the box. When just germinating, if allowed to get very dry all your work may be in vain, or if not shaded when just peeping through the surface they may be burnt up. Skillful and proper management in sowing is one great part of it and constant watchfulness the other.

I think the plan of roasting or baking the material with which you cover the seed is most excellent, especially for those seeds that take considerable time to germinate, for it kills the seeds and spores of weeds and mosses and other low organisms that so soon take possession of an unoccupied surface. A piece of sheet iron over a brisk fire will enable you to quickly roast sufficient soil to cover a great many flats of seed. And if the whole mass of soil in which you sow as well as cover has been baked so much the better.

ASTILBE JAPONICA.

This plant was known for years as Spiraea japonica, and by the commercial florist is still almost universally called spiraea. It is a perfectly hardy herbaceous plant, and there are few plants so hardy or that will stand more rough usage than this astilbe. On dry sunny borders the feathery spikes are far less beautiful than those we grow under glass, but I have seen some very fine spikes this spring on plants that were in deep, moist soil and partially shaded by trees. It is, however, as a pot plant or for cut flowers in early spring that we are most concerned with the astilbe. At Easter, though by no means so profitable as many other plants we grow, they seem almost indispensable, and again on Memorial Day they are in good demand. When used for cutting we find the flower is not the only useful part of the plant, the foliage is always cleanly used up in cheap bunches of flowers.

The clumps of roots that we force are all imported from the rich, fat lands of Holland, and so long as the Holland growers can supply them so cheaply it will never pay us to bother with their cultivation. They usually arrive about the middle of November and should be unpacked and placed in flats or boxes with an inch or so of soil or litter over them. Then give them a good soaking and place the boxes outside, anywhere.

The astilbe can be forced into flower in eight weeks by giving it great heat, but I much prefer giving them twelve weeks, and the first three weeks they can be under the bench. If not previously done, when potting them give the roots a good soaking; there is

Asplenium Bulbiferum.

inch apart. If sown middle of March it is near the middle of April before they are established in the flats after being transplanted, and they then go into a cold-frame, where in May the glass can be removed. If very large quantities are handled they can be transplanted at once into a cold-frame if the soil is dry and warm. If you have no greenhouse the whole operation can be done by the help of a hotbed.

When extra early asters are wanted they can be taken from the flats in which they were transplanted and put into 2½-inch pots. In this way they will transplant with safety to the open ground. A great many asters are now grown on greenhouse benches. For this purpose sow middle of February. For our general crop we sow middle of March. Some of the varieties grow very tall when flowered under glass and need staking and lots of head room. They pay for the labor because you get fine, long-stemmed, clean flowers. Under glass they must be given plenty of water and frequently syringed—well syringed for red spider and thrips are ever ready to attack them in the hot weather.

For cuttings we plant our asters in

during August. We have also thrown out a bed of Daybreak carnations and filled it up with asters. No fresh soil is needed; in fact the asters grow so rampant under glass when well supplied with water that too rich a soil is detrimental. But out of doors they want a deep, rich soil.

There are many strains and varieties of asters. The large, strong growing, branching variety raised by Mr. Semple, of Pittsburg, is excellent for cutting. Vick's Branching is of about the same character. Then there is the Truffauts Paeony-Flowered, very fine if true, and grand colors; Victoria, finely formed; Comet, finely curled petals; Jewel, very compact, incurved petals; Betteridge's Quilled, a dense mass of short petals with a fringe of larger ones; and many other strains, all good if well grown, but Semple's though a few weeks later than some others, will be found to be grand.

Under this heading I have dwelt at some length on the operation of sowing seed, for I consider raising many of our plants from seed the most important part of the grower's occupation. It is the most delicate, and if not requiring the most skill it certainly taxes your patience and demands closer

Astilbe Japonica.

shaded frame with some heat under the sand, either from pipes or manure, would be the most favorable condition. They are slow to root, and in our climate the little plants or cuttings are so liable to the attacks of thrip and red spider during the summer months, and so difficult to remove, that propagation by cuttings is not worthy of consideration, either to produce a fine plant or for profitable operation. All the plants we handle in our business are grafted. Desirable and popular varieties are grafted on stocks raised from the seed of some strong growing varieties. Our chief interest in the azalea is how to handle them when they arrive here, and how to care for those unsold, which should make, by good care, a fine plant for the second or third year.

Soil.

It is generally acknowledged that a soil containing lime is very unsuitable for azaleas or any of the order ericaceae, which includes the heaths, rhododendrons, etc. It will be noticed that in some soils the plants imported and potted in October have made scarcely any young roots into the soil we give them. The Belgians grow them in fibrous peat, which in most parts of our country is difficult to obtain. But peat is not entirely essential. Two-thirds of turfy loam, not sifted, but just broken up, and one-third of leaf mould, will make a good compost in which azaleas will thrive. If to the above is added one-tenth of finely sifted decomposed cow or sheep manure, so much the better. When unpacked, the roots are often found dry. They have also rooted so freely that to pot them just as received would want an unwieldy sized pot. The ball of earth can be reduced one-third by shaking off the soil and this appears to do the plant little or no harm. Considerable of the ball can be reduced by slicing off an inch or so with a sharp knife or hatchet. When the ball is reduced to the required size—and it should only be done when the roots would require a pot out of proportion to the plant—soak the ball of roots in a tub of water for a few seconds. Pot firmly. If the soil is left loose, it will only be a channel for the water to run down and escape the roots that need it.

For the first two or three weeks after potting, the plants are best in a cool, shady and rather close house or frame; after that, a cool, light house for those you wish to flower the following Easter. By cool I mean 40 degrees at night is ample, and to retard them still more, anything above the freezing point will do. Some varieties cannot be kept for spring, and it is well to bring early varieties along, so that at all times during winter you have some plants in flower.

At no time should the roots of the azalea be allowed to get extremely dry. They will not bear it; and it may be well to state right here that the many complaints of our customers

nick mass of roots that the watering does not thoroughly l. They are the simplest of l to force. Pot them into 5, :h pots, or whatever size will roots. A temperature of 55 trees at night will suit them an a higher one. Water is essential, for by the flower-the little soil that you give one mass of living, hungry is labor saved and far more ry all around to stand each 7 or 8-inch saucer, in which instant supply of water, and s weak liquid manure your id plumes of flowers will be er.

tilbe is not troubled by aphis, thrips, or any other of our t when the growth is young matured they are easily burnt co smoke and that must be either by covering the as-giving them a good syring-'e you fumigate, or best of all 'e them in a house that must ated.

is a variety known as com-iich requires two weeks more orce. Also A. japonica varie-iich has the leaves prettily id with yellow, and bearing anicles, like compacta. But inal species, japonica, is the all for commercial purposes, the most graceful panicles of

wanted for Decoration Day

we keep out of doors till April 1st; they come into flower easily in two months thus late in the season. When sold to a regular customer you will do well to either sell or give with them a 7-inch saucer with instructions to place under the pot and keep water in it. If this is done the astilbe will be satisfactory, otherwise they will shrivel up.

AZALEA.

Of all the species of this beautiful genus, the Indian or Chinese are the most valuable. The growers of continental Europe have made such a specialty of growing azaleas that it is not likely that we shall for some time look to any other source for our supply. They may have neither soil, climate nor labor more suitable than we have in many parts of this continent, but certain it is that with our present facilities or methods we cannot begin to raise an azalea at anything like the same cost and quality as those imported. New varieties are, of course, raised from seed, and at the third season you will be able to see whether you have any improvements on existing varieties.

They can also be propagated from cuttings by inserting the cutting in sand. A cutting of 2½ or 3 inches of what is known as half-ripened wood is best; that is, the young growth of spring, not in too green or succulent a state, as you would a verbena, nor too much ripened and hard. A closely

that their azalea has shriveled up or the flowers are wilted is nothing but the insufficiency of water. Especially is this the case with the plants when sold the winter following their importation. When in a temperature of over 50 degrees or when any forcing is attempted, the plants should be well syringed at least once, or better, twice a day.

Mealy bug often attacks azaleas. Plenty of syringing will keep them down. Thrip and red spider are also very bothersome to them, but neither of these would appear if syringing were faithfully observed. They can be removed by a syringing of the tobacco extract. The Rose Leaf Extract

previous summer's growth. Place them in a light, warm house, and syringe frequently. When cutting back, see that the soil is in good shape and the drainage in order. By the first of June they will have made a good growth; that growth is what gives you the bloom the following winter. From the first to the middle of June plunge them out-of-doors in the broad sun. The pots should be plunged in some material to the rim, but in a place where water won't remain during heavy rains to unduly soak the roots. Over the surface of the pots spread an inch of rotted refuse hops or rotted stable manure. In this position they will do

appear in great abundance before the leaves are developed. They are now imported in large quantities for Easter sales and are very handsome plants. If forced early enough for Easter the flowers are fairly durable, but in the warm days of May they drop quickly. The shades of color are all beautiful and range from pure white to red. Many of the pink and orange varieties are grand in color and when decorated with suitable ribbon are most attractive in our stores and sell well.

The plants arrive with the Indian azaleas and should receive a soaking at the roots and then be potted and stored away in a cold-frame till they are wanted to force. The time needed to bring them into flower will depend upon how early the season is, and more still on the temperature of your house. In a house with a night temperature of 55 degrees allow about seven weeks, as it will not pay to carry them over the season unsold. It will be much cheaper to import fresh stock. Our nurserymen recommend them strongly for planting out, and where the rhododendron does well the hardy azalea will also thrive, but in many places they are an entire disappointment and you should be careful about commending them to your patrons.

BALSAM.

In Europe, or the more northern parts of it, the balsams are often seen grown in pots. With us they do so well out of doors that they are not thought of enough importance to cultivate except for the borders and large beds. Twenty years ago when more flowers were used with short stems the white balsam was largely grown by all of us for use in designs. They were then carefully kept free of side shoots and bore on their main stem fine double flowers. They are seldom grown now for that purpose, but are still favorites with many on account of their freedom in flowering, strong growth and gay appearance in the mixed border. In large grounds where to fill up is the chief object the balsam is most suitable.

For cultivation of young plants see Aster, but remember that the balsam is a very tender plant and instead of the cold-frame should have a light, warm house or the hot-bed. They are very strong growing and should have a deep, rich soil, plenty of water, and they deserve a space of at least 18 inches each way. The seed is most easily saved and if you select your flowers and save from the finest you will in a few years have as good a strain as can be procured anywhere.

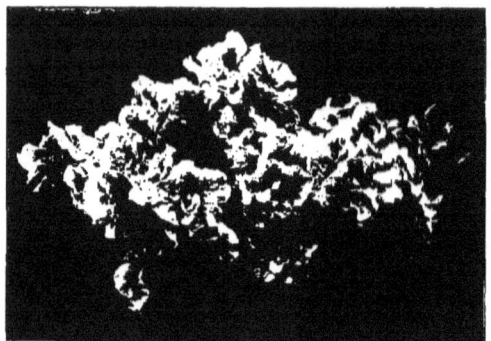

Indian Azalea.

diluted 50 to 1 will do. It is a general belief that tobacco smoke injures the foliage. It may be so, and it is well to avoid it, but I have seen little evidence that it injured the azalea.

During January, February and March the plants imported the previous autumn have a great inclination to make a growth before they develop their flowers. If this growth is not rubbed off the flower will be so weakened by the strong young growth that it will amount to nothing.

Many growers would rather import every year, and if they had plants left over in the spring, throw them away. To the man who grows but a few dozen this is likely to be the most profitable way of doing business; but where there is enough to warrant systematic care, it should not be done, for the second, third or even tenth year they are a more satisfactory plant to the purchaser than those just imported. With good but not necessarily costly care the azalea attains a good size and flourishes for many years.

Plants of the previous autumn's importation that are unsold the next spring, and are frequently in bad shape from neglect in stores, should be cut back quite severely, even to the

till the end of September, or till there is danger of frost. They want faithful attendance in watering, never to be killing dry and in hot weather a daily syringing.

If it is desired to grow on some plants a number of years to make fine specimens, the above treatment in most respects will do, but there are a few exceptions. Plants established in pots will seldom need those early growths rubbed off, for they have not the inclination to make them; neither will they want the hard cutting back every spring, the growth they make after flowering being sufficient for the next year, and stopping strong growths to keep the plant in good shape is all that is needed.

Azaleas by training and tying easily conform to almost any shape. They are beautiful if left to grow quite naturally. They are easily kept by pinching and stopping in what may be called umbrella form, but are grand when trained in pyramidal form. Few cultivated plants can equal a well flowered azalea four or five feet in diameter at base, tapering to a well formed top and six or seven feet high.

The Ghent or American azaleas are hardy deciduous shrubs. The flowers

BAY TREES.

The Sweet Bay (Laurus nobilis) has been imported from Belgium to this country in large numbers the past 15 or 20 years. Although the rather stiff, formal shapes into which they are trimmed and to which they so readily conform are entirely inappropriate in the decoration of a drawing room, yet there are many situations where they

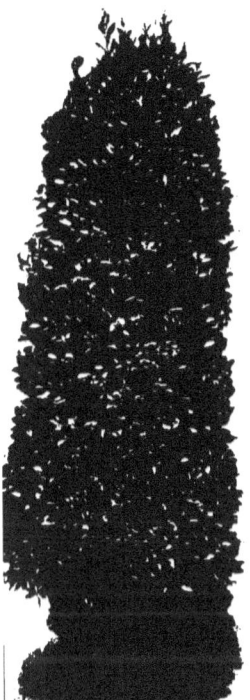

Columnar Bay Tree.

...ve a striking effect and are certain-
not out of place. A single pair of
...rfect form could be admitted to any
...urch ceremony or at the decorating
a large hall. In the summer time a
...ndsome pair stand—one on each
...le of the broad granolithic walk,
...ding to a stately mansion on one
...our fine residence streets, and very
...te their appearance is. Too much of
may get tiresome, as clipped and
...otesquely-shaped Norway spruces do
overdone, but the chronic grumbler
...o in his ignorant and prejudiced
...ndness objects to these handsome
...y trees because "they are not nat-
...al" should be confined to the back-
...ods eternally. Their formality sets
the brighter the natural grace of
...e birch, the elm, the maple or lin-
...n and the more or less freedom
the hardy flowering shrubs.
...nother place I found the Bays to
useful was when asked to decorate
a store opening and wagon loads
palms were expected. They are just
...e thing to fill up, and a fine pair or

half a dozen of them on the sidewalk
is just what Mr. Goldstein wants to
attract the attention of every passer
by, and what could you put there
equal in appearance and withstand
the ordeal unharmed? Considering the
years they must be grown, the labor
entailed and great skill in producing
such a large tree in such a comparatively small tub, their cost to us is, I
think, very moderate.

It is often a surprise to us that such
a stout stem and large head of
branches and leaves can subsist on
such a relatively small quantity of
soil. From early spring till fall they
want an abundance of water. They
are out of doors all summer, or should
be, so the hose can play on their
heads freely and over watering of the
soil is about impossible. From November to April a cold shed will keep
them in good order if it is not too
dark and where they won't get more
than 10 degrees of frost. A coach
house is an excellent place. It is usually light and seldom too cold. Less
water will do than in the summer
time.

The Sweet Bay is a native of Southern Europe. All good boys should have
read in the good book that if they are
righteous in their lives they will
"flourish like the green bay tree." But
they must not become a millionaire by
keeping a department store or they
will be more like an aged pumpkin,
hollow, mushy and slushy inwardly.
This fine evergreen grows well and
is much planted in the milder parts of
the British Isles. I expect that all
over Ireland it grows finely and is seldom or never injured by frost. In the
South of England it grows and flourishes for years, but a winter comes
occasionally and kills it to the ground.
Such a winter was that of '60 and '61.
The best time for us to cut back
growths or to keep it in that splendid
form that they are sent to us, is in the
spring just before they start to grow,
but if you wished a still more trim
appearance you would have to pinch
the young growths as they develop. A
new tub and more root room is needed
every three or four years, but keep
them in as small a tub as possible.
Liquid manure will help them much
in April, May and June. To those who
have not made bows of their strong
bottom growths or hunted rabbits
beneath their branches, they may appear a cumbersome plant to occupy
valuable greenhouse room. They don't
want it. If never coddled up under
glass they will stand 15 degrees of
frost without harm, but rather give
them a little higher temperature.

BEDDING PLANTS.

Although directions for the management of all our familiar bedding
plants will be found under their respective heads a few words on the
general subject is in order. The earliest bedding that the writer can remember was not very unlike that of
the present day.

Fifty years ago we had (I am speaking now of the gardens of Great Britain, for the American flower garden

had then scarcely an existence) beds
of verbenas edged with a variegated
geranium, beds of heliotrope, beds of
Tom Thumb geraniums, masses of
yellow calceolarias, in fact it was
masses of flowering plants, and that
is largely the taste of the day, though
not exclusively so because we have so
many foliage plants now which were
not then known and which now make
beds equal in color effect to many of
the flowers. The coleus and achyranthes were unknown and most of the
small plants that afterwards came into
favor for carpet bedding were not introduced, or were neglected because of
no value in the economy of the flower
garden. It seems to me that those
gardens of old with their circles and
squares and ovals of showy plants,
just as well kept as our gardens are
to-day, were fully as beautiful as any
we now have.

Then came the ribbon border—long
strips of flower garden, perhaps six or
seven feet on each side of a path. This
often began with the blue lobelia next

Pyramidal Bay Tree.

the margin of grass or box edging, then a variegated geranium, next Calceolaria annua floribunda, back of that Salvia patens (a most beautiful blue), then a row of dahlias, and, if the border was wide, backed up by a stately line of hollyhocks. The ribbon border was well done in this country in many places, but as some of the flowering plants could not be depended upon here we had the coleus, which does finely with us and is a poor, stunted, dull colored plant in the gardens of Great Britain.

Then twenty-five years ago, or perhaps a little more, the carpet bedding was evolved and was carried out most elaborately in many places, both private and public. Perhaps in no place in the world was it carried to greater perfection or more ingeniously than

the leading plants used in carpet bedding. They do better in our climate. I cannot believe that the alternantheras would grow there as they do with us, except in the warmer parts of Southern Europe, and if you take the alternantheras out of carpet bedding you leave a large hole. Carpet bedding never was a great item with the commercial florist simply because it was too expensive for the great majority of our patrons. A bed that could be well filled with geraniums or coleus for $15.00 would cost $40.00 if well done as a carpet bed. The plants we always had to grow, for there was sure to be a demand from people who wanted to try their hand at a fancy bed.

The prevailing taste to-day is to use flowering plants as much as possible;

hot house plants that are bedded or plunged out during the summer months, including crotons, palms, bamboos, etc. They are interesting beds, more interesting than handsome, but are instructive and to those who love plants are attractive.

A very simple and well known arrangement of a bed that I saw very recently pleased me very much, and still more when the "Missus" of the grounds said: "Mr. S., we are delighted with the bed this year. Don't you think it is beautiful?" It was surrounded here and there, but not densely with a few trees and the bed was some thirty yards back from the street. It was simply a center (about two dozen) of a tall, narrow leaved, dark—almost blood red—canna (I wish I could give you its correct

Bedding in a Public Park.

In the South Park system, of Chicago, under the direction of Mr. Frederick Kanst. It was admired by millions and criticised by a few. The minority are often in the right, but in this case the critics were only wasting their words. It was gratifying to the millions, and harmless surely, and therefore served its purpose. On a visit to the "Old Country" in 1885 we noticed much less carpet bedding than we expected to see and remember the remark of one head-gardener who was lord of a large domain: "No, we have given it up and gone back to the old geraniums and calceolarias." It was then in its greatest popularity with us, but was on the wane across the water.

As with the coleus so with some of

even the coleus is not as popular as it was a few years since. To be candid the zonale geranium, with its splendid habit and beautiful trusses of flowers of brilliant and pleasing colors, is such a universal favorite as was the horse Eclipse in the mythical story: "It is the geranium first, the rest nowhere."

There is, however, another style, or rather another arrangement, of bedding that is particularly suited to our climate, and on a lawn that is not wanted for croquet or tennis what can be more cheerful than a bed of cannas, caladiums and coleus. Perhaps this style of bedding is not worthy the name sub-tropical, perhaps the latter term is more properly applied to a bed that contains a great variety of our

name) surrounded by Caladium esculentum, then two rows of Coleus Verschaffeltii and next the grass a circle of Golden Bedder coleus. This is quite a conventional arrangement with us, but hard to beat and generally pleasing.

The landscape architect, especially of the most approved style, would, I feel sure, declaim against this bed on the lawn and say it was bad taste, not in harmony with the grass and the shade of elm and maple and linden. The up-to-date landscape artist don't want you to plant a golden elder or variegated cornus or Prunus Pissardii in shrubbery groupings because the coloring is abnormal and not in accordance with nature. What does the proprietor care about such things? He

Various Styles of Bedding.

Combination Canna and Carpet Bed.

wants to be cheerful. This sticking to nature is carried to excess. To be true to nature we would have to undergo a great change. We would not cut our hair or pare our finger nails or use knives and forks and would retrograde to the days of the fig leaf. Our early ancestors when crawling or leaping from limb to limb or wading through bogs when emigrating to the northern regions of the globe found the natural coats of the animals they had slain very comfortable on their own backs, and now clothing has developed into adornment and frills as well as becoming a necessity.

It is the mission of the florist to suggest the most appropriate style of bedding to his customers where ad-

your ability to keep a good stock of flower garden plants in a comparatively small space till after Easter. From fall till after Easter our benches are wanted for successive crops, but Easter sales largely clear them except those planted with roses and carnations. Geraniums can be then given their last shift, and so can ageratum, feverfew, heliotrope and salvia. Coleus can be grown from a cutting to a fine bedding plant in eight weeks. Cannas and caladiums can be kept in flats till middle of April and then make fine plants by June 1st. Petunias can be pricked out in pans and then in six weeks will make the best of bedding plants. Centaurea, coleus, achyranthes, verbenas, heliotropes, many of

must have attention when it is needed or it is too late. How often you hear the remark: "No, I am short on this or that. Was too busy and neglected them." This attention is not science; it is only close application and good management; and having sufficient help at the right time, and setting the men at the work most suited to them, is the very best of good management.

I don't know any business where neglect to do work at the proper time will bring about worse results. A tailor, a jeweler, a printer or a parson can lock his shop or office for weeks; his business may suffer, but his goods will not. Ours must be fed and aired and moved and shifted as they need it.

Design Bedding.

vice is asked for, and poor policy to crowd in more than is discreet when it is left to his judgment. In residence streets a flower bed between the house and the street is not good taste and should not be advocated. At the side or slightly to the rear of the house is much better. Houses of a moderate size with verandas at side and front have often a row or two of the flowering cannas in the border surrounding the veranda, and very handsome they look.

Florists are now divided into several classes. The strictly store man has no interest in bedding plants, nor has the wholesale grower more than to dispose of them, but the great majority of the florists of the country raise bedding plants for their spring crops and depend upon their sale for a good part of their income. If well and carefully done and a fair and just charge made your customers will be very unlikely to leave you and you can depend on the order from year to year.

The profit will largely depend upon

the geraniums, lobelias, aloysias, and all the carpet bedding plants, are far better in the hot beds than in the greenhouses, giving you plenty of room for the spreading out of your fine zonale geraniums, cannas and caladiums.

A great mistake made by too many florists, especially by those who have only three or four houses, is to be short of help just at the time it is most needed. For the first two weeks after Easter a man with 20,000 feet of glass occupied by a general run of plants could use twenty men with profit, though during February and March only five men were needed to keep up with the work. I am aware of the fact that you could not get the right kind of men even if you wanted them, but many times you allow a batch of plants to spoil for want of handling when a little more help would have saved them.

Bedding plants are all soft-wooded and while they rest largely, or can be just kept slowly growing during winter they feel the suns of spring and

Half the success with bedding plants depends upon the planting out. We charge nothing for planting if the bed is dug and prepared and the plants to fill it amount to $10.00 or more. If not prepared we charge for labor, manure, etc. We always prefer to plant where there is only a coachman kept, for then it is properly done. Sufficient plants are put in to make a good appearance. If enough are sent on the wagon there is none left over to call for another day, nor three more to be delivered to fill up. Nor is four dozen stretched out over a bed where six dozen should be planted. If the bed looks skimpy you don't want it to be known that they were your plants, and you will perhaps get the blame for poor general effect, for there are plenty of unreasonable people about.

We insist on our men arranging the plants carefully, just placing them in the holes, but not filling in the soil, and then when all are in place giving each plant a good soaking and in a few minutes filling in with the dry ground. That watering is worth ten on the surface. Tell your customers that cannas and caladiums can be soaked every dry evening, but that geraniums and beds of coleus and most everything else should be left alone except in very dry times when a thorough soaking should be given once a week, followed by a hoeing the next morning if the plants are not touching each other.

In charging for the bedding plants, whether contract or not, you should put down in your day book just how many plants of each variety it took to fill the different beds. Then, if Mrs. Goodpay orders her large circular bed filled with geraniums again this year you will refer to her charge of last year and find that it took 75 Mt. of Snow for a double row on the outside and the center required 140 Ernest Lauth. These figures are at random. But whether you plant the same or vary it you will know exactly how many is needed. Again you are asked a hundred times this question: "I have a flower bed eight feet across. How many geraniums will it take to fill it? Or how many coleus will it take?" We reckon ten inches apart for our 4-inch geraniums, about nine inches for coleus, fifteen inches for cannas and caladiums, and some specified distance for all the plants we commonly use. You can have a card with the sizes of the beds and quantities needed all made out so that you can give an answer in a few minutes, whereas, if you had not the thing figured out you would have to begin a sum in mathematics while somebody else is waiting for an interview.

The bedding plant business is not going to die out and you should cater to it. There is a good profit in it and it does not conflict with other branches of your business. With a clear head you can do it all.

A Long Geranium Bed.

BEGONIA.

There are few more familiar plants than the begonias and few so widely grown. The most popular section—the shrubby sorts—are many of them most excellent house plants. The Rex or stemless section make fine decorative plants and the tuberous rooted class are grand bedding plants. There are hundreds of species and numerous hybrids obtained by crossing many of the species, and among the varieties there are some beautiful plants. The begonias are all from warm climates but do not require a great heat, most of them thriving well in a night temperature of 50 to 60 degrees during the winter months. A good loam with a fourth of leaf-mould and rotten cow manure will grow any of them. If the soil is heavy add some sand, but they are really not very particular as to soil.

The Shrubby Section.

The shrubby section is the most popular and the most useful to the florist, the winter flowering kinds being in good demand. They flower for

Various Styles of Bedding.

months and the flowers are generally double while the plant is always ornamental. They are propagated in sand during the winter months, and during April and May, if properly shaded and watered, they root quickly. Any part of the shoot or stem will root except that which is hard or woody. During summer they are best kept under glass but should have an abundance of air and not too dense a shade. A close, damp, dark house will produce a rust on the leaves of many of them, which is hard to overcome, spoiling the leaf as well as flower.

There are so many species and varieties that but a few can be enumerated.

Fuchsioides: A tall growing, graceful species with scarlet flowers.

ers are of no particular value, not being produced in sufficient quantity to be profitable. Manicata aurea, is, however, a most desirable plant and I have yet to see any place or firm who have had an over supply. Like most variegated plants it is of much slower growth than the type. Few plants are so satisfactory as a window or house plant, the dry air of a room suiting it fully as well as the more moist atmosphere of the greenhouse. A native of Mexico, it will thrive in a high temperature, but a winter heat of 55 to 60 degrees will keep it in good order. To bring out its rich golden variegation, the leaves being always most irregularly marked, it should not have very rich soil. Pot firmly, and except in

Vernon: A splendid bedding plant. Dwarf, bushy habit and the plant covered with pink and white flowers. This variety does well in the broad sun and we find it one of the best of vase plants. It is easily raised from seed. Sown in October it will make a fine bedding plant by the following May. Fifty degrees is warm enough and the plants should have at all times a light bench or shelf.

Weltoniensis: An old variety that is inclined to be herbaceous. It does well planted out in summer and is largely used in vases and veranda boxes.

New varieties are being constantly sent out, all worth trying. For the amateur few plants are more easily managed or more interesting than many of the distinct species.

Tuberous-Rooted Section.

The tuberous-rooted section comes from the cooler parts of South America and are very distinct from the shrubby sorts. They are entirely deciduous. They make fine bedding plants as well as splendid pot plants for the greenhouse from June to October. As a window plant they are not to be commended, soon dropping their showy petals. It is as a bedding plant they are chiefly valuable. When I say that I have seen in our city large beds of these begonias surpassing in brilliancy of color, and certainly in variety, any bed of geraniums, it must be recognized as a good bedding plant. The cooler the summer the better they do and in localities where the heat is excessive they may not be desirable.

They are easily raised from seed, which should be sown in January or February. The seed of all begonias is very minute and no covering of the seed with soil can be done. Water the soil in the pan well before sowing and then sow on the surface, covering the pan with a pane of glass till the seed germinates. When large enough to handle prick out the seedlings into flats, keeping them on a light shelf, and when grown so as to be nearly touching put into 2-inch pots and grow on. The seedlings hardly make bedding plants the first year, but can be planted on a good piece of soil and will make fine bulbs for the succeeding year. When the tops are killed, before there is any danger of frost at the root they should be lifted, dried in a sunny place and then stored away in some perfectly dry material (dry sand will do), till it is time to start them again in the spring.

For the busy florist it is, however, advisable to leave the raising of seedlings to the specialist who grows them by the hundred thousand and be content with buying the dormant roots each year. It is cheaper, for the price is now lower than you could afford to raise them for. The double varieties are about twice as costly as the single ones and are no more effective as bedding plants.

The middle of March is early enough to start them, which is best done by

Begonia Manicata Aurea.

Glorie de Lorraine: A very recent introduction bearing rose colored flowers and blooming the entire winter.

Gracilis: Very fine summer flowering sort.

Incarnata: This name has been disputed but I can not find it described under another. It is an erect growing species, flowers most freely and is always in bloom by the holidays, but if not cut then it makes a beautiful plant when its rosy pink flowers are fully developed. The variety incarnata grandiflora is a great improvement on the species.

Maculata: Spotted leaves and handsome drooping coral pink flowers.

Manicata: This has a fine, green leaf, but is of little value to a florist, as it occupies much room and the flow-

the very hottest months it should have the full light. Its thick, fleshy, crooked stems are slow to branch, and propagation by shoots is too slow, but it will propagate from sections of the leaf precisely as do the Rex begonias, either by laying a well developed leaf on the sand and pegging it down, making a cut here and there through the mid-ribs of the leaf, or by cutting up the leaf into small pieces and putting them in the sand. When you begin steady firing, say in December, is the best time to propagate.

Metallica: Foliage very handsome. Pink and white flowers.

Nitida alba: Very pretty white flowers.

Rubra: Large coral pink.

Saundersonii: Bright red flowers; a very useful variety for cutting.

Bed of Begonias.

putting the tubers into flats of sandy soil. Half leaf-mould and half sand is a good mixture and two inches of it in the flats is enough. Place the tubers just below the surface and an inch apart. We place the flats on the hot-water pipes and remove to the bench as soon as the young leaves are showing. By middle of April the leaves will be crowding and every tuber will have made a mass of roots. There is now only one place for the plants and that is a mild hot-bed. No great heat is needed. We pot into 4-inch and plunge in the bed. By middle of May the glass can be removed except on cold nights. By this method you will have fine, sturdy plants inured to the weather and broad sun and they will receive no check when bedded out.

As a bedding plant they need lots of water and for that reason the beds should not be rounded up, but should be flat so that the water will soak in and not run off to the sides to nourish the grass. They should not be watered overhead as you would a bed of geraniums, but the hose, running an unobstructed stream, should be guided among the plants. I said unobstructed because the different kinds of sprayers and attachments they have for spraying with a hose are an abomination to a gardener. A good light soil into which has been dug a liberal dressing of rotten cow manure will suit the begonias.

Plants grown in pots want a liberal sized pot and plenty of air, and to do them well they should be shaded only from the brightest sun. Few insects trouble the begonias.

Rex Section.

Begonia Rex: The Rex or leaf begonias were a great and expensive novelty when first introduced some 50 years ago, but are now so common they are worth no more than a geranium. Occasionally you see one in the window of a humble dwelling, giving the passer-by a full view of its fine leaves, so it can not be a very poor house plant.

Nicholson's Dictionary says this handsome species of begonia was introduced into Europe from Assam in 1858. With due respect to that grand work I can swear I saw a small plant introduced into a private garden from London as early as 1856, at the modest cost of $5.00 a leaf. There were two leaves on the plant. But this is of little consequence.

Besides being a fine decorative plant for the conservatory it is very effective in vases and veranda boxes where not exposed to the afternoon sun, their large leaves having a striking effect. It is really a tough plant even if it is royal. A good light loam with plenty of leaf-mould and rotten manure will grow it finely. It likes more shade than the shrubby section, in fact will grow in very shady positions, and luxuriates in a warm, moist atmosphere. It can be syringed daily, contrary to general practice, and delights in it.

There are two methods of propagation. Either will do. You can cut the leaf (a mature, but by no means an old yellow one) into pieces two or three inches long, cutting the pieces wedge shaped to a mid-rib and putting upright half their length in warm sand; or, the entire leaf can be laid right side up on the surface of the sand, pegging the leaf down close to the sand, having previously cut through from the underside at every inch or two the principal nerves or ribs of the leaf. In the last named method the young plants will spring from the ends of the cuts. As with those struck the other way keep well shaded when first potted. If plants are wanted for spring sales the leaves should be put in as soon as firing commences, as it will take them all winter to make useful plants by the following May.

BELLIS.

The perennial daisy is a favorite garden plant with many and some of the improved varieties are grown under glass, in a cool house, for cutting. But we have so many better flowers for all purposes that as cut flowers they are little used.

We are frequently asked for plants in the early spring as we are for pansies. They are easily divided either in spring or fall. The commercial man who has need to grow them had better divide the roots in September, plant in a cold-frame a few inches apart and cover with glass during the coldest months.

There are many fine varieties, red, pink and white.

BILLBERGIA.

See Bromeliads.

BOSTON IVY.

See Ampelopsis.

BOTTLE BRUSH.

See Metrosideros.

BOTTOM HEAT.

In all cultural notes there is more or less occasion to refer to bottom heat. There was a time when few cuttings were thought to root well without the aid of bottom heat unless it was the cuttings of the ericas and conifers. Practice has taught us that to have the heat of the sand or propagating material greater than the temperature of

well if well laid in cement. Heat and moisture quickly rot wood, so use brick, and a few inches from the top, according to the purpose for which you want to use the bed, lay in, or rather build in, some strong strips of iron. A strip two inches by half an inch will bear a good weight of sand if the bed is not more than 3 feet wide and will give a good bearing for the slates. If 6 feet wide you must have a center support for the irons, and 1-inch gas pipe with 1-inch uprights every 3 feet will do well for that. Your cross strips should not be more than a foot apart. If you want bottom heat don't attempt to get it through a 1-inch board.

showy bracts are of great value for decorations.

The plant should be in a large pot or tub, or may be planted out in the border, but where it has unlimited root room it grows too freely and does not flower so well. During winter the supply of water can be diminished till the plants start growing again in March, at which time the plants can be cut back to within a few eyes of the previous year's growth.

The variety of glabra known as Sanderiana is small and is much the best for plants of medium size in pots. We were very successful in flowering plants of this the past spring but are disappointed in it as a house plant. The great majority of our flowering plants are sold to people who want them for their windows or rooms and unless a plant has fair keeping qualities under such conditions it will never be popular. The bracts of B. Sanderiana, while hanging on the plants for months in the greenhouse soon drop with the leaves when removed to the dry heat of the living room.

The following is our practice and plants of various shapes, averaging two feet above the pot and eighteen inches across were covered with the flowers and bracts. Cuttings made from the young growths strike freely in the sand in January or February. The first year they are planted out in light rich soil out of doors, where they make a vigorous growth. They are potted in the fall and kept rather cool and dry the following winter. In the spring they are put into 5 or 6-inch pots and plunged outside where they make a moderate but rather firm growth. Before there is any danger of frost they are removed to the greenhouse and are kept in a light house with a night temperature of about 50 degrees. In January we move them into a warmer house (about 60 degrees) and begin to syringe them and give more water. The flower should soon appear on the growth of the previous summer.

When growing or flowering they like an abundance of water and the soil should always be in a condition that will allow the water to pass freely away. Good fibrous loam with a little leaf-mould or old decomposed hot-bed material suits them well.

I will take this opportunity to say that this old hot-bed material is of great service and it is one of the reasons we like to put up a few dozen sash each year. There can be little ammonia left in the manure, but the manure with the soil and leaves, and perhaps refuse hops, thoroughly decomposed and well mixed together, is an excellent thing to add to the compost for nearly all our soft-wooded plants and takes the place of leaf-mould with our hard-wooded ones. It must be the excellent mechanical condition more than the fertilizing qualities that makes it so valuable an addition to all our soils.

Bougainvillea Sanderiana.

the house is with many cuttings entirely unnecessary. Ten or fifteen degrees hotter will certainly hasten the rooting of most of our soft-wooded plants, and with some it is a decided advantage while with others (carnations and geraniums for instance) it is not desirable.

Where bottom heat is essential there is no way so inexpensive or durable as having the hot-water or steam pipes under the benches and inclosed so that the heat will remain under them. The hot-bed (primitive greenhouse) is ideal as a means of affording bottom heat, but it is of short duration, being available only during the spring and summer months and is always liable to neglect. Years ago in growing plants requiring bottom heat many a day was laboriously spent in carting into the houses tan-bark, leaves and other fermenting material to afford heat to plants. That, however, is past and only the hot-water and steam pipes are now used.

Whether it be for the propagating bench or for plunging plants that require bottom heat let the walls of the bed or bench, be of brick. A 4-inch brick wall back and front will do very

Wood is one of the poorest conductors of heat and slate is one of the best. Half-inch slates (or thicker) in large slabs are very expensive. For a propagating bench roofing slate 24x12 will do very well and will last for years if you support it in the middle by having one of the iron strips every foot.

If all your heating pipes are under the bench it will be necessary to have sliding openings in the wall to let out some heat in very cold weather, but in most houses there will be an independent pipe with which you regulate the atmospheric temperature. Don't use wood for these beds. Use brick, iron and slate, and in ten years you will have saved money and much vexation.

BOUGAINVILLEA.

The most useful species of bougainvillea is the well known glabra, which makes a fine greenhouse climber in any house where the temperature does not go below 50 degrees at night. The flower is inconspicuous; it is the showy rosy purple bracts of the flowers that give the plants such an ornamental appearance. Long sprays of the bougainvillea covered with these

BOUVARDIA.

The bouvardia can be classed as almost a tropical plant, most of the species coming from Southern Mexico and South America. The hybrids of some of these species are what are of value to the florist. Twenty years ago the bouvardia was one of the most important of the plants we grew, but of late years, with the advent of long-stemmed carnations, the wonderful roses, the chrysanthemum and other more durable flowers, the bouvardias have been much less grown, and in commercial places they generally occupy but a small place, if any, notwithstanding they are beautiful and easily grown, and that the flower has grace and refinement. In these days of keen competition, the question is, "Do they pay?" That you must judge by experience in your own locality.

The best time to begin propagation is early March, with the roots of plants that have been grown on a bench for winter flowering. The bouvardia roots very slowly and unsatisfactorily from the young top growths, and in ordinary practice that is not considered a practical method of propagating this plant. We will begin with the young roots. Don't take the large roots near the base of the plants, nor the thin, thread-like roots of the widest growth. Choose the growths between these. Cut them into pieces about one-half or three-fourths of an inch in length and distribute them on a propagating bench, where you have a good heat, as you would coarse seed, pressing them into the sand. Then cover with at least an eighth of an inch of sand, pressing it down after covering. Water sufficiently to keep moist, about as you would other cuttings. In three or four weeks young plants will be springing up. When they have made two or three leaves and are an inch high, lift them from the sand and pot into 2-inch pots.

The bouvardia is a tropical plant and at no stage of its existence should it be exposed to a low temperature. This accounts for the very different treatment we give it from what is considered right in Western Europe. Plant out in the open ground about the first of June, or earlier, if you are in a latitude where no late frosts appear. A very light, rich soil is much the best adapted to the wants of the bouvardia. Unless there is a very long spell of hot, dry weather, no watering is needed after the first good watering when planted. The growth that has started in the greenhouse will continue to grow out of doors, but that is of little consequence, and can before lifting be entirely cut away. It is the strong, vigorous growth that will spring from the roots after being planted out that you will depend on to give you flowers. They want stopping about twice during the summer.

The lifting time will vary according to where you are. In Buffalo we used to lift about the second week in September. If later, and the weather

should be cold, they are much slower in taking hold of the soil in their new quarters. A very good plan is to do the last pinching a week or so before you lift them. The break from this last stopping will then come in about right for the holidays. Plant in five inches of good loam, and as to distance apart, be guided by size of the plants. A foot apart is little enough for any of them. Anybody, with almost any temperature, can get the first crop of bouvardia, but to get them to make a growth and a profitable crop of flowers again in March requires heat. Unless they are kept in a night temperature of at least 60 degrees and syringed daily, they will just stand still after their first crop is over. The rampant way they grow and flower when the warm sun of April comes shows you what they want.

They can, of course, be grown in pots, but do far better and are more easy to manage planted on a bench in a light warm house.

If after the end of March you need the bench for some other crop you can cut down the bouvardias to within a few inches of the bench, lift them, shaking off all the soil, and place them close together in flats with three or four inches of moist soil around them and put under a bench where there is not much drip, and they will do there all right till planting out time. The old plants will of course be much larger than those propagated the first year.

Red spider attacks them, and so does mealy bug, but their presence is inexcusable, for a proper use of the hose will prevent both. Green fly will appear if fumigation is neglected, but be careful to smoke lightly, particularly when the plants are first housed, for they burn readily.

In lifting, I cannot say as you can about carnations, "let all the soil tumble off if it will," so long as I save every fibre," for they do not lift so well, or rather, do not recuperate so quickly. Lift carefully with a good ball of earth and for the first week shade and syringe frequently.

BROMELIADS.

Except the variegated pineapple (see Ananas), there are few or none of these curious plants that are of any commercial value, though among them are some beautiful and interesting plants. The Buffalo Botanical Gardens now possess the very valuable collection brought together by the late firm of Pitcher & Manda, with several additions, making it the most complete collection in this country, and it is in the finest possible condition.

Besides the ananas, the most familiar genera are the tillandsia and the bromelia. The leaves are stiff, variously colored, and fluted or concave, always carrying the moisture to the base of the leaf. The flowers are often handsome. They are mostly from tropical America.

Propagation is by offsets or suckers,

which, when separated from the old plant, should be potted and plunged in a good heat. They are grown in pots or baskets, which should be drained with a third of crocks, and the compost should be fern roots and sphagnum. They require heavy shade in the summer and must be frequently syringed. It is the moist atmosphere they delight in.

By their channeled leaves they accumulate water, which remains in quantity at the base of the stem, and it should not be disturbed, as it does no harm. In nature the water would surely be there, and in this respect at least we cannot improve on nature. A compost such as described, plenty of moisture, and a minimum winter temperature of 70 degrees, is what they want. Following are named some of the most distinct genera and species:

Tillandsia utriculata and T. fenestralis.

Guzmania fragrans and G. tricolor.

Aechmea fulgens and A. crocophylla.

Karatis spectabilis and K. Moritzianum.

Vriesia musaica and V. splendens.

Billbergia zebrina.

For the culture of the variegated pineapple (Ananas sativa variegata), see Ananas.

BROWALLIA.

The best known species is elata of which there are two varieties. One has white flowers but the variety grandiflora is a fine blue. They are often used as flower garden plants but are more suitable for the mixed border as they are liable to go out of bloom just when their color is most needed.

For the flower garden sow the seed in March and transplant into flats or small pots and plant after all danger of frost. As a pot plant for winter use (and they will flower during our darkest days) sow in July and August. A pan six or seven inches across and four inches deep with half a dozen plants makes a nice show and many of them could be sold as Christmas plants. When once established in the pans they are better kept out of doors in a frame and given the open air but covered with glass in case of a storm. They must be syringed daily and will need pinching once or twice to induce them to branch. Remove to the greenhouse before any danger of frost.

BULBS.

Under this head, instead of under their respective names, is given the culture of those bulbs that are generally forced, especially those known as Dutch bulbs, and which have been so important an item with us for the past twenty years.

Roots that are often called bulbs are really corms and not bulbs. The crocus, caladium, richardia and gladiolus are corms. The true bulbs are the lily, hyacinth, tulip, etc. It is only of the Dutch bulbs that this article treats.

The tulip, hyacinth and narcissus all want about the same treatment, with some variation, which will be noted. There is little doubt that the lilies (or what may be called the loose-scaled bulbs) are subject to injury through being long exposed to the air, and they really should not be long in a perfectly dormant state. Notice the Lilium candidum in our gardens. Soon after the flower stalk is gone the plant begins to throw up a young crop of leaves, showing it is but a short time dormant, if at all. Not so with the more fleshy bulbs, like tulips, which remain out of the ground four or five months without the slightest harm.

bed, as desired. If lifted, the tops should be about ripe before the bulbs are disturbed. If lifted as soon as the flower is faded, you have arrested the formation of the bulb that was storing up its strength for the following year.

The early tulips and hyacinths bloom with us early in May. As our bedding plants do not go out till nearly or quite June 1, there is nearly time to give the bulbs a chance to mature. Two weeks later, however, would be much better if the welfare of the bulbs was the main consideration. When

In planting a bed of bulbs to any set pattern or design, look out for time of flowering of the several sorts. Crocus are always best alone and should not be used with the tulips and hyacinths. Von Sion narcissus is about as early as the hyacinths, which are several days ahead of the earliest tulips, and should not be in the same group. The early single tulips (except Duc Van Thol, which should not be used) all flower about the same day and go well together. The early double tulips are all right with the early single tulips. We noticed La Candeur, the inexpensive double white, planted with the early tulips. That was a mistake, as it is ten days later than the early tulips. If a double white is needed with the single varieties, Murillo is the sort; it is early, and a grand flower. Yellow Prince, Chrysolora, La Belle Alliance, all the Pottebakkers, La Reine, Kelzerskroon, Proserpine, Vermillion Brilliant, Cottage Maid, Tournesol, in fact, all the early single and double tulips, can be planted in one combination and will make a fine display. The little blue scilla can be planted with the crocus. It blooms with the crocus, soon after the snow is gone.

Bulbs for Forcing.

Within 25 years, and with many more recently, the forcing of tulips, hyacinths and narcissus has become a most important part of our winter operations. About 12 years ago it was at its zenith, but as the best methods of forcing became widely known and in consequence vast quantities were imported and the blooms thrown on the market the public began to tire of the flowers till during the last few years they have dropped seriously in price, and during the last winter hundreds of thousands of fine flowers were sold at about the cost of the bulbs. We predict a much smaller importation each year.

These remarks do not apply to the good old Dutch hyacinth that we grow in a 4-inch pot. They have been grown in pots and glasses for a hundred years and always will be. There are few sweeter flowers for the price than a nice spike of hyacinth. People know them and don't ask "How long will they last?" They think rightly that they have received good value for their money if they have had a pot of hyacinth in their window for ten days. Large quantities of fine hyacinths are also grown for Easter in pans, from three to a dozen in a pan. The latter quantity of some fine distinct variety in a 12-inch pan is a rich affair and generally attracts the purchaser who is looking for something nice to send his or her friend on Easter morn. The Von Sion narcissus, or daffodils as they are familiarly called, make also fine pans.

Roman hyacinths are still flowered in immense quantities and fashion has not changed the demand. They are graceful, waxy white flowers and can be used in several ways, either by

Single Tulips.

Bulbs for Bedding.

The hyacinth, tulip and hardy narcissus are usually planted in the open ground in October and November. They should always be planted a good six inches deep. The closer together the better the effect. A thinly planted tulip bed looks badly and is not worth doing. I call a foot apart thin. Six inches apart will make a gorgeous bed. Any soil will flower the bulbs one year, for the flower bud is already formed; it merely comes with you. But to grow them so that they will flower again the following, or third or fourth, year, a good, deep, rich soil should be given them.

The great majority of our bulbs when planted to succeed the flower garden plants are intended to flower only one year, and that suits the florist who supplies the bulbs very well, but that is no reason why the bulbs should be neglected or thrown away. The bulbs may either be lifted or left in the

first lifted, expose the bulbs and tops to the air till they are ripe and the tops wither away, when the tops can be pulled off, the bulbs cleaned, and stored away in a dry, cool place till fall. I noticed this spring about as good flowers produced by tulips the second year as by those freshly imported. The bulbs will do very well if left in the ground, which it is sometimes convenient to do, in the mixed border, for instance. If in beds, you can sow some summer annuals over them, such as California poppy, without much harm.

There are always some inquiries as to "When shall I cover my tulip bed?" These and the hyacinths are perfectly hardy and no covering is necessary till Christmas, when two or three inches of stable manure or litter can be put on the bed. It helps not so much to keep frost out as to prevent the surface from continuously alternating between a freeze and a thaw, which often occurs in the month of March.

Dutch Hyacinths.

themselves or in combination with roses, violets or carnations.

If you want tulips or Von Sions, Paper white narcissus or Roman hyacinths at the earliest possible date they can be got in flower you should not delay a day in getting a portion of your shipment into the flats, and they should be well watered and covered at once. The Romans arrive in August, the Paper White a little later and the tulips, hyacinths and Von Sions along in September. As I remarked about the soil for the beds, the soil, providing it is of a loose texture and easily handled, is of little consequence. Heat and water force out the flower spike and that is the last you care about the bulb. We generally use the soil that has done duty the previous year on the carnation benches.

I found out many years ago that boxes and flats of every size and shape for forcing bulbs was a poor plan, however cheap, and for years have made boxes of one pattern, which is 24 inches long, 12 inches wide and

3 inches deep, all inside measure. I buy strips 16 feet long (any length will do, but you don't want waste), 3 inches wide and half an inch thick, and some strips 3 inches wide and 1 inch thick. Four of the thin strips make the bottom with a little space between them, two of them make the sides and the 1 inch thick strips make the ends. They are nailed together with 6-penny nails, and two or three boys will make 150 of them in a few hours. These boxes will last several years if cleaned out and piled with their bottoms up, but not if allowed to lay around the yard half full of soil till the following fall, or run over by the wagon, or when used to carry plants to a bedding job to be left there and not called for.

Oh, florists, I am not immaculate myself in this respect, but how many dollars you do waste in letting your boxes, pots, flats, tools and implements lie around in disorder. You are about as bad as the slovenly farmers in a poor, poverty stricken farming district which is always to be

found without going very far. It is well known, and admitted by the manufacturer, that if the American farmer took good care of his agricultural implements and tools half the factories could and would close down. The scythe is hung in the apple tree, the plow is thrown out at the end of the last furrow to bleach and rot in the sun and rain, the harrow may be dignified by being tilted up against the fence, and the costly reaper lies out in the yard for the children and chickens to perch on. There is no time to clean and put things away. The gossip of the village smithy or rural post-office must be attended to. The prosperous farmer's place is all contrary to this, and as the florist is farming on a high grade and costly plan where the outlay and receipts to the acre are enormous, it behooves him to take care of all his implements and have them ship shape and in place where they are always ready to his hand.

Some men can do twice as much on an acre as another. It is order, system and cleanliness that enables him to do it. "Dirt is matter out of place." That is a true definition. I once found fault with a man, who was then a partner, that his rubbish pile contained everything from decent potting soil to broken glass, hoop iron and empty beer bottles. He rather peevishly replied that he had no time to spare and was glad to get rid of the stuff out of the greenhouses. That "time" excuse is the worst of all, and the man who lets his wagon stand out in the sun till the hubs are cracked has always the most time to spin a yarn, or see how much old Bill Jones' cows bring at the auction. If my friend had had a pile for stuff that was purely rubbish and another for old soil and plants and vegetable matter that would come useful some day it would have been much time saved in the end and some money.

With this diversion we will return to the bulbs. The flats as described will hold 60 Romans, 50 Paper White, and from 60 to 72 tulips, according to the size. Yellow Prince is a large bulb, La Reine is a small one. I believe, as Mr. Ernst Asmus said at Chicago years ago, that it makes little difference in the flowering how close the bulbs are. Even if touching they will flower all right, and save room.

We always do our bulb boxing outside on a temporary bench where the soil can be brought to the men by the cart load. We fill the flats nearly full, very loosely, and squeeze the bulb into the soil till the top of the bulb is even with the edge of the box. A few handfuls of soil fill up between the bulbs and the job is done. All this is a very quick operation. A good man will box 8,000 to 10,000 a day if supplied with boxes and soil and another man to take the boxes away when filled.

Bulb houses have been spoken of, but I never saw the need of them. We once tried our earliest tulips under the bench of a very cool house, covered with an inch of soil. It was an entire failure. There is no better place for the flats when filled than the surface of the open ground. We smooth off a piece of ground and lay out beds six or seven feet wide and any desired length, leaving the same width between beds. We lay down strips of old boards to keep the bottoms of the flats away from the soil. When one bed is covered with flats we get out the hose and thoroughly water the soil in the boxes. When the water has soaked in we dig up the ground between the beds and cover the bulbs with this soil about three

In many years we have never had any difficulty in getting them in to force. A mild day is sure to come and you can then get in enough for several weeks, keeping some of them in reserve in a cool shed. If unprotected by snow and the covering of soil is frozen we bring in covering and all and clean them off when thawed out. Out of doors is their natural place and I believe it is better for the bulbs to make their roots there than in any house or cellar you could build.

Paper White narcissus we do not allow to freeze, giving them the protection of glass in addition to the ma-

April two weeks in any house will bring them into flower.

The Von Sion narcissus are forced in precisely the same way as the tulips.

For years we struggled to get tulips in flower at Christmas and with the Duc Van Thol, and even with some of the finer early tulips, we were successful. But what is there in it when you have succeeded? There are plenty of other flowers for all purposes, and fancy trying to sell a dozen forced and sickly tulips when a dozen fine carnations can be had. So we have left tulips alone till after New Year's, when, if brought in, they can be had in fine quality by end of January or a few days before, and that is as soon as they are wanted.

The earliest tulips want a strong heat; 75 degrees is not too much, with plenty of water, and they need shading with cheese cloth or some such material to produce a good stem. Up to first of March they need heat, lessening shade, after that they flower on any greenhouse bench, the last ones to flower inside wanting a light house, as they are inclined to have long, weak stems.

The conditions to produce the early tulips are heat, moisture and shade, but not heat that will burn the roots. On the pipes is no place for them; it is heat around the young growths that is wanted, not at the roots.

The varieties I mentioned for bedding are the very best for forcing. When wanted for any special date, like Easter, and they are a few days too early you can help to keep the tulips in good order by putting the flats under the bench when the flowers are about fully developed and covering with paper, which prevents the opening and closing that takes place on every fine sunny day.

Hyacinths in pots and pans need no forcing towards spring, coming on very quickly as soon as brought into the greenhouse. It is impossible to give any fixed time to allow for these bulbs to come into flower, as seasons vary so much.

There is an immense number of species and varieties of narcissus. Trumpet major and the Incomparable type all do well if given the same treatment as the tulips and Von Sion narcissus. The Polyanthus narcissus are beautiful in form and color and are fragrant. They force well, but should not be exposed to frost at any time. They are not profitable for the commercial man, but are beautiful for the private conservatory. The Narcissus poeticus, and its fine variety ornatus, are both hardy and force well, and so do the elegant sweet scented jonquils.

Hyacinths in Basket, trimmed with White Ribbon.

inches deep. We never cut down the soil nearer than a foot from the end or side of the boxes because they want to be well protected there. The frost is sure to penetrate into the beds from the sides, if anywhere.

Nothing more is done to the beds for a month or two, or till severe winter weather sets in, excepting it be a very dry time. If it is dry give the beds a thorough watering every week. Remember the bulbs are not as though they were planted out and they get none of the benefit of the moisture arising from the depths of the ground as they would if planted in it, and the bulbs will not make roots unless the soil is kept moist. About the middle of December we throw on about four inches of stable manure. It is just as well to let the soil in the flats be slightly frozen before covering with the manure, as it will stop the bulbs from growing up too long. If too much manure is put on it will encourage the bulbs to draw up to a great length before spring, which will greatly injure their handling.

nure, but they are mostly into the houses before very hard weather.

Roman hyacinths will stand as much freezing as the tulips, but must not be handled when frozen. If frozen, bring in the whole covering with them and let them thaw out in a very cool shed. If when frozen they are put suddenly into heat (as you would a tulip) they will be ruined.

The Dutch hyacinths in pots we stand in a frame on dry ashes, and after covering with soil and litter prefer to cover with shutters or glass to prevent very hard freezing. Freezing may not hurt the bulbs, but it breaks the pots and pans.

Roman hyacinths and Paper White narcissus can be had in bloom from the first of November on. They want the light and no extra heat at any time. Both are better when brought on slowly. The Paper White, if well rooted, should have seven weeks in a light house at a temperature of 60 degrees; then it will be in good order for Christmas. As the season advances Romans require less and less time under glass. During March and

CACTUS.

You can walk through many a greenhouse establishment, large and small, without seeing a specimen of any of these curious plants, and unless you are a specialist you will be wise to leave them alone. The demand for

Paper White Narcissus.

phyllum on the pereskia is very simple. Pieces of the pereskia of any desired length will root in moderately moist sand. When potted off and established in pots the top of the stem is split for an inch or so, a branch of the epiphyllum inserted, and nothing more is to be done except to tie a piece of raffia around the stem to keep the graft in place, and this must be removed as soon as adhesion takes place, which will be soon if the plants are kept in a warm moist house.

CALADIUM.

Most ornamental leaved hot-house plants that are grown entirely for their beautiful leaves, which are of almost every hue. Although strictly a tropical plant they are most useful for decorations in the months of August and September, after their growth is fully matured. They lose their beautiful leaves in the winter and must rest till the following March or April.

There are several species, of which we all remember argyrites as one of the oldest and prettiest with its small silvery marked leaf. The almost innumerable varieties that are now cultivated are hybrids and surpass in beauty the original species. The tubers can be bought at a very reasonable price from any good commercial house.

Their cultivation is easy. The tubers can be placed in 3 or 4-inch pots in March in a temperature of 60 to 65 degrees. A little bottom heat will much help their starting. Water sparingly till they begin to root. When a few leaves are made they can be shifted on. A 6-inch pot will grow a fine specimen, but they are seen occasionally of immense size in 12-inch pots. Many will remember the dozen or more plants exhibited at the New York convention in 1888 from Wootton, Philadelphia. They were grand.

While growing they should have our hottest houses, a little shade, a moist atmosphere and abundance of water; the pots should be drained so that water passes freely through. Liberal treatment as to size of pot is a requirement. The soil can be a good loam, rather coarse, with a fourth of leaf-mould and rotten manure.

In October they show signs of going to rest and water should then be withheld, but not all at once. Keep the soil moderately moist till the leaves have about gone, when you can lay the pots on their sides under a bench in a warm house. A good many fine caladium bulbs are lost from keeping them too dry in the winter, and sometimes from wintering them too cold; 60 degrees is cold enough for them and don't let the soil get dust dry; look at them every two or three weeks and if the soil is very dry give them a watering. In starting, of course you will shake off all the old soil. There is no need of mentioning any of the varieties, for their name is legion, and all are beautiful.

them is altogether too small. You will, however, be often asked: "How shall I make my cactus flower?" etc., and as the florist is supposed to know how to cultivate every green thing it is well to be able to give an intelligent answer to the old lady whose uncle sent her the cactus in question many years ago from Mexico. Grotesque and peculiar as the growth of many of the cacti is the flowers of some, notably the night-blooming cereus (C. grandiflorus) are most gorgeous. It lasts but one short night, but while open it is almost unrivalled in its magnificent form, lovely colors, the beauty of its stamens and general appearance as well as great fragrance.

The mammillarias are the most useful for bedding, making a beautiful appearance in a bed of succulents. The United States and Mexican species will winter in a very cool place and need little, if any, water in the dark winter days. All of the tropical kinds will winter very well in a night temperature of 55 degrees, and our summers suit them well.

They are about as easily grown in a window as they are in the greenhouse if proper care is used in watering. Few if any insects trouble them. Drainage is of first importance, and neither in summer when they are growing nor in winter when they are at rest should the soil ever remain saturated. So whatever the compost be let the pot or tub be filled one-third with broken crocks so that water is sure to pass off quickly. In winter when little growth is being made, especially if you are keeping the plants cool, water sufficient to keep the soil from getting dust dry will do. In April

and May and through the summer, if the soil is well drained, you can water daily.

The soil should be a good fibrous loam to which add one-fourth of coarse sand, and if that is not at hand add some powdered bricks or old plaster crumbled up. They need little pot room and should not be shifted for several seasons. All of them would do well out of doors in summer time if convenient to put them outside, but look out for heavy rains; for those that are in pots or tubs too much water will rot the roots.

Some of the genera are hardy in the latitude of New York, but a very severe winter will hurt them, and where used for bedding it is better to lift them and place in flats and winter in a cold house or protected frame.

The most valuable of the cacti grown for their flowers, and which makes a most showy winter flowering plant is Epiphyllum truncatum and its varieties. It does not make a good plant on its own roots, not being strong enough to stand erect, and when a handsome little tree is seen it has been grafted on the pereskia stock. The flowers of the epiphyllum are most numerous and its varieties have colors varying from deep scarlet to almost pure white. The type is a deep rose color.

Like all the cacti the epiphyllum wants perfect drainage and must not be over-potted. Keep cool in the late fall months till they begin to show flower when they should have more heat till the flowers are fully expanded and can then be removed to a cool house which will prolong the life of the flowers.

The operation of grafting the epi-

C. Esculentum.

Caladium esculentum is an important plant with the florist and it enters largely into his spring business. Every one knows this caladium, and some of our customers know it by the descriptive and artistic name of "Elephant's Ears."

They are multiplied by the small tubers that are always found on the large ones, but at the low cost of a tuber the size of a base ball (and that is amply large enough) it will never pay a florist to grow his own bulbs. You cannot begin to raise them as

three inches deep in which the bottom half is sifted decayed manure and the top half sand, pushing the bulb down till its top is little above the rim of flat, and the bulbs almost touching. Give them a watering and place the flats on the hot water pipes. You will save two or three weeks by this method over starting them in the pots on a cold bench and will save much valuable space. We plant them in the flats in time so they will be ready to pot off just after Easter when the pressure for space has been relieved.

When taken out of the flats they have made a growth of five or six

coachman can water to his heart's content. I mentioned a bulb the size of a base ball, but that is the largest useful size. Tubers that are 1¾ to 2 inches in diameter are large enough to make fine plants for summer use.

We hear that the tubers of this caladium are cooked and eaten in the south. Its name implies that it is edible, and its other name is Colocasia esculentum.

CALAMUS

The rattan palms, or calamus, include twenty or more species of slender growing and very graceful palms that are found in a wild state in various portions of the tropics, chiefly in India or the East Indies.

Some of the species become climbers in their native country, and are said to attain a length of stem of 200 to 300 feet, and to trail over the tops of forest trees in Java and Borneo, but the subject of our illustration is one of the smaller growing species, and not likely to outgrow its accommodations for a period of several years at least.

Calamus ciliaris is a particularly graceful palm in a young state, having a slender, reed-like stem, and finely divided pinnate leaves. The leaves of this species are light green, the pinnae narrow and arranged very closely on the stem, and the foliage is rather soft to the touch, owing to its being covered with short, hair-like bristles.

C. ciliaris is essentially a warm house palm, flourishing in a temperature of 70 to 75 degrees, with abundant moisture, its tropical jungle habitat giving us some idea as to its cultural wants.

The leaves of this species being rather thin in texture, it is liable to attacks of red spider unless freely syringed and watered, but when well-grown is very attractive, and while not adapted for all trade purposes is a valuable and effective plant for special occasions.

C. ciliaris suckers freely around the base, and by careful handling these suckers may be removed and established, but it is necessary to keep them rather close and warm for a time in order to encourage the new roots, and also to be careful that they are not allowed to get too dry.

W. H. T.

Calamus Ciliaris.

cheaply as you can buy them from the man who grows an acre. If you have any plants on your own place and wish to save them, cut the stalk off a foot above the ground after the first frost, dig up, shake off all the soil and lay them on the ground under a rose-house bench. I have found the temperature and humidity of a rose house just right providing the ground is dry.

When we receive the bulbs in the spring we cut out all the eyes and small tubers because we don't want them, and we cut off the remains of the old tuber close up to the new sound one. We put them in flats

inches and are a mass of roots. They are then potted into 5-inch pots, or extra strong ones into 6-inch. You do not want them too large when bedded out, as the wind breaks them, nor too late or your customers will be disappointed; about eighteen inches high, with three leaves, will do. Any kind of rich soil will do for them in pots, with water ad libitum, and a light, dry house. When you are growing your caladiums all houses are much alike as to temperature.

To make the best effect in any position out of doors the ground should be dug deep, with plenty of manure worked in. Here is a plant that the

CALANTHE.

See Orchids.

CALCEOLARIA.

There are few more attractive and showy greenhouse flowers than the calceolaria, and although useless as a cut flower it is of great value as a greenhouse decorative plant, or as a window plant, lasting fully as long as a cineraria and many other of our popular flowers. There are several species, both of the herbaceous and shrubby sections, nearly all from the west coast of South America and at a good elevation, for calceolarias dislike great heat at any time of their growth.

Little attention is paid to the species, the beautiful hybrids of the herbaceous section being what we are interested in. Seed can be obtained of any reliable seedsman that will produce a great variety of beautiful flowers. Sow from June to end of September. If wanted in bloom by March the earlier month is the time to sow, but they are difficult to have in bloom that early; if sown in September they can be bloomed the following May, and with less risk of failure than earlier. The seed is most minute and for directions about sowing refer to chapter on that subject. Would say here that it should never be covered, a piece of glass over the seed pan being sufficient.

When the little plants are large enough to handle place them in pans or pots an inch apart. When they are near touching each other put into 3-inch pots. By December they will be large enough to go into 5-inch pots and as they must be wintered cool they will not need another shift till the first of March, when they can go into their flowering pots, a 7 or 8-inch.

Calceolarias are not so often seen in either the florists' windows or the private garden as their great beauty should warrant, and the reason is that although they cannot be called a difficult plant to manage, they are easily ruined by neglect or mismanagement. The following conditions if faithfully observed will insure success.

Watering: At no time must they be allowed to wilt for want of water, and

of winter 40 degrees at night is plenty warm enough. In Europe they are largely grown in cold-frames. Here that is not as practicable, but from seed sowing till middle of November a cold-frame is much the best for them. Let them at all times be so situated that they can have light, room

nent one till they are near flowering time.

Soil: A rather light loam, not chopped or sifted too fine, with a fourth or fifth of thoroughly rotted manure, will grow them well. If the soil is heavy, add sand to the manure. I am sure it pays well when they are in the larger pots, the 5-inch and upwards, to drain with a few crocks and a piece of green moss.

Insects: They are seldom troubled with any but the common greenfly, but to those the calceolaria is a choice morsel, and too often a fine batch of young plants is utterly ruined by them. Don't wait till you see the fly, but smoke mildly every week at least without fail, and till they are taken to the show-house should always have tobacco stems strewn among the pots. There is no feature in the cultivation of the calceolaria so important as this; never let aphis be seen on them.

The shrubby section of calceolaria is used in Europe largely as a summer flowering garden plant. The writer has tried it here several times, but always with failure, and that I believe is the general verdict; our hot summer is the obstacle. As a flowering plant for the greenhouse they are not nearly as ornamental as the herbaceous varieties. The same cultural directions will apply to them, excepting that they are usually propagated by cuttings, which root readily in the fall in a cool, shady frame.

CAMELLIA.

This once universally cultivated plant has gone largely out of fashion and for the last twenty years is neither seen nor spoken of. The cause is not far to seek. Our largest and best tea roses are as beautiful in form, of

Herbaceous Calceolarias.

like the cineraria must never be over watered or that will kill them; avoid extremes both ways. No syringing is needed.

Temperature: In the dull, dark days

to grow, plenty of fresh air and a low temperature. Bright sun coming suddenly in early spring is liable to burn their leaves, so a temporary shade should be provided, but not a perma-

3

warmer tints of color and fragrant. Then again all cut flowers must now have their natural stem and that largely bars the camellia. There was a time which all older florists remember in the first days of the use of elaborate mechanically made designs, when camellias were indispensable, and more than one of us can remember the request or order of our patrons of twenty-five years ago: "Be sure to put in plenty of Japonicas."

They are mostly all propagated by grafting the fine varieties on seedling stocks, or stocks raised from cuttings put into sandy soil in July and August in a cold-frame that can be kept shady and cool. The propagation is better left to the specialist, and the growing of camellias to the private gardener. Not because their cultivation is at all difficult, but because the

only way to get them into bloom early is to start them growing in the spring early. At that time they will stand a good heat with plenty of moisture on leaf and root. As soon as they have made their growth and show the small flower bud on the end of the growth they should be kept as cool as possible during the remainder of the summer. The hot summer is what they don't like, and there is no better place in summer than out of doors in the shade of a building, or what is still better a summer house covered with lattice-work, which gives partial shade and coolness. They will do very well in winter in a temperature of 40 degrees at night.

When I say they are hardy in the south of England and the milder parts of Ireland you can form an idea as to their hardiness. I remember about

CANNA.

The canna was of old often called "Indian Shot" because the seed is excellent as a charge for the shotgun when a stray dog is the game in view.

Few plants have undergone such a change and improvement of late years as the canna. Thirty years ago cannas were grown almost exclusively for their handsome tropical foliage, but since M. Crozy introduced his wonderful hybrids the flower is of more importance than the leaves. Our summers are admirably adapted to the perfect development of the canna, and as a decorative plant for our summer gardens it easily takes the front rank. Gorgeous beds are seen in the parks, cemeteries, private grounds, and even in the humble little garden of the day laborer. In an 8 or 9-inch pot they

Bed of Cannas bordered with Acalyphas.

demand, both for the plants and flowers, is too meager.

In cool conservatories they make grand bushes planted out in the border. The writer well remembers the day when it was his duty to jar the stem of a large double white camellia every morning when in flower and then rake up from the perfectly kept border hundreds of fallen petals, but that was in a climate more suitable, I think, for the camellia than this one.

They like a good, strong yellow loam and should not be overpotted. The roots should be moist the year round and in the spring and early summer (their growing time) should have plenty of water and an occasional syringing. They can be had in bloom from October till May, but endure no such thing as forcing. The

the year 1864 a large plant of the "Lady Hume's Blush" that was badly covered with white scale. It was left out of doors all winter with the intention of applying the radical treatment of kill or cure. The camellia came through the winter unharmed. I forget whether the scale was killed or not. The scale is about the only pest that troubles the camellia, and that can be destroyed by washing with the kerosene emulsion.

The hybrids were raised from the several species are the most useful if you grow them at all. The single colored varieties are fine decorative flowers. I learn from a Philadelphia firm that a great many camellias are now sold to go to the southern states. Where planted out they would be very fine. Last winter, however, would about do them up.

make grand plants for the decoration of a large conservatory, where you can see the fullest perfection of their grand flowers.

Since the introduction of the Crozy type (or, as they are often called, "Flowering Cannas"), the old species and types whose showy leaves were the attraction and flowers small and few, have sunk into desuetude and are rarely cultivated, because the newer varieties have not only splendid spikes of flowers but all the variety in color of foliage also. There is one of the old type still left that for effect of foliage I have never yet seen equalled by any of the large flowering ones. We call it La Grande Rouge. It grows six feet high in any ordinary soil, has narrow, long, pointed leaves, in color a deep, almost purple, bronze, and

Carludovica Atrovirens. (See page 44.)

June 1st, which is planting time, they should be in 4-inch pots.

The readiest way, and that by which all fine varieties are propagated, is by cutting up or division of the root. The old stools that have been stored all winter are divided in March. If the piece of root is three or four inches long, with one good eye or bud, it is large enough to make a fine plant. We place the pieces of root in three or four inches of sand and old hot-bed manure in flats about the middle or end of March and place the flats on the pipes where the heat is not too violent. They start to root and grow immediately.

By middle of April you have presumably got rid of your lilies, etc., and can find room to pot off the cannas into 4 and 5-inch pots. They should have a light bench in a light house and no shade, but abundance of water, and by the first of June they will be fine plants, many of them sending up their first spike of flowers.

Any soil that is one-third half rotten manure will do for the cannas. You cannot give them too deep or too rich a soil and they require a great abundance of water. They are usually planted 15 to 18 inches apart.

When the foliage is destroyed by frost the tops are cut down to within six inches of the ground and the clump of roots lifted and removed to beneath a dry bench. On the ground beneath a carnation bench is an excellent place, or anywhere the temperature is between 40 and 50 degrees, but it must not be wet or they will start to grow. Neither must there be a drip; the latter is, I know from experience, very bad for them, as the roots will rot. It is better when placing them under the bench to put boards under them for the moisture of the soil, however dry it may appear, will start them growing. A root-house for the purpose, where dahlias would keep, would be the best place, but few of us have that, and beneath the benches is amply good providing you guard against drip on them.

We always treat the canna as an herbaceous plant, and it is called so by high authorities, but in their tropical

very upright habit. For the center of a large bed we don't know its equal.

Our own American florists have raised many grand varieties, equal to any of the imported ones. The canna seems well adapted to our climate and environment. In the north in winter, outside the greenhouse, our vegetation is largely hibernating. The sombre pines keep green 'tis true, but we are without the broad-leaved evergreens of the south. Our giants of the forest are bleak and bare and the snow-bird flies noiselessly across the waste. Our woods are solemnly still. Our wild animals have scattered their seeds and herbaceous plants are covered with their welcome overcoat of snow. Except for man and his necessities it would be a quiet scene. The bear slumbers in the hollow tree and dreams of honey; the squirrel stops at home and enjoys the fruits of his frugal care, and the marmot curls up in his deep burrow but peeps out in early March to see how prospects are, and about the time he takes his first peep is the time to sow canna seed. When spring once comes our vegetation awakens and grows apace. Trees leave out it seems in a night, our

woods and fields are clothed with leaf and blossom, and music is everywhere and free to all from the tireless throat of the frog and the sweet call of the meadow lark (which is not a lark at all, but a starling), and it seems to me that the quick and stately growth of the canna is in keeping with all this, and is our ideal decorative plant.

Cannas come largely true from seed, and good plants can be raised by sowing in February for the following summer's use. The seed is so hard that it is well to not only soak it in a bag suspended in hot water, which you can renew occasionally, but are all the better if you take each seed, held firmly by a pair of pincers and slice off a small piece of the hard covering of the seed. Sow in pans in three inches of soil, covering the seed half an inch or more. We place the pans on the hot-water pipes, which quickens the growth of the seed. When the plant is three inches high we remove it and start it growing in a pot; but don't throw away the contents of the pan, for there are always more to come, and they will likely keep straggling along for months. Grow the seedlings along in a light, warm house and by

home they are by no means herbaceous, spreading and growing and flowering the year round. You can lift, divide and propagate new and rare varieties the year round, and you can lift large clumps before frost has touched them and use them in decorations.

It is difficult to pick out even a dozen varieties, for new sorts are constantly appearing and what is considered the finest this year may be eclipsed by seedlings of next year. Cannas that do not flower abundantly and hold their flowers well will not do for bedding, and those minus these qualities will soon be lost sight of. Italia and Austria, so beautiful as individual flowers, are useless planted out as is most likely all that type. Some of the best bedders, if not new, are:

Madame Crozy: Vermilion scarlet, bordered with golden yellow.

Florence Vaughan: Fine yellow, mottled with crimson.

Paul Marquant: Salmon.

Souvenir de Antoine Crozy: A grand variety; an improvement on Mme. Crozy.

Tarrytown: Rich bright red.

Trocadero: Deep crimson lake.

Charles Henderson: Deep crimson.

Egandale: Soft red; fine dark foliage.

President Carnot: Scarlet; dark foliage.

Chicago: Vermilion scarlet; fine green foliage.

President Cleveland: Orange scarlet; one of the best.

Rose Mawr: Rosy pink.

Klondike: Orange.

Admiral Avellan: Orange scarlet; fine dark foliage.

Papa: One of the best reds; immense spike.

Madame Montefiore: A fine yellow, slightly spotted.

And dozens of others. Test carefully the new varieties as they appear, unless you have a chance to see a whole bed of them growing.

CANDYTUFT.

See Annuals.

CAPE POND WEED.

See Aponogeton.

CARLUDOVICA.

Though frequently considered among palms and grown with them, yet this handsome foliage plant is not a palm, being more nearly related to the pandanus family. C. atrovirens has been in cultivation for many years, but does not appear to have become common in the trade on this side of the ocean, and as a matter of fact is seldom met with outside of private collections.

C. atrovirens is a stemless or nearly stemless plant of bushy habit, the leaves of which are bifid, plaited somewhat like those of a curculigo, and very dark green, as indicated by the specific name.

This plant grows freely in a warm house, and is not hard to please in

the matter of compost, but makes more rapid growth in light, rich soil with good drainage, the latter point being the more necessary from the fact that an abundant supply of water is needed for its welfare.

Propagation may be effected by seeds when these are obtainable, but more often depends on division, as C. atrovirens produces suckers freely, and by washing out the roots these suckers may be separated from the parent plant without difficulty, and soon become established plants.

The carludovicas are said to be natives only of tropical South America, where a number of handsome species have been found, one of which, C. palmata, possesses additional interest on account of its leaves furnishing the material for the so-called Panama hats, those luxuries of summer dress that are unfortunately beyond the purse of the average florist. But we may be permitted to grow a plant of Carludovica palmata, and by exercising the imagination we may see the patient South American native selecting one large young leaf, carefully removing the stiff veins or ribs from it, then slitting it into narrow strips, and finally plaiting it into a shapely head cover without separating the strips at the stem end. Such ingenuity deserves a proper financial reward, but in all probability the larger portion of the profit is secured by the European or American hatter, who ultimately retails the product. W. H. T.

CARNATION.

If not the most important flower we grow, the carnation certainly stands next to the rose, both in area of glass

devoted to its culture and value of the flowers sold. Of all our commercial flowers the type of carnations we grow are most distinctively American. They are very different from the tree carnation of Europe, which had the reputation of being perennial bloomers there, but the flowers were few and far between and had no such stems as our present day carnations. Nor are they like the garden carnations which come with a grand burst of bloom in June and July, but have no tendency to flower again for another year. It is certain that our strain inherits the blood of more than one breed, for seedlings often revert back to varieties that produce a strong growth and few flowers, and some again are croppers.

The splendid varieties we have today have been produced not suddenly but by the slow operation of the law of evolution, aided by artificial selection. The first carnations that I attempted to flower in the winter months were La Purite, carmine, and Edwardsii and President Degraw, both white, all very free bloomers, and the flowers were always used with short stems. If we had disbudded and picked the flowers with long stems I doubt whether they would be as free as many of our present varieties.

Astoria was a pioneer among carnations and a cross between it and Edwardsii produced Buttercup, which was a wonderful flower in its day and which for years had no rival. From 1875 to 1885 there were no carnation specialists and the few varieties introduced during that time are gone and forgotten. About the latter date appeared Grace Wilder, the first of its

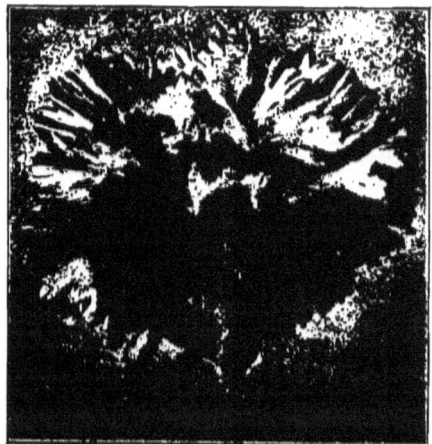

Carnation Mrs. Geo. M. Bradt.

House of Carnations.

color (Scott is almost the same shade). Then Mr. Simmons, of Geneva, sent out his famous varieties, several of which were a great advance on existing varieties and some of them are standard sorts today. Silver Spray, J. J. Harrison, Portia, Tidal Wave, and greatest of all—Daybreak—were sent out by him.

To trace further the subsequent introductions would make too long a chapter. It is about ten years since the carnation was taken up and specialized by many of our best horticulturists with the result that we have attained what ten years ago would have been considered the absolute ideal. But who can tell what Dorner, Hill, May, Nicholson, Fisher, Ward or other enthusiasts will do. Size has been attained almost or quite to the desired point. Jubilee, Pingree and America have a two-foot stem of sufficient substance to hold their heads quite erect.

Fragrance should be an attribute of all varieties. In color we have shades from deep maroon to purest white, and yet perhaps it is in color that the future promises most for the raiser of new varieties. I would say just here that when any good variety does well with you don't discard it till you are sure you can grow a better variety of the same color.

There are few plants that accommodate themselves so readily to a great variety of soils. Yet from quality of soils, or more likely methods of handling, good gardeners fail with some varieties while entirely successful with others.

Whether we have reached the limit in the improvement of the divine flower or not is a question that it is not at all essential to worry over because we shall want the disseminator of new varieties always with us. Whether under our continuous winter culture varieties should gradually lack health and vigor is a question that has led to some controversy. We don't "force" carnations by any means, yet to a great extent we reverse the seasons, and propagating by cuttings is not raising a new individual as growing from seed. We are merely divid-

ing and perpetuating the old original plant. And my experience is that after eight or ten years a variety loses its vigor and is a prey to all carnation diseases. And even if it did not it would be superseded by improved varieties.

Propagation.

In cultural hints the proper place to begin is with the cutting. Let me repeat that the plants from which you take the cuttings have not been forced. They have been subjected to a lower temperature than that in which it would flower in its native habitat. So the plant is not exhausted, and there is no need of having any plants in a cold-frame to propagate from. No better material can be had than that from your flowering plants.

Cuttings root readily from November 1st to the middle of April, or even earlier or later, but except for special purposes, such as plants to flower in early summer, which can be propagated in November, or in case you are very short of a variety, from January 1st to March 1st is the best time to put the cuttings in the sand. No special propagating house is needed. An ordinary bench such as you would grow carnations on, is as good as the most expensive arrangements and the temperature of the house can be just the same. Avoid a direct draught, either from a door or ventilator. Carnations want the light and little shading is needed during January and February. When the sun gets high enough to wilt the cuttings we tack cheese cloth up to the glass. That is far better than laying on and taking off newspapers. The cloth is heavy enough to shed the rays of the sun at any time and is far enough above the cuttings to give them sufficient light at all times.

For the cutting bed three inches of coarse clean river or lake sand is sufficient. As a consolation to those who do not have lake sand near them I will say that for the past five years I have

every day. If hot water or steam pipes run beneath the board bench, there is no harm done, but what we know as bottom heat is not at all essential in propagating carnations.

In the early days of carnation growing, before flowers were picked with long stems, we used for cuttings only the young growths from the bottom, those that would grow up and produce flowers, and I am not sure but what they make the finest plants. They are not, however, the quickest or surest to root. The propagator of large quantities, or those wishing to raise the largest possible number of a new variety, may take every green shoot that will make a plant or root. But that is not the way to perpetuate your plants for the best results. Cuttings should be taken only from the healthiest plants, and it will pay to also choose from the plants bearing the largest and best flowers, for like begets

with an old knife a perfectly straight line across three or four feet of propagating bed without the aid of a straight edge should be sent back to washing pots.

In a temperature of 50 degrees at night the cuttings will root in 25 to 30 days. They do not all root equally in the same time. Some cuttings (of roses for instance) are started up as soon as the roots have started out a fourth of an inch, but a carnation I would rather have with roots an inch long. I have occasion every year to put some in flats in two inches of sand and some in 2¼-inch pots, and I see no difference in results in the field. The flats (mine are small, holding only two dozen plants) are much the cheapest, requiring less care and being easier to handle than pots.

After the first week from the sand they will be well rooted in the pots or flats and should be given full sunlight and plenty of air. As planting out time approaches you will have stopped firing in the houses, so a good light exposure there will do as well for the plants as anywhere, but if crowded for room a cold-frame is quite as good a place and even better as you can remove the sash entirely on mild days and thus prepare in the best way for planting in the field. We always like to have the plants early enough to have pinched or stopped them once before planting out time.

Field Culture.

Don't put off planting time. The carnation is not a tender plant; it is almost a truly hardy plant. In our latitude the end of April or very early in May is late enough. If you defer planting till end of May you have lost a month's growth. Perhaps no crop should be grown year after year for many years on the same spot. We know this is very wrong for some, but we have grown carnations three consecutive years on the same ground and have not noticed the slightest ill effects. We use a light dressing of stable manure every spring and plow deep, not less than eight inches.

We plant 12 inches between plants and 15 inches between rows and leave out every sixth row. Be sure to plant in straight rows both ways; that allows you to run your Planet, Jr., cultivator both ways. This little cultivator saves you lots of labor and does about all the work, yet two or three times during the season you must go over them with the hand hoe and loosen up the soil close to the plants. We don't hoe primarily to kill weeds. We hoe or cultivate to keep the soil loose, and incidentally we of course destroy all the weeds. After a heavy rain when the ground is just friable seems the best time of all to hoe. Then the operation is a pleasure and it's a blessing to the plants. You can almost see them grow. Yet we do not always wait for a rain. In long dry spells in June, July and August we cultivate once a week.

Bench of Carnation Cuttings.

propagated in bank sand, containing even some loam in fine particles, and I have not lost on an average 5 per cent. of the cuttings, and in free rooting varieties, like Scott and Daybreak, none. There is little danger of the troublesome fungus among your carnation cuttings because the temperature should not be high enough for its vegetation. But as a preventive and for another reason we always water the sand with the ammoniacal solution before each batch of cuttings is put in.

Watering is a matter of pure sense and judgment. If the glass is covered with snow, or the weather is dull and sunless, we water every three or four days. If the weather is bright and sunny, allowing plenty of ventilation, then every second day. And if you have occasion to propagate late in March the cuttings will take water

like. The offshoots from the flowering stem make fine cuttings, but they should be taken not too low down, where they are hard and woody, nor too near the flower, where they are small and spindling.

Some growers just tear off the cuttings and put them in the sand as they are pulled off. I prefer to cut the smallest possible piece of the bottom. As to trimming the leaves, generally the two lower ones are best removed. Shearing off the tops of the leaves does not hurt the cuttings, nor does it help them to root; it is done merely to allow you to get more cuttings into the same surface of sand. The distance apart to place the cuttings in the sand is merely a question of variety. Some need more room than others, but the cuttings should be at least one inch into the sand in straight rows, and the man that cannot draw

The last week in August I would call the ideal time. If it could all be done then so much the better, but the quantity handled compels large growers to extend the operation from Aug. 15th to the first or second week in September. The question is often asked and discussed—"Is it best to lift carnations with a ball of earth?" It is a foolish question to an old carnation grower. If your soil is of a light texture it will be impossible to lift with any ball, and most undesirable if you could. If planted in a clay soil you must wait for a rain or thoroughly soak the plants before lifting. Clay when wet is as friable as sandy loam and will drop off and leave the roots and fibers intact. We do not want to retain any of the soil that they occupied in the field, but we do want all the roots, and to preserve these we raise the plants with the aid of two digging forks, each on opposite sides of the plant and six or seven inches from the plant. It is a job you can work hard at, but it should not be done in a hurry.

As soon as the plants are lifted and the soil shaken off the roots they are laid in flats and the flats carted to the door of the greenhouse and then carried to the planter so that the roots are exposed very little. It is not un-

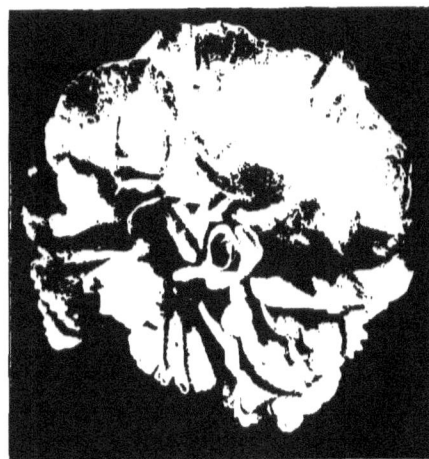

For years I practiced and preached watering when the plants were put out. Not surface watering, but a little water in the hole around the plant and then filling up with dry soil. That is the correct way to plant anything from a geranium to an oak tree; in fact the only way. But for the past two seasons we have not done that with carnations and never will again; there is no need of it. There is plenty of moisture in the ground and rising from its depths to keep the plants in good order till we get a rain. There is another great advantage in getting the plants out early. The weather is cool and you will catch the spring rains. I have always condemned watering during summer under any conditions and know that it is unnecessary and wrong.

Stopping the plant by pinching out the leading shoots is one of the most important operations connected with carnation culture. If not stopped once before planting out they will need it very shortly afterward. By stopping the leading shoots the intent is to produce a greater number of growths. A few years ago we discontinued stopping the plants early in August and did not lift them till the end of September. The plants would then be full of buds and we expected to go right on cutting flowers from the newly lifted plants. Such flowers as we then produced would not sell at any price today. With hardly an exception (the Scott may be one) no carnation should show buds at lifting time. All flower bearing shoots should be made inside, then you will get a fairly good stem and a clean flower. The plant should have its powers taxed as little as possible when undergoing the trans-

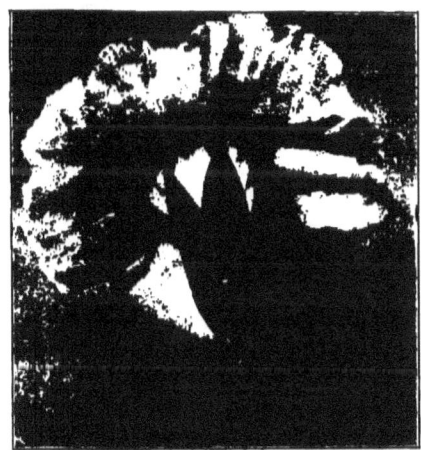

Carnation White Cloud.

planting from field to bench and the buds and flowers would be the greatest hindrance to a speedy and successful start under the new conditions.

Transplanting.

Large growers cannot fix any one week as the time for lifting, but have to begin early to get done in time.

usual for us to just strike a very hot spell for this operation. I have been planting carnations more than once in the first week of September when the thermometer under the apple tree's shade was 90 degrees and under glass 110 degrees, but we did not postpone the work "on account of the inclemency of the weather." Oh, no, we kept right on, and I don't remember of losing or injuring any plants by so doing.

At the risk of being thought egotistical I will say that we do not lose any plants through transplanting. I have time and again noticed that in houses holding about 2,500 plants we have lost none up to the following May; in others, perhaps one plant. I

I have had to listen more than once to an ex-farmer carnation grower who would inform me with pride and pleasantry that his boy could plant four carnations to my one. The best answer to that is: "You don't say so!" with pleasure and surprise on your features. When you notice in a month's time that half of those "My boy planted" are dead or dying you

A Bunch of White Carnations.

have read of growers who thought they had fair success if they did not lose more than 10 per cent. A loss of 5 per cent would worry us. When we consider the crude and ungardenerlike way in which transplanting is done by some of the smaller growers, or men who have perhaps taken to the business after a failure at many other callings, it is no wonder that the losses are 10, or even 20 per cent. The great evil in this simple but important operation is that the beginner who is without a gardener's education attempts to attain speed before he has gained the knowledge "How to do it."

are reconciled to your old slow ways. I am not by any means encouraging slowness (far from it), but learn to plant and pot and shift and tie properly first, and then when performing any of these operations speed will never interfere with the quality of the work.

The distance between plants on the bench will vary some with the varieties and also with the size of the plants. McGowan used to do with eight inches between the plants and ten inches between the rows. Scott and Daybreak, when fine plants, should be ten inches apart and twelve

inches between rows. Two years ago it was very rainy and our carnation plants grew so fast during July and August that both the last mentioned varieties needed 14 inches between rows and by Christmas were quite as thick as health would allow. Your good sense must guide you in this. To plant too far apart is not economical, but it is better to err in this direction than to crowd them overmuch, for that means mildew and rotting of the lower growths, a weakening of the whole plant and poor, weak flowers. I have seen them so closely packed in (because the owner had more than he needed and hated to see any perish in the field) that half the plants rotted and the rest were useless. Air and daylight should have access to the plant on each side if you expect good flowers, and only fine flowers will return a profit now-a-days.

Twenty years ago we used six inches of soil in the bench and later five inches was found to be enough. I believe that four inches is ample to grow any carnation, and some of the finest flowers we see at exhibitions are grown in less, but I would say four inches is about right.

Carnations seem to do fairly well in a great variety of soils. Such sandy loam as they have on Long Island is undoubtedly the ideal for most of the varieties, but if properly handled a varied texture of soil suits them. Mr. W. N. Rudd, of Mt. Greenwood, Ill., grows prize-takers in the fat prairie land of his state, and my neighbors, W. J. Palmer & Son, grow magnificent Daybreaks and several others in a stiff loam that is almost a clay. At the organization of the American Carnation Society in Philadelphia there was a discussion as to renewing the soil annually in the benches. I was surprised to hear any one say that they grew them several years in the same old soil. We had never dreamed of such a thing, but always renewed the soil every summer. Now that we have come down to only four inches of soil I would certainly advocate a change of every particle of soil annually.

Our method is to plow up a piece of clover sod towards the end of May when the clover has made a good growth. We plow five inches deep and plow and cultivate this piece frequently during summer, and early in July spread the manure on the surface and plow it in, and then add the bone flour and harrow it in. We will most likely have had a rain before hauling in the soil and if so it may need another run over with the cultivator, which helps to distribute the manure and bone. It is then hauled to the door of the house and wheeled on to the benches or got in by the most expeditious method that you can devise. It should, however, be a wheelbarrow or small tramway and truck; the old hand-barrow is killing, and not fit work for bipeds, black or white, male or female.

We try to get about a sixth or sev-

House of Armazindy Carnations.

enth of the well rotted stable manure into the soil. The horse manure is much preferable to that from the cow stable. The bone should be of the best quality and very finely ground. What we know as bone meal is often too coarse and it does not dissolve in time for the plants to have received the full benefit of it, so we get the bone flour. A 5-inch pot of bone flour to an ordinary wheelbarrow of soil is not too much, but less may be needed. You can find out how much this is to the square yard or rod.

It is a fact that occasionally the finest of carnations are grown without the aid of any manures, either artificial or animal; it has happened so with me. Last year, running short of bone, we used a grade of superphosphate known as potato phosphate and the result was quite equal to that from the bone and it was much less expensive. Bone black is also excellent, and many growers highly prize wood ashes. If I were unable to procure both bone meal and the stable manure I would much rather depend on the bone meal or superphosphate and dispense with the animal manure, too much of which produces a strong, but soft growth. For the different composts and their ingredients I must refer you to the reports of Professors Taft, Arthur and Bailey, or to our expert growers like Dorner & Sons.

To return to the planting. If the soil is very dry when put on the bench I prefer to give it a thorough soaking a day or two before planting. Make a wide hole with the trowel (but your hand is the best trowel) and spread the roots out in a natural way. Push in the soil on the roots, and I like to press the soil firmly around the roots, and be sure not to put the plant any deeper than it was growing in the field. Deep planting has killed lots of carnations. While you are making the hole, arranging the roots and filling in the soil with the right hand, the plant is firmly grasped, with its growth inside your fingers, by the left hand, so you can see that the plant is at the right depth, place and position, and is finished off neatly in every way. An earnest workman will do all this well and neatly much quicker than I can describe it. Some may ask what may be considered a good day's work for a man planting, supposing the plants are delivered right to his hand and other hands water them. I would be quite satisfied with 1,500 in ten hours' work. Any faster than this would raise doubts as to the quality of the work. Soil, however, makes a difference, and an upright grower (like Scott) is quicker to handle than Daybreak, which is spreading.

House Culture.

The first week in the houses is the most critical time with the carnations.

If you get them well established it will take a lot of brutal treatment to kill them, although continued skillful management is needed to insure best results. I am very particular about the first watering. It should be sufficient to thoroughly wet every particle of soil on the bench, and I am not satisfied till I see it dripping through the bottom of the bench. The quantity of water will depend upon the dryness of your soil when planting. We shade the first week after planting (and I think that is of great benefit) by simply throwing some muddy water on the glass. A lump of stiff blue clay dissolved in a tub of water and the water thrown on by a tin dipper will answer every purpose. The rain soon washes it off and if you don't get a rain the hose will do it with little trouble. In a week, or at least in ten days, the new roots will be active in the benches and no more shade is wanted till the following May or June.

If the weather is hot and windy I prefer to let the houses be hot rather than draughty. A cutting wind is bad for any plant when its roots are inactive, so keep the ventilators almost closed for the first few days, and if the nights are still give all the ventilation you possibly can then. You will see the carnations stand up in the morning as if they had grown there all summer. The cool night air is their salvation and the hot, dry air of daytime, is their severe ordeal. We throw water around the house and lightly spray the plants for the first few days, and we believe (contrary to scientific exponents) that the plants are greatly benefited by so doing. After the first week, and the plants have taken hold, we ventilate all we possibly can day and night and entirely discontinue all syringing.

No part of my endeavor to impart

Plant of Carnation Jubilee.

my simple knowledge to the reader is done more earnestly than that regarding this fall management of the carnation. It is during the months of September, October and November that so many houses of carnations are ruined, and there are lots of them that have too little ventilation supplied them, and many growers don't avail themselves of the means of ventilation that they have. A strong, sturdy, healthy plant in the latter part of November will endure a lot of mismanagement for the next three months, but a forced up, weak plant at that date will never repay you when the dark days come. Give all the air

you can, day and night, till winter sets in. There are thousands of carnation houses throughout the country most inadequately furnished with ventilation. Get them altered, or grow something else.

In a week or ten days the second watering of the beds is needed, but no subsequent watering should be so copious as the first one. To attempt to tell you how often a bed needed watering would be preposterous. If you

can't tell by sight or touch when the beds are dry and will take a watering, I might as well try to describe by words a sharp or a flat in music to an ear that cannot observe it when heard. You should not attempt to keep a bed or potted plant always at one degree of moisture. Extremes are bad, but it does not hurt to let them get slightly on the dry side or in that healthy state when a watering will be greatly appreciated by the plant. We try to keep the surface of the beds slightly loosened up and entirely free of weeds at all times.

Some growers tell us to keep the beds free of weeds and "dry leaves,

which should be removed." I am happy to state that we have not had occasion to remove any dry leaves for some years, and there is no occasion to have any if the plants are properly treated during the first month on the bench, particularly the first week. Some of our best growers clean the surface of the beds thoroughly in October and November and then put on a half or three-quarters of an inch of mulch, which feeds surface roots, prevents the drying out of the beds and the necessity of continually stirring the surface of the soil. It is an excellent plan. We prefer to do it, however, in February, as with our frequent snows and dark weather the beds dry out slowly. For the mulch we use rotten manure and loam, half and half, and before putting it on the bed we stir the surface and sprinkle on a good dusting of bone flour, covering the bone with the mulch. If you are going to carry your carnations on into June or July this mulching will be of the greatest benefit.

I don't think I have yet said anything about temperature. If a house is very light the day temperature is not of great importance providing it is high enough. It is certain that some varieties do better in lower temperature than others. Daybreak flowers freely in a night temperature of 45 degrees, Jubilee wants 55 degrees at night, or does very well at that, but 50 degrees at night will be found to suit the great majority of varieties very well, and is high enough for any if first class flowers and a continuous supply is expected. All of them should go up to 65 degrees in the daytime, unless the weather is very cold and it is all fire heat; then stop at 60 degrees. If the sun is shining let the house go up to 70 degrees; that is only the carnation's natural temperature. Some growers attribute bursting of the calyx largely to a very uneven temperature; that is, letting the house get down some nights as low as 40 degrees or less. But this may be theory only. The nearer you can keep the house to 50 degrees at night and to 65 to 70 degrees in the daytime, or noon, the better success you will have. A little ventilation should be given for a short time every day except in the very severest weather. On cloudy days when the outside temperature is perhaps 35 to 40 degrees it is economy to fire up and give ventilation.

Disbudding.

Disbudding, which was practiced by few ten years ago, is now universally done by all growers. It seems a great labor, but when the expense is spread over every hundred carnations you pick, the cost is extremely small, and more than that, it is now an absolute necessity. Disbudding should be done every week. The buds develop very quickly, and they should be rubbed off when quite small, not left on till they are almost showing color, or disbudding will be of little avail. The object of disbudding is to have only one bud receive the whole strength of the shoot. If you allow two or three buds to share its strength till they are nearly full size you have done little good.

Tying.

The matter of tying is of the greatest importance and a considerable part of the expense of growing carnations. Thirty years ago and for many years thereafter nothing better was thought of than the primitive straight stick, and in the days of short-stemmed, or really stemless, flowers, it did very well. Now-a-days it is useless, and the advent of the long-stemmed flower has compelled us to use some better method.

A great many devices have been thought of and many arrangements in the shape of wire supports invented, mostly all useless. There is, however, one device of wire that seems pre-eminently ahead of anything yet invented, and which it seems to me is about perfect. I do not say this to favor any manufacturer, but in justice to my readers must say that the support known as the "Model," made in Brooklyn, is about perfection. The immense quantities used by our largest growers is evidence of this. The straight, simple stake, the large stiff

each row of plants crosswise two strings are needed, one against each row. The common white string used by grocers, which is very inexpensive, is good enough for this purpose.

Each plant is then confined in a square made by the wire and string.

its cost spread over three years would make it the cheapest of all methods.

Insects and Diseases.

For many years we had no pests to contend with except our common enemies, the aphis and red spider. A few

Mr. Dorner's Method of Tying.

wire, bent into a gigantic hairpin, the wire netting and many other schemes are good.

The plan used first by Mr. Dorner, and now generally adopted, is very good, and with many varieties answers the purpose well. It is to stretch a strong wire (No. 14 or 16) along both sides of the bench about six inches above the soil, and between each row, lengthwise of the bed, a lighter wire. Then from the two outside wires a string is run across the bed and near the plants, carrying the string around each wire as it is passed. Between

To keep the wires from sagging you will want a lath across the bed at intervals, and strong wooden supports to fasten the wires to at each end of the bed. Another tier of this arrangement must be added as the plants grow, and with some varieties even a third will be needed 18 inches above the soil. This plan answers every purpose, is very inexpensive, is quickly applied and altogether satisfactory, but it is not nearly equal in neatness, convenience, or for the growth of the plants as the "Model" support, whose only defect now is its first cost. But

years ago the "Rust" was imported and became a great scare. Several other diseases were lectured upon, and the disease and its causes illustrated till we thought the cultivation of the carnation was doomed.

Tobacco smoke destroys the aphis and a light fumigation should be often given. The fly is often very troublesome to the buds. We have not seen red spider for several seasons, although never syringing. More air, more room, and perhaps the sulphur which is put on the heating pipes every fall, may have helped to prevent the spider from flourishing. If it does appear in May, syringing is the best cure, but it is difficult to dislodge.

The rust was a few years ago most discouraging. There are few varieties that it does not attack, but there are some; Flora Hill and Scott are two that I have never yet seen troubled with it. There have been many mixtures advocated for its cure or prevention, chief of which is the Bordeaux mixture with which we sprayed the plants. Little heed is now given to any cure for the rust, many believing that the cure was as bad as the disease. yet the rust is disappearing, and troubles us little; not because we have killed the disease or its spores, but because we have better understanding of the conditions least favorable to the rust's existence, chief of which are absence of moisture on the leaf, air and light between the plants, more and better ventilation, earlier planting and more vigor of growth.

With the exception of dipping the cuttings before and after being in the sand we leave fungicides alone. We

An Exhibition of the American Carnation Society.

use the ammoniacal mixture for the purpose, but if you prefer the Bordeaux mixture you can obtain it in pulp form and dilute it as you need it. Benj. Hammond, Fishkill-on-Hudson, N. Y., prepares the pulp in convenient sized cans and saves you the trouble of making it. I believe that one pipe on each side of the house painted with sulphur is of great assistance in keeping down both red spider and rust. I saw this demonstrated in the case of a house of Daybreaks in my neighborhood. They were in a house formerly used for roses and overhead was a 3-inch flow pipe, which had been about covered with sulphur for the benefit of the roses. While several establishments on every side of this house had their Daybreaks black with rust not a grain of it appeared in this house, and this was for the three years during which the rust was most troublesome. No other preventive than this unconscious one was used.

Varieties.

It would be futile to mention or recommend any particular varieties. Grow what you can grow best and that suit your soil best. Flora Hill and White Cloud are grand whites; G. H. Crane and Jubilee are fine scarlets; Mayor Pingree and Gold Nugget are great yellows; Mrs. Geo. M. Bradt is a wonderful variegated flower, and so is Helen Keller when well grown; old Wm. Scott and Daybreak are still standards in many places. In pinks there is a host of new aspirants for favor and the most promising of all I have seen grown and flower and sell is The Marquis. In every shade, from the dark Gen. Gomez to the beautifully tinted J. Whitcomb Riley we will have a chance to please our patron's fancy.

Sub-Watering.

Sub-watering, by Prof. Arthur's plan, with the watertight bench and bricks on edge is yet in the experimental stage. It seems to me almost impossible that saturated bricks can impart to the soil sufficient moisture. We must wait for further trials before going to any great expense in this direction.

The method of sub-watering adopted and explained by Prof. Taft, of the Michigan Agricultural College, has proven a great success. He makes his bench nearly water tight by nailing sound boards or planks as tightly together as possible and runs cement over the benches and between joints. In a 5 or 6-inch width of bench he lays two runs of common 2-inch drain tile. The last tile at the end is raised to

Carnation Gold Nugget.

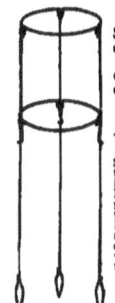
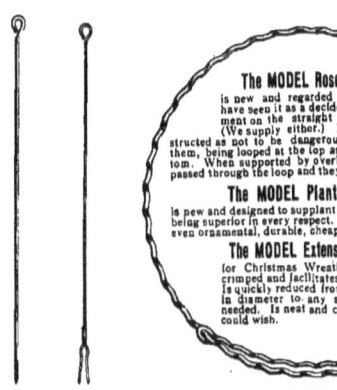
the surface so that the hose can be put in when watering is needed. The water runs through pipes and out at every joint, thoroughly wetting the soil. This is real sub-watering. Every 50 feet there should be the means of supplying the drain tile with water, and do not expect the water to run too far, as you might overwater near the inlet and leave the further end on the dry side. This plan has given the best results, and its advantage in spring and summer can be easily seen, as then is the time the roots want a soaking, and for applying liquid manure it is excellent. There is no wetting of the foliage nor baking of the surface by heavy overhead watering. This plan of sub-watering is worthy of trial by all of us.

Houses.

When the carnation first became an important flower with us any house was used to grow them in. Now thousands of houses are built expressly for the purpose. There is none better than a 22 foot house (22 feet from outside to outside of posts). This will give you three benches, each 5 feet wide and four paths, each 1½ feet wide, with heating pipes on the side wall where there is no contact with the plants. The ridge should run east and west, or better still, northeast and southwest. Ample ventilation should be given by continuous ventilating sash on the south side of ridge and in both walls.

This side ventilation will be of the greatest benefit in fall and spring. Some growers prefer to plant in solid beds on the ground. It may save material, and in late spring they don't dry out so fast, but the benches produce quite as fine flowers and are much more convenient to work. And liquid manure can be applied to the benches easier and with better results than to the solid beds.

CELOSIA.

Celosia cristata (the cockscomb) is not as often or generally seen as its striking and novel appearance deserves. It is seldom seen in our greenhouses, perhaps because when at its best the glass structure is a hot, sweltering place, August and September being its usual time of flowering. Our hot summers suit the cockscomb as it does all of the celosias, for they like heat. Last year we saw a large oval bed, the surface of which was covered with Tom Thumb sweet alyssum, and every two feet was dotted in a cockscomb. It was a "pin cushion" bed, and very striking and pleasing it was.

When to be used as a bedding plant, sow seed of this celosia in March, and as soon as the little plants can be handled transplant into flats one inch apart. When still larger they should be shifted into 3-inch pots, from which they can be bedded out.

If grown as a pot plant, shift from the 3-inch to a 5-inch pot, which is as large as they should have, or a 6-inch at most. In growing a specimen in a pot, the prime object is to get a fine, broad head on a very dwarf plant, and it is almost impossible to attain perfection unless they are grown in hot-

pots, but here our summers suit them finely out of doors. They can be planted out in the border after all danger of frost has passed.

Celosia pyramidalis makes a fine plant. It grows 18 inches to 2 feet high and should not be planted closer than 15 inches apart.

C. Huttoni has very beautiful red spikes of flowers and crimson foliage. It is worth lifting and growing in pots.

CENTAUREA.

The plants the florist grows under this name are both white and silvery leaved plants.

C. candidissima (this I think should

C. gymnocarpa, the kind with divided, feathery leaves, is not as clear and distinct a bedding plant, but is more generally useful. It is used largely in our vases and veranda boxes as well as for the edging of large beds.

It is always raised from seed, which sow in flats in January. They should be grown on light and cool, but not starved for want of pot room. A hot-bed makes them jump, but produces too rank a growth. By middle of April they should go into a 3 or 3½-inch pot and be plunged in a cold frame where they will make sturdy, useful plants.

CHEIRANTHUS (Wall Flower.)

If it were not for seeing a plant of this old favorite perennial occasionally in our public markets we would forget them entirely. The Germans have raised some fine strains of these most fragrant flowers and their people are always fond of them.

If you buy seed of the best double-flowered strain you will be sure to get some singles among them. The prevailing colors are red, brown and yellow. Were it not for its odor the flower would not be highly prized, but few flowers have a fragrance that pleases everybody as does the wall flower.

For the border the seed can be sown in August and the seedlings planted out in a cold-frame, protected during winter and transplanted to their permanent quarters when the ground is dry.

For raising in pots sow in April and May and plant out in the open ground in June. Lift in October and winter them in a well protected cold-frame, or better yet, in a very cool house, where they will throw up their spikes of flowers in May or earlier.

Cockscomb (Celosia Cristata.)

beds, with their heads near the glass. When the heat of the bed is entirely gone, shift and remove to a fresh one. They like heat at the roots as well as at the top. When growing freely, and particularly when forming their immense "combs," they must never be stunted from lack of water; and from the time they are in 3-inch pots, to insure a more even moisture at the roots the pots should be plunged. They want little shade, and that not till the end of May; then it should be only during the hottest hours of the day. Their successful culture can be summed up thus: A very rich soil, abundance of water, perfect light, and a warm, humid atmosphere.

Few insects trouble them. If aphis appears, manage to give them a mild smoking, even if they are in a frame. A cockscomb poorly grown is a very commonplace plant, but when done to perfection it is a wonder.

Besides C. cristata there are other celosias that are very handsome for the mixed border. In Europe they are grown for indoor decoration in

be ragusina) is a very fine, silvery leaved plant and was once more largely grown than at present. Its fine entire leaf was grand for the edge of beds or long ribbon borders.

It is an almost hardy plant and except when being propagated requires but little heat in the winter time. The reason why this good bedding plant is not more often grown is that it has the bad habit of rotting off in summer and leaving an unsightly gap in the bed or border.

If raised from seed sow not later than September and grow along on a light, cool shelf all winter. By bedding out time you will have a plant in a 3-inch pot, which is none too large. If propagated by cuttings lift a number of old plants in October. A good many of the old leaves can be shortened or cut away. During winter cut up the old plant, from which you will get a number of cuttings. They are really more nearly divisions or offshoots. They root with ordinary care in the sand, and must be grown on cool and light.

CHRYSANTHEMUM.

For a hundred years the chrysanthemums have had periods of great popularity and then of neglect. Perhaps it would be safe to say that with the American public the tide of present popularity is now just at the flood and the craze of 10 years ago has slightly subsided, yet not to any great extent. There is no longer a dozen firms each sending out a new set annually at Klondike prices, for which we must be devoutly thankful. An aspirant for public favor now must be about perfect and a slight advance on preceding kinds. A few new ones are offered at a price that allows us to give them a trial. We do not believe that chrysanthemums will ever drop from public favor, as say for instance the camellia, for it has many noble attributes to make it annually welcome. The perfection to which they are now grown is something former generations knew nothing of and the flower-buying public of 30 years ago was so insignificant compared with to-day that it could be truthfully said to be non-existent.

The commercial florist is interested

Exhibition Chrysanthemum Plants.

mostly in the cut blooms and in a much smaller extent in a medium sized plant in a pot. Cultural directions for both will be found below. The standards and large specimens are left to the private gardener who has time, money and space.

A Commercial Flower.

Take note during flowering season of varieties wanted for your next season's crop and remember that if few varieties are grown it simplifies labor and expense, and there are so many to choose from that one color, form and season can be all covered by varieties that you have found easy to grow. Select plants for future stock that have produced the best flowers, marking them before the flowers are cut. Lift sufficient plants and place them in flats, keeping them after first watering rather on the dry side in a cool house until time to start them growing to produce cuttings. Do not use any weak shoots for cuttings. Throw them away, it will afford room for the stronger to develop. Chrysanthemums root readily in sand or finely sifted coal ashes in an ordinary propagating bed until end of May or early June. After that date you will be more successful with a bed in a cold frame, shaded with cloth, lath or shaded glass, tilted back and front to insure a free circulation of air; and the bed must be kept copiously watered; this is very important. You often see chrysanthemum cuttings drying and wilting in June and July. They have been allowed to get dry or the sun has been shining on them, so water copiously twice a day in fine weather.

The best time to propagate varies with the different varieties and the

size of flowers wanted. For large long stemmed flowers of early varieties. such as Ivory, Bergmann, Bonnaffon (Bonnaffon can be grown early) and other dwarf sorts, February is not too early to put in the first batch. From that time on propagating can be continued until August. For late flowers, many of the free growing varieties do well and produce fine flowers on side benches from late cuttings. Those propagated as late as August can be planted on the benches direct from propagating bed without any potting, and will grow from the start if kept sprinkled and shaded for a few days during the hottest hours of the day. Earlier rooted cuttings that have to be potted will want a 2 or 2½-inch pot. Let them be well rooted before potting. Use a moderately heavy soil and not too rich. When well hold of the soil in the pots a side bench of a carnation or violet house will suit the young plants of most varieties finely, always giving them as much air as possible and room to grow without drawing up. The earliest struck batches will require a 3 or 3½ inch pot before planting out time. Some of our finest varieties which have a tendency to produce a flower larger than the stem can hold erect will be greatly benefited by having three or four weeks out of doors before planting on the bench. Such varieties which are weak necked should be grown slow and hard wooded and should never from the time they are rooted be allowed to attain a soft, rank growth. The early varieties should be planted on benches in four inches of soil; raised benches with good drainage will enable you to control the growth and ripening of the wood. The late varieties are all right in solid beds, provid-

ing the texture of the soil and drainage is right.

A heavy, free loam that the water will pass through freely, with the addition of one-fifth of rotted cow manure and a liberal sprinkling of pure bone flour will be an excellent compost. A "liberal sprinkling" is rather indefinite, so I will say one pint to a bushel of soil can be used safely. If it were mixed with the soil a month or two months before planting, so much the better. The chrysanthemum is called a free and even rank grower, but over rich soil produces very large soft flowers. The flowers produced on a soft forced growth are in poor condition to withstand the handling they have to undergo before they reach the retail counter and to produce durable, firm flowers a well matured growth of the wood is as necessary as is a good, dry house and abundance of fresh air.

This unnaturally stimulated growth may not be the whole cause of the rust, which is fatal to some of our best varieties, but it is certain that it puts the plant in an excellent condition to be attacked by the disease. The rust usually appears in September and later when there is promise of great flower buds. It is then that we are subject to great changes of temperature. If the growth is soft it is due to either too rich a soil or too much water at the roots or even too much moisture in the house, produced by water not draining off freely under the paths and benches.

That grand variety Golden Wedding has been grown in the neighborhood of Buffalo since its introduction. We hear of its failure in many places, but where there is no stagnant water in the house, and the roots have received it sparingly, and planted in a soil that water passes freely through, I have never seen a vestige of disease on it. This grand golden yellow will hold its own with any new varieties, particularly when the grower will learn to withhold water. It cannot be done right in a soil that the water does not pass freely through.

To sum up this particular point, encourage a free growth till buds are selected, then gradually withhold water which matures the wood and assists bud formation. To the inexperienced let me say that no serious check in growth must be given but merely less water than formerly, which will firm the growth.

For early varieties, where crown buds are used, care must be taken not to resume free watering until the buds are well formed, otherwise we will not get perfect flowers, but many unsalable ones. After the buds are well formed the judicious use of animal manure, either in the shape of a mulch or liquid, is safe and beneficial. I prefer to apply it in a liquid form, as we can keep better track of the condition of the soil.

While a free circulation is at all times necessary as well as keeping the house dry, from the time the buds show color till the flowers are cut, a gentle fire heat should also be put on as soon as we get cool, damp weather and the ventilators kept open day and night as long as possible. A sprinkling of air slaked lime at intervals through the growing season under the benches and walks will keep the atmosphere sweet and help the plants.

The chrysanthemum is afflicted with most of the plant enemies we have to contend with. The black, yellow and green aphis can be kept down with a moderate but regular smoking, but make sure to clear them of all aphis before the buds are far advanced. Thrip and red spider sometimes make their attacks during hot spells, but can be kept down by a proper use of the hose.

When the young plants are set in the soil of the bench give them a thorough watering to settle the soil around the roots. Plant all varieties firmly. For tall growing sorts inclined to weak stems, a uniform pounding of the soil after the plants have made new roots will make the root action slower and stronger and the stem will be correspondingly stronger and shorter jointed.

Be always very careful when watering, particularly with the early varieties, and a good look over the bench before you begin will make you aware of spots in the bed that may go another day or two. I have often noticed that where all parts of the bench were watered alike, the outside rows came into flower considerably earlier than the interior plants. The outside rows getting more light and air dry out quicker, thus hastening bud formation. By care in keeping the bench at an even degree of moisture you can bring in a crop evenly, which is a consideration both as to price you get for your flowers and your ability to clean up the bench for succeeding crops. Syringe during the growing season once or twice a day, as the weather may require, but always allow the foliage to dry before night. In using liquid manure do not apply when the soil is very dry. If applied after a moderate watering there is less danger of over feeding and feeding should be discontinued entirely after the flowers show color. In concluding these rather lengthy remarks on watering I will say when you do water be sure that it is enough to wet the soil clear through to the boards of the bench or bottom of the pot as the case may be. When you have acquired the science of watering and practice it carefully, wisely and faithfully you will have gained about 17 points out of 20 towards being a good gardener.

August the 10th is as early as it is generally advisable to take the buds of the earliest varieties and those will be "crowns." In taking or selecting buds the side growths must be taken out as soon as large enough to rub off with the thumb and the plants kept quiet until the buds are well formed. The crown being an unnatural bud re-

quires considerable care to insure its producing a perfect bloom. Terminal buds are the safest and in most varieties produce the best flowers, while crowns are earliest and should be used for that purpose, if properly understood.

All flowers should be cut and placed in water at least 18 hours before being put on the counter or shipped to the retailer. Varieties that easily drop their petals, as some of the most beautiful do, and yet desirable, should be in water 36 hours. This will harden the flowers and hold the petals. If the flowers are to be shipped it is time well spent to pack with the greatest care so they arrive at their destination as perfect as when they were cut. I know of no better way to tie or support the stems of chrysanthemums than by running wire across the bench near every row and a corresponding wire above the plants, keeping the upper wire well up. From the wire on the bench to the one above run a string for every plant. The cheapest string you can buy is good enough. This is easily disposed of when the crop is cut. You may throw away the bottom wire but the upper one is not likely to be in your way and will do duty for several years. Anyone adopting this plan will never again resort to stakes of any kind, unless it is for late struck batches on side benches.

Chrysanthemums can be planted much closer than they often are, but that will depend on how many flowers you intend to grow to each plant, and that again is controlled by what your trade demands. Three at the most is all you should expect from any plant, and I believe it most satisfactory all 'round to grow but one stem and one flower on any plant, and then plant thickly. The rows 8 inches apart and the plants 6 inches apart in the rows will do for all the moderate-sized flowers; for very large specimen flowers, 10x8 would be better.

Pot Chrysanthemums.

For several years the demand for these has not been at all satisfactory. I believe there is only one way to profitably grow a moderate-sized, healthy pot plant, that will keep its foliage and really be respectable in November. Choose healthy, young plants, that have been propagated in April. If they have been stopped once and are in 3-inch pots, so much the better. By the middle of June you will have some vacant benches to spare by the clearing of bedding plants, or you may throw away a bench of carnations. Five or six inches of soil on the bench will do, and even if it has grown carnations the previous winter, is good enough, with the addition of bone flour and a little rotted manure. Plant 15 to 18 inches apart. They will make a fine growth during summer and should have all their growths stopped at least twice before lifting. You have them under perfect control by this method, and can keep them

watered and syringed, as well as keeping the aphis subdued. The first of September, neither three days before nor after, is the time to lift them, which should be done with a digging fork, and by getting the fork down flat on bottom of bench you need not lose a fiber. These plants grow a great deal after lifting, so don't crowd them into too small a pot. We find a 6, 7 and 8-inch suits the different varieties. A few days of shading and a frequent syringing and they will have taken hold of the new soil, when you must give them a light, airy house.

These plants on an average have 12 to 20 buds, each branch disbudded to one flower. Most of them can be tied by one stake in the center and thread or raffia leading to each branch; larger plants, such as Lincoln always makes, will require several stakes; but let them be always small and inconspicuous. Only a few varieties are adapted to this purpose. The short jointed, dwarf varieties are the ones, and of all varieties that I have tried, Ivory and Lincoln are the ideals. Maud Dean is pretty fair, and so is Bonnaffon.

CINERARIA.

What florists understand when we speak of cinerarias are those which have originated from C. cruenta. The hardy species, although acceptable plants for the herbaceous border, where hardy, are not of much value to the florist. Since the introduction of the cineraria, or rather since its common use as an ornamental plant in our greenhouses, a wonderful improvement has been made in size, color and form of flower as well as in the habit of the plant. They are of easy culture and it may be said that any glass structure, where it does not actually freeze, will grow cinerarias. But like many other of these soft wooded plants which can be called "a cheap plant and easy to raise" a slight mistake or neglect will ruin the whole lot. A palm or an orchid will be much less liable to permanent injury by neglect or mismanagement, for what is a cineraria but an abomination unless it has broad, stiff, healthy leaves, and if it has those it will be sure to have a handsome head of flowers.

It is quite possible that some choice varieties are still perpetuated by cuttings, as they commonly were years ago, but that with the American grower is never thought of, neither is it at all necessary, for a fine strain is readily produced from seed supplied by our leading houses. Double varieties were also a novelty a few years ago and supposed to be a great acquisition, but the cineraria, like some other florist's flowers, is not in the slightest degree enhanced in beauty, either as an individual flower or as a decorative plant by its being double. It is simply a monstrosity and the craze for the double varieties has vanished.

If flowering plants are wanted by

November and the holidays, you must
sow at end of May or early in June.
Except on private places this is not to
be recommended. For the commercial
florist they would not be very profitable for they are a troublesome plant
to carry through the hot months and
the bulk of your customers are not
ready for them till February, March
and April. It is well to make two sow-
ings, the first early in August, the latter the middle of September; the last
sown will usually come in right for
Easter. The seed is not so small but
what it can have a slight covering;
finely sifted leaf mould or sand will
do, and keep uniformly moist till the
seeds are up.

When they have made a small character leaf, transplant into a flat or 2-
inch pots. From this time on they
must be shifted on as they need it,
never by any means allowing them to
become stunted for want of larger
pots. After they leave a 3-inch pot the
soil should not be sifted. If it is a
little rough or lumpy so much the better. I have seen hundreds of cinerarias in 4 and 5-inch pots die, not with a
slow death but suddenly droop and
die, and the cause was a close adhesive
soil through which the water did not
pass freely. They may not be a profitable plant, but if worth growing at all
will surely pay to grow well. They
must have room to spread their leaves,
and until flowering time 40 degrees at
night will suit them better than a
higher temperature. You will often

hear instructions given to "keep plants
near the glass," in other words this
means light. They must have light,
room to spread out, a cool temperature, and although a stagnant state of
the soil is fatal to them should never
be allowed to wilt from dryness or
they will lose some of their best
leaves. After light, air and a low temperature, the remaining great object
to watch in their successful culture is
never let a greenfly be seen on them.
Fumigate regularly and faithfully.

Those that are summered over do
much the best in a pit or cold-frame,
but it should be deep enough so that
when ventilation from the raised
sashes is given it should pass over
their tops and not be playing too freely on their soft leaves. Specimens can
be given an 8 or 9-inch pot, but the
commercial florist will find that a 6-

inch will flower them sufficiently well.
I have seen some growers pinch out
the leading flower shoot to induce a
broader head of bloom. If grown cool
and light this is entirely unnecessary.
It is seldom that cinerarias are
troubled with thrips or red spider, but
a dusting of water in summer and fall
is beneficial to them.

CLEMATIS.

Although more properly belonging
to the nurseryman than the florist we
are continually asked to supply plants
of several varieties and species of
these free flowering hardy climbers.
Some of the species are readily increased by cuttings. The paniculata
type root freely from pieces of the
young growth and there is no better
place than the gentle heat of a hot-
bed. They all are, however, bought
very cheaply from the nurseryman.
The large flowered Jackmanii type are
usually grafted on the roots of `C.
flammula`, the common European, or

the root of any strong growing variety. The florist buys his clematis and
is more interested in knowing how to
make them grow satisfactorily than
how to propagate them. Very strong
plants of Jackmanii and other large
flowering varieties are imported every
fall, arriving here early in November
or perhaps a little earlier. They have
usually a good growth with a great
bunch of roots. Thousands of these
are sold and thousands die, and pro-
vokingly after living one or two or
more years.

We spread out the roots and lay
them in trenches in the cold-frame
during winter and in severe weather
cover with glass, removing it before
they get anyway forced by the suns of
March. We believe they are more
satisfactory to our customers planted
this way than potted and given any

time in the greenhouse. The potted
plants look well when sold, but are
more liable to suffer from neglect after
planting. In very strong plants there
is such a mass of roots that it is impossible to spread them sufficiently
for all to get some earth around them,
so we cut out about half the roots,
which enables us to get some soil
among them.

You dare not guarantee the clematis.
If you do you will have to make good
your losses on some other article. But
you can plant them with care and
give good advice as to the attention
they need. They are nearly always
planted against a veranda, whose overhanging roof often keeps the rain
away, or they may be on the side of
the house or an aspect from which the
prevailing rains are infrequent. They
should during summer receive copious
waterings. When planting out each
clematis should receive a barrow load
of good, rich soil and not be put into
a small hole and have clay or brick

Cineraria.

4

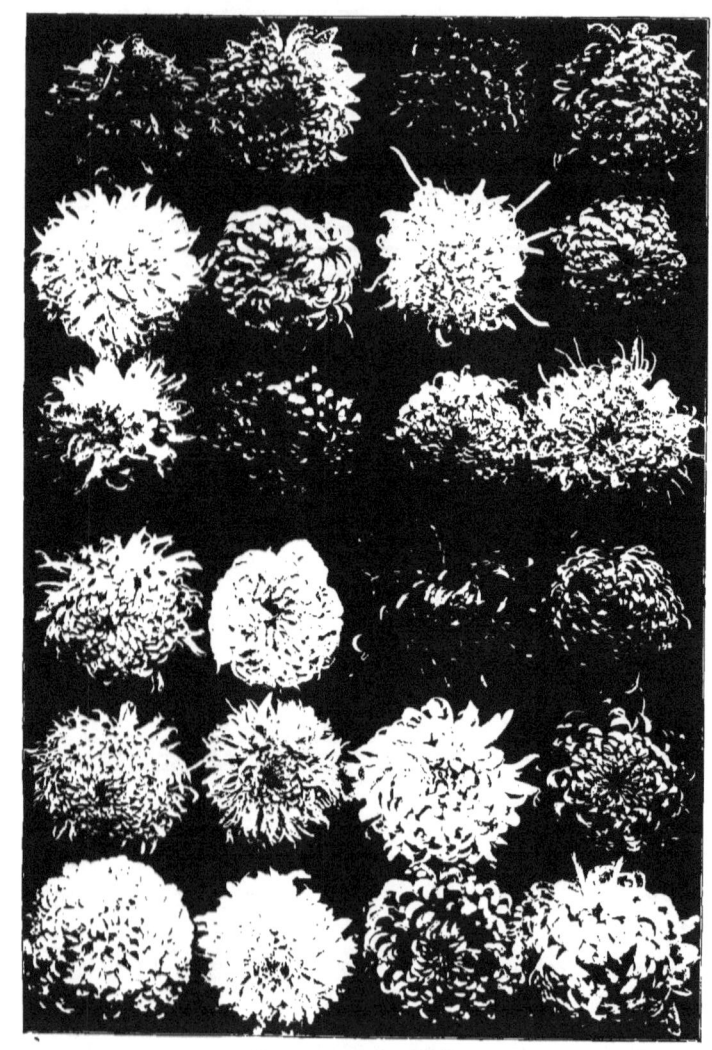

Various Types of Chrysanthemums.

bats to feed on, which is often the result of the grading and sodding that
is done around a pretty house.

In milder countries the gorgeous
Jackmanil and its kindred varieties
may retain their stems through the
winter; with us they do not, but when
well established the roots have such
vigor that the young shoots spring
from the ground in a very few weeks,
and by end of June are a gorgeous
mass of bloom 7, 8 and 9 feet high, and
5 or 6 feet across. All these flower
from the growth of the same year.
The past severe winter has injured
a few, but the majority of the clematis
have come through none the worse.

Plants of Jackmanil, Henryll or any
of that type make splendid decorative
plants grown on a balloon or flat
trellis in large pots. For this purpose
they should not be cut down, as the
frost does our outside ones, but wintered in some very cool house and
merely thinned out and tied in spring
before starting into heat.

There is a great number of species
and some of them are very distinct.
A few of them are natives of North
America and make splendid plants for
covering fences, railings, etc.

C. paniculata is very hardy and is
covered from July on with its white,
finely divided flowers, resembling almost balls of cotton.

C. coccinea is a very distinct species
with yellow and vermillion flowers of
an odd shape; fine for verandas.

C. flammula has white flowers, is
very hardy and one of the strongest
growers.

C. Fortunei: small, white, fragrant;
fine hardy climber.

C. virginiana: a very strong growing climber with small white fragrant
flowers.

The five species last mentioned do
not require any special care and when
once established live for years. It is
what is known as the Jackmanil type,
one of the first hybrids of which has
immortalized the name of the raiser,
Mr. Jackman, of Surrey, England, that
need the best of attention in planting,
etc., and which are to many people
the only clematis. An old species
from China with pale lavender flowers
five or six inches in diameter must be
one of the parents of Jackmanil. Of
this beautiful type there is a number
of varieties and among the best are:

Jackmanil: Still one of the very
best color; a rich purple.

Jackmanil superba: Violet purple.

Star of India: Reddish plum color.

Sieboldii: Lavender.

Henryll: The best white; very large.

Mme. Edouard Andre: A very distinct variety, approaching a bright
red.

Miss Bateman: An attractive variety; white flowers with dark anthers;
medium flower, dense grower and free
bloomer, but not continuous.

COBEA.

The species best known and most
useful is C. scandens and plants are
annually raised in large quantities to
be used as out door climbers. It is
a perennial, but it is much better for
us to treat it as an annual. As a
quick growing plant of fine appearance
to cover verandas, summer houses and
stumps of trees it has scarcely an
equal. It flowers profusely in August
and September, but the large, bell-
shaped flower is not conspicuous as in
color it is of little contrast to the
leaves. Where people want permanent
vines such as honeysuckles, bignonias,
etc., and are impatient of results we
recommend the cobea for immediate
effect, or till the hardy vines make
a show. When this is done be careful not to let the cobeas smother the
permanent vines when young.

The variegated form of Cobea scandens is a beautiful plant and makes a
fine greenhouse climber, but is not of
value outside. The variegated sort is
always propagated by cuttings which
strike root in the sand at any time
you have good young shoots ready.

Cobea scandens is always raised
from seed. We sow in March in flats
containing two inches of light sandy
soil, and keep in a temperature of 60
degrees. Press the soil down evenly
and moderately firm, and press the
seeds into the soil, always on edge. No
covering is needed; the upper edge of
the seed can be even with the surface
of the soil. Give them a good watering and keep moist till the young
plants are up an inch or two when
they should have plenty of light and
be soon potted off singly in small pots.
They grow rapidly, and when five or
six inches high we shift them into a
4-inch pot and put a stake two feet
long to each one. If not staked and
tied they get entangled with each oth-

er and it would be impossible to get
them apart. There are few of our customers that don't know the cobea and
a few hundred are asked for early
spring. And when you have to buy it
is one of those things difficult to get
in satisfactory shape.

COLD-FRAMES.

What we call a cold-frame (low
walls of wood or brick supporting
some glazed sash) is a miniature
greenhouse without any artificial heat.
Every grower should know the great
value of them and how much they add
to his capacity for raising many plants
and temporarily increase the area of

Clematis of Jackmanii Type.

his glass. There are times, especially
with the man who raises bedding
plants, when his place is fearfully congested and the addition of another
thousand feet of bench room is the
greatest relief.

Cold-frames are used for many purposes. In the fall and winter for pansies, to store away hybrid perpetual
roses, to winter pot carnations that
are wanted for next summer's bloom,
to winter many herbaceous plants that
have been raised from seed the previous August, to protect Roman hyacinths, and also the Dutch hyacinths
are as well under glass where they
don't get so wet, and the severe frost
does not crack the pots.

Some of our common little vase
plants we winter in cold-frames, viz.:
the sedums, lysimachia (money vine)
and the variegated glechoma. In the
spring these frames are of still greater use; not only do they relieve our
crowded benches, but many plants do
far better in them than in a green-

house. In the frames you have perfect light, an abundance of air, and on fine warm days the sashes can be removed when full exposure to sunlight and air can be given.

Carnation growers can put their young plants into the cold-frames about April the first and a few weeks in them will condition the plants for the open field much better than a lofty hot house. By the middle of April all the annuals in flats or planted can go into the cold-frames, and many of our bedding plants will be greatly benefited by a few weeks in the cold-frames. It is a far better place for geraniums than a shaded house without fire heat.

In the summer, without the sash, we find great use for the frames for plunging out our azaleas, acacias, hardy roses and many plants that are kept in pots during summer. Boards fastened up to keep your plunging material in place may do as well, but the frame is all ready to hand.

I had forgotten one very important use and that is for the longiflorum lilies in the fall. Both the Bermuda and the Japan grown are potted and placed in the cold-frames, and in case of very heavy rains are much better covered with the sash. Those you keep for Easter and later flowering must be kept in the frame till New Year's or later, and there is where your cold-frame will come in right, in fact is a necessity.

The ground on which these frames are stood should never be in a place where surface water will stand, even if only during heavy rains. If it is not a naturally dry position make provision to carry off the rains from the surrounding surface. Where a large lot of sash is used for this purpose some of the frames at least can be permanent. By that I mean they can be built of cedar or cypress posts (4x4 is a good size) driven into the ground every 8 feet for the back and front line of the frame, which can be any desired length. I have one of 30 sash in length devoted to violets. Where they are built to fixed posts in this way it is best to use 2-inch plank for the walls. Where the frame is movable and is made in length to fit three or four sash, one inch lumber will do. The sashes are made of various sizes, but it is wrong to have them an awkward size; 6 feet long by 3 feet 6 inches wide is large enough, and some prefer 3 feet wide.

For a great majority of our frames, whether permanent or portable, the height at back is 18 inches and the front 12 inches, giving the sash a slope of 6 inches to the sun; that is plenty. For a few larger plants we have some frames that are 2 feet at back and 18 inches in front. I prefer the cypress sash, butting the glass. Always use double thick glass; these sash get a good deal of handling and occasionally one blows off in a gale. They run risks of breakage far more than a fixed roof; they are moved repeatedly to ventilate and are raised to enable

you to water, so the double thick glass will save the extra price in glass in one year.

Always have a rafter for every sash to rest on and slide on. They are very simply made by nailing a piece of pine 2x1 on to another piece of pine 4x1, and have a hook and eye for every sash, to keep them from blowing off in a storm. There are always enough spare sash in the dark winter days so that you can overhaul the whole lot, mend them where needed and give them a coat of paint. And then when you put on the sash over a young batch of carnations there won't be a glass out in each sash, which you often see decorated with a piece of board, and which blows off to make a hole in the next sash, to chill or drown out the plants beneath, to disseminate profanity and vex all around. Some men may take all the little accidents that ensue from neglect quite placidly, but depend upon it when they do they are sluggish, good natured fellows that won't get far ahead.

A hail storm that knocks out all your glass is no cause to get irritable. The writer has been through it and knows how it feels. It can't be helped, no power could hinder it, and therefore you should be cheerful and clean up and find out the best place to buy glass as quick as possible. But these so-called accidents which are purely neglect are what vex a man.

A good part of your frames should be made to take four sash, because they are what are used on the hotbeds. You seldom need those deeper than 18 inches by 1 foot and the ends should be fastened to a 2x4 post in the four corners. All sash should have a strip of iron running across the middle on the underside, to which each bar should be fastened with a screw. It helps greatly to strengthen the sash and keep it from winding. The strip of iron can be ¾x1¼ inch. In summer when of little use see that the sash are laid or stood on timbers, off the ground, not winding, and that a door or some such thing be stood up and tacked to the last one covering the glass, so that your sons or sons' friends when showing you how they can curve a ball will be satisfied to break the windows in your barn and not go through three or four depths of sash.

COLEUS.

For the past thirty years, and still is, and perhaps always will be grown an immense quantity of small plants of coleus for our flower gardens. Verschaffeltii is a variety raised from Blumei, which species is also the parent of the thousands of varieties that have been raised, disseminated, and many now forgotten. The coleus as a bedding plant is finely suited to our warm summers and those that have not seen it struggling along, dwarf and scrubby looking, in the gardens of North Britain, don't realize what a grand plant we have in this tropical herb.

In climates where they make but a poor growth out of doors they are appreciated as decorative pot plants for which they make fine specimens. They can be pinched and tied to most symmetrical forms and for pure beauty of form and color are as handsome as any plant. But here, where we see them growing so luxuriantly outside they are not appreciated as pot plants unless it be for filling up in the summer and fall. It would not be at all difficult to start with a 4-inch plant in February and by the following October have a plant 6 feet across and as even in outline as an umbrella, but few would stop to admire it. They would only remark or reflect: "How long it must have taken John Smith to grow that plant!" The plant is not worth the pains.

To digress a moment. To me it is no pleasure (simply a bore in fact) to see an elephant on a tub, a horse waltzing, or a dog walking on his hind legs. I feel very tired if it lasts long and instead of being amused by such monstrosities am continually thinking how many weary days and weeks it must have taken to teach these lower animals the tricks. That's all there is in it; it shows the patience and untiring perseverance of some men, the result is nothing when attained. I will go a long ways to see a dog chasing a rabbit or a fox, a horse's neck stretched out to pass the winning post first, or an elephant pull a ten-ton cannon and show his majestic strength and it's about the same with these specimen coleus. It only shows the patience and skill of the workman; the result is meager after all the labor and cost.

To obtain a good stock of coleus for bedding purposes it is better to carry over a few each of the leading varieties in pots during summer, say in 5 or 6-inch pots. If you should have a cool spell in October and November, when firing but little, the fair sized plants can stand it, but small plants in 2-inch pots cannot. By starting these plants in good, strong heat after New Year's you will soon get plenty of cuttings. As is known to every florist the coleus roots most easily in sand the year around, and in the months of March and April when you are doing your heaviest propagating a bottom heat will save several days.

Coleus are sold cheap and must be raised expeditiously or there will be no profit. We endeavor to have several sizes. The largest are in 4-inch pots. Perhaps these have been stopped at least twice, their cuttings having been used for propagation. The 3-inch pot plants were stopped once and the smaller plants in 2½-inch had the top pinched out. We find customers want different sizes. Some are willing and able to pay for the largest plants; others think the smallest plant just as good; "They grow very fast you know." We keep on propagating to the middle of May.

I have seen, in fact I have had, a poor lot of coleus, for sale at the end of May, just when they should be

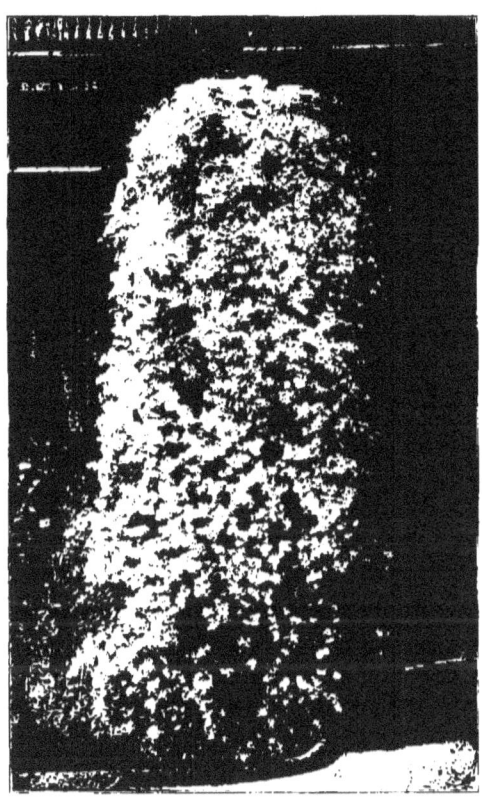

Clematis Paniculata.

looking fine, and the reason was I thought it a saving to buy no more fuel after the end of April or first of May, and perhaps to add to the trouble had some whitewash on the house. A sudden drop in temperature with a cool damp house is the very worst thing for coleus. They lose their leaves, grow decidedly smaller, and instead of showing their fine colors, all assume a brown paper appearance. Full sunlight and heat is what they want and must have.

I must refer once more to the hotbeds. There is no place like them to grow good bedding coleus. They need not be built up as if you were growing cucumbers in the month of March, but one foot of solid stable manure with four or five inches of loam or

refuse hops on top and some clean glass over them will produce in three weeks a better bedding plant than you can make in ten weeks inside. Have a big batch of cuttings so that they are ready to pot off middle of April. By first of May they can go into the hotbed in 3-inch pots, and that is their finish. One more great advantage is that on warm days toward bedding out time you can remove the sash, which finely prepares these tropical plants for their next and last move.

We use coleus of several varieties for veranda boxes and vases. They always do well. The only trouble with them is that they grow so freely that if allowed they will smother the geraniums, the flowers of which are always looked for.

Any light loam with a third of sifted rotten manure will grow coleus, and if we wish to hurry them along we add a quart of bone flour to every bushel of compost.

Mealy bug is about the only greenhouse pest that troubles the coleus, and if it has been a gardener that had charge of the house, that would not be seen. A proper use of the hose will keep them down; if it does not, use the kerosene emulsion in the mildest form, and if your plants are very bad throw them away and start with a clean lot.

Verschaffeltii I can remember very well watering as a rather choice exotic about the year 1863. It is by long odds still the best of them all, and Golden Bedder is such a fine golden yellow that nothing is equal to it in its color. If you grew 5,000 coleus for bedding plants, 2,500 should be Verschaffeltii, 2,000 Golden Bedder, and the rest your own fancy. For vases, etc., the fancy sorts are useful. Klondike is a yellow with a few dark markings, a very strong and useful variety. We have long since neglected to keep record of the names of the fancy coleus, and grow only half a dozen that are most distinct and keep their color and markings outside in the broad sun.

COSMOS.

The annual varieties are now great favorites, not only for the flower border but more especially for cutting. Its finely divided foliage and handsome flowers are now produced of various shades, there being now crimson, pink, white, and last a yellow. The only drawback to the cosmos was its late flowering habit, early frosts in our northern gardens coming before it had scarcely bloomed.

By selection an earlier breed will soon be produced, some seedsmen now advertising a strain that will begin to flower in June and be in full bloom in August. We have noticed cosmos in bloom this year by middle of July. While a tendency to early flowering is produced, the later strains are also more compact in growth; that, however, to the florist who grows for cut flowers is not so important, as it is in the long sprays that it is particularly graceful, and for decorations few flowers surpass it in light, airy beauty.

Only moderately rich soil should be given it or it would grow too strong. Plants that have many blooms yet to open can be lifted and planted in boxes and placed in a light position at the end of a carnation house, and will be greatly appreciated after all outside flowers are killed. Grown in a position where a deep cold-frame could be put over them in fall to protect them from the first severe frost will well repay the trouble.

They are best sown end of February, and transplanted into flats and kept in cold frame and planted out middle to end of May.

COTYLEDON.

These now include what we have so long known as the echeveria and sempervivum. They are dwarf succulents, a few of them forming stems, mostly perennials. Very few are of any value as flowering plants. Many of them are indispensable for carpet bedding. In fact, the rage for carpet bedding of twenty-five years ago brought several species of the echeveria into great prominence and millions were grown. They will always be most interesting plants for the rockery.

They are of the easiest culture, all the useful species sending out a number of offsets which can be removed from the parent plant in fall and planted into sandy loam thickly in flats. If you wish them to grow during winter you can give them a temperature of 55 to 60 degrees, with perfect light, and keep moderately moist. But for wintering most of them a much lower temperature will do; and give them little water during the dark months. The echeveria section should not be exposed to any frost.

While propagation by offsets is much the easiest plan, they can all be raised from seed, which is best sown in very early spring. The following list includes the most useful as well as handsome species:

C. sempervivum: House leek; perfectly hardy.

C. Gibbiflora metallica: Fine for center of carpet beds, or worthy of pot culture; broad thick leaves of a metallic hue.

C. agavoides: Beautiful form, resembling an agave, with sharp points to the leaves; one of the handsomest.

C. californica: Fine form; good for carpet bedding.

C. glauca: Leaves form a dense rosette; largely used.

C. secunda glauca: This is the one most in use; does well in any soil, is easily and rapidly propagated and for carpet bedding is unequalled; there are several varieties, all useful.

C. Peacockii: This is perhaps the most ornamental of all, and much less common than most others.

C. Ruthenicum: Good for rockery; quite hardy.

C. Verlottii: A pretty species, and hardy.

C. rosea: A fine form; suitable for large designs in carpet bedding.

C. retusa: This is the only one we have grown as a flowering plant for fall and winter sales. It sends up several flowering stems thickly covered with very pretty flowers. Being a succulent it is a most satisfactory house plant, and twenty years ago we grew it largely. It is well worth growing. Plants that have flowered should be cut down within a few inches of the ground and from the stem you will get several cuttings, which will root quickly in the sand and can be potted, and when there is no longer danger of frost planted out of doors a foot apart in good rich earth. You want these plants to grow, unlike those you have

crowded into the carpet beds. They will grow fast, and if inclined to flower too early pinch out the flowering stem till September. They lift, of course, with the greatest ease. We like to put them into a 5-inch pot. For inside arrangements of plants such as are often seen in the dining rooms of hotels this plant is of especial value, and the species metallica would also be for its grand leaves. A cold dampness is all that will hurt them.

Some of the species do not make offshoots, or not in quantity enough to propagate sufficiently fast. The leaves can be pulled off when perfectly mature and very slightly inserted in sand and kept dry; on the ends or base of the leaf small plants will form, which when of sufficient size can be potted and started growing.

You frequently see the bedding species used in frames or on the margins of beds where the edge of the bed is nearly perpendicular. Ordinary soil would wash down at the first rain. For these positions a mixture of clay and cow manure is used, and the plants put in when it is moist, the compost afterwards hardening as the fresh moulded brick does when exposed to the sun, and the cow manure binds it.

CRINUM.

Evergreen bulbs which send up a handsome mass or flower in a more or less showy umbel. The prevailing color is white. They are not of any commercial value, but are handsome plants for the private conservatory. They make strong, fleshy roots and to do well should be given plenty of pot room.

They require good drainage and a mixture of rather rough, turfy loam and decayed manure. If the pots are full of roots and you cannot shift them give them a top dressing of manure in the spring. When making their growth in the spring they require lots of water and syringing to keep down thrip and spider. Though not so much water is needed in winter, they want a moderately warm place and must by no means be dried off.

Seed is easily saved from the flowers and should be sown singly in small pots and shifted and grown on. They also can be propagated by off-shoots, which can be taken off when small.

The handsomest are nearly all tropical and flower during the summer months.

CROCUS.

This pretty little flower is alluded to in the article on bulbs. It is not really a bulb; it is a corm, but we always class it among the Dutch bulbs. We have never forced them profitably, but they are of course the most easy of any of the bulbs to force. In small pans they are the most salable; the demand for them, however, is very small and not worth bothering about. A great many crocus are sold every fall for planting in cemeteries, where they are dropped into holes four or five inches below the surface and will grow and flower every spring for years. They are not suitable for grouping with the tulips and hyacinths, being much too early. In fact, they appear as soon as the snow disappears and are often caught in a snow storm after they are in bloom.

They will thrive in any soil that is not too retentive of moisture. Dotted into the grass or in beds under the wall of a house they brighten up the first days of spring. Annuals can be grown over them during summer with-

Croton Reidii.

Cycas Revoluta.

out any harm if you don't disturb the soil too deep. There is no need of transplanting them; they will take care of themselves for years.

The varieties which we grow are named, but the color is sufficient, and of that we have yellow, purple, blue, white and striped.

CROTON.

These highly ornamental leaved plants can best be described by calling them hot house evergreen shrubs or trees, which they really are. As large decorative plants for the conservatory they have few equals. In the latitude of Philadelphia and southward they make beautiful beds out of doors, or add greatly to the appearance of the sub-tropical or mixed bed, but even in that latitude they should be in protected situations.

For decorations they are valuable, but not in cold weather, for a chill (even a low temperature) soon takes off their beauty, and a croton must be in perfect condition or it is useless. They also dislike to have their roots chilled with cold water, and repeated doses of cold water will soon show by a drooping of the foliage.

They are rapidly propagated from the tips of the young growths in warm sand in March and April. The sand must be kept moist and sun and draughts kept from the cuttings. Growers of large quantities plant out on a bench in five or six inches of good rich soil, the young plants in a light house, where during the summer months they make a fine quick growth and in the fall they are lifted and potted, and when established are ready for sale.

Where expense is of little moment they make splendid plants for the mixed baskets of flowers and plants

now sold in our largest cities. To grow crotons at their best they should not go below 70 degrees at night at any time of the year, but for a short time will endure 20 degrees lower than that. Unlike a palm or dracaena, however, anything near the freezing point for an hour or two will greatly damage them.

They are subject to the ravages of the mealy bug, red spider and thrip, but there is no excuse for either, as they delight in syringing; the proper use of the hose should banish their pests, or rather they should never appear.

For soil they like a strong, turfy loam with a fifth or sixth of rotten cow manure, and be firmly potted, and when the water passes properly through the soil, which it always should, they want lots of it. Bone meal has been added to the compost (about one pound to a bushel of soil) with the very best results.

The following will be found very handsome and satisfactory varieties, and without describing each variety, they can be depended on to furnish both variety and form, habit and color of the leaf:

Aurea picta, acubaefolia, Baron Rothschild, Day Spring, contorta, Challenger, Disraeli, elegantissimus, Johannis, Mortii, Langii, Ruberrinum, Sunbeam, Reidii, gloriosum, Lady Zetland, voluta.

Picta is remembered as one of the oldest and is probably the parent of most of the present varieties.

These plants are so universally known as crotons (and probably will be for a long time to come) that it is not worth while naming them any-thing else here. Yet modern horticultural dictionaries say that they are not crotons but codiaeums.

CYCAS.

There is one species of this handsome palm-like plant that is known to all florists, the C. revoluta. It is not only one of the finest of our decorative plants, but its handsome leaves are largely used simply tied together or with the addition of roses, etc., for funeral designs. Cycas leaves of all sizes and perfect in outline and color are now imported either from China or climes where this plant grows freely out of doors the year round. Although they are beautifully preserved and put into fine artistic forms, they are not quite the thing with all our customers and do not entirely take the place of the home grown, naturally colored leaves.

The cycas is quite a tough plant. I mean by that that it withstands a good deal of rough usage. I have seen it do well the year round in a light room where gas was used, and if you have no better place it will thrive in a temperature of 50 degrees all winter, but that is not the way to produce fine leaves. It will burn under the focus of glass, but will stand out of doors unharmed in the broadest and hottest suns if plentifully supplied with water. It makes a grand specimen for a lawn during the summer months.

They should not have a larger pot or tub than is necessary, but must have a shift every two years if they are making a strong growth. The soil should be a strong turfy loam, lightened up with leaf-mould and sand, or a fifth or sixth of well rotted cow manure. In the spring if you have no occasion to shift them give them a mulch of not over decayed manure. When in good health they will always make one whorl of leaves every spring. If water passes freely through the soil you cannot very well overwater them, and they like syringing at all times.

Their greatest enemy is the brown scale, and to remove this (or rather prevent it) they must be sponged with the kerosene emulsion. Mealy bug will attack them, but there is no excuse for that, as the hose should keep them down. A temperature of 60 degrees will do very well in winter and as hot as you like in spring and summer. When cutting the leaves for use never cut very close to the stem; leave three inches of the stem of the leaf on the main trunk.

There is no need of discussing the method of propagation of the cycas, as the young plants or stems in a dormant state are now imported by the ton and sold by weight. When first received they should be put into pots not much larger than the diameter of stem and plunged into bottom heat. They will in course of time throw out a small whorl of leaves, but their root action is slow. At this stage they are easily hurt, and although not wanting bottom heat after a few months, the plants should not be put out of doors or used for decoration, or by any means sold to a customer till they have made a good growth of

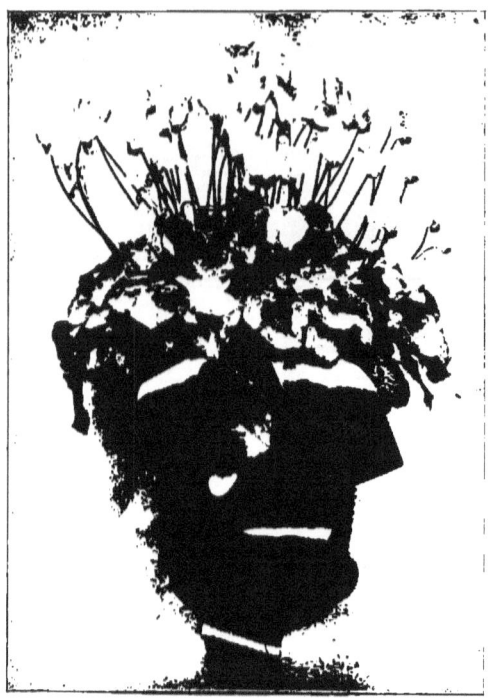

Cyclamen, in basket dressed with ribbon.

Keep moderately moist and they will germinate in three or four weeks. When the small leaves are up you should give the pan or flat plenty of light in a temperature of about 55 degrees. When the little bulbs (as we will call them) are the size of a small pea they should be transplanted into pans, or can go singly into 2-inch pots. If kept light and healthy they will need a 3-inch pot by middle of April, and the best place of all for them is a mild hot-bed. The manure should be well firmed into the frame and on it place four or five inches of soil or ashes, into which plunge the pots close to the glass.

A permanent shade is very bad for cyclamen, as they only want a shade which can be applied by throwing over a thin cloth in the hottest hours of the day. Never let them suffer for want of water. A slight syringing every bright morning is necessary. If aphis appears and fumigating is not practical, syringe with one of the tobacco extracts. By middle of June they will want another shift, and a slight bottom heat will still help them very much. They should be raised in the plunging material till the rims of the pots are even with the top of frame, so that they can be syringed thoroughly. They will now be in 4 and 5-inch pots.

By the middle of August they should have their last shift, a 6 or 7, or even an 8-inch pot, if large enough. They should never be crowded in the frame, never neglected for water and syringing and never shaded except in the hottest hours. Some narrow strips can be run along the frames above the plants and on these some lattice shading or cheese cloth can be rolled on and off. The full exposure to the air except during the brightest hours (from 10 to 4) is what they want. If wanted early some can be moved to the greenhouse middle of September, others can remain a month or six weeks later.

The cyclamen is by no means a tender plant, but it is not well to expose them to frost.

I have spoken before about what I consider good rdainage. For cyclamen in the last shift I would say a good handful of broken cocks covered with a layer of green wood moss. In the greenhouse, as at all times, they should have the fullest light. Horticultural writers use the phrase continuously "near the glass," which is equivalent to saying "perfect light," but plants that are near the glass often get a better circulation of air around them (a great advantage) than those near the floor.

If well drained the cyclamen is not very particular about soil. A good yellow loam with a fourth of well decayed cow manure and a fourth of leaf-mould, rather firmly potted, will grow them well. Some growers mix a little broken lime rubbish with good effect. Sometimes the beginner is puzzled to know how deep to put the

roots, which will be two years from the time they are started.

We often get an old cycas on our hands that has been abused and lost its leaves. By shaking off the soil and potting in small pots and treating as you do the imported stems you will in time get a good plant.

C. revoluta is by far the most valuable to the florist for all purposes. Of the other species for private collections, media and circinalis are fine plants.

CYCLAMEN.

Of all the winter blooming greenhouse plants as well as a plant for a customer a well grown cyclamen takes the first rank. It is second to none. It is so pretty in leaf and beautiful in flower that few of our customers can resist buying one, and when to that is added its good qualities as a house plant it is worthy of our greatest care and attention. There are several species of cyclamen, but only one that is

of importance to the florist. We often hear people from Central Europe (not gardeners) when they see the cyclamen persicum in our greenhouses say that they grow wild in Europe, and they call them the Alp violet. It is Cyclamen neapolitanum they have seen, a native of that country. All the beautiful varieties we grow are from C. persicum.

The writer can remember when these plants were coddled up, starved largely and kept from year to year. That day is past, and they are now rarely kept over, but are grown annually from seed. Anyone having a good strain should save his own seed; it is best fresh. It will be ripe in May and June and should be sown in September. If you don't save the seed, get the best strain. The form that is known as giganteum is not as good for the florist as the type known as C. P. grandiflora.

Sow in light soil and press the seeds into the soil and then cover slightly.

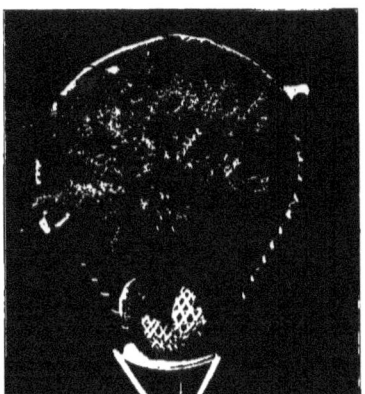

Small Plant of Cytisus in a Basket.

growths in February and are pinched and grown on by shifting during summer. We never plant them out because they lift badly. Keep them under glass and keep them plunged on a bench where there is very little shade. To make compact little plants they want their strongest shoots often stopped, the last stopping or clipping should not be later than December. In winter they can be kept in a very cool house; 40 degrees at night will be plenty.

They are of most use as an Easter plant and if not kept very cool will be too early for Easter unless that festival comes on an early date. Unsold plants can be sheared off and if kept warm and syringed will soon make a fine growth, and when shifted they can be plunged outside in summer and will want at intervals an occasional clipping. They can be made very round, compact, handsome bushes or allowed to grow more freely if you wish.

Canariensis is a trifle darker than racemosus but the latter is the best grower and best plant.

DAHLIA.

These magnificent herbaceous plants have long been favorites of the garden and were, I think, once more frequently seen than at present. They do not reward you with their grand flowers if just shoved into the ground as the useful geranium does. They want cultivation and they are well worth it. Excepting as to odor what flower is more perfect than a dahlia?

There are several classes: The Show Dahlia is the large double flower. The Fancies are identical excepting in the markings of the flower. The Pompon are perfect little double flowers, not more than one-half or one-third the size of the Show flower. The single section are very handsome and are used more for bedding. Some twenty years ago they were very much in fashion.

With the exception of the single class, or in case you want to raise new varieties of the double ones, the dahlias are easily raised from cuttings. The clump of roots which has been resting all winter should be placed on a bench in February or March on an inch or so of soil. If there is heat under the bench so much the better. The house can be about 60 degrees. Scatter some light soil among the roots, just sufficient to cover them and keep moist. From the crown of the roots will spring a number of cuttings which when two or three eyes long can be cut off and put into the sand; or you can put each cutting in a 2-inch pot, with a little soil at bottom and sand on top; the latter plan will save disturbing the roots. Always make the cuttings at a joint. This may be of little consequence with the majority of plants but is important with dahlias.

When well rooted in the small pots shift into a 4-inch pot and give plenty of light and air, and as planting time

bulb or corm. When shifting you can keep the top of bulb about even with or a little above the surface of soil. With the watering and growth the bulb will soon elevate itself to the surface.

If syringing is properly attended to the thrip and spider are seldom troublesome, but the aphis is a persistent enemy of this beautiful plant, getting down among the young leaves and flower buds. A faithful weekly fumigating must be followed up. I tried one winter an experiment on the best temperature to flower them; 45 degrees at night was too cool and 55 was too hot; 50 degrees seemed to be just right, opening the flowers fast enough without drawing them up. If once clean of aphis when brought into the house a good plan is to stand every pot on an inverted 6-inch pot and place three or four inches of loose tobacco stems between the pots. This will keep down the fly, but it should be renewed every three or four weeks.

Plants are seldom carried over the second year. If you wish to, lessen the supply of water after the flowers are gone and keep cool till May, when the pots can be placed outside, in July shake off the old soil and start growing in smaller pots and shift again as required. Old plants, if well managed, give an enormous lot of flowers that are usually not as fine as those on the year-old plants, and the plants are not as perfect. If a plant can in fifteen months be grown in an 8-inch pot, the foliage 15 to 18 inches across, with 100 fine flowers, what better is needed?

In Europe they use the soot of bituminous coal as an ingredient of the compost; it adds to the size and color of the leaves. A liquid application of nitrate of soda would possibly have a similar result. You can buy cyclamen

seed in distinct colors, and where largely grown should do so. The mixed strains, where only a few hundred are needed, will give you a fine variety. Seed can be sown as late as January with good results, and if grown cool in winter can be had in bloom for April and May.

The crested and so-called double forms are curious, but no improvement in beauty over the older forms. The double is in fact a monstrosity without beauty. The colors range from deepest crimson to purest white and in many the colors are finely blended.

Finally, what is true of most soft-wooded plants is more particularly true in the cultivation of the cyclamen; they should have no check, no setback of any kind from the time the seed germinates till they are in bloom, but should be continually growing.

CYTISUS.

These are often called genista, but cytisus is the correct name, of which the beautiful tree or shrub Laburnum is one. They are profuse blooming, branching evergreens. Small plants in 4 and 5-inch pots are most useful, but a limited number of the larger plants are very fine for decoration. Their bright yellow color, the plants covered with flowers, makes them very attractive, but we do not consider them at all a good house plant, the leaves and flowers soon dropping, and the reason must be the dry air of the room.

Any ordinary loam with a little rotten manure will grow them. They are sometimes troubled with red spider but never when they are kept syringed during the summer.

They root readily from the young

Single Dahlia.

approaches they should be in a cold-frame, where they can be hardened off. The planting time will depend on when you are sure of no more frosts. The dahlia is a cold blooded plant yet it can't endure the slightest frost. The first frost of fall kills our dahlias, so a late frost in spring would put you back with the plants for weeks or kill them.

If it is a bed you are going to plant then the whole ground should be deeply dug, and a fourth of its bulk of manure added. The single varieties can be planted 2 ft. apart, the Pompons 2 ft. 6 in., and the Show and Fancy kinds to do them real well should have 4 ft. All should have stakes to support them and in a dry time an abundance of water at least twice a week—not a sprinkling, but a soaking. Growers of good dahlias pinch out the earliest flowers and all lateral growths till the plant is 3 or 4 ft. high.

The single varieties are easily raised from seed sown in February or March. When well up pot into 2-inch pots and shift on, giving all the light and air you can as planting time approaches.

Being assistant to a good Scotch dahlia grower (the late Wm. Vair) in Toronto some 30 years ago, I have not forgotten his method and from plants propagated in March he showed and won a prize the following July 1st for the "best 12 flowers of Show dahlias." By the end of May the young plants were 15 to 18 inches high in 4-inch pots. For every plant on a long border (5 feet between plants) he dug a hole 18 inches in diameter and 15 inches deep, working in a third of manure. The surplus soil was spread on the border. Near the center of the hole he drove down a stout stake which

was left 4 ft. above the ground and close to that the plant was set. The surface of the soil was left in such shape that when watered the water would run to the plant, not away from it. I think it was the 20th of May they were planted. Frequently they

were watered and you could almost see them grow. July the 1st is extremely early to cut dahlias but there was a flower or two on several of the plants and after that they were a gorgeous sight.

It is my good fortune to see and frequently to judge the wonderful dahlias shown at Toronto's great fair in September; no better can be seen anywhere and for years the superb flowers of Grainger Bros., Toronto, have been exhibited faultless in shape and color.

It would be useless to give a list of varieties. The catalogues of our leading florists and nurserymen describe them all and the varieties are innumerable. The Show varieties have the magnificent self colors of crimson, red, yellow and white and intermediate shades. The Fancy flowers are most beautifully blotched, spotted and striped. The pretty little Pompons are all colors; some of the pink shades among them are fine for florists use and the singles are of every color. For cut flowers the Pompon class are the most useful.

Anything but a very stiff clay will do for soil. The best I ever saw were grown in a sandy loam with a third of good manure added. Deep soil, plenty of manure and abundance of water are the three essentials.

When the tops are destroyed by frost cut down to within six inches of the soil, shake or pick off all soil when lifting the roots and store in a cool, dry cellar or under a bench. Where

Vase of Double Dahlias.

Dwarf Dahlias in Pots.

potatoes will keep so will dahlias; cool as you like but no frost.

If the amateur has no means of propagating, the old root can be planted or divided, leaving an eye or two to each division, and placed in the ground by middle of May; but look out for late frosts if the top has started.

ONLY A SELECT LIST OF THE BEST....
FLORISTS'
Dahlias
Are grown by us.

Remember that in ordering from us you have the advantage of selecting from a stock which has been thoroughly culled; consequently you buy good varieties as well as good plants.

THE COTTAGE GARDENS,
QUEENS, N. Y.

DECORATIONS.

Keeping step with our business in other lines, the decoration of the house, the ball and the church has evolved apace and is with many a florist a leading feature of his trade. Looking back twenty-five or thirty years we can hardly imagine what material we then had with which to fill an order when we were favored with a decoration. Smilax we had, and some flowering plants of very common sorts. With the exception of the chandelier the decorations must have been of cut flowers, and they were hardly worth calling cut flowers for all were short stemmed and jammed into frames and designs in a very conventional way.

We can all remember (at least all those whose hair is grey) that at a wedding or reception the chief decoration was the banking of the mantelpieces with cut flowers, and I think I have seen such a bank of flowers, 6 feet by 2 feet, that contained as many orders, genera, species and varieties as are usually found in a botanical garden. Of palms there were scarcely any. A few old latanias and occasionally a shop worn Seaforthia elegans comprised the stock in trade. Of the ornamental kentias and arecas there were none, and it would not be far wrong to say that with the great majority of those who undertook a decoration, of palms or decorative plants there were none at all.

To trace the progress and improvement in our style of decoration would be of no avail. What it is today and what we can look for in the future is what we are after. The basket filled with moss and stuffed full of a variety of flowers on toothpicks is gone forever, and so is the bank of moss (often made on a board to fit the mantelpiece) gone never to return. The passing away of that style, as well as the bouquet described in Peter Henderson's fine little work, "Practical Floriculture," is not a change of fashion; not at all. It is the awakening and the throwing off of a crude, semi-barbaric education in that particular line. And as pronounced traits of barbarism are occasionally cropping out among the most refined and polished peoples you occasionally see a bouquet that in form and make up reminds you of the dark ages.

It is a question what brings about these great changes. Was it the supply of better material that suggested a more natural and refined style of decoration, or was it the good taste of our patrons that stimulated the

taste and originality of the florist? We think decidedly it was the latter, for material of some kinds we always had, and flowers too, but a knowledge of their proper use came by education and it came slowly. Did it ever occur to you how much we are all imitators? There are in our line only a few men of bright and original ideas in the whole country and I am without the postoffice address of those few, but at the risk of offending some mighty good people I believe these few bright lights lived (and I trust yet live) in New York and Boston.

All reformers are abused and reviled, or considered cranks by the common herd. All discoverers and demonstrators of everlasting truths are held in contempt and spoken of by fossilized brains and robed hypocrites as enemies of mankind. Saints never lived; they are saints when they die. Linnaeus, the colossal brained Swede who demonstrated and published the facts about the sexes in plants, had to eat his words at the command of the church. Just fancy; he had to deny a great truth in nature which is today taught to every student at a high school. Happy is the man (for his mind is his great consolation) who will grasp the truth as great minds reveal it. Let him be penniless, he is yet rich, and a king compared to ignorant affluence, who, ostrich-like, hides its head to all true knowledge except that of acquiring wealth far beyond its necessities. This is a deviation from floral decorations, but I will apply the argument to show that reformers in our line, men who were not afraid to step out of the beaten track, have likely been sneered at by hundreds of fogies who perhaps had nothing to say in argument against a new idea only that the author was "getting gay," or "thinks he's smart." Every time some man of bright ideas bring out an artistic move we ought to be thankful, for by slow degrees our ideas of the artistic part of our business have been moved upward and onward. A move in the wrong direction will soon die out, for upward and onward and progress are as sure to come as that we have progressed from the savage, and have lots of room for improvement yet.

The last twenty years have given us material that was not dreamed of in the early days. We had smilax, but we did not have Asparagus plumosus. We had, but did not then avail ourselves of the Magnolia grandiflora sprays, the Mountain Laurel (kalmia). Holly was scarcely ever seen. Lycopodium (ground pine) was little used. Leucothoe sprays were unknown; also the southern wild smilax. Adiantum cuneatum was used, but in no such quantities as now. And in cut flowers we did not have our long-stemmed carnations, or our magnificent American Beauty rose. And the glorious buds of Mermet and Perle or Cornelia Cook were very scarce twenty-five years ago. We had to be content with Safrano, Isabella Sprunt and Bon Silene. As for palms, the use of them with the majority of florists began about twenty years ago and has yearly increased till it would be safe to say that compared with twenty-five years ago palms are bought up and sold or used up at the rate of at least ten thousand to one.

The rather stringent times of the past five or six years among many wealthy people has cut down the price of decorations and no great advance in style has been made. And the prevailing style is a very natural and simple one, but good amounts can be obtained for good jobs. It is quality more than quantity that is asked for.

Wedding Decorations.

At a wedding decoration there is often some particular color that we have to follow, and while in details we must use our taste and skill, in the general plan we must follow the wishes of our patrons, if they command. At a home wedding there is usually an opportunity for the florist to show his skill in arranging a fine bank of palms as a background to the happy pair. This should be high and broad and light and graceful, not thick and dense. If the chandeliers and mirrors are ornamented with greenery, asparagus should always be used and no attempt be made to follow the outlines of the chandelier, but thrown on very loosely. Instead of clearing off all the costly and beautiful ornaments from the mantel piece, as we used to, and putting on a slab of flowers, they are now decorated with two or three vases of the finest long-stemmed flowers, such as roses, carnations or chrysanthemums. All flowers are wanted on long stems, and all can be so supplied with one important exception, i. e., orchids; and orchids will be asked for in increased quantities, depend upon it, and if you can't supply them your customers will go to some one who can.

Orchids are so desirable when cut, and it being impossible to cut any stem with some of them, cattleyas particularly, that wherever there is an arrangement of them they are used in baskets or some low arrangement, and nothing accompanies them better than maiden-hair ferns.

Instead of banks of palms, except when occasion demands such, the plant decorations are made by standing singly in every available spot a perfect specimen of palm or dracaena or croton. No such thing as a flower pot, however clean, should be exposed. The florist should have on hand handsome jars in which the single specimens should stand. And in the groups, if the pots are not hidden by the smaller plants, then small plants of the Boston fern, or better still, Asparagus Sprengeri, must finish the bottom edge of the bank.

In regard to the vases of flowers. You are often asked to furnish vases, and you should always be able to supply them.

None will differ with me when I as-

sert that nothing embellishes a flower like its own foliage. Roses should have nothing more, nor lily of the valley, tulips or any of the bulbous stuff, or chrysanthemums. If your chrysanthemum foliage is not good cut some that is. Anything else would be ridiculous. But carnations are weak in foliage and sprays of Asparagus Sprengeri go well with them.

Christmas Decorations.

Christmas decorations are of many kinds. Many good society people prefer to rent a public hall or assembly room when they are going to give a dance to 500 people, rather than turn their home upside down for a week. Perhaps the "old man" kicks. I don't blame him. If well heeled I should say, "Go and have your fun; all you want; but don't disturb my easy chair. I will pay the bills, but be careful, my dear wife and daughter."

At these events the florist has a great chance to display his skill and taste, and his work shows to the greatest advantage, as the halls are generally bare of any permanent decoration and well repay the florist's work. Here is where your wreathing of laurel the best of all comes in. Pillows and balconies are draped with wild smilax, chandeliers and gas jets are adorned with holly branches, the mistletoe bough hangs in some convenient nook, and the evening has all the features of old England (except the accent of the people) a hundred years ago. Christmas, once so coolly kept in this country, is now the great festival of the year with Jew and Gentile alike. We often hear from our patrons when we are taking an order: "We want it to look and feel real Christmassy, you know." They hardly know themselves what that is, but the feeling runs in song and legend, and that Christmas is associated with holly and red berries. "The mistletoe hung in the castle hall, the holly branch hung on the castle wall."

Laurel and leucothoe are always used in wreathing and are very effective, looking much richer than wreathing of ground pine. The magnolia sprays are fine on panels or walls and should not be crowded, but should show their fine outlines.

Holly is prettiest in branches and sprays, and there are lots of places to use it.

The wild smilax is the greatest acquisition of all. Just wound around pillars, covering ceilings, or on the outlines of arches, it is grand and becoming.

There is usually a stage in the hall and there is a place to make a palm display of the finest kind. If flowering plants are used they are usually colored azaleas and poinsettias. The latter is now a standard decorative plant in many cities, and always wanted in decorations around the holidays. It is associated with Christmas as much as the holly berries, and with us is known as the Christmas flower.

Church Decorations.

Church decorations are sometimes very elaborate, palms being of the greatest service, and many times the flowers used must be only white. There is where our Lilium Harrisii and L. longiflorum are of so great a value, and early white chrysanthemums in the fall. In addition to the palms, some perfectly fresh, clean, handsome bay trees, both the standard and pyramidal, can be used with great effect, their formal shape, that might look stiff and awkward in a drawing room, is in keeping with the solemn tone and architecture of a church. Easter decorations have undergone a great change, and it has been largely by the will of the pastors. In addition to their sacred ideas they have also secular notions, and among them is one that it is a waste of money for the congregation to donate a hundred dollars, more or less, for flowers; they believe it would be better added to their salary or given to the poor, as if the florist was not poor enough. So many a church decoration no longer exists among our regular orders, but there are just as many plants sold which are sent as offerings to the church, and "the ladies of the congregation, assisted by the deacons, arrange the donations," and then the Monday morning paper says: "The interior of beautiful St. William's was a bower of beauty, blending its incense with the heavenly music so ably rendered by the efficient choir under the direction of Prof. Flat."

Some churches still give you a fixed sum and ask you to make as good a show as you can for the money. And as no flowering plants should ever be loaned they ask that the plants be those that can be given to the poor and sick of the parish after the festival is over. A very beautiful practice. You have given joy to the poor who received them and helped the poor who grew them.

Designs as memorials to those who have gone before are now entirely out of fashion. Even the Easter cross, once so universally used on this occasion, is now not asked for, as the altar is furnished with a gold or silver cross presented by some wealthy member of the congregation. With all this our churches are beautiful with flowers sent by members of the church, and what is good and sensible about it is that it is not confined to any one or two denominations, but Episcopal and Methodist, Presbyterian and Unitarian celebrate with flowers and music. This is right. If it is a glad day for one sect it must be for all.

Other Decorations.

I have made mention of the leading events at which the florist and his material is called for to make the home, the hall or the church radiant with flowers and foliage. Any little social event, from a progressive euchre party to a grand reception, wants some little decoration, even if it is only a bunch of flowers. The use of palms, however, is getting to be almost overdone. At the most commonplace dance they want palms for the stage. That is all right. And in the house of mourning or the room where the departed rests a few palms stood around cannot be bad taste, but for every grammar school commencement, every political meeting, a few palms are wanted, and the first thing you know there will be a group of palms in Sharkey and McCoy's corner. Even this would be good taste above that of giving a half dead six day bicycle rider a basket of flowers, or presenting Mike McSluggum with a bouquet when he goes to bat. When that occurs and I am in the grand

add to the beauty of the home, the church, the hall, and to the enjoyment of all, but when shabby and shoddy they are an abomination. There is nothing so beautiful as a flower, and it is more beautiful on the plant than anywhere else. A faded flower can be cherished only for some sentiment and is kept in the leaves of the book you refer to when receiving a curtain lecture from your second wife.

You will expect me to say something about prices, but it is impossible. Seasons alter prices. There is, however, one thing we should observe. The charge for loosing palms in January should be double that in June. You may think it all right to cut down your neighbor's price on

The great use of our wild or native plants for decorations dates from about twenty years ago and is ever on the increase. An incentive to it was the much greater observance of Christmas day as a church festival and our greatest and most joyous holiday. The hundreds of car loads of holly used in our northern cities today had a very small beginning. It is just twenty-two years ago that a patron of mine, a lovely woman, one of those who make you glad you live and contented with your lot, sent me a holly wreath on Christmas eve. She had brought it from New York City, and thought it would be a novelty and a pleasure to me. It was both. It brought vividly to mind the days of "auld lang syne" and the mother country, which, however true and loyal is your allegiance to your adopted country, must and should forever remain a warm spot in the heart of every man worthy of the name.

For a few years the use of holly increased slowly, but for several years past immense quantities have been sent north, and it must grow in unlimited areas to stand the annual drain of our holiday wants. Most florists who grow and retail have to handle these native decorative materials, and how to preserve them in good order is of chief importance.

Holly arrives from beginning to end of December. It is made into wreathing, but much larger quantities are used as sprays and branches. Holly wreaths, either all holly, or ground pine and holly, are made and sold in enormous quantities. The large wreaths of holly, two and three feet in diameter, are handsome and look well in large decorations. It should when received be kept in the cases and they should be stored in a cold shed, but not where they will get zero weather. When frozen so hard the berries drop off when thawed out. Cool but not too cold is right. I have never found a better place for the wreaths when made than a cold, dark cellar, but in the absence of that a cold frame with some coarse paper to lay them on, and not more than three or four deep will do, and cover the glass with mats or boards to keep out the light and excessive cold. You can't make these wreaths all on Christmas eve, you have to begin making up a week or more ahead.

Ground pine or lycopodium, which Mr. and Mrs. Poor Lo and family gather in the woods of Wisconsin, is easily kept. It comes in crates and should be always kept outside, but covered with a cloth of some kind, or the exposed parts quickly get browned. It will keep a long time, fresh and green in the crates or made into wreaths or wreathing, if kept cool and dark; beneath a bench in a cool house or in the cold frame will do. When we bring in the bundles to prepare for making up, dip each bunch in water for a minute or two; it will make it

Galax Leaves.

stand I am ashamed of my calling and wish I was a walking delegate.

The basket of flowers for Miller and the bouquet for Mike are always paid for, and generally at a good price, but there are scores of times when our dozens of palms are not paid for. The public seems to think the cost nothing, nor the carting either. We must close down on it. If they paid $3 or $4 for the loan of a dozen palms it would stop them, and it would be just as well if it did. The common use of these ornamental plants will turn our wealthier people against them.

Decorations of any kind, plants or flowers, great or little, when well done,

palms and so get the job by a lower figure. You will find it is not all profit. Every time your palms go out they are of less value, however well you protect and guard them.

One other thing. Get a reputation for having clean, healthy, perfect palms, and above all have a reputation for having the job done at the hour you agree to. If the wedding is at 6 p. m., say to the lady of the house: "Madam, I will be out of your house at 4 p. m., all cleared up, and you will have no occasion to worry." See that you keep your word and you will feel as good as I do at finishing this rather long chapter.

Copyright 1899 by H. P. Kelsey.

Leucothoe Sprays.

more pliable and easier to work up, but don't leave it in the tub over night or it will turn black after you have made it into the wreaths.

Mistletoe is imported from France. We have the southern mistletoe, but it is not the kind the Druids worshiped and has no such associations, and although it may answer the purpose (the pleasant purpose) of kissing your wife's sister beneath, it is not the real thing. It seemed in better demand than ever last year, and as its privilege powers are better known it will be a favorite with young and old of both sexes. I think last Christmas was the first season that we had any more than realized the cost of it. It had been in other years mauled about in a dry store for a few days till there was nothing but the bare twigs left. We placed it in a cool, moist, dark cellar, and handled it just as little as possible, only to sort it over into 25 cent, 50 cent, $1, $2 or $3 sprays, and in that way were not only able to furnish nice berried pieces, but made a little money besides. It's not a large commercial transaction, but you may as well do it right.

Laurel, so called (Kalmia latifolia), is the finest material for wreathing, and thousands of yards are used for many and various kinds of decorations. It lasts a long time in good appearance, fresh and no dropping of leaves. It is clean and pleasant to handle. Though not so cheap as the ground pine wreathing, it is a hundred times richer in effect. Laurel is procured from the Allegheny mountains at any time and is widely distributed. It will keep after cutting a long time in any cool place.

The branches of the noble Magnolia grandiflora, which grows in latitudes

where the thermometer does not go below 15 degrees of frost, makes a fine decoration, and should always be used in sprays or branches. The fine, bright glossy green of the leaf is seen to great advantage contrasting with the bronze old gold color of the underside of the leaf. The branches when received should be kept cool and moist and not exposed to hard freezing or allowed to shrivel from dryness.

The leucothoe sprays are a more recent introduction and are very ornamental. They make magnificent wreaths or wreathing, being exceptionally easy to handle for this purpose. Their use is not confined to the holidays; like the laurel, they are used thoughout the winter months. Keep cool and moist.

Though small in bulk, the greatest in value of all the wild plants is the galax, the leaves of which are used for wreaths, panels, all designs em-

blematic and of good luck. It is, however, for funeral designs that the greatest quantity is used. They have grown steadily in favor till last year an aggregate of twelve millions were sent north. The small, green leaves are now largely used to encircle a bunch of violets. They have one great quality, for whatever purpose used they are most lasting, and when a design has to be sent away a few hundred miles they are often chosen for that excellent quality.

Mr. Harlan P. Kelsey, of Boston, who introduced the galax leaves to our northern market in 1890, says the sale has steadily increased till last year he alone handled some seven millions, while the price has come down from $3 per 1,000 to $1 to the retail florist, and inferior leaves much below that even. There has been a considerable lot exported to Europe the past two seasons, and Mr. Kelsey says Germany takes the bulk of them.

Florists who have not the conveniences for keeping them over winter in large quantities had better get them in moderate quantities occasionally from those who understand keeping them in cold storage. We saw a case of twenty thousand put down in a warm cellar last November, just as they arrived in the box, and we saw most of those come up the cellar stairs again at intervals this winter and spring heated and useless. If they had been unpacked, the bunches laid out and a little damp sphagnum laid between each layer, this careless and ignorant mistake would not have occurred, but the cooler the cellar the better.

This instance of how not to keep galax leaves was not an accident; it was neglect, for which in the old harsh days men used to lose their jobs; but since store clerks (alias shopmen) wear five-inch stiff collars and part their hair in the middle, it hurts their feelings to instruct them.

There are besides the southern material, evergreens from our northern woods that we use for different decorations. The common hemlock (Abies canadensis) is quite graceful in wreathing, and the American arbor-

Exhibition Group of Decorative Plants.

vitae, often called white cedar, is useful. A drive of a few miles to the music of sleigh bells and frozen toes brings us to the home of our evergreens, and the white spruce, so much used for Christmas trees, is also found, although the well-grown Norway spruce makes the ideal Christmas tree. Fancy what beautiful Christmas trees they get in Leadville, Col., where the beautiful Colorado blue spruce grows on the mountain side, and with us it is about $2.00 a foot. We will not be jealous of their noble conifers, for perhaps their rocky slopes are not covered with golden rod as are our fields and lanes just now, and how beautiful.

DECORATIVE PLANTS.

Besides the plants that are grown and kept for decorative purposes for special occasions, much of our glass, and acres of glass in large establishments, are devoted to the growing of plants used in a decorative way, either as permanent adornments of the house or for the florist's use when filling an order.

Generally when plants are known as decorative it is meant those whose foliage is ornamental rather than their flowers, and my remarks under this head will be confined mostly to those of the former class.

Palms.

Palms are pre-eminently ahead of all others for this purpose. Of the species or varieties adapted to the purpose there is at present not a great number. They must be of fairly quick growth, not easily hurt by a low temperature and able to stand a good deal of rough handling.

The Areca lutescens I place ahead of all as the handsomest. It is light and graceful. Next the Kentias Forsteriana and Belmoreana. These, like the areca, are fine in effect whether used singly or in a group. The Phoenix, especially rupicola, comes next, although these do not blend in a group and are best as small or medium sized specimens, where they can show off their graceful outlines. The Latania borbonica is fine where you can find a suitable place. We are sometimes (in

fact often) asked to place a palm in a fire-place, and there is the spot for a latania. Like the phoenix, its spreading growth makes it not so well suited for mixing in with the tall growing palms, however handsome it is individually. The graceful little Cocos Weddeliana is very valuable on many occasions. When two or three feet high and in good order, there is nothing more beautiful.

There are many other palms that are just as ornamental as the well-known kinds mentioned, but their variety and value forbid their use. And again, the kentias and arecas have entirely displaced such quick-growing but soft kinds as seaforthia.

Cycas revoluta makes a grand ornament where it can be used in a very large plant vase, perhaps at the end of a room or hall, but should be so placed that its perfect outline can be seen or it will not be appreciated.

As to the hardiness or ability to stand rough usage, of these palms I think there is not the slightest doubt that the phoenix are the best. We have a pair of P. rupicola that in the course of five or six years must have heard the congratulations of the bride's friends, or endured the orchestra's strains, the Easter and Christmas sermons, the orator's eloquence, and the chilly ride to and fro, a thousand times, and still they come up smiling. There is nothing like the phoenix in this respect.

The kentias come next for keeping in fair order, but kentias, grand house plants as they are, do not like the slightest frost.' I have noticed that where latanias and arecas have been carelessly exposed to a degree of frost they will recover, but not so with the kentias. The arecas will answer the purpose for a long time if the leaves are carefully tied when they go out, and this care should also be given the kentias. The latanias suffer most, not because they are more tender, but their broad leaves get more easily broken and become unsightly.

I remarked under the head of decorations that the charge should be about twice as much in January as in June. This is quite true, after May 1st till November 1st it does little harm to palms to give them a day and a night or more in a hall or room, and if the leaves are drawn up and carefully tied with raffia they can be sent out in an open wagon. When the thermometer is 10 degrees below zero it is very different. In addition to the wagon that is heated you have to tie up each plant and cover with paper or a bag, for the distance from the curbstone to the door of the house is frequently enough to ruin your palms if not protected. Others use long boxes, each holding a half dozen plants. As these are packed in the warm shed and the tight cover put on, and the box carried into a warm hall or vestibule before they are unpacked, the palms seldom get injured by cold, but careful and thorough tying up of the leaves is more of a necessity even than when sent in a heated wagon. Never scrimp the time in tying up the palms. If you do you will soon have to buy more, because yours will be shabby, and the price of one good areca or kentia six or seven feet high will pay for many hours' labor on the palms.

Dracaenas.

Next to the palms the dracaenas are most useful and effective. On mantels, side-boards or tables, perfect specimens of D. terminalis stricta, D. amabilis, or any of the beautiful hybrids, can't be equaled. And for situations wanting larger plants well-grown specimens of D. nova-caledonica, D. fragrans and D. Lindenii are superb, and they should always be so situated that the entire plant can be seen. D. indivisa is, of course, very common, but it is so hardy and tough that it is for many places one of the very best decorative plants we have. Dracaenas of the terminalis and fragrans type want no exposure to the cold, but they are easily packed and their leaves can be brought up and tied close to the stem with strips of tissue paper without doing any harm.

Crotons.

On all occasions except during cold weather crotons are gorgeous and grand plants for decorations, but they must not be chilled. My experience is that if a croton is exposed to a temperature of 40 degrees for an hour it will drop its handsome leaves, and in the winter we sometimes expose our palms and dracaenas to a lower temperature than that without much or any damage. So large plants of crotons had better be kept at home.

Small plants of crotons are now raised and sold almost as cheaply as fuchsias or geraniums, and if you do lose them you have possibly charged enough for the job to consider it no loss. For a mantel decoration with vases of flowers, or for plants for a banquet table nothing can be finer than the many grand varieties of crotons.

Adiantums.

Several species of ferns are among the leading articles of our decorative stuff. It must depend upon how elaborate and expensive the decoration is whether you can use the very choicest ferns. Sometimes at the bottom of a mirror a bank of Adiantum Farleyense is made as a background to a display of orchids, and what could be finer? Adiantum cuneatum, besides its great usefulness in supplying cut fronds, is many times used as a fringe or bank, and if the fronds are well matured will keep pretty well, but if young growth they will soon shrivel up in a warm, dry room.

Asparagus.

The Asparagus Sprengeri is a great acquisition, and is and will be largely used. Its pendent growths make it just the plant to hang from mantels or book cases, or to cover unsightly pots. Some plants in four and five inch pots, with a good growth, should always be on hand, and so should baskets of this useful plant. There is scarcely a plant that so readily adapts itself to the very unnatural conditions of a hanging basket. Such freedom of growth and hardiness under neglect and abuse may make it too common, but not just yet. It is unnecessary to say that this plant thrives under the most unfavorable conditions—sun or shade, wet or dry. I have tried it in many places and find it endures the gas, the wild exaggerations, the anecdotes and classical quotations of a suburban barber shop; and the aspidistra is the only other plant that is known to have lived through that ordeal. The Ficus elastica has been tried in tonsorial environments, but says: "I have got some credit as a stretcher, but that last yarn kills me."

Nephrolepis.

Most of our ornamental ferns are too tender for decorative purposes except that splendid genus, the nephrolepis.' N. tuberosa is now superseded for indoor use by N. exaltata and Bostoniensis. The latter is one of the greatest acquisitions that we have had for years. Whether in a mass or a large specimen, or in a large hanging basket, it is most ornamental, and receives not the slightest harm from an occasional trip to a party or ball-room. It is in fact a first-class house plant, so it must be valuable as a decorator.

Flowering Plants.

Unless you are well paid for the decoration you cannot afford to loan many flowering plants. For a church decoration we are never asked, but for a private function we have to, and must make out our bill or estimate accordingly.

Beginning in the fall the chrysanthemums are most in favor. Groups of yellow or pink or white varieties are often called for. However good the care given these plants they are shaky after a night in a room where there has been a strong glare of gas and a crowd of people.

Here will be a good place to mention that the cause of carnations (and perhaps other flowers) closing up in one night in a room or hall that has been crowded with people is the fact that there has been such a crowd of people. We have noticed this in both large and small rooms, and it was also noticed in one of the plant houses at Schenley Park in Pittsburg, where many thousands of people passed through in one day. The carnations collapsed, other flowers did not. But if it has this effect on carnations the breath of the multitude in one room can't be good for any flowers. And as a rule when a plant goes to a decoration we expect it to return much the worse for wear.

Azaleas, from December to May, are the finest of our decorative plants, and after a few days for recuperation are again of service.

At the holidays the poinsettia is with us a leading article and is now closely associated with Christmas. They droop quickly if they receive anything like a chill.

From November on the Liliums Harrisii and longiflorum are always in demand.

Spiraea wilts worse than any other plant, and should receive an extra soaking of water before going out.

Plants of lilac, deutzia, Ghent azalea and cytisus are used largely in the late winter and spring months.

Whole flats of tulips, narcissi and hyacinths are often used, with ribbons to match the colors of the flowers. There is no variety of tulip so fine for decorating, either in pans or flats, as the double Murillo, almost pure white when first opening, but assuming on its velvety petals the finest shade of blush pink, and so large.

Conclusion.

I can't be expected to exhaust the full list of the many plants, both

Plant of Deutzia Gracilis, trimmed with ribbon.

foliage and flowering, that are useful in decorating. There are few plants but what have a distinct beauty if well grown. And you will have many tastes and many grades of purses to accommodate.

No plants should go to a decoration unless they are clean and in good order. No dirty pots should ever go, never mind whether they are to be hidden or not. It's enough to turn the hostess against you when she sees them enter her door.

One very important thing is this: All plants that are taken out and expected to keep their heads up and look well all the afternoon and evening should be well watered an hour or two before they are packed for their dress parade, which the entertainment is to them.

We find it unwise to mix up the palms and dracaenas that we use for decorations with the stock that is kept for sale. However careful you are some little marring will be sure to occur, and if you are not careful you will have your whole collection, perhaps a fine one to look at in the aggregate, but when you want a perfect kentia, green to the very tips, you won't find it among those that have been out visiting.

Let the line be drawn between those you loan and those you want to sell,

and if you do much decorating you will want every summer a good house cleaning. Give your worn-out palms to the nearest botanical garden, or to the rubbish pile when beyond a certain degree of shabbiness. It is most unprofitable to occupy space with useless old runts.

DEUTZIA.

Several of the species are among our earliest and best known flowering shrubs, and gracilis, the smaller growing pure white species, is largely forced as an Easter plant. It is sold in pots or used for decorations, or the cut sprays are used. There is a new form of gracilis called Lemoinell, quite double, a beautiful flower and more lasting than the single. The double form is not yet quite so common and consequently is more expensive, but it will soon be grown as plentifully as gracilis. Plants for forcing of any size can be imported so cheaply and so well and compactly grown that it is useless to attempt to grow plants for forcing; they would cost you far more.

Those wanting to grow them to raise in the nursery for flowering shrubs can root them most easily from the young tender shoots taken from forced plants in February or March and put into the ordinary propagating bed or

from outside cuttings in June put into sand in a hot-bed.

When you receive the deutzias in the month of November don't expose them to zero weather. They are a hardy plant, but after their sea voyage are poorly prepared for a hard freeze. The stems are studded to their tips with their flowering buds, so they want no pruning or you will get no flowers. Keep them protected by a cold-frame and their roots covered till you pot them up for forcing. They should have about seven weeks under glass in a night temperature of 50 degrees, then they will be nicely out and not unduly forced.

For forcing we prefer to buy every year, but unsold plants if planted out make good bushes for selling with other hardy shrubs.

DIANTHUS.

To this genus belongs our Divine flower the carnation, which has been treated at length as its value deserves. D. barbatus is the well known Sweet William, a splendid border plant while in bloom but not of any commercial value. Perhaps because seen too often in the humblest gardens, or for some reason not apparent, it is not a flower that can be used in the commonest bouquet, though in June and July it makes a splendid show of bloom of the richest tints and markings.

The seed of the Sweet Williams can be sown in May in a cold-frame and when the plants are large enough transplanted into flats or placed at once in the borders where they are to flower. They will make fine spreading plants, and being entirely hardy will send up a mass of bloom the following spring. They are biennials, but a few straggling plants and flowers are often seen to survive two or three years.

The Dianthus chinensis and its splendid varieties, Heddewigii and its many forms, are the most useful to the florist. They also are biennials but are invariably treated as annuals and sown every spring. For their culture follow instructions given under the heading Aster and you will have no trouble. They look well in either the mixed border or in a solid bed.

DRACAENA.

In garden nomenclature the names Dracaena and Cordyline are interchangeable, but I prefer to call them dracaenas, by which name they are commonly known, although botanical authorities class some of our dracaenas as cordylines.

The dracaenas are noble, erect growing foliage plants, grown entirely for the beauty of their leaves and stately habit, for the flower is small and inconspicuous compared to the plant. They do not usually flower till they attain considerable size, although occasionally they flower when quite young, possibly through some check to the vigor of the plant.

Though not of equal commercial value to the palms as greenhouse and hot house decorative plants, they certainly rank very high. Some of them are excellent plants for the house. I have in mind a plant of D. fragrans Lindenii some 3 feet high in a 9-inch pot, furnished to the pot with its beautiful leaves, that has stood several feet from a window in a sitting room for the past six months, and is to all appearance in perfect health. Pandanus utilis, the ideal house plant, could not beat this.

Some of the species may grow 6 feet or 30 feet in their native habitat, and with age have bare stems crowned with a tuft of leaves, but our object in growing them as small or

Except in the darkest days of winter dracaenas should have a thorough daily syringing. By thorough is meant that every particle of the underside of the leaf should receive a good force from the syringe or hose. This necessitates a good condition of the soil that the water will pass freely through. The moisture arising from the syringing is conducive to growth, but a necessity as well to keep down thrip and red spider, which are very fond of dracaenas, especially the terminalis type, and will soon ruin the appearance of the leaf if allowed to commence their work.

Propagation in nearly all species is by cuttings, which grow from the ripened stems. The leading shoot will

and a fourth of leaf-mould, and the plants potted moderately firm. The pots, which should never be larger than necessary, should have an inch of broken crocks covered with a layer of green moss; this is as near good drainage as you can get.

Some of the species are very beautiful, but more suitable for the private collection than for the commercial man.

D. Draco: Very suitable for subtropical gardening or for vases.

D. Goldieana: Beautifully marked with dark green and silvery grey.

D. fragrans: This is one of the finest species, requiring a good heat in winter and shade in summer.

D. fragrans Lindenii: Same habit as fragrans but the leaf has a series of stripes of creamy white or yellow on each side of the green center.

D. Massangeana: Another variegated form of D. fragrans, the chief distinction from Lindenii being that the variegation appears in a broad band of yellow or cream color throughout the center of the leaf.

D. australis: A fine plant for outside decoration.

D. Novo-Caledonica: A fine bold species with large bronze leaves.

D. Sanderiana: An upright striped green and white species of recent introduction which has proved very good for the center of large ferneries, and which stands the dry air of rooms admirably.

D. terminalis: Green or bronze when young. With age the leaves assume fine shades of scarlet or crimson. Most generally cultivated of all dracaenas and the parent of scores of the finest varieties. The following will be found to be beautiful and distinct sorts: Metallica, dark purplish bronze; amabilis, fine habit, glossy green suffused with pink and white; Baptistii, green margined with yellow and pink; imperialis, broad deep green leaves, the younger leaves crimson and pink; terminalis stricta grandis, the most highly colored and best of the terminalis form; Youngii, bright green streaked with deep red; and Lord Wolsley, Gladstonei, Rebecca, Bella, Scottii, and Annerleyense, are all beautiful varieties.

D. indivisa: A distinct species from New Zealand. It will thrive in a much lower temperature than any of the others except Draco. There are several varieties of indivisa, the best of which are Veitchii and lineata. Unlike the other dracaenas this one is easily and quickly raised from seed. If it were propagated only by cuttings how highly prized it would be, for no dracaena has more grace. What makes it most valuable to the commercial florist is its ability to withstand the sun and drought to which it is exposed throughout the summer in our cemetery vases. It not only lives under these unfavorable conditions but flourishes. When three or four feet high if in good order it makes a splendid decorative plant that will endure

Dracaena Lindenii.

medium sized decorative plants is to preserve the leaves to the very bottom of the stem and with the best cultivation they will carry their bottom leaves for some years.

It is noticeable that the fragrans type (tropical Africa) will bear and require 10 degrees more heat in the winter time than the terminalis and the high colored varieties. The terminalis type will do very well in a minimum winter temperature of 55 to 60 degrees, while fragrans and its varieties and Goldieana require 10 degrees higher. Fragrans also wants a good shade in the summer months, while the varieties of terminalis need shade only from the brightest rays of the sun.

root freely but this would be a very slow process, so stems are imported, or the ripened stems of old plants are used. They can be cut up into pieces one to two inches long, or the whole length of the stem can be laid in the propagating bed. A good mixture for the propagating bed is coarse sand and chopped sphagnum in equal parts, and the heat of the bed should be 80 degrees. Let the stem be even with surface of bed. From the eyes or joints will spring young shoots which when two or three inches long can be cut from the stems, and they quickly root in warm sand and are soon on the road to make young plants.

The soil for dracaenas should be a good loam, not too finely broken up,

any amount of hard usage, in fact anything but freezing, and we know that it even comes out of a slight frost unhurt. The seed, which is very cheap, should be sown in flats in winter or spring. We prefer to grow them the first year under glass, and the second spring plant them out in some good light, rich soil. The following fall they are lifted and potted in 4 or 5-inch pots and used largely the following spring for our vases and veranda boxes. I know of no plant of its value that is so easy to grow and of so great a use to the florist. If short of room we have stood the small plants under a light bench in a cool house and kept them rather dry, where they have done well, but if you want them to grow during winter they should have 50 degrees at night, plenty of syringing with the hose, and they are troubled with nothing. In a few hundred seedlings you will see quite a variation of character; some with leaves almost a bronze red. They should be put aside and grown on with care; they may turn out to be of great beauty and value.

DRAINAGE.

There is nothing much more puzzling to the beginner in floriculture than the word "drainage" when applied to

Dracaena Fragrans.

Dracaena Massangeana.

potted plants, especially as some authors of recent years have ignored the theory of drainage entirely and pronounced it wrong in theory and a waste of money and time in practice. There are few farmers, nurserymen or market gardeners who do not believe in the practice of draining. Some land may need it more than others but all are benefited by a system of drainage except it be a good loam lying on a gravel.

I am not going into the art of draining land but the principle, if right

with land is right in our flower pots. Years ago it was carried out to an absurdity. A piece of crock in the bottom of a 4-inch geranium or canna is absurd and no one does such a thing now. If a plant is going to stop in a pot but a few weeks or even a few months and is necessarily a quick and strong rooter like a lily there is no need of any drainage. In the case of plants that may stop a year, or perhaps two or three years, in the same pot, if you were sure that the water was always going to pass freely away as it does at the first month or two, there would be no need of drainage, but worms get in and work the soil into a putty state, or the soil gets so packed at the bottom of the pot that water does not pass away freely.

Much as plants enjoy the watering when in need of it, terrestrial plants don't exactly feed on it. The water passes away, leaves the soil moist and full of moist air spaces, which the roots are continually absorbing till it is gone and they want more. See how easy it is to kill most any plant when the water remains in the pot and keeps the soil for a few days saturated. So plants want water to pass through the soil but not remain there, and with all plants that are going to remain any time in the same pot (azaleas are a good example) they should have what we call drainage.

With pots not over five inches in diameter a broad crock at the bottom covered with a piece of green moss, and with larger pots in addition to the piece of crock covering the hole an inch or so of broken crocks and the moss. The green wood moss is much better for the purpose than sphagnum because the sphagnum soon rots and the compost gets down among the crocks. You will sometimes see the healthiest and strongest roots of a plant down among the crocks. I believe it is because they find there the conditions to suit them best—perfect drainage.

How particular we are that the benches of our carnations and roses are drained by simply keeping the boards ½ or ¾ inch apart, so that if watered heavily it can pass quickly away. And so long as our flower pots are made with that one small hole we will have to make provisions to let water escape freely. The author who 30 years ago laughed at the "old fogy" notion of draining a flower pot lived to alter his opinion and freely acknowledged it.

just in perfection, so much as at Easter. Nine-tenths of all the plants are delivered on the Friday and Saturday, and must be at their best on Easter morning. If a batch of flowering plants are at their best one week ahead of time, they will be very unsatisfactory to your customers, and if a few days too late it is often nearly a total loss. Many of us can remember having some hundreds of lilies that would have sold for one dollar each on Easter morning, or rather the day before, had they each two or three flowers open, but were sold the following week at 10 cents a stalk, and the same with other plants. The quantity grown for Easter, if attractive, would bring a good price, but if late the supply is ten times in excess of the demand, the day is over, and they

many more will be added to the calendar.

Life is a continuous holiday to some and endless and hopeless drudgery to others. This is all wrong and was never ordained so. We have only recently (for five centuries is but a speck in the history of man) emerged from the feudal system, and but yesterday emancipated millions of slaves. Hopeless starvation wages is also slavery with a tincture of uncertainty added to its bitterness. The "white man's burden" is not so much the care of millions of a race or races who never yet have evolved to a high state of civilization and are still happy in their primitive life. The great burden of all of us is to bring about a better and happier condition of the fellow being whom we meet and see

Lilies, in celluloid basket trimmed with white ribbon.

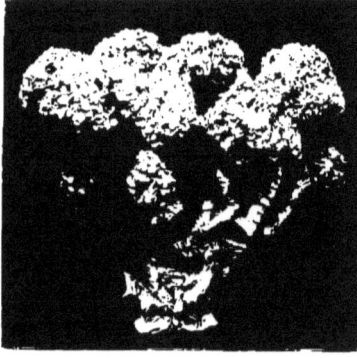

Hydrangea, trimmed with crepe paper.

EASTER PLANTS.

Easter day is undoubtedly the greatest floral festival of the entire year. For many years it has been the custom to trim and decorate our churches of all denominations with plants and flowers, but, apart from that, it is the custom now to give and receive from friends a pretty plant or box of flowers. The Easter card is gone and a plant has taken its place. It is the day on which thousands visit the cemeteries, perhaps the first visit of the spring to the resting place of the departed, that for months has been covered with snow. So several causes tend to make this a busy time with the florist, but the most commendable fashion of remembering friends near and even distant with a pretty flowering plant and Easter greeting surpasses all other demands for flowers and plants, and I see no reason why this virtuous practice should ever drop from public favor.

There is no other occasion when plants and flowers must be just right,

are given away. Another feature of the Easter trade is the fact that it is a movable festival and occurs any time during the month of April, and we have seen Easter Sunday a day of ice and snow, and again on the 25th of April I remember having nights of 70 degrees and fanning ourselves on the veranda.

To digress a moment. Why can't Easter Sunday be fixed for a certain date, say the second Sunday in April? In these days of common sense this ought to be straightened out. Easter Sunday and the days preceding it are supposed to commemorate events of solemn moment to sincere Christians, but as the moon, or the tide, or something else, dodges these anniversaries all over the month of April, how can they have any significance? We believe that ages after the events that gave rise to Easter and Good Friday are lost in oblivion, there will still be holidays kept, and let us hope that in the coming century the date will be fixed for that holiday and that

every day. Although in a wretchedly imperfect state as yet, a better time on earth for every man, woman and child must surely come. And then there will be more holidays for all. "Man's inhumanity to man makes countless thousands mourn," but every age brings more humanity, and justice and right will follow and equality for all must come.

I consider the ability to get in crops just when the market is ready for them quite equal to that which produces the plants and flowers, and at Easter time is when you want to exercise that particular line of ability to the greatest extent. It will tax your knowledge and experience, however great they are. Not only is the day of the month variable by two or three weeks, but the weather also is never two seasons alike. It is a question whether it is better to be what is called on the safe side—that is, have your plants a little early, or have them rather backward, so that they will improve from the day they are delivered. Of course, the ideal is to have them in their best appearance on Easter Sunday. If people wanted these plants for their own conservatory or house, then a lily with one flower open and four or five buds would suit the great majority. They ask for a lily or azalea "not so much blowed out." But 90 per cent of all the plants bought are sent as presents, and a good showy appearance is demanded, and for church decorations it is entirely appearance and effect that is wanted; however well grown a plant may be, it is not wanted unless well in flower. I may add here that flowering plants greatly predominate at Easter. Occasionally Mr. Goodman buys a seven or ten-dollar palm for his dear, plump little ducky, but that stops in the family, and the vast majority of plants sent as presents must be flowering. It is a cheerful morning with all Christendom and flowers are the thing to add to its joys.

We find a novelty goes well to a limited extent, but they must have some good merit to take well, and you had better try them in moderate quantity the first year. Wealthy communities in our very large cities will purchase a basket or collection of plants put up in a fancy basket and decorated with ribbon. In this arrangement there would be no end to the varied combinations to tempt the corpulent purse. These baskets of plants are sold for ten, fifteen or even twenty-five dollars, and are works of art, but they have not yet reached the general trade. We find a few customers willing to spend ten or fifteen dollars on a single plant, a great many willing to purchase a five-dollar azalea, but a far greater number whose limit is two dollars. Then there is the school child, or the poor person, who want to make their window bright and who can hardly afford twenty-five cents for a hyacinth. Our trade is made up of all these classes, and if you do a general retail trade, you must cater to all of them, and be just as pleasant and attentive to the delegation of little girls who have clubbed together to buy their school teacher a fifty-cent plant as to the millionaire who orders a dozen Beauties at eighteen dollars per dozen. A little different manner, you know, but just as attentive.

The delivery of plants at Easter, should the weather be cold, as it too often is, makes it the most trying day of the whole year. At Christmas we are prepared for cold weather and expect it, and most of the trade then is cut flowers, which are easily and safely delivered in boxes, and the plants are carefully and securely wrapped; but we never know till dawn breaks what kind of a day it is going to be on the Friday or Saturday before Easter. A cold Saturday is a great loss to our trade, not only in the great expense of wrapping and delivery, and breakage of our plants, but we miss hundreds of sales that never come again. A man may put off buy-

Easter Lilies, dressed with pink ribbon and Asparagus.

ing a hat or gloves this Saturday, but he will get them sure soon, because he needs them; but if his coat is turned up and fingers cold, he is thinking more about a cocktail and forgets that his wife told him to buy a plant and send to her friend, Mrs. Expectant. In many ways a cold time at Easter is a calamity to us.

Great rush as it is, much can be done by organizing your force. Men or women that make sales should not be expected to wrap up the plant. If the address and card is handed to the delivery department, that's all that should be expected of the salesman, and the cash or charge handed to the gentleman who presides at the desk. The man who makes change and slaps the charges on file is not so busy but what he can keep an eye on what is going on; like a man who looks on at a game of cards, he can see the right card to play better than the participant, and he can notice whether a clerk by mistake (?) drops $1.75 into his own pocket instead of the till, or whether that azalea that Mrs. Smith

so kindly said she would carry out to her carriage herself was paid for or charged. If we had an Easter Saturday every week, we should be able to keep trained help to manage it, but we have not, and it is a trying time, and a time above all to keep cool. It is a busy time, and your customers see, and all sensible ones will make allowance for a short but civil answer, and it is all they can get. Woe betide the fool of a man or woman clerk who wants to chin and chat and be funny and extra affable to the customers on these crowded, busy days; turn the hose on them if practicable. We have found that in the greenhouse, where many of us do our biggest Easter trade, much confusion can be saved by devoting a good big bench in a house adjacent to the door where the wagons are loaded to the plants that are bought ahead of time, as many are. We make room on the bench and cover it with strong, thick paper so that the pots when washed won't get mussed up again with sand or ashes. Thursday begins the delivering. Customers often say when buying a plant: "You can send it home Thursday or Friday," or another will say: "Saturday or Sunday morning, whichever you choose." Always choose the earliest moment they allow. You are sure to have plenty for the last. So on that part of the bench nearest the door is all of Thursday's deliveries, the card of the donor fastened on with baby ribbon and the address very lightly fastened on with wire. It is not safe to fasten that address card on securely till you see the weather, as

know the city well and also know a great many of the residents. Never send a load of twenty or thirty different deliveries with one man. It is waste of time. The driver knows the route to save time, and the house in most cases, and tells his helper that, "Here is Mrs. Brown's, who gets that lily and that deutzia," and while the Ann or Kate to receive the plants my driver is studying out his next call. Drivers or delivery men are just like those of any other calling; there are

warm the weather, without some wrapping paper around the pot.

The lily certainly occupies the most important place among Easter plants. The Bermuda grown longiflorum is the favorite; a single plant in a 5 or 6-inch pot or three plants in an 8-inch. It is seldom that the longiflorums are too early, and should they be a week or ten days ahead of time they keep finely in a cool, shaded house, but should not be put there till at least one flower is open or the whole plant and buds will get stunted.

Azaleas are next in importance and perhaps in value of plants sold equal the lilies. There is no excuse for having the azaleas out of date because they can be kept almost to the freezing point during winter and open quickly when put into a heat of 60 degrees at night. There is always a good demand for azaleas from Christmas on, but don't have many left after Easter, for people have seen so many then that they are tired of them.

Rhododendrons are seldom too early and you do not want many of them. A warm house with abundance of syringing will bring their fine flowers out.

The Ghent or hardy deciduous azaleas want seven or eight weeks in a moderately warm house. They are very attractive and do not drop their flowers at Easter as they do later in warmer weather, and the colors are such beautiful shades of yellow, orange, red and pink that when decorated with suitable crepe paper they sold well last year.

Lilacs need about four weeks in the greenhouse and always sell well, and are so good for cutting if not sold.

Metrosideros (bottle brush) is very odd and finds favor with a few, but the sale is limited. It should be always grown one year with us before being sold.

Acacia armata, called often Mimosa paradoxa, is a beautiful plant, but should not be offered for sale the season that it is imported. Cut down and grown in pots during the summer it makes a beautiful plant the following winter or spring. It will be too early for Easter unless kept very cool. A. Drummondii is also very pretty and can be treated the same way.

Deutzia gracilis is most easy to force and should be given seven to eight weeks in the greenhouse.

Cytisus, although a poor house plant, is so floriferous and makes such a compact, pretty plant that it is always worth growing. Keep very cool or they will be over too early.

Spiraea (astilbe) is always wanted for church decoration, and when people learn that a spiraea should always be stood in a saucer with an inch of water in it, they will find it a long-lasting house plant.

Mignonette in 4 and 5-inch pots sell well and should command a good price, as it takes six or seven months to grow a good pot. They can't be forced; they must come along slowly

Azalea, dressed with crepe paper and lace ribbon.

It may have to be pinned on to the wrapping paper that protects the plant from chilly blasts. When Thursday night comes all of Thursday's deliveries should be gone, the space devoted to Thursday should be clear, and so with the other days. Friday's orders should be looked out and got ready on Thursday and what is sold on Friday to be delivered that day should be put on the table to go out with the next load. As long as plants are on that Friday bench your wagons have not done for the day.

The delivery man is a very important personage these days. He should

good and bad, but a good one is a jewel. Only smile at calamities that can't be helped, such as hailstorms or cyclones, but swear to your heart's content at the lubber who comes home with damaged plants and says, "The lilies blowed over and I let that big azalea fall."

There is always a great number of plants that you are reasonably sure you will sell, and these should all have their pots washed a day or two ahead. Nothing can be more disgusting than a greasy, dirty pot, and no plant should be delivered, however cheap, or

Easter Plant Arrangements.

with a strong, sturdy growth in a cool house.

Lily of the valley in pots and pans sells well.

If made up out of a bed when in full bloom they are just as lasting as if grown in the pot and a much finer show can be made. It is just water they live on.

The old Dutch hyacinth always will be a favorite with many people. We believe only good bulbs should be used for this purpose. They are grown singly in a 4-inch pot, and in groups of three or more. A 10 or 12-inch pan containing a dozen grand spikes of one variety of hyacinths and trimmed with the right shade of paper is a rich affair and attracts the well-to-do.

Tulips and daffodils are grown in 6, 7 and 8-inch pans and find a ready sale because they are inexpensive.

Roses there is always a demand for, especially hybrid perpetuals. Plants that are lifted from your own grounds after the wood is ripe and carefully and gradually brought along, need from ten to twelve weeks in the greenhouse. The best pot roses I have ever seen of this class were a lot of American Beauty that had grown on a bench the previous summer, slightly dried off during October and lifted during November, potted into 6-inch

pots and kept in a cold pit away from severe freezing till middle of January, when they were brought in and started very cool. By Easter, which was then in about eleven weeks, they were a great sight: Five or six good blooms on 18-inch stems, with lots of buds to come. They outsold anything we had and would have been a splendid paying crop had we not cut a rose the previous summer.

The Crimson Rambler is, and perhaps the other ramblers will become, a standard Easter plant. Our experience is that if the plants are lifted from the ground the previous fall they must be brought along very carefully and slowly, so you must allow thirteen or fourteen weeks under glass, the first half of which they must be cool. If the plants have made their growth the previous summer in pots the wood will be better ripened and the roots not being disturbed they can be given more heat at the start so that ten weeks in the houses will do.

The white Marguerite, if well pinched in the field and kept cool during winter, makes a grand plant for church decorations. It is truly decorative and is one of the very best house plants known, blooming and flourishing in the dry air of a room for weeks.

Hardy shrubs of many kinds are occasionally tried as Easter plants, the snowball (viburnum) particularly, but we have not found people willing to pay for cost of room they have occupied.

Don't forget the 25 and 50-cent customers. A good 4-inch zonal geranium, a hyacinth or a 6-inch pan of pansies fills the bill.

There is a small and select demand for a pot of violets. If the spring is mild and early you can get them from the cold-frame two or three weeks before selling time, but if the season is backward lift from the beds the plants that show the most buds and only lift them a week or two before you want them. I may have missed some plants that many readers grow in their locality, but remember that if I have failed to notice them here I have under them due notice if in my opinion they are worth growing especially as an Easter plant.

It is always well to be supplied with a stock of moderate sized palms, pandanus, ficus, dracaenas, ferns and ferneries, but these plants are of value the year round and do not need any special mention here.

Don't think you can bring in a lot of lilies or azaleas in the fall and by

Easter Plants.

giving them a certain temperature have them in good order for Easter. Plants in the same batch treated just the same will be a month later or earlier than others. They must be moved as their condition requires. I think one winter some years ago that I moved my Harrisii at least six times, every plant, and many of them a dozen times, but it paid, for out of 1,500 plants I don't believe there were ten that did not open precisely a few days before Easter. It can be done, but not without thought, earnest thought, and active work.

EPACRIS.

These beautiful heath-like plants are not much seen in our greenhouses, although much grown as a winter and spring flowering plant in the gardens of Europe. The same general treatment as that given the ericas will suit them. Good peat (not fern root) if it can be procured is what they like. In its absence half turfy loam and half leaf-mould will do. For propagation refer to Erica.

Most of the species are from Australia and New Zealand, but the hybrids from these species are the most valuable. The colors are mostly white, pink and red of many shades.

Plants that have flowered should have the last year's growth cut down to within a few inches of the older wood, and till the young growth gets a good start the plants should be kept syringed and away from draughts. They make a growth of several stems one to two feet long, which give you the flowers the following winter. When the growth is matured the plants can be plunged outside for a

month or two, but are best in partial shade.

Till flowering time a temperature of 40 to 45 degrees at night will do very well. Like the heaths they dislike extremes of moisture, but if properly drained will take plenty of water, and must at no time be allowed to get very dry.

Although not often seen the epacris is a beautiful and aristocratic greenhouse plant and whoever can grow heaths should grow epacris. They are seldom troubled with any of our greenhouse pests of any kind.

ERICA.

This is a large genus of hard-wooded evergreen shrubs, often called Cape Heaths because they are largely from the Cape of Good Hope. Few greenhouse plants are finer as specimens than a hard-wooded heath. A plant of E. Cavendishianum, covered with its large, waxy, yellow flowers, the plant tied out most neatly, I can remember to this day, although many years since I had the honor to paint the handmade wooden labels for naming some of the plants in the heath house.

Heaths have small leaves and are slow growers. The flowers are sometimes terminal and sometimes axillary. The hard-wood section is seldom seen except in a private collection. They want most skillful watering the year round, good drainage and nothing like a sodden soil, but must never be very dry. They do not like fire heat, and a greenhouse where the night temperature is not over 40 degrees will do very well.

After they have made their growth in the spring they would be best out of doors, but shaded with lattice work from the strongest sun. A good peat and loam compost suits them best, and they should be potted firmly. But in the absence of peat a good fibrous loam with a third of leaf mould and some sand will do very well. The hard-wooded, slow-growing heaths are never likely to become of importance with the commercial florist. They are troubled with none of our greenhouse pests.

The soft-wooded, quicker growing section is now largely grown as a market plant for our eastern cities, and large quantities are raised on Long Island, where the fine loam found in many parts of the island suits it fine'y. It is generally believed that the order Ericacea, which includes the azaleas,

Erica and Epacris, in fancy basket and silver jardinieres.

Erica, in celluloid basket dressed with red ribbon.

rhododendrons and kalmias, is much averse to lime in either the soil or water, and this should be remembered.

They are propagated by cuttings from the tips of the young growths in spring. They do not want bottom heat, but should be put in well-drained flats or pans with a layer of light loam and leaf-mould, and on the surface an inch of clean sand. They should be kept rather close, away from draughts or too much ventilation. Give them a good soaking when first put in. If the cuttings are 1 or 1½ inches long of the young, tender growth stripped of the bottom leaves they will root in seven or eight weeks. As they show signs of growth give them more air. Don't pot off till they are well rooted, and keep them only just moist till they are rooted.

The young plants will do very well in a cold-frame during the fall months and in a cool, dry house during winter. In May they can be planted out in the open ground, where they will make

a good growth, and must be lifted in September or October. When first lifted and potted be careful not to let them wilt. Careful lifting, to get all their roots and fibres, is the essential object. They will do finely in a temperature of 40 degrees, but will do with more heat as their flowering time approaches.

Two-year-old plants that are unsold should be cut down to within a few inches of the pot after flowering and again planted out. The young plants will need stopping when they first begin to root, and perhaps again when planted out, but not after that.

Some of the best ericas for florists are E. caffra (small flower, but very free), E. gracilis, E. hybrida, E. hyemalis (a beautiful pink that flowers in early spring; one of the best), E. melanthera (flowers in winter), E. persoluta (May), E. ventricosa, E. Wilmoreana (spring; a grand hybrid). All of these are fine commercial kinds.

ERIOSTEMON.

This beautiful plant belongs to that class of Australian shrubs that for years were called New Holland plants, of which the pimelia is another well-known member, and there are many more. With us they are seldom seen in commercial places, but they are fine, interesting plants and are not difficult to grow. In Europe the long sprays of eriostemon are much valued for cut flowers, but with us that would not pay.

The leaves are small, and the flowers, which are mostly white and pink, are borne in great profusion. All the species flower in March, April, May or June. As small plants they are not atttractive, but when of a good size, and slightly trained to stakes, they are fine ornamental plants. Like most hard-wooded shrubs, they root freely from the young growths in spring.

Though coming from Australia these shrubs want by no means a tropical temperature. They are much the best plunged out of doors in summer, and in the winter 40 to 45 degrees will suit them. As with the acacia, metrosideros, pimelia and all that class, a good turfy loam with some rotten manure or leaf-mould will grow them. As they will remain several years in the same pot they should be well drained.

There are many species, and Nicholson selects the following as being the most desirable: E. buxifolius, pink, April to June; E. intermedius, white and pink, April; E. neriifolius, rose, April; E. salicifolius, pink, June; E. scaber, white tinged pink, April and May.

EUCHARIS.

Hot-house evergreen bulbs bearing beautiful, fragrant flowers, which either cut as stalks bearing four or five flowers or as single flowers, are invaluable to the florist. Their white, star-shaped, elegant flowers are admired by all, but are not seen in quantity, as they should be. In Europe they figure most prominently in all the cut flower markets, but in this country I have not heard of their being grown systematically in large quantities any-

where, and I believe there is a great opportunity for their cultivation, for as long as designs of flowers are used (and they will always be to some extent) there is no flower more beautiful for the purpose than the eucharis. There is scarcely a plant grown of

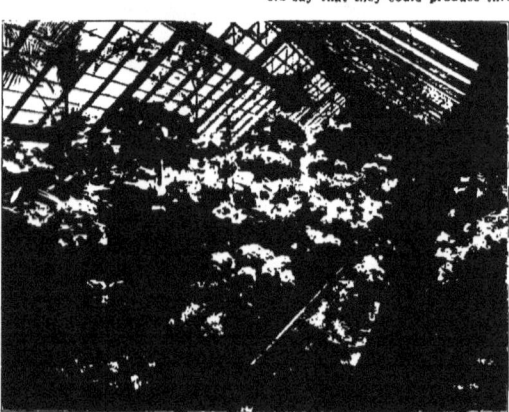

which you hear so often the same remark made, and it is this: "Yes, a grand plant. I wish I knew how to make it flower." Or, "I don't have any luck with it. It grows, but don't flower."

There are several species, all wanting the same treatment. E. grandiflora, so generally called amazonica, is the fine species we all know, bearing an umbel of four to six flowers four to five inches across on stout, erect stems eighteen inches to two feet high. E. Sanderiana is somewhat smaller and the throat or tube of the flower is yellow. E. candida is also pure white, bearing seven to ten flowers on one stalk, but not as large a flower as amazonica. I would advise the beginner to try the cultivation of the latter, as it is the handsomest of all.

Good authorities say the eucharis should have an abundance of water at all times. South American travelers and collectors have also told me that they have walked over arid plains in the dry season with scarcely a sign of vegetation and returned in six months over the same ground and found it covered with the leaves and flowers of eucharis, a gorgeous sight. This does not agree, and we have seen the bulbs dried off considerably, and when potted up send up flower stalks. But drying off as you would a hyacinth or tulip is certainly not advisable or anything approaching it.

The bulbs multiply readily by sending out offshoots, and when once you have a few healthy plants your stock is easily increased. As the plant is from New Granada, a warm house is

needed at all times; 60 to 65 degrees is the lowest they should be at any time. Disturbing of the bulbs and roots must be avoided or you will not get flowers. If established in a pot, from 8 to 12-inch, or on a bench in 6 inches of good soil, feed them when making

their growth of leaves, but don't disturb the roots for four or five years. At most times of the year they undoubtedly want lots of water, so drainage in the pot, and opportunity on the bench for water to pass freely away, is of great importance.

The soil should be a good rough loam with one-fifth of well decayed

cow manure. As the soil is to remain undisturbed for several years, add a tenth of broken up charcoal to the compost; it will help to keep the soil porous. If you receive the bulbs dormant, plant three in an 8-inch pot or five in a 10-inch, the top of bulb two inches below the surface. If on a bench, plant six inches apart in the row and the rows eight inches apart.

The principal object to observe is this: Supposing an established plant has been growing freely for two months and making a fine lot of leaves. If you continue giving it water freely it will continue to make its handsome leaves and no flowers, but if you shorten up the supply of water and keep the plants rather dry (not by any means dry enough to show any effects on the leaf), then flower leads will be formed in the bulb instead of leaves, and after a rest of two months apply again an abundance of water and up will come the flower stalks. After flowering give them only a very short rest and top dress and start again for another two or three months' growth. Remember that in cultivation, whatever their native conditions may be, a rest is only a lessening of the water, not a drying off, and their foliage should not suffer at any time.

We have all heard English gardeners say that they could produce three crops of flowers in twelve months. Possibly so. Two crops will do very well. I will just add that two years ago I saw exhibited at Toronto's great fair in September a plant of E. amazonica in an 8-inch pot that had nine flower stalks bearing a total of thirty-three flowers and buds, so it can be done.

A Florist's Display at Easter.

Easter Basket of Lilies, Azaleas, Hyacinths and Ferns.

Mealy bug often bothers the leaves. As the plants want and thrive with any amount of syringing, there is little excuse for that. Here is a plant that, when growing, should never be watered with our hydrant water, which is too often near ice water. The water in winter should be 60 degrees always. This, I believe, is a valuable point in their culture.

EUPATORIUM.

A large genus of herbaceous or shrubby plants. A few of them are native, hardy plants, but not of any value to the florist, although some years ago, in the absence of better flowers some of the species were largely grown to supply white material for designs, etc.

The species riparium is the most valuable for the florist, but the quality and value of its flowers are not sufficient to pay for the trouble and the space under glass.

After flowering in March, cut back the stems and from the young growths make cuttings, which root most easily. After frost is gone plant out 18 inches apart. Pinch the shoots as they grow during summer. They grow freely in any soil. In early October, or before frost appears, lift with a ball of earth and plant on the bench in six inches of soil.

As before stated, the panicles of pure white flowers would be useful if we did not have other flowers of more beauty. It has not the beauty or finish of the bouvardia, and occupies the benches a long time.

EUPHORBIA.

In almost every private collection of greenhouse plants of years ago you would be sure to see a plant of E. splendens and E. fulgens, generally known as E. Jaquiniaeflora. The poinsettia also belongs to the euphorbias, but it is so generally known as poinsettia that under that name I have described it.

The peculiarity of the euphorbias, at least those we grow, is that the flower proper is very inconspicuous, but the bracts, scarcely noticeable in many flowers, are in the euphorbias highly developed both in size and color, and by a casual observer the bracts are mistaken for petals.

E. splendens can be dismissed by saying that it is of no value to the commercial man. It is easily grown, rather slow of growth, should be stood out of doors in the hottest months, and needs a warm temperature in winter. The stems are covered with sharp thorns. The plant needs training on stakes or a trellis. When in flower its bright red clustered bracts make the plant very showy. But leave it to the private establishment.

E. fulgens is a beautiful plant and twenty years ago was one of our standard winter flowering plants, thought then to be indispensable. When baskets were made of a variety of flowers, it was a favorite with us for an edging, and it is a rich looking, graceful flower wherever you use it. They make annually long growths, and the flowers, which are orange scarlet, are placed close to the stem, forming long, handsome wreath-like flowers. Plants that have flowered during winter can be cut up into cuttings. Anything but the old, hard wood will root. If cut back in April, young shoots will start, which, of course, root the quickest. April and May are good months to put in the cuttings, and keep them wet and shaded. Be careful when potting off to not let them wilt from sun or dryness.

Grow on in a warm, light house, and

Bench of Eucharis Grandiflora.

in July, plant them on the bench in four or five inches of good, rich soil, six to eight inches apart. In a warm, unshaded house they will make a good growth during summer, and should be stopped two or three times to produce more shoots. They should not have a less temperature than 60 degrees at night at any time. If the sprays are cut at Christmas they will break and give another growth and flowers in March and April.

Like the poinsettia, they do not like their roots disturbed. If grown in pots they can be plunged outside in summer, but never allowed to get too much of a soaking of water. No insects trouble them. Unlike the poinsettia, the plants that are two and three years old are the most valuable. After the flower is cut they can be lifted and stored away in dry soil under a bench and started growing again

Japan, Persia and Syria, the Polynesian Islands, Cape of Good Hope, Natal, Abyssinia, Mascerene Islands, Nepal, Simla, Assam, and 6,000 feet up on the Himalaya mountains, in Thibet and Afghanistan; in the United States it grows in North Carolina and westward to Arizona, and in the Amazon valley and in the Cape de Verde Islands, as well as the Azores, Madeira, Teneriffe—in fact, throughout the world, except Australia and New Zealand. Many others have almost as wide a distribution.

Those people who may wonder and conjecture at the closely allied species of animal life existing in countries far removed from one another, and between which till a very recent date communication was impossible, need not wonder at finding the same species of ferns in many parts, because it would be quite possible for the spores

are mostly all deciduous, but they make handsome plants for the rock work or against walls or fences.

The collection and storing for winter use of the fronds of a few species of our native ferns is now quite an industry, and many millions of fronds are preserved for our winter demands.

In Europe the hardy fernery is usually a part of every well regulated garden, and a most interesting place it is for those who have a cultivated taste for these beautiful plants. It is not hazardous to say that it is superior minds that have a taste or make a hobby of ferns or any other class of plants. Retiring people, and perhaps considered cranks they may be, perhaps poor hands at swapping horses or even making money, careless in fashion and not up in golf and poor in politics, yet superior minds far above the common herd. Not those who keep an expensive gardener and pride themselves on having the finest garden to please their friends or surpass their neighbor, but the man or woman who knows their pets, their wants, and when they are flourishing and happy, there is where you will find the intelligent, honest and contented individual.

A hardy fernery in our latitude would have to be confined largely to our northern species; still, for six or seven months it would be highly interesting. They are best shaded by lofty trees and sunk some few feet below the surface, and cut out with winding paths, with rocks and mounds for the ferns. The cool as well as the tropical fernery is usually found in all fine gardens of Great Britain. There may be some here, but as yet they are not common, although there is nothing to prevent their perfect success. They are usually sunk a few feet below the surface of the surrounding ground, simply to insure a more uniform temperature. With a proper selection and planting these ferneries are most beautiful and interesting. When planted out where the roots enjoy a uniform degree of moisture, many species display a beauty that it is impossible to produce in a pot.

All students of ferns or those interested in their culture, whether for pleasure or profit, should most assuredly avail themselves of that good work, "The Book of Choice Ferns," published by the same firm as Nicholson's Dictionary of Gardening, J. Arnot Penman, New York, agent. It is in seven handsome volumes, most comprehensive, and in paper, type and illustrations magnificent. To it I must often refer, for no better authority exists. The author makes a classification of ferns for "decorative purposes" which is a guide to those who are seeking species for any particular purpose.

Prize-winning Group of Ferns.

in May or June. Any good loam with a fourth of manure will grow them, but it should be of that texture that water will pass freely through. The essentials are light, heat, plenty of water when growing, and when in leaf no disturbance of the roots.

FERNS.

This large and ancient order of plants is known botanically as Filices. They are found throughout the globe in every land, and what is remarkable is that not only is a single genus widely spread in many parts of the world, but a single species is found on every continent and island of the sea. One instance will suffice. The well known Adiantum Capillus-Veneris, the British Maiden Hair fern, is found in the warm parts of England and Ireland, and so it is a native of Central and Southern Europe. In China and

to travel hundreds, perhaps thousands, of miles by currents of air. Ferns have no flowers, and that is their great distinguishing mark from all other plants that are perennial, evergreen, or arborescent. The order includes the lowly, creeping selaginella to the majestic giant, the Dicksonia and alsophila of the Australian forest. Ferns are first of all the most graceful of plants. A few may be called more curious than beautiful, such as the platycerium (stag's horn fern), but all are handsome and interesting, and many so graceful that both as ornamental plants and cut fronds they are now indispensable, and hundreds of thousands of feet of glass are devoted to their culture alone. This is a branch of our business which cannot change except to increase. The graceful ferns we must have, whatever flowers we use. The native ferns of our latitude

He classes them as follows: 1, Tree ferns; 2, gigantic, non-arborescent; 3, small growing; 4, ferns with colored or tinted fronds; 5, variegated and crested; 6, gold and silver; 7, climbing, trailing and drooping; 8, filmy or

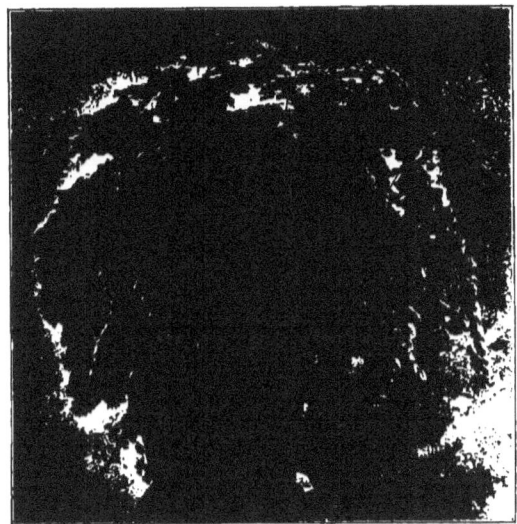

Adiantum Farleyense.

transparent; 9, viviparous or bulbil bearing; 10, curious ferns.

A selection of a few from each class of the more familiar kinds will illustrate the wisdom of the classification.

No. 1. Tree Ferns.

Alsophila australis, Cyathea dealbata, Dicksonia antarctica, Lomaria Gibba. Of these, Dicksonia antarctica is the best known and easiest to manage. Cyathea dealbata is a magnificent tree fern, large spreading head, and under side of the fronds silvery. Lomaria is seldom seen of any great size, and alsophila, although a graceful, quick growing fern, is very soft and entirely unfit for commercial use, as it suffers much in a dry heat and from neglect in watering. They can all be grown in large pots or tubs, or planted out, where the dicksonia and alsophila attain a great size. Any of these will thrive in winter, when the temperature does not go below 50 degrees, and a few nights lower will do no harm. None of the tree ferns could be called commercial plants, except for large and costly decorations, where they would be grand objects.

No. 2. Gigantic Non-Arborescent Ferns.

This includes many of the ferns that are most useful to the commercial florist. Though many ferns of this class are classed as tropical, there are only a few that will not thrive in a minimum temperature of 55 degrees.

A few of the most familiar are: Acrostichum aureum, Adiantum trapeziforme, Asplenium caudatum, Blechnum brasiliense, Davallia divaricata, Nephrodium macrophyllum, Nephrolepis davallioides, Nephrolepis exaltata, Polypodium aureum, Pteris tremula, Woodwardia orientalis, and hundreds of others, both genera and species. In that class are our large decorative plants of pteris, nephrolepis and polypodium.

No. 3. Small Growing Ferns.

As the larger growing ferns are mostly from the tropics, so the dwarfer, more compact growing ones are natives of colder or more temperate zones. There are not many commercial ferns taken from this class and, except to the student of ferns, they are less familiar. A few examples are several forms of Adiantum cuneatum, Asplenium formosum, Asplenium flabellifolium, Cheilanthes fragrans, several davallias and many other genera. Some of the tropical species of these smaller ferns make excellent material for our fern pans. A list of the most desirable for this purpose will be given later on.

No. 4. Ferns with Colored or Tinted Fronds.

As is obvious from the above description, these form one of the most ornamental class, and in classifying no regard to size has been considered.

All are acquainted with the exquisite tints of Adiantum Farleyense, the bluish tint of Polypodium aureum, the variegated Nephrodium (Lastrea) opaca, and the beautifully colored fronds of Pteris tricolor. Several of the selaginellas have a most beautiful bronze and metallic hue, and S. rubella has a golden form that is much valued. Many genera have species in this class, among them the adiantum, blechnum, davallia, doodia, nephrodium, pellaea, polypodium, pteris and selaginella.

No. 5. Variegated and Crested Ferns.

Here the author of the "Book of Ferns" remarks that "If we consider the many crested, variegated, congested, truncate, depauperated, revolute, cornute, marginate and other forms found in many genera, we feel bound to acknowledge that there is little, if any, doubt that ferns are as much addicted to variation as any other members of the vegetable kingdom." We readily believe this, for in this city there lived an old Englishman, a shoemaker, we believe, who, when emigrating, had brought with him from the Cumberland hills his beloved ferns, and had in cultivation alone fifty different forms or varieties of the very common British fern, Scolopendrium vulgare, the hart's tongue fern of every English roadside. Several of these forms the old gentleman claimed to have discovered and named, and we believed him. He found the public were not craving for distinct and odd forms of his scolopendriums, and being withal too honest for this country, returned to his native land.

Just here an innocent little story occurs to me in connection with these formidable names for so innocent a plant. A gentleman with a taste for hardy ferns was annoyed with tramps and beggars intruding on his grounds, so he set up a sign which read, "Beggars Beware! Polypodiums and Scolopendriums Set Here!" It was the simple truth and had the desired effect.

The author above quoted goes on to say: "The creation of new species, especially amongst ferns, is mostly the result of a slow process of evolution, by which naturo produces new types inheriting more or less of the parental characters. To these same variations or freaks of nature we are indebted for the majority of our decorative trees and shrubs, as also for a goodly number of flowering and foliage plants of an herbaceous nature." Just so; that is plain, truthful language, and had the author been writing on zoology he would most likely have said the same about the variations in the species of animals, and back of species have not genera been evolved in the same way, but not with animals as freaks of nature or ornament to the individual, as by their development in some direction that best suited them to their environment, and which comes back exactly to that great truth, "the survival of the fittest."

The variegated ferns exist in a number of genera. Perhaps the most familiar to us is Pteris argyrea, a fine free growing fern. The variegated form of Adiantum cuneatum is only interesting to the specialist. Variegation is found among adiantums, aspidiums, aspleniums, nephrodiums, polypodiums, pteris, scolopendriums and others.

Crested Ferns.

While variegation is found mostly among ferns belonging to the tropics, cristation, as this form is known, is largely confined to the European or cooler species. Cristation consists in the subdivision of the extremities of the frond, forming a tassel, sometimes

Adiantum Decorum.

grotesque and sometimes very ornamental. And sometimes the tips or outline of the whole frond are divided and multiplied. It has been noticed that when these forms or monstrosities occur they reproduce themselves by spores with little variation. The most familiar forms we know are the crested pteris, cretica and serrulata; Adiantum cuneatum has several forms, and the grand Nephrolepis davallioides furcans. Among other genera that give us crested forms are aspidium, asplenium, davallia, gymnogramme, polypodium, woodwardia, etc.

No. 6. Gold and Silver Ferns.

Although occurring in fewer genera, the gold and silver ferns embrace some of the most beautiful plants, and are easy of culture. They are all of exotic origin, but will thrive very well in a winter night temperature of 55 degrees. The very attractive golden and silvery gymnogrammes owe their beauty to the under side of the frond,

which is covered with a thick coating of powder, giving the plant a marvellously rich appearance.

In cheilanthes the silvery appearance is produced by scales or hairs evenly and thickly distributed over the under surface of the fronds, and in the noble Cyathea dealbata the under side of the fronds have the appearance of being painted. Of all this class, the gymnogrammes are the best known and most useful, and if I could only grow two of them it would be G. chrysophylla, a perfect cloth of gold, and G. c. peruviana, with grand silvery fronds. Other handsome ferns of this class will be found among the cheilanthes, gleichenia and nothochlacna.

No. 7. Climbing, Trailing and Drooping Ferns.

In this large class will be found many of our most useful decorative ferns. We use them for cutting, in veranda boxes, as window plants, and for the hanging baskets. Many of these have been mentioned in other classes, because their use is varied. Some years ago at Kew Garden we remember seeing baskets of adiantum and davallia three feet in diameter. They were covered on all sides, a perfect ball, and we have all seen magnificent baskets of Nephrolepis exaltata and N. e. Bostoniensis. There are at present several hanging baskets of the latter as well as of old N. tuberosum at our botanic garden that are at least eight feet in diameter; they are grand objects for large conservatories.

The truly climbing species, which climbs as perfectly as smilax, is Lygodium scandens (Japonicum). This was largely grown about twenty years ago as a decorative plant, and was used as we now use Asparagus plumosus. It is now little heard of; possibly the latter beautiful and useful plant has displaced it in public favor. There are several species of lygodium and an interesting item appears in the "Book of Ferns," which says that our native Lygodium palmatum, which grows from Massachusetts southward, was likely to become extinct in the state of Connecticut, and was protected by a law passed by the state legislature forbidding its being gathered, under a penalty of $100. It would be interesting to know whether that was a law made to be kept, or, like most of our laws, made to be broken.

The trailing ferns are of the greatest use to the amateur who has a fernery as well as to the commercial man for baskets, etc. They cover walls, trunks of large ferns and rocks.

The davallias are best known and are grand for ...is purpose, spreading out into large masses. Their rhizomes (or creeping stems) creep on the surface and are ornamental as well as the fronds. Many of the beautiful species are from warm countries, but will thrive wherever 50 degrees is kept in winter. Little soil but thorough drainage is the great requisite. Their surface rhizomes when growing should always be kept moist, and when partially resting in water never allowed to get dry.

Some of the finest of this beautiful genus are: D. canariensis, D. bullata, D. Tyermanni, D. dissecta, D. immersa, D. Mariesii, D. Novae-Zelandiae, D. pentaphylla. The last six species are especially adapted for hanging baskets. Their curious and hairy rhizomes, resembling the paw of some small animal, gives rise to their popular name of hare's foot, squirrel's foot, etc., although Polypodium aureum is often called the hare's foot.

The nephrolepis need more soil for their roots and are not so truly trailers as the davallias. They are so well known little need be said here. They multiply fast, and if given surface room soon form large masses. Their stolons, or what we would call in a strawberry a runner, spreading out in all directions, sometimes above and sometimes below the surface, but from them there spring up a few fronds, which are most easily taken off to form another plant, or left to add to the size of the parent stock.

The gleichenia is another beautiful genus that spreads by rhizomes, and for the private fernery is among ..e handsomest but not so easily managed as the davallia. Gleichenia Boryi, G. circinati, G. dicarpa, G. polypoides, G. rupestris, and varieties of these are mentioned as fine trailing ferns, as are many of the polypodiums, and of easy management. P. aureum, P. Bil-

Polypodium Subauriculatum in a hanging basket.

In many parts of the world. The same difficulty would be met with in their cultivation here as occurs with Odontoglossum crispum among orchids: our hot, dry summers and the necessity of fire heat in winter. To this class belongs the world famous Killarney fern, which grew, and if Vandals have not destroyed it, yet grows among the shady nooks and rocks about the Lakes of Killarney. What a pity travelers do not search for a section of the vertebra of some extinct saint, of which that island has been so prolific, and leave the gem Trichomanes radicans in peace.

Some forty years ago, in fact, exactly that, the writer had charge of a cool conservatory. In that house on the south side of the north path, about half way between the east and the west paths, and partly shaded by the fine heads of a Dicksonia antarctica and a Cyathea dealbata, one on either side, was a small case, perhaps about five feet long and two feet wide, with a hinged glass roof; and in this case some eighteen inches below the glass were several clumps of the Killarney fern (Trichomanes radicans) and the other British filmy fern, Hymenophyllum Tunbridgense. I have been particular in locating this little greenhouse within a greenhouse because I can see the Killarney fern now, although I have not seen one since it was my duty to lift up the lid and let in a little air if there was too great a degree of moisture on the delicate fronds. There was an older and wiser mind than mine who inspected these plants daily, and when I now read today of the most approved methods of culture of these wonderful ferns I can see that the house of forty years ago and their treatment was about right.

They are now seldom grown, but an ardent lover of ferns would surely like to have them under his care. Briefly then, the principal fact to realize is that wherever found their surroundings are charged with moisture: Light they have, but never the direct rays of the sun. Most of them have surface rhizomes and they need little soil, which can be broken up peat, chopped sphagnum and pounded up bricks or broken crocks. Moisture at the roots they want at all times and an atmosphere charged with moisture, but no syringing overhead. A dry, cutting draught, even in the greenhouse, would soon destroy them. The British species will withstand a temperature far below freezing, and the species from India and the West Indies, as well as those from China, Tasmania and New Zealand, are found at high elevations. The hymenophyllums "forming a green matting over constantly wet rocks."

A low temperature, shade and moisture are the essentials to success with these beautiful ferns, which the commercial florist will let severely alone.

lardieri, P. Paradiseae, P. repens, P. sororium and P. verrucosum are highly commended for any place where ferns of a creeping or trailing habit are desired.

The drooping ferns are those having drooping or pendulous fronds and are more valuable for hanging baskets than any other class, and none are better known or better for the purpose than the splendid genus nephrolepis. By their stoloniferous habit young plants soon emerge from the outside of the baskets in all directions. Several forms or variations in the well known N. exaltata have appeared lately and the variety known as Bostoniensis is a wonderful acquisition. It is unequalled as a basket plant, makes a grand specimen in a pot or tub, withstands the dry heat of a sitting room remarkably well, equal to a kentia palm, and does fairly well in the broad sun if well provided with water.

The best known and most desirable of the nephrolepis are N. exaltata and its grand variety Bostoniensis, N. cordifolia, known among florists generally as tuberosa because the underground stolons bear tubers. This spe-

cies, although from tropical America, lives and grows in our cool house and for vases and veranda boxes is the hardiest of all; N. davallioides, and its beautiful form, furcans. Then there are several species or varieties, one known among us as cordata compacta, shorter in the frond but making a very compact, dark green, handsome plant. A new variety has lately appeared, called Washingtoniensis, of which we have heard unfavorable reports. Several of the adiantums have a drooping form and for private collections are beautiful, but not florists' plants. A. concinnum is a beautiful species, and with it are recommended for baskets caudatum, digitatum, lunulatum, Moorei and others.

Class 8. Filmy or Transparent Ferns.

To embrace all the classes it is necessary not to neglect the above, although even if of interest to the florist they cannot be any source of profit. Yet they are considered the gems of the whole family of ferns. There are only three genera: hymenophyllum, trichomanes and todea. These three genera have numerous representatives

Class 9. Viviparous and Proliferous Ferns.

This peculiar class includes many species of many different genera.

Nephrolepis Exaltata Bostoniensis.

This last division includes only what is strange, striking, peculiar, or a species that is very unlike the great majority of ferns, but the author I have so liberally quoted does not include any of the crested, or what he calls mal-formed, varieties of originally elegant species. The species he selects for this class are so unlike ferns in appearance that they are not readily taken for ferns. The Lygodium scandens would hardly be thought a fern, and Platycerium alcicorne, the well-known stag's horn fern, differs widely from our usual idea of ferns. The Acrostichum crinitum of the West Indies must be a remarkable looking plant, for its shape and texture gives it the name of the elephant's ear. There are some species that, but for their so-called fruit, bear no resemblance to the ferns or entitle them to rank with the order.

As curious objects for the fernery or conservatory, they have their place, but that is not in the precincts of the commercial man. But think of the thousands of forms we have that are strange, grotesque, beautiful, graceful, some creeping on wet, cold rocks like a tracery of fine lace, and some of the family rearing their plumed heads 100 feet high in the tropical forest, inhabitants of the earth in the dark ages of the dim past, contemporaries, perhaps, of the giant horse tails that formed our coal, surviving the glacial period.

While in some genera of this class only two or three species are represented, in others they predominate. The large genus asplenium is of the latter. This class is known from their curious way of multiplying or reproducing their species.

They are again divided into classes from the manner or disposition of the bulbils. Two of the best known ferns that are viviparous are Asplenium bulbiferum and Aspidium angulare proliferum. We constantly see these in every place where ferns are grown. These have the bulbils or little plants scattered over the upper surface of the leaf, and are most readily increased by detaching the young plant and potting or laying the whole leaf on the surface of some pan of suitable soil where the young plants soon root and can be afterwards potted.

Another class has this proliferous character extending only to the stalk of the frond. Another class has but a single bulbil growing at the tip or end of the frond. And there is yet another which is classed as proliferous, but in a very different way from the other three. This includes the invaluable genus nephrolepis, and its proliferous character enables us to propagate it with such ease, and is also the cause of its being such a splendid basket fern. The nephrolepis have long, wiry stolons or underground rhizomes provided with latent buds which are constantly sending up fronds and forming young plants. As we all know, to sever this wiry rhizome or stolon from the parent plant is not felt by either, so our stock of the Boston fern and other nephrolepis is most rapidly increased by planting out medium sized plants in four or five inches of soil during summer. Besides those mentioned there are a number of viviparous or proliferous ferns, many of them highly interesting and handsome, but not desirable to the plant grower. These are adiantum, gymnogramme, marattia, nephrodium, platycerium, polypodium, pteris, scolopendrium, woodwardia and others; all have several representatives in this curious hen and chickens-like class.

Nephrolepis Rufescens Tripinnatifida.

All kindred because the reproduction of the species is the same in all.

Propagation.

Those that have surface rhizomes, such as the davallias and some of the adiantums (Capillus-Veneris is one), are easily and quickly divided. A rhizome that has run out and thrown up a few fronds will have also made some roots and can be severed from the parent plant and potted. Never over-pot ferns. It is true that some of the stronger growing kinds, especially the pteris, soon get root-bound and then want larger pots, but the great majority of ferns do not need so much pot room, but they always want good drainage, so that water can pass freely through.

Those that have stolons or underground rhizomes, such as the nephrolepis, are most easy of all to multiply, young plants often coming up at the side of the pot and on the aerial roots, the young plants appearing at intervals. In June, when your bedding plants are gone, select a bench that will let the water through freely, and in five or six inches of soil plant out young plants from 3 or 4-inch pots. They will by September or October have made fine plants and have sent out such an abundance of stolons that at intervals, or when you lift, you will get a number of young plants, which can be potted up, or if a larger stock is needed, replanted. There is no doubt a much larger plant of any of the nephrolepis can be obtained in a short time by planting out than if grown in a pot, and they lift with a mass of roots, perfectly, without losing a single frond.

Few of the commercial sorts are proliferous on the leafy frond, but those that are lend themselves to

Nephrolepis Davallioides Furcans.

propagation most easily, as described in the remarks on that class.

Some species that grow in tufts, such as Adiantum cuneatum, the common Maiden Hair, can be divided. The crown should be cut carefully and then the roots pulled apart. Cuneatum, or any particular form of it, is often increased by division, and sterile species, of which the most beautiful of all, A. Farleyense is one, can only be propagated by division. This should be done in early spring, when the plants are in most cases resting and before

the young growth is made, but can by care be done at any season.

Just here it is worthy of mention that this beautiful fern, A. Farleyense, is usually thought to be a sterile form of A. tenerum, but there is no definite knowledge about it, and the millions of plants now existing, or that have existed, all came from one plant found growing on Farley Hills, in the island of Barbadoes, the thickest populated island of the world, where the children's stomachs are distended like balloons by an unchanged diet of sugar cane.

Nearly all the useful species can be readily raised from spores, which is the natural way, and has the advantage of producing possibly either an improved form or variation from the parent which by division, or by proliferous stolons, or divisions of the rhizomes, never happens. The raising of seedling ferns from spores is a very delicate operation and with the beginner not always a success. You will likely get several species which you never believed you sowed and few of those that you thought were sown. We all know how ferns spring up in the pots or on the benches, if left undisturbed for a few months, if there are any spore-bearing ferns in the house. Adiantum cuneatum I have seen vegetate on a slimy, dirty brick wall by the tens of thousands and had to scrape them off for the sake of cleanliness.

Before giving any directions for sowing, just a word about these spores. The whole order of ferns have no flowers, consequently no sexual organs, and from the spore to the young perfect fern frond like its parent is a profound, complicated and mysterious phenomenon. When the spore vege-

Pteris Tremula Smithae.

Pteris Victoriae.

tales it forms cells, which are called the prothallus, and is only an increase of cells. On the under side of the prothallus (which resembles the Liverwort so often seen on the surface of our soil) with plants making a slow or stagnant growth) develop the organs of both sexes, which have the same function as the more conspicuous organs in the flowering plants. To describe the complicated and marvellous process of fertilization would require a chapter, had I time or space to quote it. From the prothallus finally springs (varying in time with the species) the young true frond. Any cross fertilization of species, as we do with flowering plants, is therefore impossible, but by sowing the spores of different species in one pan there is assurance that hybrids have been produced, and this is getting deep into science.

One word as to the fertility or fecundity of ferns. Mr. Charles T. Druery, who is quoted in the "Book of Choice Ferns," says: "We have estimated the spores upon a single frond of our native (British) Polypodium vulgare (a frond not over a foot long by three inches wide), and found that one of the sub-divisions of the same size taken from a tree fern would yield plants sufficient to form a wood as large as Epping Forest. Every frond would bear hundreds of such sub-divisions and the tree fern would probably bear thirty or forty fronds every season. A little calculation, therefore, will show that inconceivable numbers have to be dealt with." Truly inconceivable; countless millions on every frond. Another illustration by the same author was the shaking of the

spores of an asplenium out and collecting them, about filling a teaspoon, in which he estimates he had eighty million spores. So if one in ten thousand of the spores we sow vegetate, and the surface of our pan will be covered with the moss-like prothalli.

The spores should be gathered, or rather the frond cut before the spore

Cyrtomium Falcatum.

cases have burst, and if not convenient to sow at once, put them away in paper bags. The soil or material you sow on, which can be a light, sandy loam, covering an inch or so

of broken crocks, should be baked to destroy all germs of weeds or moss or eggs of insects. If not baked, water with scalding water. Make the surface smooth and scatter the spores. No careless watering must be given, but let it flow over the surface slowly. If covered with glass, which it should be, the soil will not need much watering till the prothalli appear in the way above described. When this about covers the surface of the pan they should be divided by taking small patches, say 1-4 inch square, and placing them on the surface of other pans or flats. Soon the true fern leaf will appear, when in time the little plants can be pricked out singly in small pots, or, what is still better, in flats, till they are larger and need a pot for themselves.

If a few large plants of the leading sorts are kept in a house and allowed to shed their spores, they will be carried to every corner of the house, and if some plants (like large palms) are in the house that are not often shifted, you will be sure to have an abundance of young ferns. I have noticed frequently the young plants of Adiantum cuneatum growing on the sphagnum in the cattleya baskets.

Cultivation.

It would be impossible to give any special instructions for any particular class of ferns, and there is no need of it. Those that make strong roots, such as the pteris, want root room and must be well drained. Those making surface rhizomes, as the davallias, do not want much depth of soil, but need surface room if large specimens are wanted.

It is generally conceded that in soil ferns are not at all particular. Atmospheric conditions are of far more consequence. A good fibrous loam, with a third of leaf-mould, will suit any of them. Bone meal will help ferns if soil is thoroughly watered after re-

Gymnogramme Decomposita.

putting. Some growers of Adiantum cuneatum add about one-sixth of well rotted and sifted cow manure to their compost. Pot firmly but not too solid.

As before mentioned about temperature, few plants will thrive in a lower temperature than that of their native habitat so well as ferns. Species from the tropics, where in some localities the temperature would hardly ever be below 70 degrees, will do very well in our houses if not below 55 degrees. Growers of Adiantum cuneatum or A. decorum, who grow houses of them for the market, sometimes as pot plants, but more often for the cut fronds, will, I am aware, keep them higher than 55 degrees. Cuneatum will pay best when grown in a high temperature, but should be well matured before sold or it will soon wilt.

Watering ferns does not need any great skill. All evergreen ferns, and we grow only those, require plenty of water at all times, but less in winter, when all ferns take a partial rest. We have had young men tell us that at "their establishment," where the A. Farleyense was well grown, they have seen repeatedly Jack Jones standing with the hose and giving the Farleyense a good syringing. It must have

been on the morning of bright summer days.

Almost all ferns are found as undergrowth in forests and woods, and are shaded by the trees above. Ferns want subdued light, but not a heavy shade. The ideal conditions for all the ferns we grow would be a house that could be shaded, say, by 9 a. m., and the shade removed at 5 p. m., but that great and most desirable convenience is not attained. Next to that is a north house, where light comes in, but not the direct rays of the sun. As we perhaps have neither of the above, then shade by degrees till midsummer, and remove gradually as winter approaches. Ferns will grow fast enough in a very shady house, but the fronds are weak and straggling. Plenty of water in the roots, plenty of moisture in the house, is needed, but do little wetting of the fronds; they don't need it.

One of the most important points to observe is to give the ferns a cool bottom. A bench with three or four 4-inch pipes under it is the worst possible place. A solid bed covered with ashes will suit them far better. If growing adiantum on a bench, let it be a deep one and well drained, and no steam or hot water pipes near it. Let the pipes

be on the side, where they can have no influence on the soil. The bottom heat that is so congenial to most of our soft wooded plants is misery to the ferns.

The healthiest lot of ferns I ever saw under glass was in the fernery at the Manchester (England) Botanic Gardens. Cool and moist, with water trickling over rocks, with the dicksonias in the center and their great stems covered with platycertums, you could fancy you were transported to a rocky dell of New Zealand. The most luxuriant ferns growing naturally were on the banks of the small river or inlet to Lake Chautauqua, N. Y., where the osmunda grew to the water's edge in rank profusion, shaded by the overhanging forest.

Few insects trouble our commercial ferns. Scale is often troublesome to large ferns. Old fronds, if badly affected, are best cut off and destroyed, and washing the others with soap and Nikoteen is all you can do. Thrip will succumb to the fumes of tobacco, but ferns don't like tobacco smoke, and it is much better to vaporize with the Rose Leaf extract of tobacco or Nikoteen. Do this at least once a week; it will also keep down aphis, which sometimes infests the young fronds of the adiantums and will do the ferns no harm. Wood lice, which often are known by that awful name of sow bugs, eat the tender shoots. A hollowed-out potato in which they will go to roost will catch thousands, or a mixture of paris green and powdered sugar placed along the edge of the bench will destroy them.

The small white slugs are the worst enemy of ferns, and the adiantums seem selected as their own especial diet. The old remedy of placing cabbage or lettuce leaves on the bench or pots is sure to catch many of them, but they should be examined early every morning. The slugs are said to be very fond of bran, and if small patches are put on the bench here and there the slugs will revel in it and can be caught. Large growers o. the Maiden Hair find that a light dusting of air slacked lime on the plants and soil about once a month is sufficient to dispel any visitation of the slugs.

Ferneries.

The filling of small ferneries for the table is now an important branch of business. We should endeavor to make these as satisfactory as possible, for they are short lived at best. We get them returned in the condition of mud and again as dry as a rock. It will not pay us all to be raising our young ferns, and unless you are in it with all facilities, leave it to the specialist. Ferns that are small, compact growing, would be too slow in growing to be profitable, so it is small plants of quick growing, larger kinds that are mostly used for this purpose. The spores are sown in winter or early spring and the plants delivered to us from 2-inch pots in the fall months.

A night temperature of 60 degrees,

Microlepia Hirta Cristata.

To be reminiscent once more. Somewhere about the year '60 of this century the writer had the first serious attack of the "tender passion." The cause of the attack and outbreak was much his senior, and having no funds to buy an album or a volume of Byron, he made a collection of British ferns, dried them in a book, and presented them, named, and the collection without varieties was almost complete with the exception, perhaps, of ten species. Now, I have forgotten what size glove that young woman wore, or whether her hair was in curls or brushed back a la the Empress Eugenie, but I will never forget how to write Asplenium Ruta-muraria, although I have not seen Ruta-muraria or the old woman nigh on to forty years. Look at a plant and write it down; once written and spelt correctly, you will never forget. The writer has a fair memory for anecdotes, because they can be filled in as you go along, but no good for names unless he writes them down; then they stick in that laboratory which is a mystery to all of us.

FERTILIZERS AND MANURES.

As we use the words in gardening operations, they include any substance, animal or mineral, that will add quantity, weight, vigor and size to our crops. I shall not attempt to give you any learned discourse on chemical manures, because, first, I am not able, and, secondly, you can easily obtain a report from the many state agricultural and horticultural stations giving the analyses of the several manures and the quantities used, as well as their effect on different soils and plants.

with a cool bottom and partial shade, is the place to grow on the young ferns. You don't want them to grow fast, but to fill up and be strong and robust. An eastern firm who raise several hundred thousand young ferns for this purpose gave me the following list as those best suited for the purpose, the first four being most useful in the center; Pteris cretica magnifica, Pteris cretica albo-lineata, Pteris Victoriae (variegated), Pteris argyraea, Cyrtomium falcatum, Aspidium angulare, Blechnum occidentale, Blechnum braziliense, Davallia stricta, Lomaria ciliata, Lomaria Gibba, Lastrea opaca, Lastrea chrysoloba, Lastrea artistata variegata, Nephrodium hertypes, Onychium japonicum, Polystichum corianum, Polystichum setosum, Polystichum pubescens, Pteris hiaurita argentea, Pteris serrulata, Pteris cristata, Pteris nana compacta, Pteris voluta, Pteris cretica Mayli (variegated), Selaginella Emiliana (for edging).

Conclusion.

With the exception of the list last quoted, in which the names of some varieties may not be correct, but by which they are best known, I have followed out the nomenclature of Hooker and Baker, as used in the "Book of Choice Ferns," as those names will eventually prevail. In doing so, however, I found with my limited knowledge of ferns that names have been much changed in forty years. What we knew as Lastrea felix-mas is now Nephrodium felix-mas, and many less familiar cases.

In conclusion, if you are not brought in contact with any class of plants you cannot quickly memorize their names, but all plants under your care

or that you handle you should know correctly. To ask the name in a botanic garden or at your neighbor's and forget it the next moment is waste of time and an annoyance. "Let me see; what is that fern? I forget." The professor says, "That is Onychium japonicum." "Oh, yes, yes, yes, of course; and what's that?" And before you have got to the door you have forgotten the very sound of the name.

Platycerium Alcicorne.

Platycerium Grande.

The paper read at the Cleveland convention of the S. A. F., in August, 1896, by Prof. R. C. Kedzie, M. A., of the Michigan Agricultural College, was very instructive. He said "Potassium, phosphorus and nitrogen are of the highest importance to florists for four reasons: First, they are absolutely indispensable to vegetable life, because no plant can grow in the absence of any one of them; second, because in available form they are found in smaller amounts than other food elements; third, because they are soonest exhausted by cultivation; fourth, because they are especially concerned in the early growth of plants up to and including the period of flowering." For their great value, not only to the farmer, but to the gardener, the professor called them "The Chemical Tripod in Floriculture."

The fertilizer that is a favorite with all florists is what we call bone dust or flour. There is sometimes confusion about the names of these grades. With us the bone dust is ground up about as fine as Scotch oatmeal, but there are too many coarse pieces in it to be available to the plants in one season. If the plants were to grow two or three years in the same pot or bench, then the coarser particles would be all right, because the coarser particles would be gradually dissolving and giving benefit to the soil and plants; but if not dissolved, then you have thrown out a costly fertilizer and had no benefit. So when we want "bone" for roses or carnations, or to mix with our potting soil in early spring, to give our soft-wooded plants a jump, we order the bone "flour," which is really as fine as flour.

Bone is the most complete manure we can use, because it contains both

phosphate and nitrogen. The quantity you can use is often questioned. I have heard one professor say he "thought you could not overdo it if the soil was not allowed to get dry." We have used on carnations 200 pounds on a bench with five inches of

Platycerium Willinckii.

soil, 200 feet long and 6 feet wide, and seen only the best results. For potting soil we have used a 6-inch pot full to an ordinary wheelbarrow of soil. Perhaps much more could be added with safety, but we don't think it advisable.

Phosphates produce flowers and nitrates produce a strong leaf growth, giving a rich green to the foliage. Here it may be as well to say that all manures reach the roots of plants more completely and perfectly when applied in a liquid form than in the dry state, but not all of us have the facilities for so applying them.

Last year, being short of ground bone, we used on carnations in the same quantities as bone a superphosphate of a fine grade that was sold under the name of "potato phosphate," simply being of a better quality than that usually sold to farmers for their wheat, etc.

Nitrate of soda (Chili saltpeter) is valuable for its available nitrogen and we have tried it on several plants, one pound dissolved in fifty gallons of water. It produces a rich growth of leaf and stem, but does not induce flowers (in fact, the contrary), but in the early stages of plants, young roses, for instance, where growth and size of plant is wanted, not flower, it can be used to advantage. My experience with it in mineral form was very disastrous. I sowed it on a bench of carnations and then stirred it in before the carnations were planted, about two pounds on a space 8x7 feet. It killed almost every carnation. A smaller quantity might have had a different effect, but don't use it except in solution. English farmers sow it broadcast on their grain crops in early spring, but on the surface and out of doors is no guide to us. In solution and the proportion named above (one pound in fifty gallons of water) it is a valuable stimulant to violets, producing a larger and deeper blue flower; and as we usually get plenty of violet flowers too often lacking in quality, there is where the nitrate of soda is very valuable.

Prof. Kedzie places a very high value on wood ashes, in fact places them first, and to quote him, he says: "These contain all the mineral matter of plant growth, and so far as minerals are concerned are an all round manure. Without this mineral matter in some form plants cannot grow." We have many of us a good opportunity to obtain this valuable fertilizer very near home, but do not avail ourselves of it. They can be used with ordinary animal manure. About one peck to a yard or load of soil will be found a safe quantity. As the ashes of wood contain the elements that the mature plant contained, they must furnish the elements for a full and rapid growth.

The way we use our chemical fertilizers is not similar to that followed on the farm or market garden, where a change of manure may be desirable on any one piece of ground. With a bench of roses or carnations it is a new lot of plants and new soil every year, and if bone meal is a perfect manure there can be no harm in using it year after year.

Guano was largely in use thirty years ago when the supply was greater. It is the excrement of sea birds, found on the islands off the coast of Peru. It is difficult now to obtain and what would be sold to you for Peruvian guano would be most likely an imitation. The pure guano was one of the most wonderful of manures. We have used a 2-inch pot of guano in four gallons of water and the effect of an occasional watering on soft-wooded plants was marvelous. If procurable it would, however, be too expensive and not as complete a manure as bone meal.

Of the animal manures the one mostly in use by florists is that of the cow stable. Why, I do not know, as horse manure is richer in ammonia. One of the best rose growers we know, on being asked what manure he used, answered, "Any I can get." A few years ago my neighbor, Mr. W. J. Palmer, showed me two houses of Daybreak carnations that were for general vigor, stout stem and large flowers much superior to other houses of the same variety. On being asked to account for it, Mr. Palmer said he could not, except that the best lot had manure from his horse stable while the poorer ones had only cow manure. We believe that the cause was explained.

While certain animal manures may have special fertilizing properties, for our crops of roses and carnations it would be perfectly safe, and I believe beneficial, to use them mixed. There is no doubt there is a difference in the qualities of manure by the difference in the food of the animals. Animal or farm-yard manure should not be allowed to lie in a great heap and violently ferment, or much of its value will be destroyed.

With our roses there is a difference of opinion as to quantity to use. Too much manure in the soil for carnations produces a rank, soft growth, and if bone meal or superphosphate is used a tenth of animal manure is sufficient. With roses a sixth or seventh is sometimes used, and more often less. Sheep manure is much stronger and a twentieth is as strong as it should be used. In making up our compost pile in the summer time for use in the following winter and spring we have often added a fourth of horse or cow manure, and when chopped down and thoroughly mixed with soil it was not more than was beneficial to our usual run of soft-wooded plants, such as geraniums, coleus, cannas, etc.

There is not much doubt that our animal manures, besides imparting fertilizing properties to the soil, are often of a mechanical benefit, making the soil more porous and friable.

We should remember, in discussing the quantities and qualities of manures, that there is such a wide dif-

ference, not only in the chemical properties of soils in different localities, but in the condition of soils of the same qualities. A meadow that has been used as a pasture for ten or fifteen years will give you a sod that must be rich in plant food over that which has been laid down but two years and previously was cropped year after year. Or again, the soil of a market garden that has annually received a heavy dressing of manure will grow any of our greenhouse crops, while a worn-out garden, however good naturally the texture of the soil, will grow nothing without the aid of some quick acting fertilizer.

In concluding this chapter I would remind you that soot (bituminous only) is very largely used by the plant growers of Europe, and Nicholson says: "It has the advantage over other manures that it can hardly be misapplied." No soot is wasted in the cities of Great Britain; it is all sold to the farmer and gardener. It is not, however, a flower producer, but adds size and lustre to the leaf and flower. It is used by all cyclamen growers, mixed with the soil, and as a liquid. And by chrysanthemum growers it is highly valued. A peck of it is put into a bag and placed in fifty gallons of water, and the effect on the leaf and color of the flower is most marked.

Animal or organic manures can be misapplied or used to excess in the greenhouse, but in the field seldom are, and it is generally a sign of a

thrifty florist or gardener when you see his place adorned with manure piles; it is money well laid out; it is an investment that with ordinary management is sure to come back with great interest. Millions of acres in our eastern states are crying for manure to replace the properties of the soil that lazy and careless tillage has year after year taken from it.

FICUS.

A large genus of trees or shrubs cultivated for their ornamental leaves, F. elastica, familiarly known as the rubber tree, is the species we are interested in above all others, although for private collections and botanical gardens several others are noble plants. F. repens (properly F. stipulata) is a small-leaved, very useful climbing plant, growing and adhering closely to the walls of greenhouses, making a very pretty appearance, and will withstand a few degrees of frost. F. Parcelli has a very prettily variegated leaf. It is very unlike elastica, the plant being more branching and slow growing. The leaves are sharp pointed, three or four inches long and very irregularly blotched. It is handsome when well grown, but is most horribly addicted to thrip and red spider.

F. elastica is now a plant of the first importance with all commercial plant men. Tens of thousands are annually sold. The "rubber" is known to all as one of the very best house plants.

Ficus Elastica.

We have all seen it thriving in a dark hall, and with fair treatment there are few plants that will endure unfavorable conditions as well. We get, however, lots of complaints. "My rubber is losing its leaves, etc."

I tell my customers to sponge the leaves occasionally and if the water passes through the soil freely to water twice a day in summer and once every day in winter.

They stand out in pots and tubs during summer in the broad sun and they want plenty of water. I have never seen their fine leaves burned or injured by the sun when out of doors, but they easily burn under glass in the bright days of spring before we are shaded.

The following is not quoted for my readers to·follow, but the most shiny leaves and greasiest soil I ever saw was on a plant brought to me two years ago. I think the little lady brought it for my inspection because she was proud of it. It looked bright and well and its introduction to me was as follows: "What do you think of my rubber, Mr. S.? I oiled its leaves yesterday with olive oil and last week a friend told me she thought it was troubled with worms, so I gave it two tablespoonfuls of castor oil and two worms came out."

Perhaps to Mr. Wm. K. Harris, of Philadelphia, belongs the credit of growing the finest specimen rubbers in one year of any man in the world, producing branching plants 6 feet high and 4 feet through, and furnished with leaves to the pot. I do not pretend to tell you how to emulate Mr. Harris, but young plants that are wanted to branch should not be allowed to grow 3 feet high and then cut down to the hard wood. They will break, but slowly. If wanted branched pinch the top out of the strongest young plants when not over 15 inches high.

F. elastica is a tropical tree, but will exist in our greenhouses in winter at a temperature of 50 degrees or even lower, but when rapid growth is wanted 70 degrees at night is the temperature, and when growing those specimens spoken of above it is never less than that and possibly 100 in the day time.

The rubbers thrive in a comparatively small pot and for our sales should not be overpotted. A good, open, turfy loam, with a fifth or sixth of manure, and to this compost add one quart of bone meal to every bushel.

Propagation is by two methods—cuttings and what is generally known as "mossing." The latter is much the surest way. Sometimes cuttings root very well, and again under the same conditions they don't. Cuttings seven or eight inches long, with several leaves, always the latest growths, and cut just below a joint, inserted in a 2-inch pot of sand and loam, the end of the cutting well down to bottom of pot and the pot plunged in some material where the bottom heat is 80 degrees, will usually meet with success. Keep the cuttings after the first water-

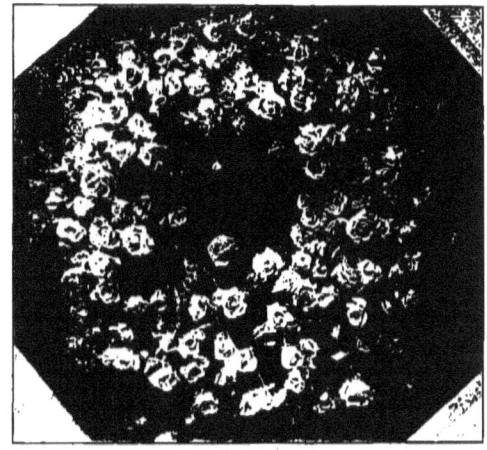

A Wreath of Roses.

ing only moderately moist. As the leaves are much in the way a small stick is inserted in the pot to which the leaves are drawn up. If this were not done they would take up a great deal of room and be inconvenient to water. They should be well rooted in the small pots before being shifted. Late spring is a good time to propagate by cuttings.

By the mossing system failure is almost impossible. August and September are favorable months for the operation because the wood is about right then, but it can be done at any time. The tops of young plants can be taken, although large branching trees are usually kept where they are propagated in any quantity. Nine or ten inches from the tip of the shoot, where the wood is not too green nor too hard, a cut is made in the wood upwards about an inch and a half long from the bark to about half way through the shoot. Sphagnum moss is inserted to keep the cut open and more moss wrapped round to entirely envelop the stem where the cut has been made. If the moss when tied on is as large as a hen's egg you have enough on. Keep the moss syringed daily.

In five or six weeks you will see roots protruding through the moss. Let them get well rooted and then sever from the plant just below the moss, and pot. The young plants should be kept from sun and draught till they take hold of the new soil.

Most florists are pleased to inform their customers· that this is the plant that produces the rubber of commerce, and a slight scratch on a shoot will soon show the milky sap, but they are

mistaken. Ficus elastica is a native of the East Indies, and our rubber comes from Brazil and from a tree that is very unlike Ficus elastica.

FITTONIA.

Very pretty little trailing plants that require a good heat at all times. They are easily propagated in the spring in warm sand. A few plants in a 6 or 8-inch pan will soon cover it and make very ornamental pans for the table. For large ferneries they are very useful. They like shade and plenty of water during summer when growing.

F. gigantea is somewhat erect, with pale red flowers and finely veined leaves.

F. Verschaffeltii and its varieties, argyroneura and Pearcei, are the kinds useful to the florist, being dwarf, spreading and compact, entirely covering the pot or pan with their very ornamental foliage. The leaves of the former are bright green, with a tracing of pure white. The latter is also green, with veins of bright carmine.

FLORAL ARRANGEMENTS.

Within twenty years there has been a great change in our floral arrangements and designs. This has been partly brought about by the innovations of the more enlightened florist and partly by the more refined taste of our customers who have rebelled against the same old conventional arrangements. Time was when the center-piece of the table was an elaborate lofty affair, very complicated in design and three or four feet high, and if the host at the head of the table

A Vase of Roses.

wished to see those at the other end
he or she had to lean over at a tilting
angle. Reason has abolished all this
and whatever flowers are used now are
in low baskets or trays or vases with
flowers on their natural stems. This
wiping out of these very artificial arrangements may be a loss to some
classes of florists, but who can regret
the more natural and beautiful use of
flowers which prevails today.

Baskets or trays are still used for
holding the roses, carnations, violets
or orchids, but we expect to see these
go soon and all flowers used in vases
of some kind for all decorations. They
last better, they look better, it is better taste and more comfort to the
guest to look upon a vase of roses
whose petals and leaves are plump and
fresh than upon those whose heads
begin to droop, for you will be of a
strange build yourself if you do not
feel a wilting come over your spirits
in a more or less degree when you
look upon a wilted arrangement of
flowers. The wilted dude rolled in the
gutter over night is not a more piti-
able sight than a basket of roses that
have collapsed. And the less our customers see of these wilted flowers the
better.

At smaller dinner parties Maidenhair fern or Farleyense or asparagus
sprays are strewn on the table and
here and there some flowers of the
choicest kinds, rose buds, orchids or
lily of the valley. This is a beautiful
arrangement and most pleasing to the
guest if not overdone. Very seldom
now that any design of flowers, whether for the table or a gift, is made of
more than one or two varieties of

A Vase of Carnations.

flowers, and more often, with the exception of orchids, it is only one variety. It is a basket of pink and white roses, or all Meteor or Liberty roses, or American Beauties, all lily of the valley, or valley and violets. Perhaps all violets and perhaps violets and Roman hyacinths. It is almost impossible to make an ugly combination of carnations, they blend so finely, yet they are most often chosen in one color or at most one or two shades. Tulips and narcissus are scarcely ever used except in one color.

Orchids are of such a fantastic shape and pleasing colors that a variety is prettier than a mass of one sort. A basket of all Cattleya Trianae would be very rich, almost too heavy, and the addition of cypripediums and oncidiums would be an improvement and entirely in keeping with the nature of the flowers. The orchids are from the tropics where the vegetable kingdom is all jumbled up and thousands of species to the acre, while the natives of a cooler clime, our roses and carnations and violets, grow in colonies as do the wild flowers of the northern temperate zone.

It is difficult to foresee any great improvement in the arrangement of our flowers for decorations over the prevailing taste and customs of the present day. There need not be less used because the arrangement is simple. Flowers on their own stems is the order of the day and the longer the flowers last in their beauty the more there will be wanted, for in many homes now and in the future, in every home, humble as well as palatial, the flower will be considered not a luxury but an essential and comfort.

A great many florists in this country, especially shop or store keepers, depend very largely on the funeral orders for their living. If the prevailing fashion of sending flowers, particularly designs, to the family of the bereaved were suddenly to become unfashionable with all classes of society there are several thousand flower stores throughout the land that would be to rent for some other class of business. It is not likely to go so suddenly out of fashion but it will change; and the change has already come with many people. A large number of citizens recently handed themselves together in Cleveland and in my city and perhaps others, to protect themselves against "The enormous and extravagant expense of funerals, the outlay and display made at the funeral of the dead often leaving the survivors in hopeless debt."

Carriages and flowers of course come in for a good part of these worthy people's condemnation. There is no doubt that the expense of many funerals is out of all proportion to the means of the family; it is ridiculous and almost criminal to see such ostentation, and we often suffer from it. An instance occurred the other day. Forty dollars' worth of flowers were ordered and delivered, and a month or so afterwards the collector was told

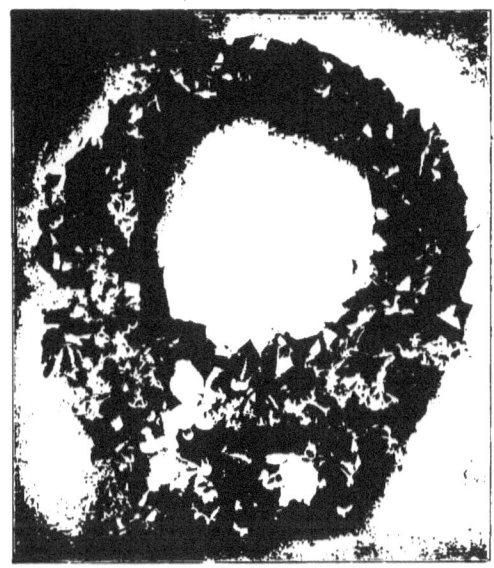

Wreath of Ivy Leaves and Orchids.

A Plain Crescent Wreath.

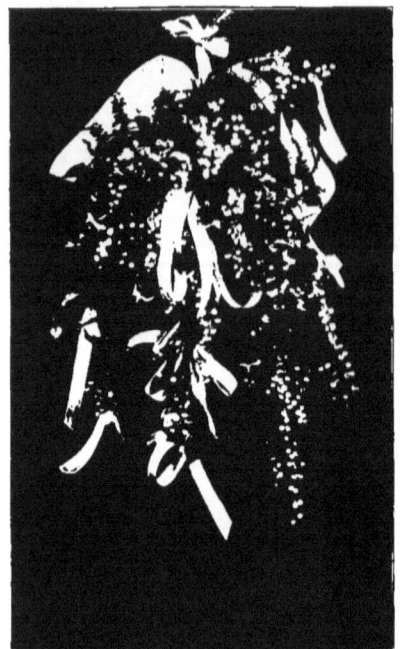

A Shower Bouquet of Lily of the Valley and Cypripediums.

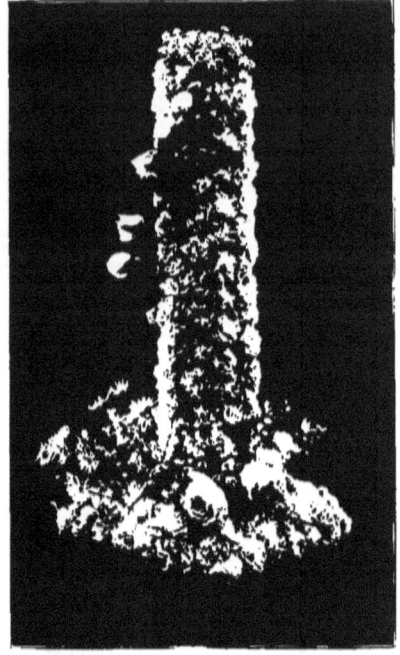

A Simple Form of Broken Column.

by the poor widow that, "The children had gone too far in ordering, and added that her husband had led a double life, having a wife in St. Louis as well as here in Buffalo, and instead of having ten thousand dollars life insurance, as she supposed, he had none, and she was penniless. And there are lots of such cases.

In those times of distress and excitement people are often careless about expenses. You can't very well ask for payment before the articles are delivered and it's hard hearted to send an order C. O. D. or to call around the next day with your bill. Looking at it in a business way, without sympathy, when you know the family is quite poor, persuade them that very little is necessary. When a number of friends are uniting together to send a deceased friend a design, get all you possibly can. They won't miss it and it's a worthy way to distribute wealth, and distributed it is, as is the outlay for all luxuries as well as necessities.

No association or legislation or advice or admonition from pastor or

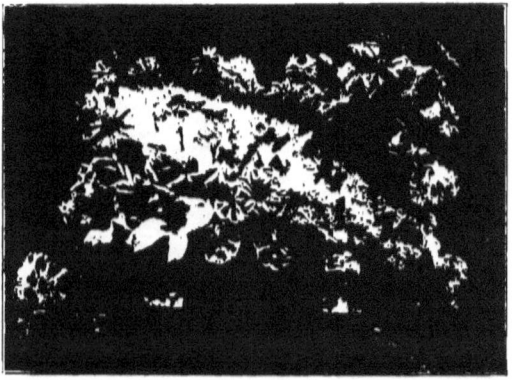

A Small Pillow.

bishop can stop or abolish the use of flowers at funerals; for there is nothing else you can do. In no other way can you show your sympathy. With some people the use of flowers at the grave is as old as history and will continue. But fashion and a more refined taste will modify and change the manner of their use.

We read constantly of the obsequies of some illustrious personage in Europe and the flowers used are invariably in the shape of a wreath. You would think they knew of nothing else but a wreath, for it is a wreath from the emperor of Germany or Queen Victoria or the "Honorable Guild of Candlestick Makers of the Ancient City of London." They never rise above or below a wreath, and when you read of carloads of wreaths, or that it took one hundred men to carry the wreaths, as it did at the funeral of the late president of France, you feel nauseated, as if you had sat down to a dinner of fourteen courses, but every course was the same old thing. I may be mistaken, but I don't think they stick to this very ancient but still most beautiful design because they haven't heard of any other; it is solely because it is simple and chaste, and they don't want any other. Yet it seems that a bunch or loose arrangement of roses or carnations or orchids would be a relief and change from the everlasting wreath.

Our best people (by that I don't mean necessarily the most virtuous, but the people of wealth and refinement and the taste and education which wealth affords) have almost entirely set their faces against the elaborate designs that were used by all classes twenty years ago. Gates ajar and broken columns and scrolls, and even crosses and anchors are never seen or ordered by that class who lead in fashion, and depend upon it the other strata of society will copy and emulate the well-to-do as they do in every particular where their means can possibly reach.

Floral arrangements for the more refined are almost entirely now limited to loose arrangements. Cycas leaves, two or three dozen roses, lily of the valley, a bunch of Roman hyacinths. A wreath is often used, but it is usually some distinct design. Ivy leaves with lily of the valley or all valley, orchids, or all roses, or valley and violets, or all violets. And in many cases the above flowers are bought and sent to the house of mourning simply with a card and loosely in a box.

It would be absurd for the florist to discourage the use of large designs where they are wanted, and in case of societies who wish to send a design to a late brother or sister there is nothing but a large design to send, and the catering to this class of business is quite lucrative with many. Where the design is a pillow, broken column, anchor or scroll, there is room for a display of skill and art, but where the design represents the calling of the departed there is no art, it is merely

Funeral Design.

Low Basket of Violets and Small Ferns.

longer do we see the solemn whiteness in bunches or designs, or any arrangements. Why should we? I think the fashion of white flowers is as absurd as the deep mourning assumed by many. A long black veil only attracts notice and attention, and surely the broken-hearted and sincere mourner does not want to attract attention.

The crowding of flowers in a design is no longer permissible. Every flower should if possible show its individuality. The whole should blend and every flower and leaf should be fresh and spotlessly clean. And let me add in conclusion that when you take an order for a design and promise it at a certain hour see that it is delivered on time. Punctuality gets a large credit mark in the public favor.

FREESIA.

These graceful, fragrant flowers are of the easiest culture. The bulbs are now sold remarkably cheap, cheaper in fact than you can save them. The species called refracta and refracta alba are mostly grown. The latter is pure white, without the yellow blotch in the throat. We too often plant a large lot of freesia bulbs at one time, thus having more than our demand makes profitable. You receive the bulbs in July, and every two or three weeks a few hundred can be started.

Their treatment is entirely different from the so-called Dutch bulbs, and sometimes mistakes are made. We usually plant seven to nine bulbs in a 5-inch pot. Put the bulb a little under the surface and place the pots in a cold-frame. Later batches you will start inside. The pots want no covering of any kind, as the top and roots start together. Water moderately till the foliage is well developed. When the pots are full of roots they should not suffer for water. They like a temperature of about 50 degrees at night and should always have the fullest light.

A good loam with some well rotted manure or leaf-mold will grow them;

A Laurel Wreath with Cycas Leaves.

mechanical, bad taste and bound to sink into disuse. It is impossible to make beautiful such a thing as a fireman's hat, a locomotive, a safe, a gun, a desk; or in case of a brewer, a quarter barrel keg. There is no skill in making those designs; the wire worker is the only man who exercised any skill; putting the flowers into the monstrosities is no more than putting on an overcoat; the tailor is the man who had the skill; if you depart from the lines laid down by the frame you spoil the imitation.

There is a wonderful change in the material used since the days of balsams and hollyhocks, when a design resembled a clipped sheep, with a Saffrano bud here and there raised above the surface a fraction over the rest; and tuheroses were a very important flower. Funeral designs are now made with great taste. Fine flowers are used and color is not forbidden. No

Hamper filled with Violets, Heath and Adiantum Ferns.

THE FLORISTS' MANUAL. 101

FERNS! Shipped in any quantity, from 1000 to 100,000 at a time. Write for prices.

FINE LAUREL FESTOONING, $5 per 100 yards.
FINE LAUREL WREATHS, PRINCESS PINE
WREATHS, for Xmas and Decorations.
FLOWERING LAUREL, 50c per bunch, extra nice. Galax Leaves, Mosses, Etc., Etc.

CROWL FERN CO., Millington, Mass.
Telegraph office, New Salem, Mass.

CUT **FLOWERS**

ROSES, CARNATIONS,
LILIES, SMILAX, ETC.
Always fresh of our own growing.
Send for cut flower price list.

J. L. DILLON, BLOOMSBURG, PA.

BENTHEY & CO.

F. F. BENTHEY, Mgr.

WHOLESALE AND COMMISSION **Florists.** Consignments Solicited.

41 Randolph St., CHICAGO.

Cut Flowers, Florists' Supplies, Wire Designs.

HEADQUARTERS IN WESTERN NEW YORK

Price Lists and Catalogues on Application.

WM. F. KASTING,
WHOLESALE FLORIST,

481 Washington Street,
BUFFALO, N. Y.

Long Distance Phone, Seneca 620.

Bassett&Washburn

76 Wabash Ave., CHICAGO, ILL.

Wholesale Growers of and Dealers in CUT FLOWERS

Greenhouses at Hinsdale. Ill.

C. A. KUEHN
WHOLESALE FLORIST.

Cut Flowers and Florists' Supplies.
Manufacturer of the Patent Wire Clamp Floral Designs. A full line of Supplies always on hand. Write for catalogue and prices.

1122 PINE STREET, · ST. LOUIS, MO.

EMIL STEFFENS, Established 1866.

MANUFACTURER OF

FLORISTS' **W**IRE... DESIGNS

...AND SUPPLIES...

335 East 21st Street, NEW YORK.

GEO. A. KUHL,
WHOLESALE
ROSES, CARNATIONS,
MUMS AND SMILAX,
PEKIN, ILL.

I HAVE IT! WHAT? Why
ANYTHING IN FLOWERS....

H. G. BERNING,
Wholesale Florist,
1322 Pine Street, ST. LOUIS, MO.

WE CAN SUPPLY

ELECTROTYPES
of most of the engraving in this book, at 15 cents a square inch.

FLORISTS' PUB. CO.,
Caxton Building, CHICAGO.

For weekly hints on the latest in the arrangement of Flowers, consult the "Retail Florist" department in the Florists' Review, issued weekly at $1.00 a year, by the

FLORISTS' PUBLISHING COMPANY,

520-535 Caxton Building. ....CHICAGO.

do not give them poor, worn-out soil as you can a tulip.

Pots that have flowered can be stored away after the foliage is ripe and the bulbs shaken out and started again the following fall, but as stated above the bulbs are now produced so fine and cheap that it is better to buy every year. Freesias will endure a few degrees of frost without any harm, but don't let the dry bulbs freeze when out of the ground.

FUCHSIA.

Plants that have been grown in greenhouses for more than a century, and a favorite with all. There are a great many species, mostly all from South America, but the true species are now seldom seen. The hybrid varieties are those of the commercial florists, and firms that make a specialty of soft-wooded plants are continually sending out new varieties. Many of my readers will remember old Fuchsia fulgens, with its clustered raceme of flowers at the end of the shoots; and many are also acquainted with F. macrostema; both true species, but very unlike.

In the milder parts of Great Britain you will see such varieties as Rose of Castile trained up the front of verandas as we do clematis, showing that they withstand a good freezing, and many of the species are treated as hardy shrubs, the winter killing the tops, but the plant makes a strong growth again in the spring, just as our basket willows are cut down and an annual growth is made. Where the thermometer does not go below 15 degrees these species will winter very well. We treat the fuchsia as a very short-lived plant, seldom growing the plant more than one year, but in its native Andes it is a shrub, or even small tree.

With us fuchsias are often used for summer bedding, but they never can be any part of a formal flower garden because they would conform with no other beds. Nor will they thrive in the broad sun. Behind buildings or hedges or where they will get only the morning sun, and where they are no part of any design, they make very pleasing beds. The soil should be deep and rich and where the hose can reach them a number of varieties can be used; one-year-old plants are always better for this purpose than the spring struck plants. Plants that have been wintered almost dormant and bedded out in early May before they are started will be much surer of success than plants out of a warm greenhouse.

Thousands of fuchsias are sold in our cities during April and May and used up among the class of people who want a few plants for their window. The latest arrivals from Europe are the largest consumers of fuchsias. Plants should be selected or obtained in the spring, not later than May, and grown on carefully. By July they should be at their best. In July these plants should be plunged outside in

Wreath of Laurel with Lilacs and Cycas Leaves.

the sun, or only partial shade. They will grow very little more, but will ripen their wood. Leave them out of doors till after the first very slight frost. By that time (say middle of October) the shoots will be ripe and the leaves off. Bring them in and for two weeks they can stand in a cool shed, or be laid under a bench.

By November 1st shorten back the lateral growths to firm, ripe wood and start them in a house at 55 to 60 degrees. Syringe daily. Soon you will see signs of new growth, when they should be shaken out and repotted in fresh soil and in two or three weeks you will get your first batch of cuttings, and successive lots to the following February. That is as late as you can propagate fuchsias and make plants that are any good that summer. Few cuttings root more freely than fuchsias. With the sand at 70 and the atmosphere at 55 you will root just five-score for every 100 cuttings you put in.

Fuchsias when grown in pots want a very rich soil; two parts loam, one part rotten manure and one part leaf-mold will grow them finely. Pot fairly firm, but not as solid as you would

with geraniums. Fifty to fifty-five degrees at night is about right. An abundance of water, daily syringing and a shade from the hottest suns in April and May is the treatment.

Most of our fuchsias are sold in 4 and 5-inch pots. From the cutting bed to a 2½-inch and from that to a 4-inch and from that to a 5-inch. With some varieties (such a one was old Elm City) they were allowed to go straight up and the plant formed a most symmetrical pyramid shape, but few of the varieties will do that, and they are generally pinched when a few inches high, which gives them two or three leading shoots and makes a more compact plant. Some varieties can be stopped the second time, which makes them fine little bushes.

In selecting varieties see that they are good growers and of a good habit; that is everything. Raisers of new varieties have produced some enormous double flowers, both white and purple or red corollas, but the plants are not good. Broadly it may be said that in producing the double corolla you have added nothing to the beauty of the fuchsia. Many of the single varieties have the most grace and beauty and are usually the finest growers.

Plants that are wanted for outside beds should be wintered over in pots in a very cool, light cellar or cool house and given only water enough to keep them from shriveling. Large specimens that are wanted for summer use are also wintered very cool, shortened back in the spring, mulched or shifted and started growing slowly. Our hot summers are against fuchsias.

Varieties are innumerable. Mr. E. G. Hill, of Richmond, Ind., and others import yearly all the newer varieties and test their merits for our climate.

A leading establishment describes the following:

Double Varieties.

Cervantes: Purple corolla, crimson sepals.

Phenominal: Dark plum color, great size.

Mme. Thibaut: White corolla, crimson sepals.

Molesworth: White corolla, crimson sepals.

Storm King: White corolla, scarlet sepals.

Pres. Carnot: Mauve corolla, crimson sepals.

Single Varieties.

Annie Earle: Carmine corolla, white sepals.

Beacon: Carmine corolla, scarlet sepals.

Brilliant: Scarlet corolla, white sepals.

Earl of Beaconsfield: Orange corolla and sepals.

Mrs. Marshall: Carmine corolla, white sepals.

Speciosa: Orange scarlet corolla, white sepals; an old but standard variety and one of the very best for use in veranda boxes or beds.

Black Prince: Corolla and sepals carmine. This is a grand market variety; the best of growers, fine habit, and a profuse bloomer.

Fuchsias should be used in vases and veranda boxes only where the sun reaches them for but a few hours during the day. They may look attractive when first put in a vase, but are soon leafless stalks without shade and plenty of water.

FUNGICIDES AND INSECTICIDES.

If it were not for our enemies the aphides, spider, thrip, mealy bug and many other minute animals, with the low plant organisms, the mildews, rusts, etc., our calling would be comparatively easy, and we are not the only ones. The fruit grower, market gardener and farmer all have their foes, compelling us to keep up a continual watch and fight against their attacks.

It is really half the battle to keep our minute enemies at bay, but think what would be the consequence if there were no greenfly or red spider, no mildew or rust. What would be the profits of flower growing? It would be small, for every careless fellow would have what is called "Good luck." As it is it is not good luck but good reward for continual care, watchfulness and industry. Perhaps it is just as well as it is, for although you can scarcely imagine in a past or future paradise that white scale will trouble the orange trees, or some future Eve will have to apply kerosene emulsion for mealy bug, the present time is one that rewards the gardener for his industry and faithfulness to his duty, and no little part of his thoughts are taken up repelling the attacks of the many afflictions he is heir to in the fungoid and insect line.

Peter Henderson wrote more than thirty years ago that the least excusable of the gardener's failings was allowing his plants to become infested with aphis, because it was easily remedied. Quite right. Yet you see men today walk through their carnation houses where every shoot is covered with aphis. If any remark is made the reply is usually: "Yes, I must smoke." Or: "I am all out of stems. I must get some." Alas, the greenfly is the least to be dreaded. It succumbs to tobacco in several forms. Not so with all our insects and as for the mildews

and rusts it is more the condition of the plant that we must improve than to combat the diseases. Keep the plant vigorous and its environments right and the mildew and rust will not appear.

Some years ago I attempted to grow Mermet roses in a house that could not on cold nights be kept at over 50 degrees, and very cold nights perhaps not over 47 degrees. I did not pick many roses, but the plants looked healthy. One morning I discovered the end ventilator open six inches and the thermometer down to 10 degrees outside. I thought to myself frost inside sure, if not, then a good dose of mildew. It was nearly a frost, but not a sign of mildew appeared. The plants were making a slow, firm growth and could stand the chill they got. If the house had been kept steadily at 58 or 60 degrees mildew would have appeared for certain. The above is not quoted to instruct you in rose growing by any means.

Man and other animals hate a draught and so do plants. Man can stand for a while in a gale of wind and the mercury at zero with no more damage than cold fingers and chilled

Cross of Eucharis Flowers.

nose, but let him sit in a warm room with a draught of cold air on him, even if it is only a few degrees cooler than the room, and the result is often pneumonia. And so, I believe, it is with plants, and why not?

In no part of the exercise of our business is the old adage, "Prevention is better than cure," so true as it is with our minute enemies. With the fungoids that come because the vitality of the plant is checked, guard against any neglect, day and night, and with the insects that will attack our plants even in the best of health apply your remedies regularly, not to cure but to prevent.

The formulas for several of the following solutions and fungicides are copied from the bulletin issued by the Cornell Agricultural Experiment Station, by E. G. Lodeman, February, 1895, a copy of which all growers should avail themselves of.

Bordeaux Mixture.

Copper sulphate, 6 lbs.
Quicklime, 4 lbs.
Water, 40 to 50 gallons.

Dissolve the copper sulphate by putting it in a bag or coarse cloth and hanging this in a vessel holding at least four gallons, so that it is just covered by the water. Use an earthen or wooden vessel. Slake the lime in an equal quantity of water, then mix the two and add water enough to make 40 gallons. It is then ready for immediate use, but will keep indefinitely. If to be used on young, tender leaves, it is advisable to add an extra pound of lime to the formula. When applied to such plants as carnations it will adhere better to the leaves if about one pound of hard soap is dissolved and added to the mixture.

The above is for rots, moulds, mildews and fungous diseases.

Ammoniacal Copper Carbonate.

Copper carbonate, 1 oz.
Ammonia enough to dissolve the copper.
Water, 9 gallons.

The copper carbonate is best dissolved in large bottles, when it will keep indefinitely, and diluted with water as required. Used for the same purpose as Bordeaux mixture.

Copper Sulphate Solution.

Copper sulphate, 1 lb.
Water, 15 gallons.

Dissolve the copper in the water, when it is ready for use. This should not be used on any foliage, but can be used on the wood of trees and shrubs before the buds start.

Paris Green.

Paris green, 1 lb.
Water, 200 gallons.

This will do for poisoning all insects that chew, such as caterpillars and worms. We have found that in applying the paris green it was necessary to add something to make the solution stick to the leaves, and you can use with the above quantities two or three

pounds of hard soap, dissolved, or add two quarts of the Rose Leaf extract of tobacco, which is of a sticky nature.

London Purple.

This can be used in the same proportion as paris green. To make this safer to use on the foliage of chrysanthemums add one pound of slaked lime. This also is for insects that chew.

Florists do not always remember the distinction between the chewers and suckers. The aphides bore into the tissue of plants and suck the juices, and although they may be drenched with the paris green solution would feel no ill effects from it. The worms and caterpillars eat the surface of the leaves and must consequently get the poison into their stomachs.

Hellebore.

Fresh white hellebore, 1 ounce.
Water, 3 gallons.

Apply when thoroughly mixed. This poison is not so energetic as arsenites and may be used on the more tender growths for insects that chew.

Kerosene Emulsion.

Hard soap, ½ lb.
Boiling water, 1 gallon.
Kerosene, 2 gallons.

Dissolve the soap in the water by cutting into thin slices; add the kerosene and agitate with a syringe till thoroughly mixed. In this condition, when cool, it will become of the consistency of sour milk and may be kept indefinitely. Dilute twenty to thirty times with water when applying. Use strong emulsion for all scale insects. This is used for all insects that suck, as green, black and yellow fly (the latter the most troublesome on chrysanthemums), mealy bugs, red spider, thrips, and all worms with soft bodies will succumb to this.

It should, however, be always used with caution. It is best to try the weakest emulsion first.

Hydrocyanic Acid Gas.

Water, 1 quart.
Sulphuric acid, 1 quart.
Cyanide of potash, 5 oz.

The above quantities are right for 1,000 cubic feet of air space in your houses, and measurements and quantities must be accurate. As many thousand cubic feet of air as your house contains, so many vessels you must have. Butter jars are the best for the purpose and they should be placed on the floor of the house, not among or near the plants. The house must be shut down closely and must be opened again in half an hour. As this gas is very deadly you must contrive to let the cyanide down through a small hole in the glass, or through a crack in the ventilator. As the 5 oz. parcel is a small affair a very thin piece of string attached will do. We suspend the cyanide to the end of the string, as many as required, and divided equally in the house. Beneath place the jars, each containing 1 quart

of the acid; then add 1 quart of water, and when each jar is ready the cyanide of potash is lowered into the jars. An explosion, as it may be called, immediately follows, the gas is generated instantly, and that is why you would not dare to be in the house, for you would stop breathing in an instant. This gas is death to every insect that breathes, and does not hurt the most tender foliage.

Mr. Saltford, of Poughkeepsie, who gave me the formula, showed me a Maidenhair fern that was in perfect health that had frequently been exposed to the gas. I used the gas several times last winter on violets with the best results.

As compared with tobacco smoke it is quite expensive and some trouble to apply, but if it saves a crop of violets from the ravages of that minute fly that punctures the leaf, laying an egg which destroys the tissue of the leaf and produces what we call curl leaf, it is certainly worth ten times the cost and labor. It is applied principally to destroy the almost invisible insects so injurious to violets, but while doing that it utterly destroys green fly, red spider, centipedes and all else that breathes. It leaves no objectionable odor.

Have the jar in which you generate the gas four times as large as the mixture of water and acid, and when purchasing the cyanide of potash have each 5 oz. package well wrapped in double paper.

Sulphur.

Sulphur in different forms is the great antidote for fungus, and our chief rose enemy, the mildew, is a fungus. The flour of sulphur is often dusted on the plants. This is perhaps the least useful method, and sulphur should never be allowed to reach the soil. It is sometimes sprinkled on the pipes, and sometimes placed in shallow pans and placed where the rays of the sun will strike it, as when at a high temperature it gives off its fumes that destroy the spores of the fungus.

I think it is most beneficial, most easily applied, and the least harmful to the plants when it is mixed with linseed oil and painted on the pipes. Don't overdo it. Where there are eight or ten hot water pipes, or twenty small steam pipes, paint the upper surface of one pipe; that will be sufficient. We think the oil does some good with the sulphur. This is an excellent preventive of mildew.

Sulphur is sometimes burnt on hot bricks or an old shovel made red hot. I have done it and it is of course a very effective way of applying the deadly fumes, but you must be very careful and directly the odor of sulphur is plainly noted you must move on a few yards. When the carnation rust was at its worst a few years ago we burnt a great deal of sulphur in the houses when they were entirely empty in the month of August. We made it strong enough to kill a Kilkenny cat and trust it killed all the spores and germs of the rust and other fungous diseases.

Sulphide of potassium, known as "liver of sulphur," is a good preventive and possibly a cure for mildew. I have used it dissolved in water and then mixed with clay till it was the consistency of molasses, and on the pipes put a dab of the paint here and there, say every three feet. It is stronger than the common sulphur. Or the roses can be syringed with it; 1 lb. in 50 gallons of water.

Tobacco.

What could we do in the absence of this wonderful weed? As a luxury it is possibly dispensable, and so are tea and coffee, but as an insecticide it is a great essential. Till we find something better it is the great cure-all of many a florist's establishment. Where fumigation is not possible or permissible, as in conservatories attached to dwelling houses, it is used as dust or in the liquid form, but "smoking," as the gardener calls it, is the way it is universally applied; most effective and cheapest.

Most florists in or near a large town get their stems from the cigarmaker and pay for them with a plant occasionally sent to Mrs. Havana Filler. If you have to purchase the stems they cost little. Every florist knows his own way of fumigating. I for one don't believe in placing it on the floor to burn itself out. I prefer it in an iron or galvanized iron vessel that can be moved along. If you can't stand the smoke, learn to; go to a New York Florists' "smoker," and after that you will survive not only tobacco smoke but the fumes of sulphur. Tobacco stems get very dry in our sheds and are apt to flare if not moistened. The stems should be shaken out a few hours before you intend to smoke and sprinkled. They will then be moist, without being wet.

How thick or dense tobacco smoke should be is a matter of experience. It is experience that allows us to endure it when it is so thick you can scarcely see your hand before you, and would quickly suffocate the tenderfoot. Lightly and often is the motto always to follow. This has been often preached before, yet how true and wise it is. Don't wait to see three generations of green fly sucking the life blood out of your plants, but have a day to smoke and remember that day, or rather night, to keep it smoky.

There are a few plants that are easily injured by tobacco smoke, and plants having flowers with thin single petals should not be exposed to fumigation when in flower. Those plants that are hurt by tobacco smoke will be noted in their respective cultural directions.

I never noticed that it was any injury to carnations except that it destroyed their odor and left in its place that of stale tobacco, which will last on the flowers for twenty-four hours. There is a difference of opinion about its effect on roses that are producing

buds. Some large growers say they fumigate and see no harm, but the majority of good rose growers keep down the aphis by other methods, and the writer sides with the latter. I have on many occasions seen the petals of our best tea roses, Brides and Bridesmaids, malformed and discolored from no cause but tobacco smoke. Rose growers who use steam have tin vessels which hold one or two bushels of tobacco stems,which are chopped up as a hay cutter would cut them. Into the bottom of this tin vessel runs a half-inch steam pipe. You can have as many of them as your house requires. When the steam is turned on a dense vapor fills the house, which of course contains nicotine. This is an effectual way of killing the fly, but is objected to by some as producing a soft growth on the roses, and vaporizing the extracts of tobacco is preferred by many. Some growers profess to keep down the aphis by strewing the stems on the pipes and paths, or laying them between the plants in bunches. This will keep down the aphis if you start perfectly clean and change the stems every two weeks, but it will not kill the fly if they once have a start.

Although tobacco contains the nicotine which is so useful yet a deadly poison, the stems when rotten are not in the least injurious to the soil. I have seen tons of decayed tobacco stems plowed into the land which produced fine crops.

Tobacco Extracts.

The Rose Leaf extract is now largely used and saves the florist the trouble of making his own solution out of the stems, and it is doubtless better. It can be used diluted 75 times and will rid plants of aphis, red spider and thrip. Rose growers who heat with hot water and can't vaporize as described above can use this extract to great advantage. In a 20 or 22-foot house, at every thirty feet, you can place a pie dish, say 12x6 inches and 6 inches deep. Dilute some extract in ten parts of water and pour into the dishes to the depth of one inch. Have some old pieces of iron, 8x4 inches and 2 or 3 inches thick. We use pieces of old railroad iron of the old style, cut into 8 or 9-inch lengths. These are made red hot in the fire and carried with the help of a coal scuttle and tongs to the dishes on the walk, and when one is dropped into the tobacco extract there is directly a cloud of vapor which is very effectual in killing the aphis, and of no possible harm to the roses unless it be the softening of the growth.

The vaporizing of the extract by diluting it in ten parts of water and placing in small tin troughs are made to lay on the upper pipe of a steam coil is a method used by many growers and answers the purpose well. The tins are replenished frequently and while you have steam in the pipes evaporation is continuous. It is too

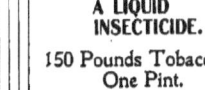
slight to any more than just notice, but so continuous that the aphis gets no chance to thrive.

The extract that is known as Nikoteen answers every purpose of the Rose Leaf extract. It is more expensive by the gallon, but it has four times the strength and must be diluted four times as much. For syringing for spider and thrip it should be diluted with water at least 200 to 1. It is cleaner and better to handle than the Rose Leaf.

Fir Tree Oil.

This is an article largely used to kill the brown and white scale. The latter is much the worst to contend with. To ten gallons of water add a half pint of the oil. If the water is at a temperature of 100 degrees, so much the better. Large palms and other plants can be syringed and in half an hour be given a good syringing of clear water, when most of the scale will be destroyed. Small palms can be dipped or immersed entirely in the water, excepting, of course, the ball of earth, and shortly afterwards syringed with clear water. That is doing it most effectually.

Palms received from Europe are often infested with this white scale and should be thoroughly cleaned before placing among your other stock.

Water.

There are many compounds and mixtures advertised and sold for fungicides and insecticides, but those quoted will about fill the bill. And finally there is plain pure water, properly applied. The use of the syringe or hose will save much labor and expense with insecticides if properly applied. Red spider, thrip or mealy bug should never be seen and never would be if a good gardener handled the hose.

All the patent sprayers and hose attachments are not worth one cent. The forefinger of either hand is a marvelous attachment and can guide and divide the stream of water in any form or direction you choose. You can't talk to a fellow workman and intelligently and faithfully water a lot of plants in pots, much less syringe them. Your work needs all your thought and attention, and I will conclude this chapter by saying that a man who chatters or smokes at his work is of little use. Work in work hours, give all your mind to your work, and when the noon and evening hour comes you will enjoy the rest far better than if you had been discussing your mother-in-law or last employer.

GARDENIA.

In the days when short stemmed flowers were used the flowers of Gardenia florida were much prized. Flowers are often sent from the southern states, but by the time they reach our northern cities they are much the worse for the journey and useless. They would not pay a florist to grow, but they are so deliciously fragrant that well grown plants are desirable for private conservatories. The gardenia is a dwarf evergreen shrub. The double form of G. florida, called the Cape Jessamine, resembles the flower of a small camellia. They are propagated from sideshoots of the half ripened wood in early spring in a strong bottom heat. Grow the plants on as quickly as possible, with plenty of heat and light. A good, fibrous, open loam with a fifth or sixth of rotten cow manure and leaf mould will do. Let the drainage be perfect, for they want a liberal allowance of water, especially when growing, and should be daily well syringed to keep down mealy bug and red spider.

In California young plants are planted on the benches under glass, each

plant having a little mound to itself to insure perfect drainage, and that is necessary where so much syringing is resorted to. If grown commercially young plants are preferred, but large plants can be grown on.

GERANIUM.

All the geraniums that are so popular with us—the show, fancy, ivy leaf, tricolor, zonal, etc., are botanically known as pelargoniums, but the name geranium is so firmly and popularly associated with our favorite bedding plants that it would be absurd for me to write of them under the much less familiar name of pelargonium. The show and fancy pelargoniums that so strangely are known to some people as "Lady" and "Martha Washingtons," I will treat under their proper name.

The geranium needs no introduction, for if there is a plant known universally by everyone it is the geranium. Within thirty years an immense improvement has taken place, both in the habit of the plant and the grand form and color of the flower. The earliest double ones were a curiosity when first they came out, but they were so double that they were of little use, and now a form called semi-double has entirely displaced them. The semi-doubles have one advantage, the petals are not knocked off by a rain storm, and they have also a disadvantage. Some of the varieties, although excellent growers and remarkably free flowering, become unsightly by the inner florets losing color or decaying before the outside florets have opened. The single varieties are still most useful for bedding. The ivy leaf section have been improved as much as the zonals, having beautiful semi-double flowers, and now we have double flowers on the bronze and variegated type. Some of the variegated kinds, such as the useful "Mountain of Snow," are as vigorous as the zonals, and so are the yellow and bronze varieties, but the tricolor type are less robust.

When Peter Greive some forty years ago raised the lovely "Mrs. Pollock" it was a great departure from any other geranium. I have seen great beds of it, or rather edgings of beds. It likes a rich soil and a slight shade. It will burn up and grow less in our hot suns with the ordinary treatment we give the flowering zonals.

Mme. Salleroi is a type of itself, forming no stems, but a mass of short shoots spring from the crown and the plant makes a compact little clump, very suitable for edging.

Propagation.

When planting out for your own stock give the plants plenty of room to grow and do not crowd or the growths will be soft and unsuitable for cuttings. Unless the season is very dry geraniums seldom want water, and if you must water give them a thorough soaking and then hoe before the ground bakes. That is pretty good ad-

vice to apply to a whole lot of things. Keep all flowers picked off as soon as they are fully developed; it will encourage the plants to grow.

About September 1st take off your first batch of cuttings and pot firmly in 2¼-inch pots. A cold-frame will do for the cuttings, but an ordinary bench is just as good and less liable to neglect. They should be shaded during the hottest hours of the day only, and that can be done with newspapers, which is better than any fixed shading because on dull days a shading would be injurious.

Potting firmly with a good sifted loam is an important point. Don't thumb the top of the soil, but get your finger and thumb down by the side of the cutting like a wedge and make the soil around the base of the cutting firm. The watering will take care of the surface without your wasting any time with your thumbs.

They want a good, thorough watering when first potted; after that only when they are decidedly on the dry side. There are more geraniums go off black and rotten through the heat and moisture than there are from dryness. In a month most of them will be rooted, and when they commence to make new leaves they should be stood over, dry leaves rubbed off and the surface of the soil stirred. From now on you will have to treat them barbarously to keep them from thriving.

Why you should wait till September 1st or about that time before propagating is because earlier propagation in a hot spell in August is not safe. I have seen 75 per cent. of can cuttings turn black in a few days when we had very warm weather. Any kind that you were very short of can be propagated earlier, but it would be safer to put them in the sand.

By taking off all the leading shoots thus early you will usually by middle of October get another good lot of cuttings, which root still more certainly. If you don't have time for another batch these plants are in excellent shape to lift and pot and propagate during winter.

Florists that grow a variety of plants had better do their operations by a system, and our system is to get all our geraniums propagated in the fall without need of lifting old plants. A light house should be given to geraniums; it cannot be too light and dry and airy. A night temperature of 45 degrees will bring them along fast enough.

After our holiday trade there is room to spread out, and then our geraniums get a shift into a 3-inch pot. It is not much of a shift, but it makes a great difference to the plants. About February 1st they have made good roots in the new pots and then we stand them over, taking off all the tops that will make a cutting, and those that are not long enough we just pinch out the center. The cuttings from the tops of these 3-inch plants will root most easily at this time of year; pot-

Bench of Bruant Geraniums.

ted in 2-inch you will not lose one in a thousand.

Pot Culture.

An early Easter is always a blessing to a man who grows bedding plants, for just before Easter he is fearfully crowded and has to exercise all his wits to keep things from spoiling, and one of the principal crops that needs attention is the geraniums. Then they are shifted into the 4-inch pots, from which they are bedded out. The February struck plants get a 3-inch as soon after the others as possible, and make good bedding plants that sell to late customers, and if you get 50 cents per dozen less than you do for your fine 4-inch plants they pay well.

We are always successful in getting our geraniums in full bloom from the 15th of May to June 1st, and believe that geraniums are grown nowhere finer and better than they are in this city. We believe this is largely because we use a rather heavy loam. The only fertilizer is about a fifth of sifted hot-bed manure, in which there can be little ammonia, but it keeps the soil open. We pot firmly, as firmly as we can, ram the soil down with our fingers, and this, we believe, is an important point in getting them to flower.

If you are a market grower, and your customers will forget where they purchased their geraniums, you can add a 5-inch pot of bone flour to every wheelbarrow load of compost. It will make the geraniums jump. But if you fill flower beds year after year for a good customer, don't use the bone flour; there is no need of it and plants thus stimulated will not do so well when bedded out as those grown without this fertilizer.

The treatment described above will do for all the geraniums of the zonal, rose leaf, variegated and bronze sections. The tricolor and more slow-growing varieties of the variegated and smaller scented kinds we prefer to put in the sand and give them five degrees more heat during winter and a richer and lighter compost.

Speaking of composts, we used to have occasion to buy some geraniums to fill late orders, and the compost they were in looked like black rappee snuff, a light sand and at least half old rotten manure; loosely potted, loose at the neck, almost needing a stake; this is the very reverse of what is right. There would surely be plenty of leaves on such plants, but a poor flower, and such stuff makes poor bedding plants.

Mme. Salleroi is so distinct in its habit that it would be waste of room to propagate it in the way we do the strong growing zonals. We lift before frost as many plants from the ground as our needs demand and pot in 4 or 5-inch pots just as they are lifted, and store away in some light, cool house. In January we cut them up and every shoot is a cutting which roots most easily in the sand. In the crowded state of our houses before the bedding out begins we put the variegated zonal, bronze, sweet scented and Salleroi sections into a mild hot-bed. Put into the beds by middle of April they make fine plants by bedding time. In these varieties it is leaf growth you want, and they are greatly benefited by the action of the ammonia on their leaves.

The ivy leaf section used so largely

In our baskets, vases and veranda boxes we treat entirely different. We leave them out of doors as long as safe from frost, and even if you should feel that a frost is coming it is no great job to cover them or to pull the plants up and take them into the shed to be made ready for the cutting bed next day. A few dozen old plants will give you an immense lot of cuttings and always put them in the sand, which by this time of year is probably a little warm with fire heat.

We keep them in 2-inch pots till New Year's, then shift into a 3-inch; and the demand for these beautiful plants is so great for our veranda boxes that we have to shift many of them again into a 4-inch. Their drooping habit makes them awkward to grow on a bench when of any size, so we have to put them on 10-inch shelves, a row hanging over on each side.

The ivy leaf section are beautiful plants and when their roots are confined they continue to flower a long time, but when planted out in good soil they grow so freely that blooming ceases.

In winter you are seldom asked for geranium flowers, or not enough to warrant your devoting any bench room to them, but you are frequently called upon for a geranium plant in flower, and it is just as well to have some. Should you not sell them they will make a fine lot of cuttings in February.

Select a few hundred healthy young plants in May of the free blooming varieties and put them aside as sold. When the rush is over shift into 5-inch and grow along in a light house, with the pots plunged in some material to keep them from continually drying out; here is where the portable shading would come in so good. A cold-frame would do as well with the glass tilted up back and front, and then you can shade from 10 till 4 o'clock.

Keep the buds always picked off these geraniums during summer, and in August, if they are worth it, shift again, into a 6-inch pot. If you allow the buds to come up after middle of September you will have some very cheerful, bright plants that are very attractive. These plants if wanted to flower freely should have a night temperature of 55 degrees, and the lightest bench you have.

There is a lesson to be observed about these common geraniums. If we give them more than 45 degrees at night and 55 to 60 degrees at day with our imperfect light and want of ventilation, for we can only give air to a limited extent, the plants will run up to leggy, useless plants, but out of doors in a night temperature of 70, and during the day perhaps to 90 degrees, they do not run up, they grow into sturdy, stout plants. So the nearer we can come to perfect light and air with those plants (roses, carnations, etc.) that we ask to flower in the

winter instead of resting, the greater success we shall have.

There are scarcely any insects that trouble geraniums, and it is a great thing in their favor. Tobacco smoke does not hurt any of them and only the scented leaved section is ever troubled with aphis. Too close proximity to hot water pipes will sometimes produce red spider, but that should not occur. It is a great treat to me to water a batch of geraniums that are on the dry side, and they should be allowed to get so. Then they seem to relish the soaking they get.

Specialists who grow to supply the trade with young stock propagate from stock plants the season through if possible, but their stock is not what we want to make our fine bedding plants. However, it is on such men as C. W. Ward, of The Cottage Gardens, and E. G. Hill & Co., of Richmond, Ind., that we must rely for new varieties, for these gentlemen import at great expense all the new varieties, many of which, perhaps, they do not deem worthy of sending out to the florist who deals directly with the public.

It would be useless to publish a list of varieties as sorts wear out and new ones are constantly taking their places. Neither am I acquainted with a long list of varieties. It is very unwise to grow a great variety. A dozen of the best semi-doubles, half a dozen single, half a dozen of the ivy leaf section, and a few of the standard variegated and bronze, will fill the bill for the man who has flower beds to fill. Last year the demand for geraniums was larger than ever and although we had double the quantity of S. A. Nutt over any other, we were sold out of it long before the rest, showing that you want a large quantity of the very few leading varieties, and proportionately smaller quantities of the rest. We find at present that the following sorts suit our business best:

Semi-Double Zonal Varieties.

S. A. Nutt: Crimson.
Alphonse Riccard: Orange scarlet.
J. J. Harrison: Fine scarlet.
W. P. Simmons: Orange scarlet.
Tower Eiffel: Bright scarlet.
Beaute Poitevine: Clear salmon.
Emile de Girardin: Fine pink.
Francis Perkins: Clear pure pink; the best pink we know; grand habit.
Prokop Daubeck: Light scarlet; best variety for vases.
Ernest Lauth: Rich shade of red; extra good.
La Favorite: Pure white.

Single Zonals.

Queen of the West: Fine red.
Athlete: Bright scarlet.
General Grant: Bright scarlet; one of the very best for large beds.
Mrs. E. G. Hill: Salmon; a grand truss.
Rev. W. Atkinson: Deep, bright scarlet.
Mme. Lavalle: Rosy salmon.

Well Bloomed Dwarf Geranium.

to ourselves and pleasure to our customers.

This would be a good place to say something about a geranium cutting. It is remarkable to see the poor judgment (or is it carelessness?) of some men in such a simple thing as making cuttings. We have been told that cutting at a joint was not at all essential; don't believe it. Cuttings will root, of many kinds of plants, an inch below a joint, but not as surely. At a joint is where the wood is most firm, and if you left a piece of sappy, succulent stem an inch long below a joint it is more likely to get overcharged with moisture, the walls of the cells are ruptured, decay commences and the stem turns black. If cut at a joint this is not so likely to occur. When I say at a joint I mean an eighth to a fourth of an inch below.

Then again you will see men denude a cutting of all the leaves except the small, undeveloped ones, and others will leave three or four large leaves, so that if put into the sand or potted they would be just a mass of leaves unless you placed them far apart. These mistakes are not always by the boys or beginners, but by men who ought to know better. It is carelessness, want of brains and want of thought.

Now, this pleasant little operation of making cuttings should go quickly. They should pass through your hands as quickly as the half-dollars drop into the ticket office of Forepaugh's circus, but be properly done, withal. The cutting exists largely on what the leaf absorbs from the atmosphere and sends down material to form the root. (These remarks of course apply to soft-wooded cuttings that are in active

growth.) So do not pull off all the geranium leaves. Leave one perfect leaf and one half developed; that will allow you to stand the small pots close together.

If it was any sacrifice of material to cut just below a joint there would be some reason for not doing it, but there is none. Neither the piece above the joint you leave on the parent plant or the piece you leave below the joint of the cutting is any good, and whoever thinks it takes longer to cut in the proper place is mistaken; a practiced eye and hand fixes on the proper spot in a moment.

We are well aware that tea roses root very well an inch or two below a joint, but no better, and they are hardly soft-wooded plants.

While I have stated just how I would trim a geranium cutting, that is no guide to the hundreds of other soft-wooded plants we grow. With many of the smaller leaved kinds a number of leaves can be left on, perhaps the more the better for the rooting process, but if too many leaves were allowed you would soon fill up your propagating bed, and to crowd the cuttings, covering the sand densely, is just the way to produce fungus on the surface of the sand, which is a calamity and often results in serious loss.

With the great majority of the soft-wooded plants we propagate during winter and spring. The heliotrope, ageratum, fuchsia, etc., the verbena, for example, root quicker and surer when the cutting is quick grown, succulent and brittle. I have endeavored to mention the condition of cutting best suited for propagation with every

plant for which I have given cultural directions.

GLADIOLUS.

The varieties we grow are hybrids from some of the many species of which the large genus is composed. The handsome spikes of the gladiolus are known to all, and for the flower border the gladiolus is one of the most handsome of summer flowers, but grown with such ease by everyone that the price of the spikes is now very low.

They can be readily raised from seed and will flower the second year. That, of course, is the only way to produce varieties, of which now there are legions.

They are often grown by florists on their benches among other crops to produce flowers in May and June before those outside are in bloom. They will not flower, however, till we get the warm days of spring, and no matter how early you may plant the bulbs they will in a carnation temperature grow very slowly. I have never seen that they injured the carnations if not put in too thickly.

Plant the bulb on the bench in February among the carnations by just squeezing it into the soil. It needs no covering and the watering you give the carnations will suit the gladiolus. A rose bench would suit them much better, but it would be hardly fair to the roses.

Out of doors the cultivation is very simple. The better the ground the finer the spikes, and in very dry weather they should get an occasional soaking with water. Very large growers must necessarily use only plow and cultivator. The commercial man should plant the corms (for they are not bulbs at all) in rows two feet apart, so that the horse cultivator can be run between them, and six to eight inches in the rows. Five to six inches deep is about right. When as deep as that they are not in our dry summers so likely to suffer for want of water.

The corms increase rapidly and you will frequently find two fine ones in place of the old one planted in the spring. If a succession of flowers is desired, make plantings at intervals of two weeks, but remember that you will get no more flowers after the first frost. Before there is any danger of frost reaching the bulb, dig them up and let them lie in the sun for a day or two with the tops cut off a foot or so above the corms. When the stalk is dry cut it off within an inch of the corm, and if they are not wet with rain or dew store them away in flat trays anywhere out of the reach of frost.

Any place that will keep potatoes will keep gladiolus bulbs. There is usually such a place in the greenhouse sheds. They are the easiest possible bulbs to keep; only keep them from frost. We once had a lot dug up and lying on the ground to ripen the tops when over night down came a frost, about three degrees, I thought our gladiolus had escaped, but every bulb was destroyed.

The white and light varieties are much the most valuable to the florist. There are now pure white varieties and of every other conceivable shade except blue. In buying bulbs remember that 75 per cent should be white or very light shades.

It is impossible to give a list of names. There are too many, and few florists grow them under name. The Lemoine strain are very handsome and distinct and differ from the ordinary gladiolus by being finely spotted and marked, and some of them have fine shades of orange and yellow.

GLAZING.

A most important part of greenhouse construction. Poor putty, if the glass is lapped and poorly laid, is a source of constant annoyance, waste of coal and injury to the plants. When the glass is butted, unless the house is well and truly built, it will be a botch and failure and will bring censure on this excellent method, which under most circumstances is the way to glaze a commercial house. Some critics may say if good for the commercial man why not for all glass structures? The lapped method is more expensive, but if well and properly laid is undoubtedly a good job, but the butted plan is quicker to lay, easier to repair, much less expensive, and if you ever want to alter or move your houses or wish to remove the glass you can do so with perfect ease. As to tightness for making a warm house both methods when thoroughly done will do that, with a preference toward the butted system.

Lapped or Puttied.

Where the modern iron frame houses are built the bar used is usually very light, but well supported by a number of purlins. On these houses the glass is usually lapped and there are only one or two points to observe. The putty should be of good quality and to it should be added one-fifth of white lead. The glass should be pressed down till the putty is spread out evenly and over the entire surface of the shoulder of the bar; this will save much labor when you take off the back putty, as there will be no holes to fill up.

In old style glazing you saw laps of all sizes from a sixteenth of an inch to one inch. The longer the lap the more place for dust and dirt to lodge with no means or chance to clean it out, so you have a dark strip across at the junction of every light. One-eighth of an inch is the ideal length of a lap for any size glass and it makes just as warm a house as a lap of two inches.

The best thing I have found to hold the glass down as well as to hold it from slipping down is the Van Reyper glazing point. It is a small double staple which has a shoulder in the top or end that both holds down the glass and at the same time prevents its slipping.

Houses that are glazed with putty should have a coat of paint after the glass is in, regardless of how many

coats the bars have had before they were put up. One-eighth of an inch is usually allowed between the bars; this allows only one-sixteenth of an inch on each side between the glass and the wood.

Butted Glass.

The unfavorable reports and condemnation of this system are largely from two sources, mostly by men who never tried in the right way, or perhaps tried it on an old house that was formerly glazed with putty, and by other people whose houses were not built correct enough and made straight and true. Square cut glass will not fit crooked plate and bars.

In the first place you must use the cypress cap and bar that is especially made for the purpose and your bars must be put on true and parallel. One-sixteenth of an inch is all you want for play between bars. It should be just that and nothing more or less; this is very particular. Some carpenters mark out on the ridge and plate the place for the bars, others will cut a strip of hardwood, one to be used at ridge and one at plate. If the strip is one-sixteenth inch longer than width of glass and the bar is nailed up to the stick carefully every time, top and bottom, you can't go very far wrong; yet every ten bars or so you should prove by a rod that you are keeping the bar at top and bottom parallel. You can make up any discrepancy with putty. Putty, like charity, covers a multitude of sins. With butted glass you must be correct, and it is just as easy to be so.

Don't trust to any carpenter, however many houses he has built; prove for yourself that he is right. When the bar is nailed to the plate see that the face of the bar on which the glass rests and the slope of the plate are exactly flush. If the bar is a trifle below the plate it is difficult to remedy. If it is a trifle above it can easily be taken off with a chisel. The bar can always be straightened on the purlin when you lay the glass, or straightened by a straight-edge and fastened in place before you begin to lay the glass. The glass should not be lapped on the plate more than half an inch; the less glass there is resting on the wood the less likelihood of breakage by ice. The glass should always without fail be laid with the rounding part up; all glass is more or less convex and concave. The thin edge of the glass (if there is a choice) should always lead up the bar. If you were to put the thick edge up and it butted against a thin one there would be a small space for the water to lodge. The man who lays the glass, if he has any brains at all, will be able to see these points at a glance and lay it about as quick as a boy can make it to him. Remember that is all he has to do; there is no putty and no brads, no squeezing and thumbing, no squinting and swearing, it is only to lay the glass in, and so you go on to the top.

In laying out the length of the bar we try to make it so that a certain

number of lights just fill up from plate to ridge. If that is not convenient you can always make it so that a half light will finish at the top. When you know exactly what sized fraction of a light you need (if any) you will have them all cut ready; it is just as well to use the small piece at the bottom.

Before we lay any glass we drive in two wire six-penny nails, half an inch below edge of plate, but only drive them in a small depth, just enough to hold the lights while you are laying them. This can be done before you begin to glaze and by a man standing on the ground. When the whole run of glass is in and before you screw down the cap the man nearest the bottom, with the end of his chisel handle, gives the glass a good push up, closing up any space, however small, and then drives in his bottom nails. They should be driven close down to the glass or they will impede snow and ice slipping off. Now this effectually prevents the glass from slipping, and if the bottom light does not bow can the others?

One inch round-headed screws are used to screw down the cap, the first screw two inches from the bottom and one exactly at every joint or butt. A boy can get these caps ready because you will have one cap as a pattern, and with a ratchet drill the caps can be ready with the screws already lightly tapped in, and when the two men laying the glass call for the cap up it goes and the men who have ratchet screwdrivers soon have the screws down in their place. Don't screw down too tightly, just firm and solid is enough. You will, of course, need one screw within an inch or so of the ridge.

Be sure to have the ventilators made the same way with cap and bar, and to take the same size glass. Have but one size glass on the place if possible, and as little cutting as possible. I do not like to disparage any device that is made and sent abroad in good faith by a fellow florist, but in justice to those who will follow my advice I must candidly say the zinc strips that are made to go between glass when butted are a miserable failure and a nuisance. You want nothing between them or under them; simply the cap. Any size glass can be butted. We have it on 12, 14 and 16 inch square and always double thick. We prefer to use glass that is square, that is, 14x14 or 16x16. Then you have the choice of two edges, and if one is a little rough you can use the other. If glass is laid as described above it will save you many dollars. It is a smooth, fine roof, more air tight than lapped glass. The drip is nothing, absolutely nothing, if well and properly laid; if there should be a trifle it is always at the bottom, which in commercial houses would fall in the path. And if a little dust creeps in, and it will creep in where water won't, it can be washed annually as clean as the day you put it up.

Fancy the luxury of painting such a house. Remove the glass, thoroughly paint and relay again. If you were visited by a hailstorm you have only to break out the shattered lights, shove up the sound, and before night you are whole.

Without considering these contingencies, it is the ideal way for a commercial man to build. I have ten houses glazed with butted glass. I had no one to tell me how, but I persevered, and when I had built five or six I had it down fine and have given you the mature fruits of my experience.

GLECHOMA (NEPETA GLECHOMA).

The species that is useful to the florist is called by many names. 'Ground Ivy" is one, and the Germans apply the elegant name of "Louse Kraut." The variegated form of this little weed is one of our best basket plants. It starts to grow so well and makes such a fine appearance in a vase or basket that, weed as it may be, it is well worth growing.

The ends of the growths, a few inches long, should be put into 2-inch pots in September, three or four in each pot, and placed in a cold-frame. Kept shaded and moist they will soon be rooted, and then the glass should be removed till severe weather arrives, when the glass should again go on. Leave them in the frame till end of March, when they should be got out and shifted into 3-inch pots and started growing in the greenhouse. We place them along the edges of benches or shelves where their quick growing shoots can hang down.

Few plants will make such a veil of growth to cover the woodwork of our rustic baskets or the moss of our hanging baskets as this little "creeping Jenny," but do not attempt to keep it in the greenhouse all winter or it will be useless.

GLOXINIA.

These tropical American plants are well adapted to house culture. I have seen plants with fifteen perfect flowers in the window of a humble cottage. We seldom get complaints about their failure. They are essentially summer flowering.

Gloxinias are raised in large quantities from seed by specialists, but the florist who grows only a few hundred will do much better to obtain his supply of corms (usually called bulbs) from some firm that raises them in large quantities. The price of the bulbs is now very low. Seed is usually sown in February. Sow on a wet surface and don't cover the seed; it is too small. Cover the pan with a light of glass till the seeds are up. A warm house is needed and the pans should be kept away from the direct rays of the sun.

As soon as the seedlings can be handled, transplant them two inches apart in flats in two or three inches of loam and leaf-mould. In June plant them in four inches of soil in a cold-frame, or better still, a hot-bed that has lost its violent heat. When growing they like plenty of water and should be shaded on all bright days. Many of these seedlings will flower the same summer and will make good bulbs for growing in pots the next season.

In September water should be gradually withheld till the foliage has dried up, when the bulbs should be lifted and stored away in dry sand or soil during winter. As previously said, for a few hundred you cannot begin to raise seedlings at the price you can buy good flowering bulbs from the specialist.

February to March is the best time to start the bulbs. We put them first in 4-inch pots, just covering the bulbs. One watering is sufficient till the leaves begin to start. A good loam with a third of its bulk composed of leaf-mould and well rotted cow manure will grow them finely. The house you start them in should not be less at night than 60 degrees, but as the season advances they delight in our warmest weather. When the leaves extend over the pots they should be shifted into their flowering pot, a 6-inch, and well drained. Gloxinias really want a warm, moist temperature without any water lying on their leaves, although before flowering they should be daily syringed, which should always be done

in the morning. I have had the best success with gloxinias when the plants stood on inverted 5 or 6-inch pots on the bench; you can syringe the under side of the leaves better and the plants seem to thrive much better with the increased circulation of the air they get in this position.

Shading is the most particular part of their cultivation. They don't like the dense shade that whitewash affords, neither do they want the bright sun, or their beautiful flowers will wilt and droop. A light shade, or best of all, one that could be applied only in the hottest hours, would be ideal. Never let them get dry or you will lose their flowers. This is a plant that in watering I should resort to the old watering pot, unless you have

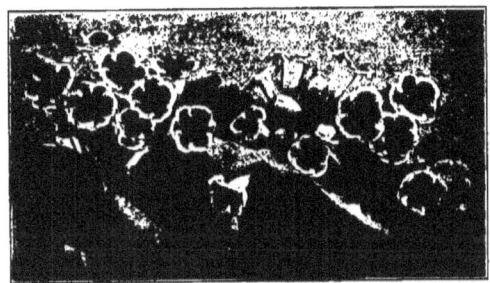

Gloxinias.

a very slow stream running from the hose and your mind intently on your work.

The fine leaves of the gloxinia are very brittle and easily broken, and when shifting or handling must receive good care or your plant will be spoiled.

When out of flower, if you wish to keep over the old corms, lay the pots on their side under a warm, dry bench and leave them undisturbed till you want to shake them out and start again in the spring.

There are now grand strains of most beautiful rich shades of color and the upright or erect flowering are the best.

GRASSES.

Several grasses should be prominent in all mixed borders of hardy plants, or make beautiful clumps on the lawn, either singly or in groups. They will thrive in any ordinarily good soil and those named are perfectly hardy. They are propagated by division and rapidly increase in size.

The finest and most ornamental of all, the Pampas grass, is unfortunately not hardy enough to withstand our northern winters. Where the temperature does not drop more than 15 degrees below the freezing point it will do finely. The Pampas grass (Gynerium argenteum) is a native of the Ar-

Border of Pennisetum Longistylum around a bed of Cannas.

gentines and temperate South America, thriving grandly in California, from whence we get our plumes. It seems as though with the protection of a stout box filled in with dry leaves and with a movable cover, this ornamental plant could be wintered safely, and in the decoration of fine grounds well repay the labor. We assuredly go to greater expense in preserving some plants that are not of so much value.

Arundo Donax: This is the noblest of the hardy grasses, growing in one summer eight to ten feet in height. It needs no protection. In the spring cut off close to the ground the last year's canes and mulch with a few inches of manure.

A. Donax versicolor or variegata is not quite so hardy, but is much more ornamental. It should be protected in the winter months with a covering of six inches of litter over the crowns. It is identical in every respect with the type except that its leaves are beautifully variegated.

Eulalias are the most useful grasses and are so hardy they need no protection. The tops are usually left standing during winter and removed by cutting or burning off in the spring.

Eulalia japonica: The flower is ornamental but it is the long, narrow, 4-foot leaves that make this grass such an acquisition to the garden.

E. j. zebrina: The leaves are very handsome, having bars of yellow across them.

E. j. foliis striatis: In this sort the creamy band runs lengthwise of the leaf.

E. j. gracillima univittata: This is

the narrowest leaved and most graceful of all, but not such a robust grower as the others, and is more suitable for a choice place in the border than to form a mass on the lawn.

Erianthus Ravennae: This might be called a small Pampas grass, throwing up handsome plumes. It is quite hardy.

Arundinaria tecla: A very ornamental grass, but should be planted in moist ground or given water very freely. It does well on the margins of lakes.

Pennisetum japonicum: Well worthy a place in the mixed border and perfectly hardy.

Pennisetum longistylum: This pretty plumed grass is very effectively used in bedding. It can be grown from seed, but is usually propagated by division. Take up several clumps in the fall, trim off the foliage, place in a box and set under a bench in a house with a temperature of 40 to 45 degrees. In March shake out the soil, tear the clump to pieces and pot two or three runners in a 3 or 4-inch pot. Place in a house with a temperature of 60 degrees. They make plants in a short time and may be bedded out the latter part of May or early in June. The accompanying engraving shows a border of this pennisetum around a bed of cannas.

GREENHOUSE BUILDING.

In step with the growth of our business, the demand for flowers and their rapid production, and the high quality now demanded, the science of building our greenhouse structures has kept well to the front. When we see the old

dark structures of twenty-five years ago, with their heavy wood work, 8x10 glass, and 4-inch cast iron pipe, we feel a chill, especially if we own them. We believe it would be almost impossible to produce the roses and carnations of to-day in the quantity and quality they are, had not our flower growers the modern houses of to-day.

Houses for the private establishment I shall not mention. They can be built with all the ornamentation as well as substantial and useful appointments that the owner desires, and should be always in keeping with the grounds and mansion with which they are associated. I will say this much: That whenever a range of glass is to be erected, let it be a costly and extensive range or but one small conservatory, it is far cheaper in the end and a hundred times more satisfactory, to have them built by horticultural builders, whose specialty it is, and who have made a life study of the business, constantly devising new and better methods, employing expert workmen, who know accurately every detail of the structure.

Building a greenhouse or conservatory is as distinct a business from the ordinary house building as is ship building, and the local carpenter, glazer and steam fitter are the most unfit people to employ. I have had local painters put a piece of tin against the bar when painting the roof, "to keep the paint off of the glass," thereby entirely neglecting the one important place for paint, the space between the glass and wood occupied with putty. The local steam fitter is learning some thing about steam, but his knowledge

of hot water circulation is yet awfully crude, and the carpenter, who is perhaps capable of building a winding stair case, is a failure at greenhouse building unless you are able to tell him "just how you want it." So the amateur or man of wealth should always employ one of those firms who make a business of glass structures. Perhaps there are many such firms. Of my acquaintances, who are masters of their business as well as honorable men that are bound to perform all they agree, there are Lord & Burnham Co., of Irvington-on-the-Hudson, N. Y.; Hitchings & Co., and Thomas W. Weathered's Sons, of New York. All of these firms are constantly building, not only private establishments, but commercial houses all over the country.

Shape and Aspect.

Plant houses, i. e., houses for raising palms, pandanus or ferns, *or* flowering lilies and azaleas, or growing the bulk of our bedding plants, in fact for any purpose except for roses and carnations, can run north and south. A house with its ridge running north and south with good sized glass will give you all the light that these plants need, and in the summer when too much sun is the trouble they are not so hot.

There is no doubt that houses that are built communicating, or simply a partition wall between them, are a great saving in fuel, and in latitudes where we get great snows, and often weeks of zero weather, it is most advisable that blocks of houses be built together with only two outside walls, providing you are sure you will not want to change your business and convert them into rose or carnation houses; for this purpose they would be very unsuitable.

The conventional house of this kind is usually 20 ft. wide, with a middle bench of 6 ft. 6 in., and two side benches of 3 ft. 6in. each, allowing 2 ft. for each path and keeping the benches away from posts 2 or 3 inches on each side to avoid any drip on the plants. Whenever I speak of the width of a house as 20 or 22 ft., I always mean the dimensions to be from outside to outside of posts if detached, or from center to center of posts if attached. For the general run of our plant houses the top of the posts from outside grade of ground is usually for these equal span houses 4 ft. 6 in., with the plate on top of post and the bar about 11 ft. 6 in.; this gives you nice head room for the paths.

The middle bench is used for tall growing plants and the side benches for the dwarfer ones. Often the space that would be occupied by the bench is used by standing the plants on the floor or planting them out, as you do with smilax, etc. If four or five houses are used for the same kind of plants, for instance chrysanthemums, ferns, lilies, then geraniums, or maybe all palms, then there is no need of a partition wall, but unless you are in a big way of business you will find it

much safer to have a partition between them. You so often want to keep one house a little warmer or cooler than others, or in fumigating you may find it very inconvenient to have to fill the whole lot with smoke when there were plants in some that you did not want to smoke.

Another style of house for general plant growing that is, I think, more economical to build and easier to work, is one of 22 ft. This will allow an 18-inch path against each wall, three benches a little short of 5 ft. 6 in. each, and two more paths of 1 ft. 6in. each. The heating would be but a trifle more, the first cost of glass and bars but a fraction, and the walls and the gutters no more. In these houses the heating pipes, whether of steam or hot water, are against the walls, away from the plants, where there is no danger of encouraging red spider. Where the houses are built in this way the posts should be 5 ft., so as to give head room in the outside paths. The benches in these houses could be any height to suit your plants.

Benches.

I will say here about benches, that it is often thought necessary to raise them up, sometimes to an awkward height, with the view of getting more light. "Keep plants near the glass," is an old maxim oft repeated. What is intended by this advice is give them light. In our modern houses where the glass is never less than 12 inches wide, and the light is unobstructed, the plants receive as much light eight feet from the glass as they do two feet from it. Years ago violets were always grown in a pit near the glass. They are grown as well today 10 feet from the glass.

Board benches are continually wearing out; even if made of 2-inch plank their life is short. For roses and carnations there is perhaps no substitute for wood as when their roots touch the moist wood it is congenial to them, which slate and cement are not, but plants in pots are quite different, as they are seldom stood on the bare boards but usually stand on a layer of ashes or sand. Heavy slate is too expensive for the commercial man and roofing slate would need so much supporting.

We saw at the South Park, Chicago, an excellent device for the plant tables, the invention of Mr. Kanst, we think. The frame of the tables was angle and T iron. For the floor of the bench he had a composition flagging. They were about two feet square and if I remember correctly one inch thick. It is obvious they could be made any reasonable length and breadth, and thicker if desired. It would be only a matter of making a mould. A frame of inch strips of wood was made, or a number of them, the frames were set on a surface of boards and a mixture of fine gravel and cement thrown in and struck off with a straight-edge. After the concrete, as we will call it, had set, which cement quickly does, the frame and bottom boards were re-

moved. I am not certain that I am exactly clear how the boards and frame were removed, but that is a trifling part of it, and will quickly occur to any ingenious workman.

When dry there was a lot of everlasting material for the plant tables, and as most of the tables were so constructed with the iron supports and concrete flooring they were practically indestructible. And to show us that a large plant would not break these slabs of cement and gravel Mr. Kanst jumped on the middle of one about two feet square and gave us one step of the Highland fling. These tables cannot be expensive and where the material is near by cannot exceed the cost of a 2-inch plank of pine or hemlock, and would in ten years be much the cheapest.

Often, though, we have not the time to do these things and turn to the readiest and quickest methods, so we resort to the same old boards. The uprights should be 2x6 and the cross pieces of the same dimensions. I think it cheaper in the end to use for the surface of the table 2-inch plank. The pulling out and rebuilding is half the cost, and that you certainly save. We mix up a pail of hydraulic cement, which with us is called water lime, and with a whitewash brush give the top of planks or boards a thorough coat of the cement, and on top of the cross pieces and top of uprights, in fact wherever wood is laid on wood, for that is where we find decay first begins.

Wooden benches are supported on iron frames made of gas pipe. They are most easily put up, look neat and are of course long lasting. It would take too long to describe here, and unnecessary, as you have only to send to the Jennings Bros., Olney, Philadelphia, for their illustrated circular which shows you the whole thing.

Where the bench is not over eighteen inches from the ground we believe the bench should be solid, that is walls built up with 4-inch brick walls laid in cement or concrete walls, and filled in with stones or ashes, and surfaced with any material you choose. It is easier for the workman to handle the plants when the benches are about three feet high, but no better for the plants, and saves much repairing and "fixing" of benches; and what a fine bench for palms, azaleas, lilies and later for cannas, in fact for anything.

Ventilation.

The ventilation of these houses, or any house, should be ample always. You may not need it except in summer, but you want the means for the largest amount of ventilation that is of benefit to the plants in the hottest weather. Our prevailing winds are from the west, and a large proportion of the country is the same. So we ventilate on the east side. There is also another advantage in ventilating on the east side. In February and March particularly, the thermometer may indicate 15 degrees of frost, yet the sun be very bright, compelling us

LORD & BURNHAM CO.
Horticultural Architects and Builders,
STEAM AND HOT WATER HEATING ENGINEERS.
Send 5 cents postage for Greenhouse Heating and Ventilating Catalogue.

RANGE OF ROSE HOUSES ERECTED BY US AT SCARBOROUGH, N. Y.

Plans and Estimates furnished on application for Greenhouses, Conservatories, etc., erected complete with our Patent Iron Construction; or for material only, ready for erection.

Estimates furnished also for Cypress Greenhouse Material.

Largest builders of Greenhouse structures. Plans and construction embrace latest improvements.

Six highest awards at the World's Fair.

Latest greenhouse construction catalogue mailed from New York on receipt of five cents postage.

We make special greenhouse PUTTY. Price on application.

WRITE FOR CIRCULAR OF CYPRESS HOT BED SASH AND FRAMES.

NEW YORK OFFICE: GENERAL OFFICE AND WORKS:

St. James Bldg., Broadway and 26th St.   Irvington-on-Hudson, N. Y.

to put on a crack of air by 9 or 10 o'clock. The ventilators, if on the west side, would be frozen and could be lifted only with great trouble, while the sun has thawed the ice on the east side. We do not think that ventilation on both sides is necessary if ample is given on the east side.

The dimensions for ventilators on a 20 or 22-foot house should be 2 ft. 6 in. deep from ridge to bottom of ventilator, and continuous the whole way along the roof. It is plain to everyone that a 3-inch opening the whole way is far better than a 6-inch opening for the length of four feet and then a space of five or six feet with no opening. We have seen some very clearly defined cases of failure of late that were unmistakably traceable to very inadequate ventilation. It costs no more in glass and little more for the machines that operate the sash.

In rose houses the best method is doubtless that where the ventilator opens at the ridge, and with plants of a tropical nature, like our palms, dracaenas, orchids, ferns, etc., it must also be the best system. For carnations and the more cold blooded plants, such as azaleas, lilies, and our geraniums, the ventilators hinged at the ridge will do, but if all the ventilators open at the ridge for every house you won't be far wrong.

I cannot see any use in cutting off the bars where the headers go in for the ventilators to be hinged on, or it may be close, on. Let all the bars run up to the ridge; you will get as much ventilation, the bars will be stronger, you will have a straighter roof, and the labor is only a trifle more, if any. Usually these plant houses lead out from a continuous shed, which is of course on the north end of them, so that there is not a square foot of bench room that has not the full light; more particularly is this true of the 22-ft. houses, where the benches are removed from the walls.

Where several of these houses are built parallel and attached, only the two outside ones can spread, and this brings us to the question of

Posts.

Some men with sufficient capital can afford to build brick walls on stone foundations, and when the stone work is 2 ft. 6 in. or 3 ft. in the ground and dry work to near the surface of the ground it makes an excellent drain, keeping the surface of the house dry, which is an excellent state of affairs. I doubt whether an 8-inch brick wall is much warmer than two thicknesses of boards, and a 12-inch wall is quite expensive. However, with those that can afford it it is certainly to be commended. Wooden posts will for a long time be used, and if of the right material outlast any other portion of the house.

Locust is the nearest to cast iron of any wood we know of, but good locust posts are difficult to obtain and very hard to work. Red cedar is most durable, light to handle and easy and pleasant to work. Next in quality

comes cypress, which, when of good quality will last in the ground many years, and the only other wood I know of suitable for posts is what is generally known as white or yellow cedar, which for the purpose is far inferior to the red cedar, although one-half the cost of the latter.

A post that is dressed 5x5 or 6x4 is large enough for ordinary houses. It is well to have all parts set firmly in the ground, especially the outside ones, although the posts must not be trusted to keep the walls plumb, however well set. If the post hole is dug a few inches on all sides larger than the post and when the posts are set perfectly true and straight by the aid of two lines, one near the top and one near the bottom, and the excavation filled in with concrete, gravel and cement, which should be carried above the surface as high as possible, you have fastened the posts as firmly as it is possible to do.

The tops of the posts should be cut off square. Now, how do you get this line so that the plate shall be a perfect line? Not with a swinging line, surely, for you can never get a perfect line by any cord, however taut. With a 10-ft. straight-edge and level you first get a level on the two end posts, the two extreme ends, then if you wish to drop two or three inches to the shed, or the same from the shed, you measure down the number of inches on the end that you wish to drop, tack on a strip of wood a few inches broad with a straight top edge, and when it is nailed on the post temporarily let it project a foot or so outside the line of posts and perfectly level. Nail a similar piece on the post at the other end and the height you have decided on, dab a little black paint on one of the strips and on the other some white paint.

Then a man (two men are better) with a 2-ft. spirit level held to the side of all the intermediate posts will give you an exact line. One man should hold the spirit level, level and raise or lower by order of the boss, who is sighting over one of the end strips. When the top of the level is exactly even or in a line with the tops of the strips make a pencil mark on the post and move to another. You will have a line when your posts are cut off that is not pretty near a line, but correct to a hair. Why the strips of wood should be white and black is to help you sight, and it would be difficult to sight truly if it were just the ordinary planed pine.

I have described this operation seemingly at some length, but twenty posts are marked quicker than I have described it. It is the only way to get a true line, and when established it is a guide for your pipes and benches, or you can level across to another run of posts if need be, although your corner posts once correct this sighted line is much truer than any straight edge.

The top of post should be cut off square and on it spiked the plate, which should be broad enough to pro-

ject an inch over the post on the inside and four inches outside of the posts, then when the matched boarding and novelty siding is nailed on there is still a projection of two inches.

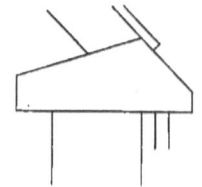

The plate should be beveled both ways and the heel of the bar being cut to the bevel it affords good solid nailing. The outside bevel should be the same as that of the slope of your roof. Posts that support a gutter should never be more than four feet from center to center. For outside posts we have got along very well with posts eight feet apart. There is no great weight on the outside plate and the two thicknesses of siding help support it.

The posts for partitions, or that will support the gutter, should be sawed at the same level as the corresponding posts outside, and the gutter plate project equally on either side. If the center posts are of red cedar 6x3 is just as good as square.

Gutters.

Many a good dollar has been thrown away in the days gone by in the wonderful construction of the gutter. Good pine boards nailed in all sorts of complicated ways and then covered with zinc, tin or galvanized iron, only put up to rot. The gutter now is a simple affair and promises to last as long as the ridge. It is simply a plank of the clearest and soundest cypress and 1¾ inches thick when dressed, and either eight inches or twelve inches wide. If eight inches then the gutter pieces which the bars butt against and are nailed, are screwed on the side of the gutter plate, thus:

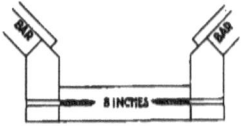

Or if a foot wide then the pieces are nailed on top of the gutter, as below:

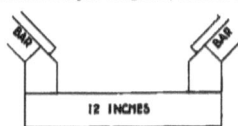

I prefer the latter plan, and after six years' trial of it have no fault or failure in the least. You should have at least a clear eight inches in width of gutter, and the side pieces, whether nailed on the side or on top, should not be less than 2½ inches above gutter before the bevel begins. The plan for joining the gutter plates, explained and illustrated in the work "How to Grow Flowers," by the late Myron A. Hunt, is excellent, and again I say, after some years of adoption, I can see no better way.

A coarse saw groove is made in the center of the thickness of the plate three inches deep and one-eighth or a trifle less wide. Both planks where they will butt will be sawed, then get a piece of sheet iron six inches broad and the length of the breadth of the gutter plate and the thickness of the saw cuts, and after smearing it with white lead drive it home in the saw groove of one plate that is already in place, and when the next plate is laid that is also driven home. If the planks have been sawed perfectly square, this is an absolutely tight joint. We never look for these joints to be over a post, as the joint is as strong as any part of the gutter.

The Ridge.

The ridge is 8x1¾ dressed. This allows ample face for the bevel of the bar, the groove for the glass to enter, and three inches above the bar for the ventilator if hinged at ridge, or bevel of ventilator to close against if opening at the ridge.

The main support to keep a house rigid and perfectly straight and true, as long as it will stand, and that is, we trust, a long time, is a 1¼-inch iron pipe straight under the ridge. If the ridge is thus supported the whole weight is really taken off the walls. In wind storms the roofs of our greenhouses are severely tested, and this center support should be screwed into a fitting which has a shoulder that fits under and screws on to side of the ridge.

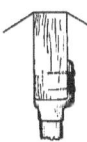

At the bottom or floor this should be screwed into a circular plate which should be screwed into a short post securely set into the ground a couple of feet. Some only rest the bottom of this iron pipe on a stone. That is good enough for all weight from above, but in case of great wind storms, when a vacuum is formed in the house, I have seen the iron supports lifted clear off the stone, which is a wrenching of the roof and conducive to cracked glass. In houses such as we have endeavored to describe, intended for plants in pots, if planted out to smilax or as-

paragus they would be on the ground, and wheeling on the benches would not be necessary.

The neatest way to support the purlins is by getting the fittings made by Jennings Bros., of Philadelphia. They are made to go over a 1¾-inch pipe with a branch, one in each side, with a socket for a 1-inch pipe. They are fastened at any height on the center 1¼-inch pipe by a set screw and have knuckle joints so that the 1-inch pipe leading from them can be set at any angle.

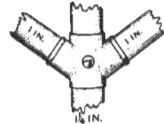

It will be readily seen that the weight from the purlins pressing to a common center must be the best of support. The purlins, one on each side of the ridge, should be situated about half way between ridge and gutter or plate; or if you use a heavy bar let it be a little nearer the ridge than the gutter, because it will keep the bars more rigid near the ventilators. There should be 1-inch gas pipe set every eight feet (same distance apart as the center posts). You must put in a T into which will screw the 1-inch pipe that leads from the fitting on center post.

The bars are fastened to the purlins neatly and quickly by a steam fitter's galvanized iron clip, which you buy by the weight. The clip is screwed into the bar with a ⅞-inch screw and

holds the bar firmly, but not so firmly but what a rap with the hammer will move it either way when you are glazing. Be sure that you get the pattern for the bar the exact bevel both for the ridge and plate. Nothing looks worse than an ill fitting open joint at the heel of the bar on the plate. Once get your pattern correct and the mitre box laid out right and you will have every joint correct.

When putting on the bars we put up the ridge the whole length, nailing up a bar on each side every five or six feet, but only temporarily, and then the iron work is put up. By sighting along the bars the fitting that controls the purlins can be raised or lowered till you can get an exactly straight roof.

Glazing has been dealt with in another chapter.

Cypress.

It is a great pleasure to build houses nowadays. You know you are putting them up to stay. It is quickly done and much of the pleasure arises from the fact that you are building with a material that is well nigh indestructible, and that is cypress lumber. Cypress can be procured in any lumber market, but for greenhouse building we should be afraid to trust it, and we prefer to get our supply from firms who make a specialty of greenhouse material and have the facilities for getting out material of any dimensions you wish.

In the material furnished for ten houses during the past seven years by the Lockland Lumber Co., we have yet to discover a single knot; and what is more, neither in gutter plate, wall plate, ends of bars or any part or piece of the material have we seen decay, even to the depth of a sixteenth of an inch.

Painting.

When you contemplate building get the wood work on the ground at the earliest possible moment, and get a priming coat of paint, mostly linseed oil, applied at once. And as soon as the plates, ridge and bars are cut to their lengths, another two coats should be given. You can paint on the ground just ten times as fast as you can on the roof.

As we butt our glass, there is no need of any painting after the roof is up and the glass in. The ends of the bars are always given an extra dab of thick paint just before they are nailed up, and this should be done by a boy who hands them up to the carpenter.

I will mention here that no part of the wood work where moisture can lie should be flat. All parts should have a bevel either in or out.

General Notes.

The length of a house is largely your own choice. If for plants there is a continual running backwards and forwards to a shed at the end, carrying often heavy flats of plants, and I think 150 feet is long enough, and 125 feet is better.

The soil or site on which greenhouses are built differs widely. I have some covering a light loam and the subsoil is gravel and shale. If a hose were left running a whole night on the floor of these houses the water would have entirely disappeared a few minutes after the faucet was shut off. I have other houses where if the faucet only leaks a trifle there is a pool of water for hours. For several reasons I think it very injurious to have the surface of the green house a wet, damp soil, retentive of moisture. This may be all right for orchids, but for the great majority of our plants, especially roses, carnations, violets, and the bulk of our plants, a stagnant moisture is just what we don't want.

If your soil is a retentive clay, there should be provision for draining it before you put up any structure. Dig a trench two feet deep and at its bottom put in a 3-inch drain tile, and instead of filling in the trench again with the clay, as you would in draining a field, fill up to the surface if possible with stones, clinkers and coarse gravel. You will find this money well spent. You can always find some outlet for the pipes at one end, running them all into one cross drain and dropping into the stoke hole if you have no other system.

Just a word here about houses that are connected and form what are known by builders as valleys. Some may say they are bad for the snows. Now, the writer certainly lives in a district where the supply of "the beautiful" is most bountiful, and we have noticed year after year that we are no more troubled with snow in the valleys than we are on the outside roofs. It seems to melt quicker in the valleys and the gutter than it does on the outside plates, and runs and melts as quickly off the glass unless it be on the almost perpendicular face of the short span to the south, which, of course, is always clear. Ordinary snows (a fall of five or six inches) don't bother any houses on any kind of roof, but when we get four feet in twenty-four hours, as we did last December, or the visitation to the eastern cities in February last, that upsets all calculations, and it is a case of dig out, front, back and middle.

The worst condition is where one of the avalanche-like falls have come suddenly. The heat of the glass will melt the snow some five or six inches from the glass and then its power is lost and there hangs a covering of snow a foot deep. This we found as troublesome on the outside slope of the roofs as in the valleys, and with our modern wooden gutters it is easily broken up, and when once disturbed soon goes.

I never could see any use in outside gutters unless you wanted to save the water from the roofs. If made of metal they are continually breaking down with the ice and bad better be made of wood. The ground surrounding houses should always be so graded that surface water will flow off where it will do no harm. If the water of the gutters is saved be sure to tap your gutter plate two feet from the farther end, if the houses grade that way. A conductor of any sort on the end and outside of a house is a big failure and is the winter long a fantastic and ornamental miniature iceberg.

Where the water is not used the houses will of course drop two or three inches from the shed to the farther end. We let the gutter plate project six inches beyond the house, and making a saw groove an inch or two deep in it insert a piece of tin a few inches broad. This throws the water clear of the house and provision is made by the outside grade to carry it away from the buildings.

Under the head of painting we meant to say a word about painting the iron work. We have just had

some experience with some 1¼-inch pipe supporting the roof that ran through the benches on which we have frequently used coal ashes to stand the plants on. They have only been up six years. The pipes began to corrode and scale off and this summer are rusted clear through, not in holes, but an inch or two of the pipes are clear gone. We have often used coal ashes on the floor and believe they should be kept clear of all wrought iron pipes. We also believe that all our iron supports, ventilating shafts, heating pipes and all pipes of every description should be well painted with white lead and oil.

As for any porousness of our pipes, that is perfect nonsense. A friend remarked on seeing 2-inch heating pipes painted that it would prevent radiation. Nonsense; it will help it. A smooth surface is always a better conductor of heat than a rough one. Paint all your pipes everywhere. It will save them and it will help to give lightness to the house, and light means health and life. If painted in the summer time there will be no possible odor from the lead, and the slight fumes of the linseed oil are more a benefit than otherwise.

Greenhouses for Producing Flowers.

I have at some length given the directions for building, and the same will apply precisely to houses that are built to grow roses and carnations, except the shape, size and aspect. The object sought in these houses is to get every possible ray of sunshine, and besides direct sunshine, light;, for there are many days, yes, and weeks, in the dead of winter in our northern clime when we don't see the sun at all.

There are three styles of these houses and all have their champions. They are the long-span-to-the-south, the equal or nearly equal span, and the short-span-to-the-south. Twenty years ago and less the long-span-to-the-south house was considered by many as the only house for winter roses. Then came the very reverse of that, the short-span-to-the-south, and within seven or eight years many good growers have gone back to the simple equal span, and from results believe that it is as good a house as any.

All these styles when built for flower producing face to the south, or what is still better, facing a few points to the east of that. The ridge is running east and west, or a few points north of east, and south of west. It is obvious that only one style of these three can have a range of glass attached, and that is, of course, the short-span-to-the-south. If attached the equal span would shade the house to the north of it, making one-fourth at least of the north house useless, and the long-span-to-the-south connected would be still worse and out of the question.

So excepting the short-span-to-the-south the other two styles are always built with their walls some 18 to 20

feet removed from another structure. Where land is cheap and most large establishments are so situated, this is no great consideration; and if it takes more heat, but the results are sufficiently better, that also is not an objection. The long-span-to-the-south doubtless predominates throughout the country, but that does not confirm it as the best, because florists, like all other classes, are great copyists, and if one or two leaders said so the rest would follow sheep-like, notwithstanding the fact that millions of fine roses have been produced for years in the long-span-to-the-south houses.

I see nothing about them in any respect to warrant their being called the best houses for the purpose. If there is any merit, and there undoubtedly is, in the short-span-to-the-south, then the others must be entirely wrong. They are expensive to build, awkward and costly to arrange the benching in, more laborious to attend to, and do not get the direct rays of the sun to the same extent as do the equal span or short-span-to-the-south.

The front wall is usually 4 feet 6 inches (and 18 inches or 2 feet of it glass), and the back wall 8 feet, the back or short rafter 8 feet and the long south rafter 16 feet. These are the dimensions for a house 19 feet wide; if 22 feet wide the long rafter is 18 feet and the short one 9 feet. An upright 1¼-inch pipe supports them under the ridge with a branch holding a 1-inch purlin a foot below the ventilator headers, and another upright supporting another 1-inch purlin is needed half way between the plate and ventilator purlin. The ventilators of these houses are always on the south side of the ridge and open at the ridge; and as ventilation should be afforded to the fullest extent, it should be continuous and deep.

It is thought necessary to raise the benches so that the plants should be at about an equal distance from the glass, and the benches are arranged in a 19-foot house as follows: The south bench 3 feet and path 18 inches or 2 feet. The middle bench 6 feet and the back or north bench 3 feet. If the house is 22 feet the front bench is 3 feet and the back bench 3 feet and two middle benches of 5 feet each, with three paths, each path and bench being raised a foot or so till the back or north path is 4 feet from the ground. If heated with hot water the pipes are mostly under the benches. If steam is used the flow is most likely raised above the plants and the returns under the bench. It is as well to add, because it is the truth, that these houses, while getting the sun's rays in winter very obliquely, get it broadside in the summer, making them terribly hot houses in the summer months.

The short-slope-to-the-south is also built sometimes 19 feet wide and sometimes 22 feet. The walls are of equal height, usually five feet. There is a path against the north and south walls and one dividing the two benches, which are about 6 feet 6 inches each. The paths being removed from the walls gives you the ideal place to hang your pipes, whether steam or hot water.

An improvement over the house just described, and one that is giving the owner the greatest satisfaction (after a trial of several of them he has added some more of the dimensions of 400x 22 feet), is 22 feet from outside to outside of posts. The south or short bar is 9 feet, the long or north bar is 18 feet, and the walls 5 feet high. On the south side there is a path next the wall, then a 6-foot bench, then another 6-foot bench, then again a path, and against the north wall a 3-foot bench. There is a 1¼-inch pipe under the ridge with a branch from that supporting a purlin near ventilator headers, and another row of 1¼-inch pipe supporting a purlin three feet lower down the roof on the north side. The ventilation in these south-span-to-the-south houses is always on the north side and open at the ridge.

Now, happening to know several of these houses, I can vouch for the very excellent quality of the flowers that are grown in them, and having two of them myself, I am ready to accord to them the several advantages and merits they possess. They are easy and cheap to build, much more so than the long-span-to-the-south. They are cheaply heated; less pipe will heat them than either of the other two styles. When there is any sun in our dreary winter you must get the direct rays, for the face of the south slope is about at right angles with the rays of the sun in our shortest days. They are most decidedly the coolest houses in summer, which is a decided advantage, and last they can be built attached with gutter and walls only separating them.

The front or south bench being some two feet from the wall there is not the slightest shade from the ridge of the house on the south. The fact of these houses being in a block, and the roof of one largely breaking the force of the wind to the north, is a great saving of fuel. I can only say that some of the best rose growers of the country, having adopted this style of house seven or eight years ago, are highly satisfied with them and are still building more, and the quality of their product is evidence of their not being far wrong.

The equal span house is to me about the ideal. It may take more heat, but it gives the best distribution of light. An equal span of 22 ft. should always be removed from another like house 20 ft. The walls should be 5 ft., a path against each wall, and two more separating the benches, and three benches each 5 ft. wide. This house would take a 14 ft. bar, and in addition to the main support in the center would need a purlin on each side.

Ample ventilation should be supplied on the south side of the ridge and opening at the ridge. Ventilation could be put into the walls of this

house, but you would not use it for roses, and for carnations if shading is attended to, I am convinced it is not necessary, as carnations in our equal span houses with only top ventilation are often so vigorous and thriving at the end of August that it seems a sacrifice to throw them away.

We have on these equal span houses some large ventilators on the north side that are not worked by any apparatus, and not used till settled warm weather, when they are raised up a foot or so on stout blocks, fastened down with wire and left open till planting time, or in some cases till there is danger of the houses getting too cold. I am sure that in carnation houses these ventilators to be used only in our hot weather are of great use. Why a steep roof always makes a lighter house than a flat roof is not easy to explain, but it is so, and unmistakably so. Many times have I compared the light in the three different styles of houses on the same day and the equal span at an angle of about 45 degrees is much the lightest appearing house, and I believe although the short-span-to-the-south has many advantages, particularly on the score of economy of heat and space, that the equal span, using the same glass and bar, has the most perfect diffusion of light and comes nearer the ideal for producing high class flowers.

A violet house should run north and south. You get all the light you want in the winter and you would get too much sun in the early spring if the house faced south. Under the head of violets I will give you my idea of a violet house.

In conclusion all I have said about any of these houses, both for plants and flowers, applies only to those that you are going to build under your own supervision. If you have no mechanical genius at all, engage a horticultural builder. Some men have the bump of destruction and some of construction. The writer wishes no greater pleasure in this world than hossing the erection of glass structures. Poor fare and short hours in bed will do him then if he can only squint over those pieces of wood by which we get a line on the posts or hangers for the pipes.

The well known firms I mentioned in my opening remarks in this chapter will put you up most excellent commercial houses and make them any shape or design you wish. What I have tried to convey is the method by which you can erect with the help of one good carpenter and his tools substantial lasting houses that will grow flowers and plants equal to the best. And if you are a builder yourself, not necessarily able to handle a jack plane, but to boss the job, you can build first class houses at least 50 per cent cheaper than the iron frame houses of the horticultural builder, and 200 per cent cheaper and better than the local carpenter, glazier and steam fitter.

It will be asked why don't I say what would be the cost per lineal foot of a house about 20 ft. wide. As near as I could keep a record of the last house I built, 19 ft. wide, heated for carnations by hot water, using double thick glass, the Challenge ventilator, the best clear cypress lumber, red cedar posts and wooden benches, they cost about $8 per lineal foot. This was a year ago before the high tariff had had a chance to shed its beneficent blessings on the florists' calling.

Possibly at present prices of pipe and glass the same houses could not be built for less than $12 per lineal foot, but as glass is principally made of sand and fire and wind, with which we are well supplied, and there is iron

enough in our mountains to last the world ten thousand years, neither the folly of alleged statesmanship nor the greed of corporations can long keep those commodities up to these artificial and preposterous prices.

We trust lumber will not go up in sympathy with the manufactured articles. There are broad miles (and I hope thousands of miles) yet in the southern states of cypress, and its great value seems only within this 20 years to have become widely known.

The Canadians use the wood of the Larch (Tamarax) for benches, and a most excellent wood it is for the purpose, possessing largely the good qualities of the cypress. They are both deciduous conifers. The tamarax is the larch of our northern swamps, and the southern cypress is a beautiful tree, Taxodium distichum.

GREVILLEA ROBUSTA.

There are many species of these small trees or shrubs, some of them very ornamental, but G. robusta is the easiest to grow and most useful to the florist. It is often called the Austra-

lian silk oak. We use it in vases and veranda boxes, and plants a foot to two feet high make very useful plants for winter decoration. It withstands a good deal of rough treatment and does very well in winter in a cool greenhouse, subject to no insects and thriving in any soil.

It is always raised from seed, which should be sown in flats in March or April, and shifted along as required. Keep them in doors on the benches if you can afford the room, and give them little or no shade and they will make useful plants the following spring. It is best to sow seeds every spring, as the plants when over three feet high lose their value as decorative plants, or rather there are other plants occupying no more room that are better for the purpose. Avoid getting them into large pots, a 5-inch pot will do very well for a plant two to three feet high, and that is a great advantage when you are using decorative plants.

HARDY PERENNIAL PLANTS.

This term is usually meant to apply to our long list of herbaceous plants, a few of which are useful to the florist as cut flowers. The demand of late has greatly increased for hardy plants, and where the florist has some good land at his disposal he should be supplied with a collection of the leading kinds so that he can supply the demands of his customers.

The increased demand for this class of plants is to be attributed to so many of our people of means having summer homes in the country. They have usually more land than they can take care of, and not wishing to go deeply into the formal flower garden with our tender plants they turn to the hardy herbaceous perennial kinds to fill up the beds and borders.

In preparing ground to receive these perennial plants, either to produce flowers for your own cutting or for your customer, remember you cannot very well dig too deeply or manure too heavily, and with the great majority it should be well drained and dry. You can top dress and manure annually, but you can never recover by subsequent cultivation the mistake of planting in shallow, poor soil.

Although called perennials they wear out and most of them are greatly benefited by lifting and dividing every four or five years. There are so many species cultivated of this class for the herbaceous border, and they differ so widely, that no rule for their propagation and treatment will do for all. It is generally conceded that early fall, as soon as the foliage or stems are about dried up, is the best time to transplant, and hence it is the best time to fill your customers' orders.

If you cultivate a row or two of the leading kinds, keep them in straight lines and far enough apart to run the horse cultivator between them. Many thousand plants will go on one acre, but they want keeping clean and must be constantly hoed, and should be al-

Aquilegia Chrysantha.

a hot-bed. Eighteen inches of manure well and evenly trodden down, with a few inches of soil and then two inches of sand, will root any of these plants. Give air carefully, shade from sun and keep watered. When rooted give plenty of air till potted off and then grow on in cold-frame all summer. These will be good plants in 3 or 4-inch pots, either to sell or to plant out in September or October.

DIELYTRA (Bleeding Heart). Often forced, but beautiful and graceful as D. spectabilis is, it takes up too much room. A very handsome, hardy plant. Division.

DIGITALIS. White and purple and yellow; the well known foxglove. Stately spikes of flowers. Seed.

Double Delphiniums.

ways plainly labeled as they are often moved before their growth appears. One more important thing is when you plant dormant crowns of paeonies, phlox, etc., keep them two or three inches below the surface; the winter will be sure to raise them up.

Herbaceous plants are always benefited by some stable manure scattered between the rows and over the crowns. In their natural state they would at least get the benefit of their own withered tops, while most of them would get a covering of leaves from the trees whose branches covered them. For appearance sake we rob them of their natural covering.

Those most useful to the florist and which have not received notice in their alphabetical order are as follows:

ACHILLEA. Several species, good for rockwork, easily divided in fall or early spring.

ANEMONE japonica alba. This is a florist's flower, and a beautiful fall blooming plant. Division.

AQUILEGIA. The beautiful columbine. There are several magnificent species that should be in every garden. Seed.

CAMPANULA. Several species. Carpathica, the Canterbury Bell, is popular with all. Not a florist's flower, but fine for the border. Raised from seed, sown in August in cold-frame and transplanted later a few inches

apart in good soil in cold-frame, where they can be protected during winter and plant out in permanent bed or nursery row as soon as ground is dry in the spring. In other varieties when stated that they can be raised from seed the above directions will suit them all.

COREOPSIS. The best of the species for the florist is lanceolata. Graceful and beautiful yellow flowers. Seed.

DELPHINIUMS. Most every one knows the D. formosum, which is often called larkspur. The improved varieties are among the handsomest of our hardy flowers, and are decidedly of value to the florist. Their handsome spikes, from the lightest shades of blue to indigo, and even to bronze, are grand ornaments for our stores, even if they do not sell; but invariably those who see them want a plant. They flower a long time, should the weather not be too dry, and last a long while in water when cut. Seed, or divisions or cuttings.

Cuttings of herbaceous plants should always be made from the young shoots of early spring, when only a few inches above ground. The heat in our propagating houses then, which is early May, is often about gone, as firing is only then very moderate.

Where a considerable number of these cuttings are to be put in, such as delphiniums, phlox or pyrethrum, there is no place so well adapted as

Helianthus Orgyalis.

8

DORONICUM. Of service to the florist because its bright yellow flowers are among the first to open after the snow is gone. Division.

FUNKIA. The Day lily. There are several species of them, all handsome leaved plants. Division.

GAILLARDIA grandiflora. Showy bright flowers. Seed.

HELIANTHUS. There are now a number of these tall growing perennial sunflowers, many of them very useful to the florist. The variety known as multiflorus flore plena became so common that it is no longer acceptable even in the cheapest bunches of

Helianthus Multiflora Flore Plena.

flowers, but the single species are very fine. Seed, division or cuttings.

HEMEROCALLIS. Several species, mostly yellow and orange flowers. Showy for the border, but not a florist's flower. Seed or division.

HIBISCUS. Californicus and others. Fine showy flowers. Seed.

IRIS. These have such a fine spike and curious but beautiful flower that they are most desirable for the florist, and are wanted by every amateur. They do best in a rather moist soil and root so freely that every third year they should be lifted and divided. There are now many varieties. The Japanese have immense flowers, and the I. germanica, or German iris, includes now many beautiful varieties. Division.

LOBELIA cardinalis. Not a florist's flower, but most showy for the border. Division or seed.

MONARDA didyma. A native northern plant, though not common. A fine herbaceous plant. Division.

PAEONIES. See in their alphabetical order.

PHLOX. There are several species of hardy phlox, but it is the hybrids and varieties of P. decussata that are most desirable for the border and for the florist. We have found where they can be freshly cut and used they are most desirable, but will not travel well, dropping their florets badly. The many varieties are of beautiful shades and the phlox thrives in any soil. Cuttings or division, and for new varieties easily by seed.

PYRETHRUM roseum. This is not truly herbaceous but is so hardy we will include it in this chapter. The improved varieties, both double and single flowers, of this species are now truly a florist's flower. They are seen in our store windows in May and June and are bought in preference to carnations. They are sometimes difficult to divide and make thrive, and cuttings as described above are best to increase your stock. Few border plants are so well worthy of cultivation.

RUDBECKIA. The single flowered species, maxima and fulgida, are showy flowers, yellow with dark disk, and are sometimes useful to us as well as very fine border plants. But there is now a double form known as "Golden Glow," which is undoubtedly one of our finest hardy summer flowers. It is of a rich yellow. It is much superior to the dwarf double helianthus. Seed or division.

To describe the many desirable

hardy herbaceous plants would require a good sized catalogue, and have mentioned but a few of those kinds which every florist should grow.

HARDY SHRUBS.

Some years ago I was asked to reply at one of our annual conventions to the query, "Is it advisable for the florist to be in a position to supply to his customers hardy shrubs and trees?" The question was not probably just that but the sense was that. My answer was brief, and certainly not, with the knowledge of the business I have today, or to be more modest, which experience has compelled me to absorb. Division of labor is most truly the order of the day, as much in our trade as in others, but circumstances alter cases.

It would be absurd to think of Mr. Kift or Mr. Wienhoeber, or Mr. Thorley talking about the best hedge to plant, or a specialist like Charles D. Ball, or John Burton, or Dailledouze Bros., going out to plant a group of shrubs. Their specialty is all they can do, or all they need do. But in smaller cities, among the men who grow and retail and plant flower gardens, there is a growing demand from their customers that they supply them with hardy roses, hardy vines, hedge plants and shrubs, and if with shrubs why not with ornamental trees.

Perhaps there is no local nurseryman, and if there is he is too busy a man in his shipping season to bother about retail orders. So who is there to supply the local trade? The tree peddler is fast losing ground, his wonderful pictures and himself are now discredited, and the local florist is called, for he is responsible. A tree peddler who still hangs out in the same neighborhood for ten years past, once told me that "he did not reckon to make a second sale to the same person." Fancy that, and we expect to make sales to the same people as long as they and we live. We will make our sales of shrubs or vines satisfactory. If failure occurs the first time we try again.

In our growing suburbs and on our residence streets there is an increasing and continuous demand for handsome shrubs and ornamental trees, and if you have the knowledge what to buy and how and when to plant you are throwing away a great chance if you neglect this substantial part of the horticultural profession. If you can't show your men how to prune and plant a shrub get a foreman that can. but it is an enormous advantage if your early education embraced the spade as well as the pen.

We used to deplore the absence in our northern clime of what are known as the broad leaved evergreens, such as the Sweet Bay, arbutus, aucuba and laurestinus that form the shrubberies of temperate Europe, but we believe now that our vegetation in this line is just right as it is, and with our snowed up winter the true evergreen would look too sombre. How beauti-

A Field of Japanese Iris.

ful and inspiring in the warm days of spring, after the hibernating days of winter, to see willows blossom, and later the gay scarlet flowers of Pyrus japonica and the yellow wreathing of forsythia. And then the many tinted leaves of the hardy shrubs. It is an awakening, an annual treat and pleasure to the senses that the monotonous sombre evergreen cannot give. So everything is right as it is. And Japan has to be thanked for contributing a whole host of our best hardy shrubs.

Shrubs, so called, are always more safely transplanted than trees for two reasons. They are seldom in the nursery more than two or three years, and even the neglect of transplanting, of which our American nurserymen are woefully guilty, should they be left five or six years in one spot, does not prevent them from making a mass of roots, most of which can be lifted. So the percentage of loss in transplanting shrubs with any ordinary care is very low.

The time of transplanting varies a week or so with the season. With a dry season and early frosts you can plant from middle of October till late in November. If you start early in the fall and the leaves have not fallen off the shrubs, pull or rather rub them off. If they come off easily no harm is done. In spring the transition from winter to summer or hot weather is sometimes very short and affords the planter but a very brief time. Had we a month of cool, moist weather between frost and the bursting of the buds into leaf, I should say that April

and even May was the best time of all to move shrubs.

If the buds are breaking and the leaves showing, then the shrubs must be severely cut back. Even if you plant them in the most favorable time and in the best condition, it is necessary to shorten back the shoots. The larger and taller the shrub the more in proportion should it be cut back. Don't think, and don't let your customer think, there is going to be any eventual loss of growth or size on account of this cutting back. The roots are disturbed, the fine fibrous roots that are the feeders and nourishers of the plant are gone or inactive, the shortened supply of sap goes to the extremities of the shoots and a feeble break or growth occurs at the end of the shoots, and the lower buds perish, and then you have bare stems. Insist on it that transplanted shrubs and trees must be pruned more or less according to the loss of roots.

A word here about future pruning. No shrubbery is planted for all time. Perhaps where they do well a mixed belt of shrubs never looks better than from six to ten years after they are planted. Then they crowd each other. Some grow tall and lose their beauty, so a shrubbery is never finished; it is a continual thinning out and replenishing.

In pruning distinguish the difference between those that set their flower buds in the fall and those that flower on the growths of the current year. The lilac is a good type of the former, and if you prune severely in

winter and spring you must cut away the flower buds. You will readily distinguish the difference in these shrubs, and if they are to be pruned, a good time is just after they have done flowering, when they have time to make more growth and set more flower buds. The latter type is well represented by our hardy roses and the Hydrangea paniculata. The harder back this class of shrubs is pruned the larger and better the flowers.

To revert once more to planting. Many of our hardy shrubs will exist in any soil, but a quick and thrifty growth is what our customers want and expect, and when planting a group or bed of shrubs the soil should be dug a foot deep. Not making small holes for each plant, but the whole space dug deeply, and to it add plenty of animal manure. Don't believe for a moment that shrubs don't like manure. It is just what will make them jump and grow.

When singly on the lawn, let it be either a shrub, tree or any of the evergreens, it is not depth that is needed. The hole to receive the shrub or tree need be only sufficient to let the plant down to the same depth it stood in the nursery, an inch or so lower won't hurt many of the shrubs but with the trees and the evergreens this is very particular. When the ground is settled round them let it be just about as high on the stem as it was before moving.

It is width of hole you want, and if a stiff clay, not only should width of excavation be large enough to enable you to spread the roots out without any bending or crowding, but every foot in diameter you go beyond this and fill in with good soil will much assist the growth and thriftiness of your tree.

It matters not whether it is fall or spring there is only one way to plant a shrub or tree and that is to give its roots plenty of room in width, putting on sufficient soil to cover the roots, and by shaking the tree or shrub see that the soil is well distributed among the roots. Firm the soil with your feet and then give it a thorough soaking. After the water has soaked in, wetting root and fiber, fill in with more soil to the grade of your bed or border. This first watering is worth ten on the surface. If planting has been done in the spring and we have a very dry summer, they will need a soaking every week, and if the surface is covered with a mulch of two inches of stable manure it will add ten fold to the benefits of the watering.

As I cannot afford a separate chapter on our evergreens, so called, or more properly our coniferous trees, I would say that the time of transplanting them differs much from the deciduous shrubs and trees.

Evergreen conifers, such as the pines and spruces, and all of them, are best moved in the spring just as the young growths start, which is often the middle or end of May. This is a month later than the shrub planting time. The next best time is the last week in August or first week in September. After middle of September don't attempt to move evergreens.

There is often a great disappointment in planting spruce, pines, etc. It is not the fault of the plants, although in some cases it is often too crudely done. It is in most cases the fault of the nurseryman. Our American nurserymen plant a Norway spruce or Australian pine from six to ten inches high and without even transplanting let some of them grow to 4, 5 or 6 ft., and then sell them.

Whether they expect them to grow I don't know. They sell them and thus is their chief object attained. I saw this summer, every few days, several hundred nice symmetrical Australian pines, 3 to 4 ft. They looked well when planted this spring, but our summer has killed 90 per cent. These fine little trees had never been transplanted in the nursery since they were ten inches high. Had not many of their working roots had been saved when dug and sold, think you? Scarcely any.

There is, I am glad to say, a school of young nurserymen coming to the front who are alive to this crude and almost dishonest way of growing evergreens, and soon in every part of the land you will be able to buy a pine or thuya or abies or spruce and plant it with the same confidence that we plant the geranium in the beds, because every two years they have had a move in the nursery.

A local "Farmer-fruit grower-nurs-

eryman," a long title but a correct one, said the public would not pay 25 cents for a transplanted Norway spruce when they could get one that looked as good for 10 cents. He is entirely wrong. We are all looking for the transplanted tree that won't disappoint us and our customers. I find the man of wealth, or even moderate means, anxious to pay for the best. It is quite different from their canna or geranium bed, which they know is for one short season. Their trees and shrubs are for the permanent improvement of their grounds.

The evergreens like good rotten animal manure just as much as the deciduous shrubs, but unless well rotted don't put it in contact with the roots when planting. A little experience of mine of twenty-five years ago will be instructive. On both sides of a Norway spruce hedge, as near as I could get to the stems, I forked in at least two inches of rotten stable manure. It was done in May. The trees made a fine growth and in attempting to lightly fork up the surface the following spring I found on both sides at least three feet from the stem, that the roots were just a mat close to the surface, and you might as well have tried to fork up a wire spring mattress.

You should acquaint yourself with the many varieties of flowering shrubs and their habits and heights and time of flowering, so that they can be arranged properly. The tallest growing in the background, etc. Some of them make fine groups or beds when planted of just one kind. This is decidedly true of the favorite Hydrangea paniculata, which makes a fine bed of a dozen or more plants, or even a single specimen on a lawn.

A bed of shrubs that pleased me very much this summer was very gay near the entrance of our Forest Lawn Cemetery. The center was the common purple barberry with an edging of the golden philadelphus. Another bed was Prunus Pissardii surrounded with the variegated cornus. In private grounds masses of one species are often planted, but in private grounds the mixed collection of shrubs is most desirable, for with a proper selection there are always some in flower. But the flower is only a part of their beauty. I cannot afford space to give more than a list of the very best shrubs, in recommending any of which you will not go wrong, and here they are:

Althea in several varieties.
Berberis vulgaris and Thunbergii.
Calycanthus floridus.
Corchorus japonica.
Cornus (Dogwood). Several species. The variegated cornus is one of the best of all variegated shrubs.
Cydonia (Pyrus) japonica.
Deutzia crenata, gracilis and scabra.
Exochorda grandiflora.
Forsythia, several species; the earliest shrub in flower.
Hydrangea paniculata grandiflora. There are two or three new species of this type, all fine.

Ligustrum (Privet). The Californian ovalifolium is most desirable.
Lonicera tartarica. Tartarian honeysuckle.
Magnolias. These are dwarf trees and deserve a place on the lawn alone, where they can show off their great beauty; several species.
Philadelphus grandiflora. The mock orange.
Rhus cotinus. Purple fringe.
Rhus glabra laciniata. The cut leaved sumach. A most beautiful shrub or dwarf tree.
Sambucus aurea. Golden elder. Most showy in early summer.
Spiraea. This large genus has given us some of our finest flowering shrubs. Billardii, bumalda, Douglasii, prunifolia, Reevesii, Thunbergii and Van Houttei are all grand, splendid shrubs.
Staphylea colchica. The bladder nut.
Symphoricarpus. The snowberry. Several species.
Syringa. The well known lilac. Several species and varieties, and now some fine double forms.
Viburnum. The snowball. Plicatum and opulis.
Weigla. Many varieties. Rose, red and white flowers and variegated foliage.

The above is not a collection but merely a selection. Many desirable kinds could be added. I have not included any of the broad leaved evergreen shrubs, as there are so few. Daphne cneorum does deserve a place in every garden. Euonymus radicans variegata is used for the margins of shrubberies. Mahonia aquifolia, with its racemes of yellow flowers and purple fruit, is a beautiful holly-leaved like shrub, but unless shaded from the March suns it burns badly.

Neither have I said anything about the rhododendrons, kalmias, or hardy azaleas. Where these American plants do well cultivated, as they do so finely at Wellesley, Mass., and doubtless many other places, they are beautiful and desirable, but in a limestone district, without a great labor of transporting suitable soil, and again with our zero nights and bright days, they are useless, and to plant them is a fraud. They are a fit article for the tree peddler who never goes back after the bill is collected, and who is usually nomadic in his habits, like the Parthians of old.

We have not such a long list of evergreens or conifers and our winters bar us from planting many of great beauty that thrive in the British Isles, but we have yet a good variety. You are usually advised to plant small.

Garden of Hardy Plants in a Public Park.

Good advice, so long as nurserymen won't furnish you a tree that has been transplanted and furnished with a compact ball of roots.

You must remember that many of the evergreens that are hardy in the vicinity of New York and Boston are useless in land in the latitude of Chicago, and many are catalogued as hardy, such as Cedrus deodara and Cupressus Lawsoniana. They are useless in our vicinity. It is not only the low temperature but some other climatic influence that kills them or leaves them stunted, crippled objects.

Several of the abies are fine, including alba, white spruce; canadensis, hemlock spruce, and excelsa, Norway spruce, many forms of it. Several junipers, the Irish, Swedish and our own red cedar, J. virginiana. Picea pungens, the Colorado blue spruce, is the most beautiful of our conifers, and P. balsamea, P. concolor and P. Nordmaniana, are fine trees. The pines are the noblest of the conifers. The Austrian is one of our hardiest trees, and so is P. sylvestris, the Scotch pine. P. strobus, our native white pine, and P. cembra, the stone pine.

The retinosporas are dense growing, compact evergreens, and are good and hardy. The Thuyas (arbor-vitae) make handsome trees. T. occidentalis is our yellow or white cedar, and T. orientalis is the Siberian or Chinese arbor-vitae, a very compact, hardy evergreen. Taxodium distichum, the southern cypress, though deciduous,

like our American larch, is a conifer and makes a splendid specimen for our lawns, and the giants of the south provide us with its invaluable timber. For dwarf evergreens the taxus (yew) are unequaled. They are hardy and have several ornamental forms.

It is characteristic of many of the conifers that they vary much in form and color, hence the many varieties that are now known, and to this variation we owe the several golden forms we have in the thuyas, taxus and retinosporas.

I have said nothing about propagation of the shrubs because that is a nurseryman's business, and unless you are in the business to some extent you had better buy the shrubs from reputable nurserymen. Even they depend largely on importing small plants from France from specialists who raise millions of the leading varieties and supply them at a seemingly very low cost. If you have a few acres of good light soil, easy to work, it would be a good investment to buy a thousand or so of small plants of the leading kinds and in two years you will have shrubs that you can sell your customers with the greatest confidence.

The long list of noble trees I cannot enter on. Nurserymen publish descriptive catalogues of all desirable kinds. I am not in favor of transplanting large trees from the woods of our native elms and maples. They survive a few years, but generally collapse in three or four,

HEATING.

There are only two recognized methods of heating our glass structures, steam and hot water. Brick flues have gone and electricity has not come, but it may. Some fifteen years ago heating greenhouses by steam came with a rush, although it had long been used as a means of heating dwellings and large buildings. Men who had been at first most sanguine about its merits and consider whether after all hot water had not the most advantages. A patriarch of the business, Mr. Peter Henderson, being asked by the writer in 1889 which was the best way to heat, inquired what system I was then using. On being told "hot water," the reply came quick and brief, "Keep on with the hot water." But after all this ebb and flow of popular favor it is now well established that with an improved system of piping, steam for many establishments is the cheapest and best, and although by no means claiming to know of steam what I do of the circulation of water, we will first consider

Steam Heating.

Steam as applied to heating greenhouses has several advantages over water. Heat is quickly produced by steam and sent through the houses in case of a quick fall of the outside temperature. It is also quickly reduced or entirely absent in the pipes should you see in the early morning that it is going to be a bright, warm day and no steam heat will be needed. This I consider one of its very best features, for we all know how we have suffered with over heated houses when the water in the pipes would not cool.

With a number of pipes and a valve at each, a house with steam and proper attention can be kept at almost the desired degree. It is cheaper to put in a steam plant. The piping is much cheaper, sufficiently less to offset the larger cost of boiler.

Steam is undoubtedly the best system where a block of houses is devoted to one purpose, but where two rose houses and two carnation houses are heated by one boiler it would not be so economical, because a month or more after no heat was needed in the carnation houses you would have to still make steam for the rose houses.

Where a dozen houses are used for many different plants water is to be preferred. Water can be heated to a temperature of say 140 degrees, just sufficient to take the chill off the house; a very slow burning fire will do this. With steam you must have sufficient fire to make steam or you may as well have no fire at all. If you wish only to fill one 1-inch pipe the boiler may be full of steam or none will pass into the pipe. Steam is most convenient for evaporating tobacco. Altogether steam is the plan for large establishments, where four or five houses will want heat at the same time, and water is the best for houses where less quantities but greater variety is grown.

Cast iron boilers of several makes are used by greenhouse men to generate steam, but wherever there is much work to be done a steel tubular boiler is the best. If for locomotives, steamships and factories the tubular boiler is the best, why is it not the best for the greenhouse with some modification of the way the fire is applied.

I have seen some greenhouse furnaces where the fire or heat from it first passed under the whole length of the boiler, then returned to the front by half of the flues and again returned to the rear by the other half of the flues. We believe that was overdoing it. On returning the third time the smoke would be so cool that it could not help in making steam, therefore it was no help. If the draught is carried through one set of tubes and back by another you will have all out of the fuel that can be got towards making steam.

Many prefer to use old marine boilers that have been condemned for use where high pressure was needed. They may last a long time, but as in everything else a new boiler made for you is the cheapest in the end.

It is of the greatest importance that the boiler should be well down under its work. The working of a steam boiler when well down will be so much more satisfactory over one that has to return the condensed steam by an automatic pump or trap, that any expense in the way of excavation or

sewer is warranted. Keep the boiler down so that there is a perfect and unobstructed return to the boiler. If the top of the boiler is two feet lower than your return pipes in the house you are all right, but if convenient lower still is better.

The size of pipe that you lead out of the boiler and the branches attached leading to the different houses will depend on the number and size of the houses. To illustrate. If you were heating six rose houses from one boilery, or battery of boilers, you would start with a 6-inch; the first two houses would be tapped from the 6-inch, after which the main could be reduced to a 4-inch and from it feed two more houses. Then the main pipe could be reduced to a 3-inch and supply one more house; and reducing the main to a 2-inch would be enough for the sixth house. But be on the safe side and have good sized pipes for supply. I may have given even a smaller sized pipe for the supply than is judicious.

The arrangement of steam pipes is very like the modern way of arranging pipes for hot water. They are usually carried up in the shed above the doorways for convenience sake. Just here let me say that all the steam pipes should be well covered with asbestos, mineral wool, or some such material; if exposed much condensation would occur.

When steam was first used in greenhouses, and maybe in some places yet, the main pipe or flow, a 2½ or 3-inch, was carried along a foot or two from the roof, and at the end dropped into manifolds and a number of 1-inch pipes, either on the side or under the benches. From the shed or boiler end drop the pipes slightly (two inches in a hundred feet is enough) and return the same way. Drop enough back to the boiler to empty the pipes is enough. For a return a 1-inch will do for five flows. On reaching the shed let all the returns enter one 2-inch pipe and when convenient drop into the bottom of the boiler. The arrangement of steam pipes is more simple than hot water. You can drive steam but water will only flow by a natural law.

I cannot give any quantities of pipe for a given house better than one I saw working last winter. It was at Mr. John H. Dunlop's, of Toronto, Canada, remember. The house (a rose house, short-span-to-the-south), was 22 ft. wide and 200 ft. long. The pipes were 1-inch on the side wall, and two 1¼-inch about eight inches from

the roof, several feet apart. All these pipes were filled direct from the main supply (not running 200 feet and used as returns). On the two side walls there were five 1-inch on each only. There was a 1-inch return for each side, and that for the five 1-inch flows was ample.

This seemed to me remarkably little pipe, and Mr. Dunlop assured me that at 10 below zero they could keep 56 degrees with ease with about 10 lbs. of steam, and very seldom used the entire five pipes. The attached great importance to the 1¼-inch pipes near the roof in extremely cold weather, although in ordinary times they were not used. The pipes near the glass seemed to prevent that cold wave which in the best of houses seems to strike you on very cold nights and which is of course the air when suddenly cooled dropping rapidly to the lowest point in the house. This is about half the surface of pipe that would be required with hot water, however well heated. Near the manifold, where the supply enters the house, every pipe should have a valve, so that you can use just as many or as few as weather compels.

It is usual where a large amount of steam is used that two or more boilers are required. Perhaps you will use only one a great part of the season, and in several months your whole power, but one boiler should never be depended on. In case of a breakdown you may lose more in one night than two or three boilers would cost, and it is both in hot water and steam poor economy to have boilers that are just able to keep your houses comfortable in ordinary cold weather, for when extremes come, having no reserve power, you will suffer.

If your boiler is not big enough or you are deficient in pipes on these occasions you will be sending fuel up the chimney in vain, besides the injury to your crops. Put up your boiler and pipes with the understanding that you want a certain heat in your houses when the wind is blowing forty miles an hour and zero outside. Then when it is 20 degrees of frost and a clear, still night you will be in clover. In fact you will have "coal to burn." Not only on the small heating pipes should you have valves, but on all the main pipes leading to each house. I have found repeatedly that in hot water heating with small pipes it is wise economy to put in a valve wherever there is a possibility of your wanting to make an alteration or addition, or shut off one house while using others. Don't spare the valves, you can hardly tell when their need will occur.

Steam boilers with a good draught will burn a much inferior grade of coal than a cast iron hot water heater, and seldom that anthracite coal is used. The cheaper the fuel, however, the more of it, and more attention is needed.

Where steam is used a night fireman is a necessity, and one should be on the place at all hours of the night.

Heating by steam is very simple and if the water gauge is watched has no possible danger. Rise to a convenient height with your main pipe, drop from that to the time the condensed steam enters bottom of boiler again. Keep the boilers well down, and with four or five pounds of steam you will heat a large establishment with less fuel and less labor than by any other method.

Heating by Hot Water.

I beg most humbly to submit that using small wrought iron pipe in hot water heating is as much in advance over the old cast iron 4-inch pipe as the 4-inch pipe was over the brick flues. The 4-inch cast iron pipe will heat a house very well, and so did the stage coach take an emigrant from New York to Buffalo, but not as quickly or as cheaply. It seems almost irresistible now we are out of it, to smile and partly shudder at the cumbersome old pipe associated with hands covered with red lead or iron borings, Portland cement, etc., lying on your back at some difficult joint, fingers hammered up, in fact a week or two of a miserable time.

It would be useless to speak of the disadvantages of the large cast iron pipes. Just one feature, an alteration or addition to the piping, was a dreadful affair. The general use now, at least among the commercial men, of the wrought iron pipe has made that important part of greenhouse construction an easy job, in fact a pleasure. Two years ago I remember assisting at piping a violet house 125 ft. long and 20 ft. wide. At each side hung on the posts we put three 2-inch pipes. The pipes had been resting under an apple tree for several weeks and when the man hollered out that the brackets for holding the pipe were on the posts it was perhaps two hours' work for one man. Four of us lifted the pipes, put them in place and screwed them together in just two hours. Of course there was work left around the heater and a few small fittings at the end, but fancy the difference between putting up those six runs of 2-inch pipe and say four runs of cast iron 4-inch, with brick piers, etc. And how could you have got the 4-inch cast iron pipes a foot above the violets, the best place for them? I will give it up, as it would be a conundrum of which a solution is not a necessity.

A 4-inch pipe holds 16 times as much water as a 1-inch, but its radiating surface is only four times as much. So you have to heat four times as much water in a 4-inch pipe as in a 1-inch pipe, for the same amount of radiation. That is on the face of it overwhelming evidence in favor of the smaller pipe, but there may be some slight influences that bring these great advantages a trifle lower than odds of four to one. Friction retarding circulation, you will be told, is an objection to small pipe. I don't attach much importance to it, if the pipes are

laid to a true grade. Then, they will tell you that smaller pipe radiates so fast that the heat goes out of the water too quickly. So it does, but in radiating you get the heat into the house, which is just what you are after, and with much diminished volume of water you can make it hotter with less fire.

Supposing we acknowledge that there is some truth about the greater friction and the rapid cooling. If there were not, you have a superior system over the large 4-inch as four is to one. We will take off one-fourth and still the smaller pipe has a superiority of three to one. Tremendous odds. To illustrate the difference I have taken 1-inch pipe, but that is rather small. The smallest we use is 1 1-4-inch; and 150 feet is as far from the boiler as you should expect these small pipes to do good service.

One more comparison. I have several carnation houses which are heated with wrought iron pipe. Take one 19 ft. wide. On each side on the post a few inches under the plate there is a 2-inch flow running to the farther end and returning with five 1 1-4-inch pipes. They are attached to a very competent heater, and during the worst weather that house has not been below 45 degrees. It would take at least three 4-inch pipes on each side to keep that house at 45 degrees on the coldest nights. Let us see the comparative water and radiation between the large and small pipes. In the large pipes, in round figures, I have about 72 inches of radiation, or 864 inches to every lineal foot of piping. While in the smaller I have about 720 ft. of radiation for every lineal foot. Not quite so much, you see. But against that I have to heat in the big pipes about 720 cubic inches of water to every foot of piping and in the smaller pipes less than 250 cubic inches.

Now, don't you think that with less fuel I can heat that much smaller body of water to a far greater heat? I am sure I can, and do do it, and if the water comes back cooled it accelerates circulation. I will assert that by this system the pipes at 125 feet from the boiler are just about as hot as steam; perhaps it is within a degree or two. There has been a most terrible lot of rubbish and theories ventilated about hot water heating within twenty years, mostly by men who never saw a good system put up or ever studied the law by which hot water circulates. Telling people that you can place a hot water heater on the surface of the ground and get good results is wild talk, and the overhead heating craze would have been laughable if it had not misled some people. One scientist said overhead heating was right because our natural heat came from above. On that theory the gentleman should have taken when chilly a seat on Pike's Peak with an icicle for a cushion, for he would have been nearer the source of heat.

Some forty-five years ago, perhaps

before, there was published in London by Hood a volume on hot water. There has never been a better work on the same subject since. We may have found out better and cheaper modes of applying it than prevailed in his day, but all the laws of circulation which he demonstrates so finely are just the same today and always will be, for they are natural laws, and can never be altered. Hood says that the circulation of hot water was well known by the Romans, and used for heating their baths, so this wonderfully useful method of warming our houses did not originate in London, New York or Kalamazoo.

Why the hot water goes out of the flow pipe and the cold water enters is illustrated by Hood by two vessels, each holding a few gallons of water, say two 6-inch pipes, each three feet high, with a 1-inch pipe and valve connecting them at the bottom. Fill one of the pipes with water the temperature of 50 degrees and the other at a temperature of 150 degrees, filling both to exactly the same level. Open the valve and the hot water will immediately rise to a higher level than the cold, because the cold is of greater specific gravity than the hot, and has forced it to a higher level.

Now this illustrates the motive power that first starts the circulation of hot water. It is the difference between the weight of the water in the return pipe and that in the boiler. The water in the boiler being made lighter by the fire, the colder and heavier water forces it up and is replaced with cold water, so it must follow that the higher, and consequently heavier, the column of water in the return pipe the faster will be your circulation. And it follows again that the faster the circulation the hotter will your pipes be, for the water returning quickly to the fire has not time to get cool. When your return pipe near the boiler is nearly as hot as the flow where it leaves the boiler your circulation is perfect. All of which goes to prove that the lower the boiler the better the apparatus will work.

Reserve all your drop till you get near the boiler and then drop perpendicularly down. This talk about giving the pipes a rise of a foot in one hundred, or the same drop, is all bosh. If the pipes were a dead level in the house it would be perfect, but it is better to have a rise or fall of two inches in a hundred feet because you want when emptying the pipes to have a drain out. Providing your boiler is well down, and that is the very essence of the whole job, it makes no difference whether you have a slight rise in the flow pipes in the house or a slight fall. But for several reasons, matters of simplicity and convenience, I prefer after having at once raised to the highest point over the boiler that from there on there shall be a continual fall. Don't forget that one inch in a hundred feet, if truly laid, is far better than two feet, because you reserve all your drop till you get to the

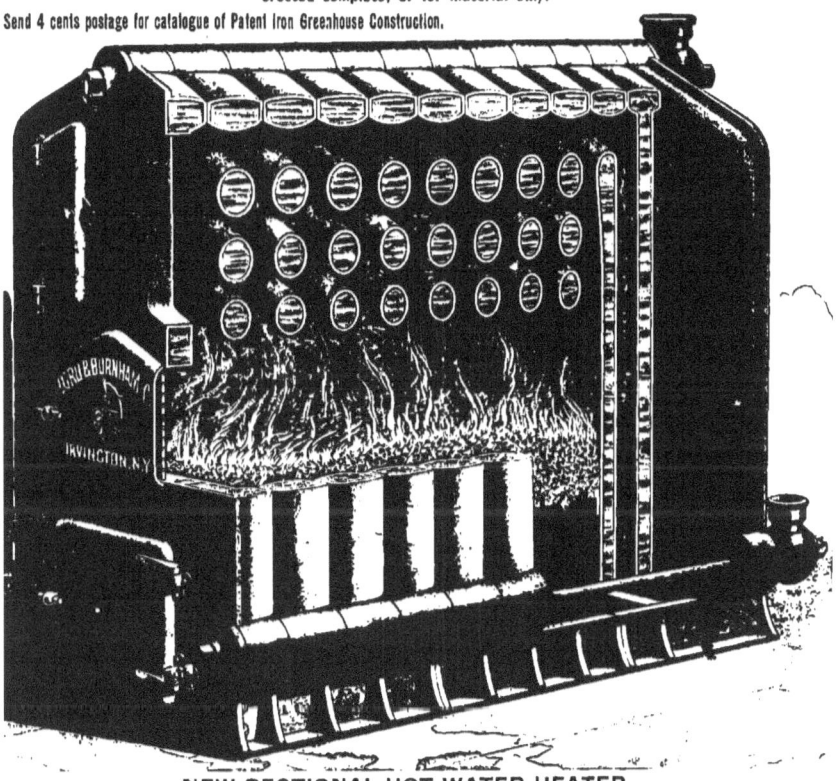

boiler. This is the most important point of all.

All kinds of boilers are used, in fact half the florists in the country have invented one of their own, and it looked a few years ago as if it was a case of "every man his own boiler maker." There are no amount in the market, some most excellent and some I have that cost a good deal of money, that as soon as I can afford it will be broken up and sold to "Isaac" for junk before they have a chance to cripple me by cracking on a cold night.

Some people praise or condemn a boiler without a fair test of what work it is doing, and unless they have houses of the same dimensions and piped alike they can't compare one with the other. Now, I happen to have four houses, each 19x125, built exactly to an inch alike and piped to one inch the same. One pair of houses leads out of the shed to the west, and the other pair to the east. As before stated everything is identical about the two pair of houses except the heaters. They are of a different make. I notice the boys attend to one twice as often as the other, I also have noticed that a third more ashes are taken from that one than the other. The damper of the first one is frequently wide open while of the other it is never more than half out. And it is also well known to my son that the one that takes the least fuel (hard coke, not gas house coke) will keep the houses five degrees higher than the extravagant one. And remarkable to say, but absolutely true, the economical one had a small violet house 125x11 tacked on to it three years ago, which is finely heated by six runs of 1 1-4 inch pipe and the following winter it took actually less fuel than it did the previous winter. That, of course, was on account of its being a mild winter.

Now here is a test. I can speak of the relative merits of these two boilers with some authority, to say that this most excellent cast iron sectional boiler is "The Royal," made by Hart & Crouse, of Utica, N. Y. For that kind of boiler it is about ideal, and the one tested with it is by no means the one I am going to sell for $1.75.

If I describe how the houses are piped it will be a better means of conveying my ideas than any instructions. The top of the boiler is about two feet below the floor of the greenhouse. It would have been lower could I have got sewerage. The flow pipe, a 3-inch (there is one on each side of boiler hut that makes no difference), rises up straight to about 8 feet above floor of shed. There is an elbow on top with a piece of 3-inch pipe leading over close to wall of greenhouse, and then a T with 2-inch openings from which a pipe leads to right and left, running over the door ways.

Now the elbow on top of the upright 3-inch pipe is the highest point in the whole system, and from that elbow there is a very slight drop till the 2-

inch pipes enter the house, one on each side, where they drop 4 or 5 ft. In the elbow is drilled in a ¾-inch pipe which runs up 20 feet or a few inches above a large tank which supplies the houses with water. The top of the pipe is bent over merely so that any drip from it would drop in the tank. From the bottom of this 150-barrel tank a 1 1-2-inch pipe leads down and enters the return pipe close to the boiler. Now, of course, the water in the ¾-inch pipe, which we will call the air pipe, is always on a level with the water in the large tank, and I think I have made out that I have about 7 lbs. pressure from that cause.

Remember it is height of water that makes pressure, not volume. There would be no more pressure at the bottom of a funnel ten feet high that was three feet wide at the top and one inch at the bottom than there would be at the bottom of an upright 1-inch pipe of the same length as the spreading funnel. How much importance to attach to this little pressure I don't know, but I am safe in allowing none. The 2-inch pipe passes through the shed wall and runs along the wall of the house about eight inches below the glass. The houses have a gradual but true down grade of two inches in their length and the flow pipe runs parallel with the plate. At the further end the pipe goes into a 2-inch manifold with five 1 1-4-inch openings from which drops a 1 1-4-inch pipe with elbows which start the five 1 1-4-inch returns on their journey back. And they have a drop back to the shed of two inches. going into a 2-inch manifold again and joining the return pipe from the other side of the house go through the wall about even, or just below, level of the walks, and then drop perpendicularly to bottom of boiler. So you can call this the down hill plan if you like, for after leaving the first 3-inch elbow at the highest point it is one continuous drop, although for 125 feet the drop is not perceptible.

Why this is better than having a rise in the pipes to the further end is because you would have to put cocks at the highest point to let out air, or open stand pipes, or a small pipe tapped in and running up higher than the tank which supplied the heater. In the way I have described there are no air valves to watch, no feeding cistern to fill, no thumping or cracking of pipes. It works smoothly and perfectly and as long as you have water in the tank your pipes are full. The big tank is no advantage and a barrel holding a few gallons, raised above the highest point in your sys-

EXPERT ADVICE
On All Matters Pertaining to
GREENHOUSE HEATING.

HENRY W. GIBBONS,
Steam and Hot Water Heating Engineer,
136 Liberty St., NEW YORK, N. Y.
CATALOGUES, FOUR CENTS.

tem, would be just as well if you kept it full.

This plan can be extended to any dimensions, providing you do not violate any of the principles. Always remember that hot water when circulating will never go down hill if there is any chance for it to go up. So let all tees and manifolds be laid horizontally, so that where the water has to be spread out into several pipes there is as much inclination for it to flow into one as another.

Like the main supply pipes in steam heating if you heat many pipes from one or two outlets only, you must start off with a 6 or 8-inch pipe and reduce by degrees as the main pipe has less water to supply. The 2-inch flows supply the five 1 1-4-inch quoted in excellent shape, but for a rose house these would take at least eight 1 1-4-inch on each side, a 3-inch flow would be small enough.

Where it is not convenient to carry the flow pipe up over the doors, but enter the house perhaps level with the floor and then rise up to the plate, or even continue along under the bench, the flow pipe would have a rise of an inch or two to the farther end and a corresponding drop back in the returns. At the highest point farthest from the boiler tap in a 1-2 or ¾-inch pipe and let it run up to the roof anywhere out of the way. This is much better than pet cocks, which are so easily forgotten, and the automatic air valves get out of order. The feeding cistern to supply the boiler can be in the shed and should of course be a little lower than the top of the small pipe, which is called the air pipe, at the farther end. Now, if the boiler is low enough this system will work admirably and would be perhaps more suited for a private greenhouse or show house than the first system described.

I have never had much experience with water under pressure, unless the pressure of our city mains constitutes that system. Our city water has a pressure of about 35 lbs. to the square inch, and my experience with it is a very cheap heating system for a store or office. Wishing to heat a flower store in this city, which is some 19 ft. by 80, I put a small heater in the cellar. It is simply three lengths of 3-inch pipe, each about three feet long, and run into a manifold at both ends. The coil is resting on two 4-inch brick walls about two feet from the floor and is bricked over top, sides and ends. One end of this coil is raised about three inches and from it rising to the ceiling is the 1 1-4-inch flow, which leads off, and by the help of some tees connects with three radiators on floor of store, and from the other end of the radiators the returns drop to the lower end of the coil. There are two natural gas burners under this very simple heater, which in the coldest weather has never been turned on more than one-third its force.

A 1-inch pipe from the city water is connected with the lowest part of the coil and the valve is never closed, so

there is always a pressure of 35 lbs. on the pipe and radiators. The highest part of the system is the top of the radiators, and in them is a pet cock which should be opened every day to let out air, but often is not for weeks, and in a radiator it is not of so much consequence.

There is nothing more about it, only the radiators can be made red hot; a great success. If a strong fire should expand the water in the heater it has to find room by driving the water back into the mains. The whole thing cost less than $50, and $5 worth of gas was consumed in the coldest month. Now this system could be used with great success wherever you have a boiler that would stand the pressure. You could use it on either the uphill or downhill systems, but you could not have any open air vents, and unless you trusted to the automatic air valves you would have to daily open the pet cocks at the highest point.

I have seen pipes arranged in many ways, including the old 4-inch pipe system, put up by the experts of New York, and well they do their work, but of the various systems the one first described is the most satisfactory in every way.

Where a considerable range is heated with one boiler, although some of the cast iron boilers are excellent there is nothing better than a tubular boiler, such as you would use for making steam, only that you do not want the large space left that is occupied with steam. You want it all tubes to the top or it would hold too much water.

I have said very little about arrangement of the pipes. Where the benches are away from the walls there is no place so good for the pipes as to be hung on the wall. The heat strikes the glass quickly just where it is needed. There is no strong heat near the plants, and there is a free radiation not hindered by benches. Sometimes this is not possible, then the pipes can be laid under the benches, but it will much simplify matters if you can always let the flow be on the wall near the glass.

I think overhead heating, so called, unless to a very limited extent, a great mistake. I have tried it to my loss and pulled it down. In the most severe weather you may get the benefit of the pipes over head, but in ordinary winter weather much of your heat is thrown away, and why have any there? Heat rises quickly enough, and if your pipes are hot the heat rising will soon reach all parts of the house, especially the top.

HEDERA (IVY).

Till the introduction of the galax leaves the ivy was of much importance to us and a large quantity is still used and possibly always will be. Helix is the common ivy and it has innumerable varieties and forms. Some of the variegated varieties make most beautiful pot plants, and if they could be produced cheaply enough

would make the best of basket and vase plants.

The common ivy is not a success here out of doors. They will do fairly well on a north wall for some years and then we get a winter that kills. In Europe, dead trees, and live ones, too, and on ruined towers and old buildings you see the ivy climbing everywhere. "Creeping where no life is seen, a rare old plant is the ivy green." And Gray says: "Save that from yonder ivy mantled tower, the moping owl does to the moon complain." So the ivy must have crept its way to the top of the lofty tower, for it mantled it.

The ivy roots easily during spring, and if planted out early in good soil will make fine plants by following October, when they should be lifted and potted in 4-inch pots. One advantage of the ivy is they will winter under a bench in a cool house about as well as on the bench. We use them largely in vases and veranda boxes and they suffer neither from heat, drought nor wind.

To produce leaves for designs I have not found them a great success beneath a bench. Although I planted a lot beneath a carnation bench in good soil, I prefer a wall where they will get the daylight, and such is generally to be found, somewhere on the place.

HEDGE PLANTS.

If you supply shrubs you will be sure to be asked to plant hedges. Some of our American cities have distinctly beautiful residence streets and the uncommon feature always noticeable to Rudyard Kipling and less illustrious "Outlanders" is the absence of fences or hedges. There is nothing but the well kept lawn, the group of shrubs and trees, or perhaps a flower bed, between the sidewalk and the residence. There is no finer specimen of this beautiful style of street in America than our own Delaware avenue, Buffalo, N. Y. We would never be guilty of advocating any other style, but whether we would or not there is a fast growing tendency to put up iron fences, or plant hedges, and when they are asked for we must be ready.

We will say in defense of a hedge that where an iron fence is used we think a well kept hedge behind it is an improvement. Or where there is a retaining wall a small hedge on the bank is a finish to it. Or where the lot finishes on the street with a terrace we think a hedge is in place. And a well kept hedge can hardly be out of place anywhere near the street. But it is all in the quality of the hedge. We trust for the credit of our city and its pride, the residence streets, that stone walls or Norway spruce hedges will never be built to prevent the passer-by from admiring the trees and well kept lawns and flower gardens of our wealthy citizens. A good and happy life on the avenue is not fostered by admiring your own lot alone. You see in a month more of your neighbor's than you do of your own, and a resident keeps his grounds neat and trim and beautiful because others shall admire them, the knowledge of which gratifies the owner. It resolves itself, like many other good deeds, into a species of selfishness; by doing good to others you have tickled and pleased your own self.

But let us get back to the hedge. There are mighty few hedges seen in our cities that are properly kept, either of the evergreen or deciduous kind. The best specimens of hedges I have seen in this country were at Newport, mostly privet. And the finest evergreen hedges I have seen are in Toronto, of Norway spruce. But the perfection of a hedge in every feature was a hemlock hedge (Abies canadensis) in the nurseries of George Leslie & Son. Hemlock is without doubt the finest and most perfect in form of all evergreen hedges. There are some terrible specimens of privet hedges scattered over our city and others. Before they are three feet high a western hog could run through them without disturbing many of their twigs. When like this they are simply an abomination. The fault is mostly with the proprietor, who insists on immediate effect and says "no, no, don't cut it down; I want some show for my money; leave it alone, we will trust to its filling out." Which it never does. And a privet hedge is allowed to run up two feet the first season and then be just topped an inch or so.

Another reason for the poor hedges you see is that they are seldom trimmed properly. Let it be an evergreen or a deciduous hedge it should not be cut up square, and sometimes you see them worse than that, even broader at the top than the bottom. If they run up square how are the lower branches going to get equal light or rains? They soon begin to lose their lower branches and then they are ruined. I would call a fine privet hedge one that was three feet at the base with the sides sloping in till the rounded top was not more than 18 inches through, and the hedge not over 4 1-2 or 5 feet high. The same with the evergreen hedges, when broad at the base and narrowing to the top they can be kept for years in perfect health and green to the bottom. Midsummer is the best time to prune evergreen hedges and they look much better cut with a knife than the shears. Hedges of deciduous shrubs like privet are best and quickest sheared, which can be done in early spring before growth and again in midsummer.

In planting evergreen hedges you must begin with small, compact, perfect trees; if you don't start right you never will have a hedge. The best evergreen for the purpose is first of all the hemlock spruce; it has a grace and droop to it that no other evergreen hedge has. Next the Norway spruce, and then the American and Chinese arbor-vitae.

The deciduous hedges will always be more planted in city lots, and for this purpose are certainly to be preferred.

The finest for most purposes is the Californian and English privet (Ligustrum ovalifolium and L. vulgaris). The Californian was considerably killed this past winter. If a fine, dense hedge is wanted, a double row of the privet should be always planted, the rows one foot apart and the plants nine or ten inches in the row. For several seasons they should be cut back to within six inches of the previous season's growth, then you will have a solid hedge that a cat would have difficulty in squeezing through.

Berberis Thunbergii makes a magnificent hedge. Its habit is spreading and the worst treatment will not prevent it becoming dense and bushy. It can be either trimmed in formal shape or left to grow naturally, when it is one of the handsomest of shrubs. Its small leaves are always handsome, coloring to beautiful tints in the autumn, and covered with its fruit. It is a most hardy, easily transplanted shrub.

There is a hedge of Pyrus (Cydonia) japonica here and there throughout the country. One I have in mind is on a retaining wall near the home of the late Mr. Parkman, the Indian historian, in the suburbs of Boston. It was in flower when I was escorted that way, and it was gorgeous. It is an admirable hedge shrub, can be cut after blooming to any dimensions, and is simply gorgeous in the early spring, and very hardy.

Other trees and shrubs can be used for the purpose. I have only made a selection and my chief object was to tell you that a hedge cannot be made in one year, and will not do unless all parts of the hedge get a share of sun and rain.

HELIOTROPE.

This old favorite has possibly been grown as long as there has been any greenhouse to protect it in winter. All we grow are varieties of H. peruvianum. It always was a favorite for our summer flower garden, either in beds or in the mixed border. As a cut flower it has its delicious fragrance to commend it, but it wilts rather quickly when cut.

You can neither lift old plants with success nor root the cuttings that you take from the plants grown outside, so you should always grow a few plants over summer in pots, and move them to the greenhouse before frost, when if the shoots are shortened back you will get young, tender cuttings that root quickly where there is some bottom heat. No cuttings root more quickly or surely than heliotrope in January, February and March, and your stock can be then increased to any extent. Young plants soon spoil if stunted in small pots, and to keep them thrifty they must be shifted on and occasionally pinched. For this reason you don't want a large stock too early in the season. This is a plant that does finely in a mild hotbed after middle of April. Thousands are sold in our markets every spring.

You often see a plant of heliotrope

planted out at the end of a greenhouse covering a large space. Such a one I have. It gets cut back to the main shoots every September, and during winter yields bushels of flowers, which are occasionally asked for. It also provides me with an abundance of cuttings at any time during winter that I may need them.

Heliotropes are often grown as standards and are used as conservatory plants or plunged out in the flower garden. They certainly make a fine appearance. Say a bed of heliotrope of the ordinary sized plants, into which plunge a dozen of the 3-foot standards; or any other dwarf flowering plant could be the groundwork. They are easily grown.

Choose a strong, healthy young plant, and without any pinching encourage it to run up 3 feet, and then stop it, keeping all lateral growths pinched off except a few near the top. You can let these plants rest in a cool house with little water during winter and start growing again in March. The head can be left to grow naturally as you would a standard rose, but they look much better tied to a wire frame as we do standard chrysanthemums. I can't say that the standard heliotrope is a good investment for the florist, but when time and space allows they are a great ornament to our flower gardens.

Heliotrope is popularly supposed to be easily injured by tobacco smoke. If a strong dose is first given it does injure it, but after a few fumigations it does not notice it more than a geranium. Why should it not get inured to it? I have noticed frequently that it does, although it does not need any smoke.

A rust is its worst enemy, which will not attack it unless it gets root bound and stunted. The heliotrope grows finely in a temperature of 50 degrees, but will not endure the slightest frost. There are constantly new varieties being sent out, a few good ones are:

LE CID: Semi-dwarf, robust, large panicles, mauve, with clear white eye.

LE POITEVINE: Great size, mauve, violet and azure; very free and continuous in bloom.

THE GIANT: Enormous panicle of bloom, color a rosy violet, white eye.

CAMELEON: Bright blue, large panicles and florets.

ALBERT DELAUX: Pretty variegated foliage, purple flowers.

WHITE LADY: The best of the white or light varieties.

HIBISCUS.

The species we see in the greenhouses is H. rosa-sinensis and its varieties. They are hardly a florist's plant, yet their bright, shining leaves and showy, brilliant flowers make them desirable for the private conservatory.

They thrive in any good, coarse loam, with some well rotted manure added. They soon make large plants and need a liberal sized pot, and plenty of water and syringing when growing. Their brilliant flowers come on the young growths. In winter they will do in a temperature of 50 degrees, and keep on the dry side. When starting them into more growth in April, shorten back the shoots; the young growths will be all the stronger. The flowers are of various colors and are both single and double.

The young growths root readily in April in some warm sand, but should not be exposed to the sun or too much air.

HOLLYHOCK.

This stately plant is seen in the large grounds of the millionaire and in the small piece of garden that the farmer or his wife devotes to "posies." It is handsome anywhere, and it is particularly suitable for a border whose background is a hedge or belt of trees. There appears to be an increased call for them of late. Some years ago the hollyhock disease discouraged many would-be growers of this old favorite, but little is now heard of the disease, and we have seen no trouble from it in several years.

Hollyhocks are of very easy culture and few plants will pay for the labor with an equal amount of flowers and fine effect. If they required the same care and labor that a dahlia does, there would be less excuse for not growing them, but they do not. When once planted out, they will take care of themselves, only requiring one stout stake to support their main stem and tying as they grow.

The best strain if allowed to remain without transplanting for four or five years will deteriorate in quality and revert back to the single-flowered form. Little regard is now paid to named varieties, because the best strains give you all the desirable colors and the finest flowers; in fact, plants less than one year old give the finest flowers. Plants that have flowered and are carried over winter are hardy in our ordinary winters, but should be protected by some litter placed around the plant and a few evergreen boughs over them.

Where the winters are not so severe seed is sown in May or June out of doors and the young plants transplanted into beds, where they remain all winter in the open ground, and are planted out and sold the following spring. This is all right for the man with a catalogue trade, but is not the way to produce the finest plants and flowers.

Sow in flats or in the cold-frame in early August. If you have no other accommodation, you can transplant four or five inches apart in the frames, and in the three or four months of severest winter weather protect with glass, and transplant to their permanent position as soon as the ground is dry in the spring. Still better, transplant from the seed beds into flats or

2-inch pots and in October shift into 4-inch pots, keeping them plunged in the cold-frame till very cold weather, and then winter them in a very cool house. A violet temperature, or less, will do. Don't defer planting till you put out your tropical bedding plants, but get them into the border as soon as you can work the ground. The latter method is the one I have seen followed with the very grandest results.

Hollyhocks like a heavy soil, dug deeply and with plenty of animal manure worked in. If the spring is dry, they should receive a soaking twice a week. As fine hollyhocks as I have ever seen were planted in a stiff clay, into which was dug a lot of cow manure. They want a good stout stake to keep the wind from blowing them over, and sometimes when the side shoots are loaded with flowers they will want supporting to the main stem.

Chater's strain was for years the best obtainable, and is, I think, still offered by some of the leading seedsmen.

When the plants are small, as a preventive of fungous diseases they can be dipped into a pail of the ammoniacal solution.

The best strains now embrace colors from the darkest maroon (almost black) through beautiful shades of red and pink, yellow and pale straw, to pure white. Three feet apart is close enough to plant them, and if strong plants, more room is better.

HOTBEDS.

These primitive greenhouses may never be seen at many establishments, and where only cut flowers are grown there is no occasion for them, but to the florist who grows an assortment of bedding plants they are of the greatest assistance. As is well known there is a number of our soft-wooded plants that grow much faster and thriftier in a hotbed than in the best greenhouse that you can possibly give them.

The vegetable grower starts preparations for his hotbeds in February, but the florist does not need to, and for our latitude the hotbed is of most use from early April on to end of May, and occasionally during summer, where plants like cyclamen want a little bottom heat.

The frames are usually 18 inches at back and 12 inches in front, and for convenience made to fit three or four sash of 6 feet by 3 feet 6 inches each. When hotbeds are used on a large scale and where drainage is good the earth is excavated to a depth of 18 inches up to a foot above the surface. There is an advantage in this because the late frost does not cool the fermenting material. Wherever you have them let them be all together, for the larger the mass of manure the slower it will cool.

The first requisite is some good, fresh straw manure, and sometimes that alone is used. If you have some

dry leaves of the previous fall you can mix in a third of those, and if you are on good terms with the local brewer the spent hops of the brewery is a splendid material for the purpose. Hops heat violently, and should not be used alone, or the heat will be too violent for a time, and will too quickly subside. I would call one-half stable manure, one-fourth leaves and one-fourth fresh hops a fine mixture.

You can not get all your material in one day, but when you have collected enough to begin operations the whole mass, whatever it is, should be turned over once into a big pile and thoroughly shaken out, mixing the long with the short. When the pile begins to show signs of heating, then form your hotbeds. Lay out a space 18 inches larger and broader than the frame or frames, and allow for an 18-inch path between the frames, but path and all to be built up with the manure.

Build the sides up square and when making the beds one man should throw on the manure and another be shaking and spreading it evenly and continually tramping on it, so that when it sinks, which it will do as it settles, it will sink evenly. If the material is dry, have the hose near at hand and every layer of three or four inches give the surface a good sprinkling. It will prevent the heat being so violent, but will make it last longer.

When the bed or material has reached a height of 2 feet put on your frames and see that they are straight and square or the sash won't fit, and above all see that the frames are not "winding." If you sight across the top edges back and front and they line with each other, then they are not winding. Continue to build up with the material till you are nearly to the top of the frame. Then throw in four or five inches of the plunging material. This could be sawdust, tan bark, or even sifted ashes, but for the sake of the hotbed material for after use, which is invaluable to the plant man, we prefer to put on four or five inches of some light soil that we have used for some other crop.

Don't plunge any plants in the soil for five or six days, or till the most violent heat has passed, and keep a little ventilation on to allow the vapor to escape. When the violent heat has subsided get in your plants and the growth they will make will be remarkable. And so will the growth of weeds from the soil. But weeding must be attended to as all other duties.

Only "the man who never forgets" should have the care of the hotbeds. A cold night is often followed by a bright, sunny day, and the sun seems to accelerate the heat of the bed, and if they are neglected till, say 11 a. m., you run a good chance of having your whole crop burnt up, which has happened occasionally to most of us. A little ventilation at first, and a little more in an hour, is the way to care for a hotbed. And close down early in the afternoon. With the uniform moisture and heat at the roots and the ammonia charged atmosphere, the growth of many plants is prodigious.

When hotbeds are started early, say 1st of April, you should always cover them nightly with mats or shutters, the former much preferred both for warmth and convenience. You must not trust to the bare glass on nights of sharp frost. The surface of the soil gets quickly cool and then Jack Frost touches the plants, whose tops are very near the glass.

The hotbeds are a great relief to us in our crowded state in April and May. And more than that when the beds are emptied the material is tossed up on a pile and chopped down once or twice during fall, and there you have an excellent substitute for leaf-mould, with some ammonia in it. If not, its mechanical condition is what you want for all of your soft-wooded, and many of the hard-wooded, plants.

HOYA.

These hot-house climbers are seldom seen now. The days of short-stemmed flowers are gone, and hoyas are only found in the private collection. H. carnosa was once a very common plant in our greenhouses, and we have all heard the dear old lady tell us hundreds of times that her "wax plant did not flower."

H. carnosa and H. bella are the two best known. The latter is a beautiful but more delicate plant. They root easily in the spring from the tops of the growths. If a specimen is wanted they should be trained on a wire frame. They like plenty of sun and ventilation in summer time, and in winter should be given a rest by keeping rather dry and in a house at about 50 degrees.

Their waxy flowers, in fine umbels, are very pretty, but they are not a florist's flower.

HYACINTH.

See Bulbs.

HYDRANGEA.

These are among the most important of our decorative flowering plants. Large quantities are sold for Easter church decorations, and later on large plants are in demand for outside decoration. The hardy Hydrangea paniculata grandiflora is one of the finest of our hardy shrubs.

H. hortensis and its variety Otaksa is the common hydrangea of our greenhouses. The flowers of Otaksa are nearly always sterile, and from that fact arise their fine, showy heads of bloom. The normal color of Otaksa is a beautiful flesh pink, but it varies with certain soil, and in some parts they assume a beautiful blue color. Iron dust or filings in the soil is said to produce this. If so, it cannot be done with one season's treatment, but must be followed up from the time the plant is first rooted. When Otaksa is well colored its beautiful shade of pink can scarcely be improved by changing to a blue.

All the hydrangeas can be readily rooted from the young growths in February and March. Old plants that are given a little heat in the winter will give you fine cuttings, and they should be short, stout pieces of the very latest growth, which root quickly in the sand. For early spring use the cuttings should be propagated in February, potted on till June and have the tops pinched out, when they can go into a 5-inch pot and be plunged outside on a dry bottom, giving them plenty of room between the plants. If they grow freely give them a 6-inch in August.

After the first few mild frosts, which does them no harm, take them into a light house. By this time you have some chrysanthemum benches empty and can give the hydrangeas a good bench. Till the New Year they do not want any forcing, but after that if they are wanted for Easter they must get 55 degrees at night, and increase it if you see they are going to be late. Plants that are not wanted for Easter can rest in a very cool house, in fact under a bench till February, and be given enough water to keep them from shriveling, after which they can be cleaned up, shifted, if necessary, and started growing. These will be in good flower about the end of May, when there is a good demand for them.

I failed to mention that the earlier forced plants should also be given a shift into a 6 or 7-inch pot when they start to grow at New Year's. Otaksa is about hardy in the milder parts of Europe, so it does not want anything but a cool greenhouse except when forced.

Hydrangeas, especially the hortensis type, are great feeders, and should have a rather heavy but good, fresh loam with a fourth of decayed manure, and some bone flour added at the last shift will help them. Water they want in great abundance when growing and flowering, and if allowed to suffer for it they soon show it, and will show it later by yellow leaves.

There is little trouble with hydrangeas from insects. You can fumigate them should fly trouble them, and although red spider will attack the flowers it should never be allowed as a daily syringing should be given them.

Plants that have not sold should have the flowers removed by cutting back the stem to within a few eyes of the pot. Remove some of the soil and give them a shift and plunge outside for the summer. They will make fine plants for another spring. The principal object to attain with any of these plants is a strong growth in summer, and well ripened wood in the fall. So bright sun, cool nights, and a lessening of the supply of water, are the requisites.

When hydrangeas get into 10 and 12-inch pots they take up too much room unless you are assured of a good sale. They make magnificent plants in tubs for the lawn, but those that have developed their flowers under glass are not valuable for this purpose, as they

soon lose the beauty of their flowers. The best plants for this purpose that I have seen were wintered for several years in the basement of a coach house. There was no artificial heat. It was not too dark, and with an occasional watering the plants remained dormant till it was time to return them to the lawn, when they came along naturally about the same as the hardy shrubs, and the flowers lasted the greater part of the summer. Some such place as this should be provided for large plants, as the greenhouse, however cool, will bring them on too fast.

Some growers adopt a different plan with the young plants. Instead of growing them on in pots they plant them out in good, deep, rich soil, and lift and pot in September or October. I have often done this, and for late spring sales it is a good plan, but for the Easter lot I prefer to grow them in pots all summer.

The kinds forced include Thomas Hogg, a pure white variety of hortensis. Paniculata is also forced in some places, but we think we have better plants. There is a finer variety with purplish red stems and highly colored pink flowers, rather a tall growth but very handsome, H. hortensis Otaksa is the finest variety, giving the largest head of bloom, and forcing well.

IMPATIENS SULTANI.

This little perennial flowering balsam is not so much seen as it was a dozen years ago. Nearly all the year it is covered with bright scarlet flowers and is chiefly valuable as a bright flower for the greenhouse in summer when most of our flowering plants are done. It roots readily from cuttings in warm sand, or can be raised from seed. A rather rich, open soil suits it, with plenty of water. Plants in 4 and 5-inch pots are most useful.

Being from tropical Africa it should not be kept lower than 55 degrees in the winter, but any greenhouse does it well in summer, and it does not want much shade.

When plants get shabby from the want of a shift it is cheaper and better to throw them away, as young and thrifty plants are so easily raised.

IRESINE (ACHYRANTHES.)

These are known almost entirely under the name of achyranthes, but iresine is correct. They, with the coleus, are the principal plants used to furnish color to the tropical and foliage beds.

Their culture is so well known and so simple that little need be said. They thrive in any ordinary good soil. They have an advantage over the coleus in that they are not nearly so tender and will grow during winter when the coleus would starve. Outside, though injured by the first frost, they will not drop their leaves when the thermometer gets down to 40 degrees, as do many coleus.

We grow them not only as a bedding plant, but for our vases and veranda boxes they are most useful, and do not monopolize the whole space to the sacrifice of other plants, as do the stronger growing coleus.

Green fly attacks them if smoking is neglected, and mealy bugs like them, but that can be thoroughly cleaned off when you start a new batch of cuttings.

Nothing can possibly root better than iresine at all times of the year. We select a few cuttings from outside that are clean and healthy in September, and from a few dozen of each kind a large lot can be produced by bedding time. A hotbed grows them thrifty and quickly and gives you a chance to harden them off. To grow fast for cuttings they should have a temperature of 60 degrees, but will thrive finely in 10 degrees less.

I. Herbstii is the useful sort we know as Verschaffeltii; finely colored, habit spreading and free.

I. Herbstii aurea reticulata is the variegated form.

I. Lindenii is more erect; narrow leaves, deep, rich color; a fine bedding plant.

There is also another variety, or I believe a species (the correct name I cannot find) with smaller, rounded leaf, of a fine "bottle green" color; in contrast with a lighter foliage plant this is the best of all.

JASMINUM.

Of the several species of these sweet scented shrubs there is only one that florists cultivate, and that now is most often conspicuous by its absence. But we all know J. grandiflorum. A plant that I can remember as long ago as I can think of any plant was a large bush of J. revolutum, which for the larger part of the summer was covered with its sweet yellow blossoms. But that was in the temperate climate of the south coast of England. Here it is not hardy.

J. grandiflorum needs a temperature of 50 degrees during winter. The young growths root readily in the spring, and if planted out after frost is gone and kept pinched they make fine bushy little plants and can be lifted and potted, and will flower in October and November. They can not be called a showy plant and would receive no attention if it were not for their delicious fragrance.

The jasmine is no more a climber than a heliotrope, but if you want the flowers the best way is to plant one out at the end of a carnation house and in the spring prune it back, and during summer keep it pinched so that the flowering is retarded to late fall, when for weddings there is often a call for it.

Unfortunately when asked for jasmine for a bride's bouquet the sweet flower is gone, and again when the flower is ready the bride is not.

Any good loam will grow the jasminum.

KALMIA.

This is known among us as the "Mountain Laurel," and is the plant that furnishes the fine glossy sprays that make such admirable wreathing for our winter festivities. This is a truly broad leaved evergreen, but as I had occasion to remark under the head of "Hardy Shrubs," it is in most soils and localities very disappointing when transported away from its native mountains. Those who have never seen a mountain side covered with the pinkish white flowers of the kalmia have little idea what a lovely shrub it is on its native Alleghanies. It is widely distributed.

For an early June wedding (about the time it is usually in full flower) we have tried it in wreathing. Its appearance is fine, but the waxy florets never cease dropping, which precludes its use when in flower.

Neat little plants, well set with buds, are now imported from Europe suitable for forcing. They can be potted and kept in cold-frame till time to start them in the houses. If wanted for Easter, give them six weeks in a temperature of 50 degrees, and near flowering time a little more. Though very beautiful when in full flower we do not attach much value to them, and nine customers out of ten would in preference buy an Indian azalea.

KOENIGA (SWEET ALYSSUM.)

The double form of this little plant is quite important to the florist whose business includes flower gardening, and particularly for the edges of veranda boxes and vases. Sprays of its small white flowers were formerly much in demand for funeral designs, and plants were often grown on the edges of carnation beds where the flowers could hang over the walks, and I have seen whole benches devoted to its cultivation. As a cut flower it is not now so much in favor, but as a flower garden plant it is most useful. We lift a few old plants in September, cutting them back, and from the young tender growths get lots of cuttings, or young, suitable growths from outside will give you stock. During winter you can multiply it by cuttings ad libitum.

Here is another plant that we find the mild hotbed suits finely. You should have a large lot in 3-inch pots early in April, when if shifted into 3-inch and put in the hotbed they make fine plants for use in boxes and vases end of May.

The large double flowering is the most useful. The single or true species is always raised from seed which is sown out of doors in spring with the summer annuals.

Tom Thumb is a very dwarf, compact form and is used for carpet bedding. Raised from seed sown in February.

LANTANA.

A genus of tropical evergreen shrubs having very pretty flowers, mostly white, pink and orange. They are

sometimes used as greenhouse plants for summer decoration, but it is as flower garden plants that we use them. Our summer climate suits them finely and they grow very freely. They cannot be used for any set design, but for the mixed border, or even in a mass, they are very effective. The odor of the leaf is not at all agreeable and the flower for cutting useless, but for all that it is a very desirable, free growing and flowering summer plant.

It is troubled with no insects or diseases and thrives in any ordinary compost. Grow a plant or two of each of the most desirable varieties in 4 or 5-inch pots over summer plunged outside, and at the approach of frost bring them in and store in any house where the temperature does not go below 50 degrees. After New Year's cut these plants back a little and start in a warmer house, and keep syringed. You will soon have a number of young shoots, which root readily in our ordinary propagating bed. From the time you bring in the plants in the fall till you start them growing, keep them rather dry. We sell them in 3-inch pots, which is large enough, as they grow very fast when planted out.

LAPAGERIA.

This is one of the very handsomest greenhouse climbers. The pendent flowers are so rich looking that when a long spray of the plant is cut with its flowers attached nothing can surpass it in beauty. Such sprays were seen at the Boston convention in 1890, being part of the decoration of the exhibit that received the first premium for wedding arrangement. The flowers are three or four inches long, resembling a miniature inverted wine glass, and of great substance. They appears at the axils of the leaves. The leaf is rather small, dark green, and the stems long and wiry.

They want a cool, shaded house in summer and will thrive in a very cool house in winter. A magnificent plant of the variety alba covers the roof (or did) in the glazed corridor at the entrance to Veitch's nursery, Chelsea, England, and I was informed it had many times had to endure several degrees of frost. It was then (August) covered with its magnificent flowers. Unfortunately, cut close to the stem the single flower would be of little use to us, and you would have to possess a fine plant to afford the cutting of flowering sprays.

It is often grown in large pots and trained on a wire trellis. It is, however, much better planted out in the border of a house with a limit to the amount of room the roots can spread. I have tried it here and find it does not like our hot summers, so it should be in a position where you can shade during summer and give plenty of air. A thorough good drainage to the border or tub in which it is planted is of first importance. A good compost would be coarse fibrous loam with a tenth of decayed cow manure, and to that add another tenth of old broken up mortar or crushed charcoal.

They are propagated by layering the ends of strong shoots or from seed. Young plants were once very expensive. They are now obtainable at a moderate cost. When raised from seed they vary both in size and color, so fine varieties are increased by layers.

Slugs will eat the tops of the young asparagus-like shoots, but cotton batting will stop them. Tobacco smoke will keep down fly and thrip, and syringing, which the plant delights in throughout the spring and summer, will prevent red spider and mealy bug. There is only one species (Lapageria rosea), but there is a pure white form and from seedlings have been produced intermediate colors. It is not a florist's plant, but yet one that any gardener should be proud to grow well for its aristocratic beauty.

LAWNS—MAKING AND THEIR CARE.

A fine, well kept lawn is a source of pleasure and pride to the owner, and how unseemly it would be to see a fifty thousand dollar mansion surrounded by a weedy, ill kept lawn. I have remarked some years ago, perhaps only to myself, that the lawns of the temperate and moist parts of Europe (such as Great Britain) were made to walk on; ours are made to look at. "Keep off the grass" is assuredly more frequently seen here than there. "The Emerald Isle" gets its poetic designation because the grass is green the year 'round. Ours in summer, such as this of 1899, is brown in color, and for months in winter an "invisible green." So we prize our lawns, spend money on them, and pay large water bills for the privilege of frequently spoiling them, but withal I must say that for trimness and neatness and greenness in our cities our lawns will compare most favorably with those I saw in England fourteen years ago. In fact, the latter were a disappointment, and badly needed the water cart or hose.

Whether you use sod or seed to make a lawn, the ground should be dug or plowed a good eight or nine inches deep; the deeper the roots can go down in the soil, the less your grass will dry out in summer. If you cannot afford that amount of good top soil you should at least have the soil dug that deep, and into it work a good lot of well rotted manure. Break it up with plow or spade, so that the roots will go down into it. If for sodding, you should have at least two inches of good surface loam, so that the roots will quickly take hold.

In grading a piece of ground you may have had depressions to fill up in some spots several feet deep. In other places you have had to take off the surface, leaving that part very solid. The filled up portion will be sure to sink, so it should be got down to its permanent grade either by ramming or by water. In small areas, such as

where excavations have been made for sewers, there is no rammer equal to the hose. Flood it with water, if practicable, and that will take it down solid. This is particularly true of clay.

Obtain the best and cleanest sod you can, and here is a chance for you to pull out the dandelion and plantain; their roots are severed in cutting the sod, and it takes little time to pull out the tops with the short pieces of root. It is seldom we get sod that is evenly cut, but if the ground has been nicely graded and the soil not too solid, you can overcome that, and a good heavy roller will flatten down small inequalities. There is nothing more to do but give the sod a good soaking of water. In a few days pass the mowing machine over it and you have a lawn pleasing to the eye, and if you are a reasonable person your eye will not see it as it is today, but will picture it after a month's growth and several cuttings, and your prophetic vision will be looking on something like the surface of a billiard table.

Where there is any quantity of lawn to make or renew, seeding is always preferable to sodding. Not alone does it make a better looking lawn, better grass and better quality all round, but it is far cheaper. The same care in digging deep and making is essential, and the top two inches of surface should be of good, friable soil, that the delicate little plants may get a good start.

You can, when preparing for seed, put on an absolutely perfect grade, whether it be for a bowling green, which is level, or a gradual fall to any point, or a pleasing slope in any direction. When I say you can, I mean you can if you have an eye and know how to handle the rake, and you are not supposed to be leveling or grading if you can't. Some men have a great gift at this kind of work and some are created to play "Golf" "Gaawf."

In small, defined areas, when seeding it is a good plan to lay a strip of sod around the margin. Sometimes a bed for flowers or shrubs is laid out on the lawns. If a strip of sod, say a foot wide, is laid around these at a correct grade, they are a good guide when leveling, or what may be called "putting on the finishing touch" for intervening spaces.

I may have rather an elaborate way of sowing grass seed, but it answers well. When you have finished raking and have the surface as nearly perfect as your eye tells you, give the whole a light rolling. You will see much plainer then any little inequalities than when the ground was left rough by the rake. Mend any imperfections and roll those places again where you disturb the soil. Then sow the seed on the smooth surface. Next pass over the surface with a rake, not raking as if you had stones and rubbish to rake or leveling to do, but let the teeth of the rake pass backwards and forwards lightly over the surface. This will just work in the seeds, or enough of

them, for if one in a hundred grows you have enough. After that light raking pass over again with a light roller.

Just one digression. How pleasant it is to see a man with his back bent (or your own) and handling the rake as an expert, for expertness can be exercised with a rake as well as with a bat, a ball, or a billiard cue. Don't handle the rake like the interesting school marm among the hay fields of her country cousins during vacation. Men that are expert with these simple tools and keep sober are never out of employment.

Sodding is done as soon after frost as the ground is dry till first of June, and again in the fall if the weather is not too dry to cut it. Seeding is also done in early spring, but not safe to do after end of May, as we frequently get a dry spell, and unless you can reach it with the hose it may be a failure. The very best time of the whole year to seed a lawn is from the last of August to middle of September; even a little earlier in August is all right. We are almost sure to get some showers the end of August, and if within reach of the hose you are not dependent on showers, and if sown end of August or very early September you have a lawn well established before winter sets in.

In fall sowing, which is the best, there is no need of sowing anything with the grass seeds. Sometimes in spring sowing a sprinkling of oats or rye is sown, which germinates quickly, and by its growth shades and protects the little grass spears till they are up a few inches. In a few weeks the oats are mowed off with a scythe and the grass takes care of itself. This, of course, is quite unnecessary where you sprinkle occasionally. Our climate is uncertain—no two seasons alike—but although I have seen many acres sown for a lawn in August which was a disappointment because there were no rains, yet it is by far the surest and best time to sow.

There are many seedsmen, leading firms, who give great attention to the preparation of lawn grass seed, and when ordering you should say whether the soil is a clay loam or sandy, whether it is boggy or moist, or high and dry. Some grasses are more suitable for shade than others. Most of the reputable firms charge a good round sum for their "extra superfine lawn grass mixture." Possibly it is not the seed that costs so much as the "extra superfine," for which you always have to pay high, whether it be in a coat or cod liver oil.

If I am asked to lay down a lawn, I just buy a good clean sample of Red Top (Agrostis vulgaris), and add a few pounds of White Clover, which is best sown separately, as the little weighty seed will find its way to the bottom of your bag or box and not be distributed evenly with the grass. The fine mixtures of the seedsman are all right and a few dollars is of little consequence in such an important and permanent undertaking as making a lawn.

Most of the grass seeds are very light and will fly in every direction, much preferring the openings in your face to the ground. When there is a very gentle breeze blowing steadily in one direction is a good time to sow. You will soon find out then where your seed is settling and gauge your distance accordingly. About 30 to 40 pounds of grass seed is usually sown to the acre and 5 or 6 pounds of White Clover. If a small plot of ground, it is easy to know when you have sown enough. In most cases you will sow far too thickly. Neither in spring nor fall is it advisable to keep the newly made lawns mowed closely, so you

idea of nourishing the roots you are mistaken. The fertilizing properties of the manure have passed through the soil while the roots were inactive and have not benefited the plant. With excessive watering the roots are often brought near the surface and at the same time continually sprinkling impoverishes the surface soil.

So one inch of good loam to which has been added ½ lb. of bone meal to the bushel, and this soil thrown on the surface of the lawn and worked in by the back of the rake just before rolling, or even after, will do more good than all the manure you can put on. Then you have given the grass something to feed on and you

public parks, and greener than it does in the sun, simply because the farmer and the park and cemetery superintendents do not water it. He has not time, and would not if he could.

This continued watering brings the roots to the surface only to perish. It produces a weak, forced growth of the grass. What better combination could you have to wear out a lawn than keeping up a continual forcing of growth by water and then clipping it off short with the mowing machine. You will ask "What better can you tell us to do, for we are determined to have a green lawn?" First, if your lawn has been sodded on a hard clay or sown on an inch or two of poor sandy soil, dig it up and dig deep, and put in lots of manure. If you can't do that and your lawn turns brown with a week of hot weather in June, then water thoroughly once a week and then let it alone. Once a week is often enough for any lawn if thoroughly done. And under the shade of trees remember that much less is needed.

If a very dry summer a good soaking once in two weeks is ample for grass that is heavily shaded with trees. Unfortunately this, in many cases, is near the sidewalk where your man or yourself delight to stand hose in hand in your shirt sleeves and nightly pour ice water (for cold it often is) on the tender grass in hot evenings of June, remarking to every acquaintance who passes: "Hot enough for you?" The struggling blade of grass would say, could it make you sensible of its desires, "Shut up and shut off and let me breathe in the warm night air; I am shivering with the cold and my feet are wet." In protracted periods of drought, such as many parts have suffered with this summer of 1899, grass will turn brown. The poorer the soil the browner the grass, but it can be green and fresh looking with an occasional watering. And leave alone this everlasting and daily sprinkling.

I should say in conclusion that all lawns, big or little, should be underdrained with tile or some other means as good. You can get on the lawn earlier in the spring and later in the fall, but more important than that, it is better for the roots of the grass than land that is boggy and saturated with moisture. All lawns may not need it, but most do.

The mowing machine keeps down all troublesome weeds except dandelion and plantain. The latter perishes if the lawn is cut an inch below the surface. For dandelion I know no cure and there is a rich prize for the man who will discover some effectual method for its extermination.

A well-kept Lawn.

must waive appearance for the benefit of the grass, at least for the first season.

The care of lawns is something I have thought and talked about for years, for I am convinced that in two features our lawns are greatly mismanaged. The only time our lawns want rolling is in the spring. Then they certainly need it. Winter and heavy frosts have heaved up places here and there, and more than that, have heaved up the roots of the grass, much of which perishes if not pressed back by the roller. Rolling (and this time it should be done with a good heavy one) must be done when the ground is drying after the frost has left it; when it is soft and pliable but not wet and sticky. The mowing machine will do the rest for the remainder of the season. Rolling is all right, and if you have time roll often; no harm done.

The practice of strewing stable manure on the grass in November with the idea of protecting it is all nonsense. It brings you a great crop of all kinds of weeds, and that's about all it does. If you put it on with the

will see great results in a few weeks. Although an inch over the whole surface may seem burying the grass; it will soon disappear when moved about by the back of the rake, and after the first good rain you will not notice it.

The other feature I object to is this continual sprinkling, and many of our citizens who have grass surrounding their houses are insane over the matter. "Henry, you had better put the sprinkler on the front lawn." I have seen this done while yet the rainbow was in the sky, the effect of a receding storm that had an hour before poured out its liquid gifts in copious quantities.

The grass that suffers most with this idiotic treatment is that beneath the shade of trees and buildings. We know scores of places that are resodded or seeded every season, or at most every alternate year, and simply because it is drowned out. "I can't get the grass to grow under the trees" is the continual plaint. It grows under the shade of trees in our orchards and so it does in our large cemeteries and

LIBONIA.

This is a very pretty little free flowering plant that has been largely crowded out by other perhaps more showy plants. It makes in one season a compact little plant from eight inches to a foot in height, with small shining leaves and profusely covered with small tubular scarlet, yellow tipped flowers. We used to grow it for selling in pots, but many a hundred we cut up and used in baskets and cut flowers. A greenhouse temperature of about 50 degrees suits it well.

The terminal growths or the young breaks of the cut down plants root readily in winter and when planted out end of May in good, light loam, grow nicely during summer. It needs little pinching, as its growth is branching. They lift well in September and by. the holidays are in full flower. They are so easily raised from cuttings that plants are not worth keeping the second year.

L. floribunda is the species we grew for years, but a great improvement on that is L. Penrhosiensis.

LILIUM.

This large and handsome genus of bulbous plants give us a few species that are of first importance to the florist. All are beautiful and where there is an opportunity for their cultivation in the garden few flowering plants can be of more interest. They are widely scattered over the Northern Hemisphere and the majority of them are hardy in our northern clime. The most important species to the florist is L. longiflorum. I will say here that there are several varieties of some species. The variated character is principally difference of color or markings of the flower. The lily that is known as L. Harrisii, or the Bermuda lily, must be a variety of longiflorum which the mild climate of Bermuda has through years of cultivation produced. There are certainly characteristics possessed by it sufficient to make it a distinct variety. The leaves are thinner and less glaucous, the petals lack the substance of longiflorum, the flower is larger, and it is more easily forced into flower. Briefly, the plant has not the substance of the true longiflorum. All of these traits are what could be expected after years of cultivation in a semi-tropical climate, for except in coloring what is it that produces variations but environment?

The following cultural directions are suitable for the Harrisii, Bermuda grown longiflorum and Japan longiflorum, except some slight differences which will be noticed. At present the Harrisii and what we know as Bermuda longiflorum (the latter is the true longiflorum taken to Bermuda and grown a few years) are all imported from the Bermuda Islands and what with the disease and the tariff the bulbs within three years have about doubled in cost to us. Doubtless there are experiments going on and surely somewhere in our southern states in the broad millions of square miles we have, some place will be found where the longiflorum can be grown and ripened early enough to give us bulbs for Easter forcing.

As soon as you receive the bulbs get them potted without delay. The bulbs are loose scaled, quite different from a tulip, and must be injured by laying around exposed to the air. We once tried (as a means of saving labor) to force our 5 to 7 inch bulbs in square boxes holding a dozen plants and about five inches of soil. It was by no means a success. They were very awkward to handle and for some reason not accounted for a large percentage came blind.

We put the 5 to 7 bulbs in 5-inch pots, leaving the top of bulb about even with surface of soil. For those we want early, say for December cutting, we put at once on the bench in a shady house and after one watering cover the pots lightly with excelsior. It keeps them from drying out and does not prevent the lily from pushing up. Remove it as soon as the growth is up an inch. Water sparingly till the growth starts. As there are few roots they don't want much water. Later batches of this size we put outside in frames and there the few inches of covering is of still greater service, as the sun would daily dry out and bake the soil. Be sure that the frames you stand them in have a dry bottom and that water does not remain under the pots.

I like to have the lilies in frames because if we get several days of copious rain, say in October, it would be altogether too much for them. And there you have at hand the means of covering them with glass.

The 7 to 9 bulbs we put into 4-inch and treat the same. We were told by a neighbor that he had found that starting the bulbs in a 4-inch and after a time giving them a shift, retarded them two weeks, or made them later by two weeks than those put at once into their flowering pot, a 6-inch. We have not found it so and shall continue to put the large bulbs of Harrisii and the Bermuda grown longiflorum first into the 4-inch and after a growth of four or five inches shift them into a 6-inch, and the strongest into a 7-inch.

We find the smaller bulbs (5 to 7) the best to grow for cutting, for the reason that you can make a better bunch or vase of flowers with stems of two or three flowers and a bud than you can a stalk of say four flowers and three buds to open.

The Bermuda grown longiflorum is now the favorite lily for Easter. It makes a finer plant and a better, and grows with ordinary care about the most desirable height, two to three feet. But it is well for church decorations to have some of the Harrisii, for if they are six feet high many people will think of them of great merit.

It is not only at Easter or Christmas or Decoration Day that we want the lilies. From November on till June there is use for them. At weddings they are often a leading feature and at funerals they are in constant use.

Although desirable to have a continuous supply, Easter is the time when your main crop will be wanted, and every effort should be made to get them right to the day. Though the great majority of plants are sold singly in 5, 6 or 7-inch pots, there is always a good sale for a number of large pots, about a 9-inch, with three plants of Bermuda longiflorum. For this purpose we would only use those bulbs. Here is where the advantage of starting them in the 4-inch is apparent. You can select three plants that are all about the same size and degree of earliness, and if carefully handled in shifting they will be all three in bloom at the same time. You may have another pot with three plants not so forward, but they also will be in flower at Easter because the heat you give them afterwards will regulate that.

If let alone in one house at one temperature a batch of lilies would vary in time of flowering a month or six weeks. It is entirely by moving them about into different degrees of temperature that you can get, say 900 out of a thousand lilies to be in flower the same week.

We will go back to the 7 to 9 bulbs we left in the frame in 4-inch pots. If you leave them there till middle of December, which for want of room you may have to do, don't let a sudden hard frost sweep down on them. Though almost or quite a hardy plant they have been grown somewhat artificially and ten to fifteen degrees of frost without any covering will hurt the foliage and greatly disfigure them. I can speak from experience on this and would rather the lilies had little or no frost.

If Easter is early you will want to bring them in by the first of November. If three or four inches above the pot we then shift into the flowering pot and this enables us to fill around the stem an inch or less with soil, which is a help to the roots, which often come out above the bulb.

We start in with a night temperature of 45 to 50 degrees and increase to 60 later. I think a night heat of 60 in a light house—and this is what lilies should always have till they open their flowers—grows them nicely, and can't be called heavy forcing. There are times frequently when to get the backward plants in bloom we have to give them 70 at night and 85 to 90 in day time. Beyond that degree of heat it is not safe, for I have seen the young buds when an inch or so long just dry up.

You cannot get your Easter crop of lilies in without a great deal of labor in moving them around, and with the experience of years you will yet be anxious as to getting all at the right time. No possible rule can be laid

A Field of Lilium Harrisii in Bermuda.

down, as Easter is a changeable date. It is sure that if Easter is in the last days of March you will have to force much more than if it were the 24th of April. Be in time and before you move lilies into a cool house let them be opening the flowers. I have noticed that when moved, say from a night temperature of 60 degrees to one of 45 degrees, when the buds were not fully developed, they would stand about still. It is too great a check at a time when they need heat, but when just expanding, they can be put in a very cool house and if shaded will keep for two weeks after being open. When the lilies are a foot above the pots they want a stake or they swing about and often get loose and frequently break at the neck of the bulb.

The soil we use for lilies is a good loam, to which has been added a fifth of old hot-bed manure, and we pot rather firmly. For the 5 to 7 bulbs which are cut during winter and are flowered in 6-inch pots we do not trouble to put any drainage in the pots, but with the 6-inch and larger we always use a crock and a thin piece of green moss. Lilies have to stand on all kinds of material and when this little precaution is taken they are less likely to get stuffed up. We frequently notice the tips of the leaves of the Harrisii, and sometimes of the longiflorum, turn brown for half an inch or so. Many times every leaf is so affected. The cause of it we don't know unless it be the effect of

fumigating, which the lilies need so much. Therefore we think it safest to evaporate some of the tobacco extracts rather than burn it. The vapor cannot possibly harm anything, and it penetrates into the thick rosette of leaves which is formed just before the buds are seen.

Lilies are much troubled with aphis, in fact against them it is a continual fight, still if the house is vaporized once a week regularly, it will save you much annoyance. The fly is always deep down among the small and tender flower buds, and if undisturbed will puncture the small bud, which causes that deformed and twisted flower. So in addition to tobacco fumes or vapor you should go over the crowns of the plants occasionally and in the center of them with a rubber plant sprinkler squirt in some "Nikoteen" diluted 200 times This may seem tedious, but it need not cost a quarter of a cent a plant and will surely pay at that price.

The Bermuda grown Harrisii wants a little more heat to bring it in early than the Harrisii. We never try to get the longiflorum in flower till Easter.

The Japan grown longiflorum are now imported in large quantities. They arrive much later than the Bermuda grown bulbs and it would be hard to get them in flower any time in April. They make good flowers for later use and if kept well protected in a cold frame are fine for Decoration Day. Last year we had two thousand

in 3-inch pots in a very cool house till end of February, when they were shifted into 5-inch and still brought plenty of ventilation on in the cool nights of April and May they were exactly right for the 30th of May. Out of the lot there was not a diseased plant. So the Bermuda disease is not bad in the land of the Mikado.

The longiflorum in good, well drained loam is hardy in this latitude, but would be benefited by a covering of litter every fall after the stems are dry. We have frequently planted out the plants of Harrisii that had been grown and cut at Easter. If a good piece of stem is left, so much the better. Many of them will send up a flower stalk from which you will get a few flowers in July and August. This is all the use you can make of them. To force any of them again is out of the question.

I know no cure for, or any means of detecting, a diseased bulb. It is to be hoped with a change of soil and care in discarding diseased plants and bulbs that our Bermuda friends will in future supply us with a higher grade of bulbs. One of the advantages I intended to mention in starting the large bulbs in small pots was that by shifting time you will be able to discover most of the diseased plants, and will not have wasted space, labor and soil on them nearly so much as you would in 6 or 7-inch.

Lilium lancifolium (which correctly is L. speciosum) is next to the longiflorum most valuable to the florist; album roseum and rubrum. They are all about identical in growth. They are not forced for winter or spring, but are very acceptable in July and August, when we are often short of flowers. With a covering of leaves over the ground during winter, they are quite hardy with us.

We receive the bulbs (from Japan) in late fall and winter, and they are well packed, losing little of their strength in the long journey. We used to try these in cold-frames during winter, but it was not a success, and now we never fail by potting them in 7 and 8-inch pots, three bulbs in a pot. Put them in dry loam a trifle below the surface, but do not water them, and place the pots beneath your coolest bench, where there is the least drip. If the soil is moderately moist the bulbs will remain seven or eight weeks without starting or making any growth. When they do start and have grown a few inches they must be given the light and grown on, but coolly.

Any of the lilies, either of the longiflorum or lancifolium, want little water till they have made good roots, but after starting they soon fill the pots with roots, and from then on they want an abundance of water.

When the lancifolium lilies are in flower, and before they are in flower, they should be given the coolest house, with all the ventilation possible. It is midsummer when these lilies are in flower, so if kept cool and shaded the plants will be stronger, the flowers larger and they will last longer. Out of doors in a sheltered and shady place will do for the lancifolium type very well for the last month.

These lilies are much troubled with green fly and need fumigating occasionally. They have a most delightful odor, agreeable to all.

The bulbs of Lilium lancifolium need not be thrown away. They are worth planting out in some good soil and will grow for years. We have also forced them the second year with good success. If you intend to do this, don't throw the bulbs under the bench as soon as the flower is cut, but stand them out of doors and keep watered till the foliage is gone and the stems are dry, when they can be cut off and the pots stored under a very cool bench during winter. In February shake them out and repot and treat as those first imported. If bulbs are not received till March, then they can be given a bench at once, but little water till they start.

Lilium auratum, most gorgeous of all the family, has flowers sometimes a foot across, with broad bands of yellow and beautifully spotted, which gave it the name of "the golden rayed lily of Japan." It grows from two to three feet and strong, healthy bulbs frequently bear fifteen to twenty flowers. We can very well remember the introduction of this magnificent lily and the sensation it created when first flowered. It has long, narrow leaves. I have never seen it here out of doors where it has been treated as a hardy

lily, but with good care and in well drained soil it may be quite hardy, as large masses of it are perfectly hardy in Scotland; and plantings of several hundred bulbs are a rich sight. We treat it precisely as we do the lancifolium section. It has a powerful odor, too much for most people, and this forbids its use as a decorative plant or as a cut flower in designs. Unfortunately many imported bulbs make but a poor growth.

Before the splendid forcing qualities of the L. Harrisii were known, and when the growing of the bulbs in Bermuda was not an industry as it now is, we used to grow and force the beautiful Lilium candidum. Its delightful, pure pearl white spikes were in great demand for cutting, as well as for Easter plants. It would be useless to describe our manner of forcing (although it differed little from that of the longiflorum), because it is entirely superseded. It should be always grown wherever you have ground to grow it. It does well in rather a heavy soil and should not be disturbed for several years. Its beautiful flowers are always in demand when in season, with us end of June and July.

There are no other lilies grown in pots for commercial use. Many species doubtless could be, but would not be profitable. Beds of L. longiflorum and candidum should be on every florist's place. And if you have the room many other species are beautiful plants for the border. The principal thing to observe with the lilies in the ground in winter is that it is a well drained soil. A good loam overlying a gravel would be perfection, but any soil that is drained will do. In the absence of peat, which many like, dig in a few inches of very rotten manure or rotten leaf-mould from the woods, and plant the bulbs when perfectly dormant. August is a good month. Plant six inches deep.

In addition to the longiflorum and lancifolium type, these will be found perfectly hardy:

L. canadense, orange, finely spotted, two to three feet.

L. croceum, yellow, four to five feet.

L. excelsum or testaceum, yellow tinged with red, four to five feet.

L. Hansonii, reddish orange, three to four feet.

L. Humboldti, orange, very fine, four to five feet.

L. paradalinum, orange with purple spots, five to six feet; of this there are several fine varieties.

L. pomponium, bright red, two to three feet.

L. rubescens, or Washingtonianum, white tinged with purple, four to five feet.

L. superbum, orange red, spotted, four to five feet.

L. tenuifolium, scarlet, dwarf and slender, but handsome, one foot.

L. Thunbergianum, red, two to three feet.

L. tigrinum, the well known tiger lily, deep orange, purple spots, very hardy, two to three feet.

And several others, both species and varieties.

LILY OF THE VALLEY (CONVALLARIA MAJALIS).

We can remember pots of lily of the valley being grown in our greenhouses in March and April many years ago. These pots (a 5 or 6-inch) contained a solid mass of roots and were not disturbed or shifted for several years. After flowering they were stood outside and kept watered till fall, when they were plunged in coal ashes and a few inches of the same material thrown over them. This was growing them in a natural way, and a very great addition they were to the attractiveness of the conservatory. As a pot plant they are of little consideration. Within twenty-five years the flower must now be supplied the year around.

When first lily of the valley was produced in the summer and fall months it commanded a most lucrative price, but nowadays at the close margin at which it is sold you must be successful or you had far better not attempt it; rather leave the growing to the specialist and buy your flowers from the grower or commission man.

A few years ago in the columns of the "American Florist" appeared several articles from the pen of Mr. R. Simpson, who can not only write plainly and explicitly convey his knowledge to us, but has been one of the largest and most successful growers of this dainty little flower, and though not copying him verbatim I acknowledge to him many of the important details on growing now given in this article, and particularly the care of the pips in cold storage, for it must be remembered that while the winter is the natural cold storage for the pips that give us the flowers from middle of January to possibly end of May, the other seven or eight months we must depend on those whose growth has been arrested by cold storage.

I never did believe that to put the original cases into cold storage and expect them to come out in seven or eight months and give good results was at all the reasonable or proper plan. When first received, which is usually in November, unpack at once. Large growers place them in trenches in cold-frames and between each row of trenches put some sandy soil or finely sifted coal ashes, and over the tops of the pips two inches of the same material. Small growers will find boxes holding conveniently the quantity they want to force weekly or bi-weekly more convenient than the first plan, because you can easily bring in the box containing just the quantity you want. When putting them outside the smallest and weakest pips should be put by themselves and labeled and reserved for the latest spring forcing, but with those that are to go into cold storage it is just the reverse, and those which are to be retarded longest should be the strongest.

Sometimes we find the roots very dry. I prefer to dip the roots for a few moments in a tub of water before putting them outside. Let a frost come, a good, hard one, so that the covering is frozen, and no harm if the roots are, then put a foot of hay or excelsior over them and cover with shutters to keep off rain. It is not well for the roots to be too wet. Glass sash would keep off the rain, but it would also raise the temperature on bright days during a thaw, and that is just what you don't want. These conditions will do for all the pips that you force during winter and up to the time that we get the flowers outside. But long before this you must have removed to the cold storage the roots that are wanted for summer and autumn.

The time to put them in cold storage may vary by a month because the weather varies. They must be absolutely dormant when removed to the cold storage, and that must be closely watched. We have tried repeatedly to store away a few thousand in our local cold storage warehouses, and if we could be always successful with them it would be a great convenience and cheaper than building one of your own. But it is very uncertain work and we have often blamed ourselves when perhaps it was the cold storage management that was at fault.

Mr. Simpson at some length gives instructions how to build a cold storage house, but were I to repeat it I am sure you could not build one by it without visiting some one who has one and seeing for yourself "how to do it." The most comforting part of it is that Mr. S. says a cold storage house that will hold 400,000 valley roots can be built for $600. The interest on that sum seems very trifling when the success of even a quarter of the above number is grown. Whether you have your own cold storage or hire it, the conditions which you should try and preserve are these:

Get convenient sized boxes, six or seven inches deep, line them with moist sphagnum moss and between the bunches of roots put moist sand, not saturated, and cover pips with an inch or two of sphagnum. To occupy little space you will have to put slats or boards on top of each box, so that they can be piled up one above the other. In renting space in cold storage this would be a great consideration. When first put in give them 10 degrees of frost and in a few days let the temperature go up to 28 or 29 degrees and remain at that.

In large cold storage houses they have rooms at all temperatures and will ask you what degree you want, so the same plan can be carried out by moving the boxes. If when removing the roots from the frame to cold storage they appeared dry, give the whole box a watering before putting it away, but it is not well for the

sand to be too wet or the roots may rot. Those small growers who hire the local cold storage for their arrested lilies may as well put them in suitable boxes when first receiving them in the fall; then with the addition of some moist sphagnum over the pips

Flower Spray of Lily of the Valley.

they can be easily removed at short notice to their cold surroundings.

There have been many ways of forcing the pip into flower. The English growers use ordinary loam as we use sand, and Mr. Simpson asserts that they (the English) produce larger spikes and finer flowers than are grown here, but does not attribute that to cultivation so much as obtaining a uniformly high grade of roots and being very particular that they

are first class. A firm that grows annually six millions of pips, as does Thomas Rochford, near London, deserves certainly to get the best there is in the market. Germany supplies them and is likely to supply them for a long time.

In obtaining the pips get the very best you can. Don't be guided by any tacked on, absurd title, but find out a good source or good man and when you are well treated stick to that man. Unless you get a well developed crown that contains a good spike of flowers in an embryonic size your most skillful and faithful care will not produce a good flower.

When brought in to force the tips of the roots are chopped off. They make no fibrous root while growing, but I don't believe the roots should be chopped off too short. So the boxes, if you use boxes, should be five inches deep, leaving the pips just above the surface of the sand. You can place the roots as close as they will conveniently go in the trench of sand and three inches between the rows. Some growers place an inch of sphagnum between the pips on the surface of the box and when the boxes are going on the pipes I think it a good plan. Large growers who use beds of sand do not bother with moss, and under the conditions it is not necessary.

I have grown fairly good valley in boxes placed on the pipes. Raise the boxes a few inches from the pipes by strips of wood. The first ten days we place over pipes that have a good, strong heat, then remove for a few days to over some pipes that are not so warm and a little more light, and when color begins to show remove them to top of bench, but still shaded from the sun. Always avoid wetting the bells after showing color, but before that syringe frequently and water the sand daily. When lily of the valley is about fully expanded (that is, the top bells) it can be cut and placed in water in bunches for twenty-four hours. They travel and keep better than those freshly cut, as do most all flowers.

Large growers (and this plan is better far than the boxes with those that want, say, from one to two thousand a week) is to put the roots at once into six inches of sand in the bed. A small, narrow house, with a northern aspect, such as you often see on the north side of an old-fashioned three-quarter span house, would be an excellent place to grow the valley. Top, or atmospheric, heat is not of consequence, but one or two pipes on side of wall or path is advisable to he used in very severe weather. The bench should be boarded up back and front. If you don't have any pipes except under the bench have one of the front boards hinged so that it can be opened in very severe weather to warm the air of the house, for in those times when you are firing so hard you can spare the heat from beneath the bench. In a section of bench in an ordinary house this is not needed because the house is always warm enough.

The bench should be of roofing slate over which you spread half an inch of cement, all of which is a good conductor of heat. Mr. Simpson says that under the bench should be four 2-inch pipes or three 4-inch. If steam, that would do, but better have five 2-inch hot water pipes and four 4-inch. There should be a 12-inch board above the bench, back and front, the front one movable for convenience in planting, cutting, etc. These boards should be high enough so that when the shading is put on it would be four or five inches above the tops of the fully developed flowers. It is bottom heat that is the great requisite, as we all know, and the earliest forced bulbs want about 85 degrees, gradually lessening the heat till in April, near their natural time of growing, 65 to 70 is enough.

For the first few days, or till the pips have grown three or four inches, they are covered with wooden shutters which almost entirely exclude the light, then these are replaced by cloth shutters; cheese cloth oiled and fastened on frames will do nicely and the last few days these are removed and they are given full light, but no direct sunlight. I have often noticed in handling valley that was in boxes that even if fully developed they quickly wilt if exposed to any draught.

This same place will do for the summer and fall growing, but little bottom heat is needed, though shade and watering are the same. In summer in addition to the portable shading over the plants the house should be shaded and made as cool as possible.

We always handle a good deal of the flowers during the short week they are in bloom out of doors, and very poor stuff it often is. A heavy shower will quickly ruin it. Every florist who has the ground should have some beds outside, planted with good pips. The beds will last for years. They should be made the size of your frames or planted in permanent frames. Then when winter was over you could put on the sash and with water and shade produce some very fine flowers and foliage several days ahead of the common, unprotected stuff.

It would be also possible with the aid of some ice and shade to retard your crop a week or ten days after the outside flowers were gone, all of which would be much cheaper than the most ready way of forcing the imported pips.

Lily of the valley can never recede in public favor. It has all the attributes that appeal to the most refined and delicate senses. Its grace and simple beauty is unsurpassed and its delicate odor is loved by all. Even supposing you don't get more than 75 per cent. of good flowers, then it is a more profitable flower to the grower and retailer than almost anything you handle, and there is no greenhouse where provision could not be made for its successful culture.

Pans and pots of it sell at Christmas and Easter. They can be treated just as described above, but a better way is to select roots with some perfect flowers and foliage and put them into the pans when in full bloom. There is no fraud about this as if kept moist they last just as long as those grown in the pans from the start and will have a better appearance. I have never had any satisfaction from the imported clumps and would not advise anyone to bother with them.

LINUM TRIGYNUM.

Some of the species of this genus are used in flower gardening. L. grandiflorum is a pretty, deep rose-colored summer annual. L. trigynum is the species that is sold for a winter blooming plant. It is not likely to become very popular as a house plant on account of its dropping its petals so quickly, although for the conservatory it is a most showy plant and is always in the best of order about Christmas time. When supplied with pot room and plenty of water it makes a shapely, rounded plant, covered with its bright yellow flowers. It is often attacked by red spider and needs daily syringing when in the greenhouse. A night temperature of 50 degrees does it well.

It roots freely from the young growths in March and should be planted out of doors in a light soil end of May. It will need constant pinching to keep it compact, and lifts with the greatest ease in September. Its flowers come in clusters at the axil of the leaf and although a flower lasts but a few days there is such an abundance to take its place that the plants for a month or more are extremely showy.

LOBELIA.

This extensive genus includes some very handsome hardy perennial plants. L. cardinalis, the Cardinal Flower, is one. They are best raised from seed sown in August and wintered in a cold-frame and placed in their permanent position early in the spring. This method is suited to a great many of our best hardy perennial plants that do not divide easily.

The dwarf tender species of lobelias are of most interest to us, although they are not of such value here as a flower garden plant as they are in the cooler summers of Northern Europe. In Great Britain some of the best flower garden effects are produced by the blue lobelia, where they can be depended on to flower all summer. Here they are very gay out of doors till perhaps the middle of July, when they will go entirely out of flower and your design is left with a streak of dark green in place of the brightest of blues.

For hanging baskets, vases and veranda boxes they are to us indispensable, and if not lasting all summer they add greatly in color when first used, and are not so much missed later as stronger growing droopers take their place.

Select a few of the best plants in September, cut them back a trifle, and before a hard frost dig up and pot and give them a light, cool place. With a little more heat they will give plenty of cuttings, and both from the old plants and the young ones you will get all the cuttings you want, which root like the proverbial weed. We like to grow them on hanging shelves, as it affords room to let them droop. We endeavor to be well supplied with plenty of lobelias in 3-inch pots with a thick growth or ten inches long and just ready to flower about middle to end of May, and this you can do from cuttings struck in February if pinched once or twice and given a good light shelf.

L. Erinus and its varieties is the one most useful to us, the variety called speciosa being most in use. If seed is sown of speciosa you will get a number of varied forms, and some of those grown by us have originated locally. A good, free growth and a fine blue flower is what we select in speciosa.

Paxtoniana is another variety of Erinus which is still more straggling in growth, with light blue flowers with white throat.

The dwarf compact form of Erinus, "compacta," which is so largely used in Europe, would be the best of all for bedding, but it is not to be depended upon here and is not of any other use.

Seed of the varieties of Erinus can be sown in January and by the help of a hot-bed in April and May would be large enough for bedding plants, but to have them in good order for our vases, etc., cuttings are much better.

LYSIMACHIA.

There is one species, Nummularia, the creeping, little, yellow-flowered "Money Vine," or moneywort, that besides being one of our best hardy rockwork plants is with us as a standard so-called vine for baskets and vases. Its long, pendant growth is just what we want for that purpose. For cultivation see Glechoma.

Don't attempt to take it into the greenhouse in any shape in the fall, or it will get rusty and be useless. To thrive it must have its freeze-up during the few hard winter months.

MANETTIA.

All the species are climbers, and used on trellises they make good summer vines in situations that have a sheltered, sunny exposure. They are not a prominent commercial plant, as we occasionally are asked for them. They root very easily during winter from tender tips of the growth, and will grow in any good loam. The flowers are tubular, freely produced and attractive.

The species are: M. bicolor, scarlet with yellow tip; M. coccinea, white tube spotted with red, yellow throat; M. cordifolia, scarlet; M. micans, orange; this species is more suited for inside.

Martinezia Caryotaefolia.

this species has been in cultivation since 1845, it is not now largely grown, but few seeds being offered in the market.

The martinezia also possesses a disadvantage in being so abundantly provided with long and sharp spines, not only the stems, but also the backs of the leaves being armed with these needlelike protectors, and nearly all plants having this characteristic receive but scanty attention from the general public, and especially so if the price is held above the average.

Martinezia caryotaefolia may be described in a general way as bearing some resemblance to Caryota urens, except that the latter is without spines, but the peculiarly wedge-shaped pinnae of the martinezia are arranged in irregular groups along the leaf stem, there being frequently from six to ten inches of bare stem between these groups of pinnae on a large leaf. The general color of the leaves is deep green, and the habit of the plant very graceful.

This palm is not specially subject to the attacks of insects, but if scale insects are allowed to infest it they are likely to fix themselves along the stems among the thorns, where it is very difficult to dislodge them. In fact, with any of the very spiny palms it becomes a severe test of patience to eradicate scale, and the use of strong insecticides can hardly be recommended in such a case, an experience with kerosene emulsion some years ago on both martinezias and daemonorops having proved disastrous.

Regarding the cultural requirements of martinezias it may be said that they belong among the warm house palms, and will flourish under suitable conditions for Areca lutescens, that is, temperature of 65 to 70 degrees, moderate shading and abundant moisture.

M. caryotaefolia is said to bear exposure very well as a plant for house decoration, but I have not seen it tested for such use, though a good sized plant of this species would undoubtedly be a very effective single specimen to be placed on a pedestal, where its spines would be out of reach of the passer-by.   W. H. T.

MARANTA.

These very ornamental leaved hothouse plants are now known botanically as calathea, but it is not likely that we shall ever know them commercially as anything but marantas. There are many species, all from tropical America, entirely grown for their handsome leaves. They have creeping rhizomes and when shaken out the roots can be readily divided. June and July is a good time for this operation. Some of the smaller growing species make beautiful plants for table decoration or for the larger ferneries, but they do not thrive long in the dry air of a living room. It is as fine plants for the hot-house that they are chiefly cultivated.

The essential to grow a fine plant is a good coarse loam, to which can be added a fifth of well decayed manure, and some sand to keep the soil open. As when growing they want abundance of water and syringing there should be ample drainage to let water pass freely through. In a shaded, sheltered place they will do out of doors, but are far better suited in a shaded house where there is abundance of moisture. In winter they will do in a temperature of 60 degrees, but as they are evergreen they must not get dry, only a less quantity of water. For a full development of their velvety leaves they should every two or three years be shaken out and divided or their roots and crowns get very crowded.

There are so many species that it is unnecessary to single out any of them. All are handsome and there is a range in size from the diminutive M. micans, with glittering leaves two to three inches long, to M. zebrina, with leaves three feet long and eight inches broad. Every gardener will remember this old species, probably one of the first introduced. Here is a description of M. veitchii, from Nicholson's Dictionary of Gardening:

"Leaves large, ovate elliptic, over one foot long, very rich, glossy green, marked along each side the mid-rib with crescent-shaped blotches of yellow, softened by shades of green and white; under surface light purple. Height of plant three feet. Introduced in 1866 from west tropical America. Probably the handsomest of the genus."

But there are any number of other species with various beautiful markings, and none difficult to grow where heat, moisture, a porous soil and shade in summer can be given.

MARTINEZIA.

M. caryotaefolia, a young plant of which is illustrated, is one of a small family of rather slender growing South American palms, the species in question having been found in parts of Peru and also New Granada. Though

MAURANDYA.

These are useful to us for summer climbers and thrive in our hottest suns. M. Barclayana is best sown in early March in a heat of about 55 to 60 degrees. When large enough to handle pot into 2-inch. In this size they are large enough for our baskets, but if wanted for outside climbing can be shifted into 3-inch and must have a small stake or they get sadly tangled up. They make a very quick growth and cover quickly a small trellis. The flower is not conspicuous, being of a greenish color, about two inches long.

M. scandens, often called Lophospermum scandens, is a larger leaved, stronger growing climber, and one of the very best vines for our vases. The flowers are pinkish violet. This can be raised from seed precisely as we do M. Barclayana, but we prefer to take a few cuttings from outside plants in the fall and grow on during winter. It roots easily from any part of the growth and by this means we get much more serviceable plants for use in large vases and veranda boxes. They winter very well in 50 degrees, but grow faster, when you want to propagate, in 60 degrees.

METROSIDEROS (BOTTLE BRUSH PLANT).

This is one of the many hard-wooded evergreen shrubs that we get from the Southern Pacific Islands. The species we import is M. robusta, and its peculiar, terminal, densely flowered

Bottle Brush (Metrosideros) trimmed with crimson ribbon, in celluloid basket.

spike is so like in form to a bottle brush that the popular name is often suggested by people who have never heard it. It has been for many years grown as a cool greenhouse plant, but only within a dozen years have the Europeans been sending us the little, compact bushes that now arrive with our azaleas. The Belgians grow it in peat as they do most hard-wooded plants, but it does very well in good turfy loam with a fourth of leaf-mold. It will root from the young growths in early spring, which can be planted out in good soil end of May. But with tariff included we can get fine plants landed here at a cost that it would be impossible to grow them as good for the same money.

You don't want a great many of them; about one to every ten Azalea indica you grow. Plants in 6-inch pots, well flowered and fixed up with a red ribbon, do look novel and at-

tractive, and a limited number find a ready sale.

When they arrive soak the ball and then pot firmly and put in a house at about 45 degrees. To bring them in for Easter you must watch them and gradually give them more heat, but not suddenly. Freshly imported plants if forced in much heat, as you can an azalea, will shed their flowers. Plants unsold the first spring will be much better and more satisfactory the second year. End of April cut them back to within an inch or two of the old growth and put them into a good heat and keep syringed. They will make a bushy growth with a number of shoots. Early in June plunge them out in the broad sun, well covering their pots, and in the hot weath-

er don't let them suffer for water. In July or earlier mulch the surface of the pots with an inch of half decomposed cow manure; this will add greatly to their robustness. Bring in before any danger of frost and keep in a temperature of 45 degrees; warmer if you want them earlier than Easter. These will be far better plants and be much more satisfactory to the purchaser than the newly imported.

MIGNONETTE (RESEDA ODORATA).

It is doubtful if there is any plant so universally known or better liked than the mignonette.

The florist sows it in his garden as soon as the ground is dry, and makes another sowing later, in shallow drills in deep, rich soil. If continuous cutting is expected the plants should be thinned out to a few inches apart and watered in dry weather.

As a cut flower in winter it is a staple article and for that purpose is grown, good, bad and indifferent. To obtain fine spikes that sell by the dozen or hundred it must have a suitable place and room to grow.

A solid bed in a light house would without doubt be the best place, but it can be grown on a bench in five or six inches of soil, very well. The soil should be a heavy loam with a fourth of rotten cow manure. A bench where the heat of the pipes would be felt would not be good as the roots like a cool bottom.

Sow early in August. We put a few seeds in a spot, about one foot apart, and when an inch high thin out to the strongest plant. When a few inches high they will branch from the bottom and four or five of the strongest side shoots can be selected; after that keep lateral growths off both the main spike and the side growths. If grown cool it will not want any staking, but if it should it is easily done, as one small stake would support several spikes.

This mignonette, whether grown for cutting or for pots, must have the fullest possible light and air on all permissible occasions. Light and air and a cool temperature will just make the difference between stout, heavy spikes and thin, spindling ones. You ought to get a good cutting at the holidays and another at Easter. In fact after Christmas you can always cut good spikes. The night temperature should never be over 50 degrees, and I should prefer it when heavy firing is going on to be only 45 degrees.

There are few plants that will fill the bill more acceptably for an inexpensive Easter gift than a well grown mignonette. A 4-inch pot will grow a nice plant, but a 5-inch is much better. For this purpose sow not later than end of August. Sow in the same pots that they are to be sold in. I have been quite successful shifting them from a small pot, and also unsuccessful. The former is the much safest plan.

Put a crock and a piece of green moss in the bottom of the pot and fill up solidly with good, fresh loam with a fourth of cow manure; make the soil quite solid. Sow a number of seeds on the surface and cover lightly. When well up thin out to three strong plants equal distances apart. We pinch the leading shoot out of these plants, which will give you nine or ten nice spikes, which is better than three or four large ones. Keep them in just such a house as you do those growing for cutting and if any preference keep in the coolest end.

If showing flower too soon stop them, but they should not be pinched for twelve weeks before you want to sell them. A neat stake would be needed for these pots, and perhaps three small stakes is better, just to hold the branches from breaking. Don't attempt to grow mignonette in a dark, ill ventilated house; you will only get weak, spindling stuff. Like

the moon flower had grown to a height of 75 feet. There are many of these ipomaeas that make fine climbers for the conservatory and hothouse, and doubtless could be used out of doors in our summers, but the moon flower is known by all.

There is the grandiflora type of moon flower with blossoms six to seven inches across, and an improved kind with small flowers, but flowering earlier in the summer. They should not be planted out till danger of frost is past, but as they are always against a fence or trellis can be easily protected from late frosts.

They are easily raised from seed sown in the greenhouse in March, but a few cuttings can be taken from the small side shoots in September, which root readily. When rooted don't try to grow them fast till early spring, when with more heat they will quickly grow and can be increased by cuttings.

There is nothing that surpasses the moon flower for rapidity of growth. It makes a perfectly dense screen, and in the evening and until 10 or 11 o'clock in the morning is studded with its noble flowers.

MULCHING.

This garden term may be new to some beginners, but it represents some very important operations in our business.

In plants in pots it means with those plunged outside in summer, such as azaleas, acacias, hardy roses, etc., that an inch or less of manure and soil, or all manure, is put on the surface of the pot. Sometimes chemical fertilizers are added to the compost. Its purpose is two-fold. It feeds the roots and encourages them to come to the surface, which they do, feeding on the mulch which is applied, and it prevents the hot sun from parching the soil, which necessitates such frequent watering. The good effects of an inch of cow manure applied to azaleas this past July plunged in the broad sun have been most marked. It is sometimes done inside, where plants cannot be shifted, but when the roots need more nourishment.

On plants in beds, such as roses and carnations, it is a most important operation. The soil is shallow and the application of half an inch of manure or a rich compost containing bone dust or sheep manure is the greatest help to them. And in spring the mulching on our beds has the same effect as that on the pots in summer; it prevents evaporation.

Not so much to encourage growth as to save the lives of trees and shrubs that are recently planted, mulching is of the greatest benefit to all trees and shrubs that are planted the previous fall or present spring. It has saved the lives of millions of young trees. In dry weather a freshly planted tree needs water, however scientifically you have planted it, and to water on the

Bench of Mignonette.

many other plants the more perfect the light and the more you can give air the less you will hurt with a higher temperature.

Mignonette does not like transplanting; that is why they are sown on the bench where they are to grow, and in pots in which they are to flower.

Simple as this plant is to sow outside as a hardy annual, we always sell a good many plants with other summer flowering plants. For this purpose we sow a number of seeds in 3-inch pots on some light bench in early March. Later we thin out to three or four of the strongest and in April plunge them in a mild hot-bed, where by middle of May they are strong, thrifty plants.

When the mignonette plants are quite small you must watch out for slugs and wood-lice, both of which relish them as fine salad. If you see the small yellow butterfly in your mignonette house in August or September get your double-barreled, hammerless Parker shotgun, or your hat, and annihilate him, or rather her. She flits over the plants depositing a small green egg, which quickly evolves into the green worm, the cabbage worm, which will, if unmolested, soon chew up your young mignonette.

I have never noticed that tobacco smoke did any harm to the mignonette, nor does it need it much. If it gets over the slugs, wood-lice and worms there is no trouble ahead.

You ought to select the finest spikes and save your own seed. The strain we grow was obtained from Mr. John N. May some years ago, and by selection it is better than when first obtained. But mignonette is very like asparagus; it is the growing and rich, heavy soil that makes the giant or colossal qualities; any of the strains are good when well grown. Besides new advertised strains, some standard

ones are: Bird's Mammoth, Miles' Hybrid Spiral, Machet, Golden Queen and Machet's Perfection.

MIMULUS.

As a boy we thought there were very few plants so beautiful as M. luteus (Monkey Flower). We don't think so now, but its yellow and spotted flower is very attractive. Our hot summers do not suit it planted out. It is often treated as an annual and can be raised from seed sown in early spring. Or it can be kept over winter and propagated by cuttings. In a shaded, moist place it will do well planted out, and in a liberal sized pot in a cool house it would thrive, and when well grown its showy flowers will sell it.

M. moschatus is the common musk plant, which in some cities is a great market plant, but in many of our cities is scarcely ever seen. It also likes to be away from the hot sun. Good light soil and partial shade and moisture suit it well. It can be raised from seed, which is very small and needs no covering, but it is a perennial, and if you have a few plants carried over winter as dormant roots you can shake them out in early March and start growing in a warm greenhouse. As they grow small pieces can be taken and two or three of them put round the edge of a three or four-inch pot, which they will soon cover with their fast creeping growth. In this way you can rapidly make any number of salable pots. They never want the cutting bed.

MOON FLOWER (IPOMOEA BONA NOX OR NOCTIFLORA).

This is one of the many evergreen ipomaeas that make us a splendid summer climber. We have seen pictures of windmills in Georgia where

surface tends only to aggravate its condition, as the ground soon becomes parched. By laying two or three inches of stable litter on the surface of the ground for a distance extending farther than the roots of the tree you will prevent evaporation from the ground. It will keep the ground cool and moist, and when you do water no baking of the ground will ensue; the tree or shrub will get the benefit of the watering for many days. This mulching of newly-planted trees is of the utmost importance. Many a young tree, evergreen or deciduous, shrubs and fruit trees, all alike, are saved from death by the simple and inexpensive operation of mulching.

It is also the only way we can fertilize our hardy herbaceous plants. An inch or two of manure laid between the rows in early spring prevents drying out, feeds the roots, and can, later in the fall, be lightly cultivated into the soil.

MUSA.

The banana plant is of the easiest possible culture; a rough, rich loam, an abundance of water, heat and room to grow, are all that is required. Occasionally we see a bunch of M. Cavendishii in our northern hot-houses, and if I had the chance of some millionaires I would raise my own bananas. That would be as reasonable as Levi P. Morton producing his own cream, which costs him the same price as his champagne.

To those who have only tasted the bananas picked green in the West Indies and ripened in the hold of a vessel or heated warehouse and finished off in the sleeping apartment of Giuseppe Garibaldi, the fresh yellow fruit ripened on the plant is as Mr. Morton's Jersey cream to a very thin sample of skim milk. You are not, however, likely to embark in the banana industry, and as our government will soon own a large part of the world suitable to their culture we will leave that to the new office which will be known as "Secretary of the Tropical Fruit and Tattooing Department."

Musa ensete, from Abyssinia, and M. superba, from the East Indies, make very ornamental plants for the sub-tropical garden or for specimens on the lawn. You can raise them from seed, or buy young plants at a very low cost. They should always be planted out where a good, fast growth is wanted.

Though a tropical plant you can store them during winter in a cool house with little water, or they can be lifted, the ground shaken off the roots and laid under a bench, or they will keep in a root-house or cellar when not below 40 degrees, but 50 degrees is better.

In sheltered places they make fine specimens on a lawn with their broad, tropical leaves, especially M. ensete, but in windy places their leaves rip and tear, giving the plant a very ragged appearance.

MYOSOTIS.

We are always asked for some plants of these in early spring. They do not last long in our hot, dry summers. M. alpestris makes a compact little tuft, full of flowers in the spring.

You can sow the seed in August and plant in cold-frames, where they will winter all right, but if you have any stock it can be divided quite easily and planted in cold-frame in September, a few inches apart.

For years we grew a very useful species of myosotis for cutting in winter. It was planted in fall along the edge of the carnation benches, and as it grew entirely outwards and hung over the sides of the bench it did no harm to the carnations except what strength it took from the soil, and that we could afford. We propagated a few dozen by cuttings in late spring,

Nepenthes.

kept them in 3-inch pots during summer, and after the carnations were planted we put in a plant of myosotis, not too thickly, one about every three feet. From them we picked sprays of their beautiful flowers all winter. I am not positive, but the species was, I feel sure, M. azorica. M. dissitiflora has large, deep blue flowers, fine for borders, but not as good for cutting as azorica.

NASTURTIUM.

See Tropaeolum.

NIEREMBERGIA.

The species of most use to the florist is gracilis, which has slender growth with pretty white and light purple flowers. They were formerly used sometimes for flower beds or long rib-

bon borders, but are more valuable as a vase plant, for which their graceful but free growth and free flowering qualities are well adapted. They cannot be called a drooping plant, yet their slender but wiry growths have a fine effect in the edge of a vase or veranda box.

Any good loam will grow them. Lift a few plants in fall and cut back hard, and keep in a cool, light house. In January start with a little heat and you will get plenty of cuttings. Or if you prefer, take off some cuttings in the fall, but they don't root freely unless the cuttings are of recent growth.

NEPENTHES.

These remarkable plants are little handled by the commercial florist, but are so striking and curious that all are interested in a knowledge of them.

They are an important genus in that family of plants which are now known as insectivorous and to which the great Darwin devoted a volume as the result of his marvelous research. The Dionaea muscipula (Venus' fly trap), from Carolina, is the most familiar of the insectivorous plants. Others are its close relation, the drosera, of our northern swamps, and again the familiar sarracenia.

The nepenthes are called "Pitcher plants," because the extension of the leaf terminates in the perfect form of a pitcher, lid and all. If they were not called pitcher plants they would remind you much of the large German pipes, five or six inches in the bowl, which usually have a cover. What part the pitcher bears to the economy of the plant is not fully determined, but the fluid held in the pitcher contains bacteria which is capable of digesting nitrogenous matter. If an insect, a fly or bee once explores the depths of the pitcher he is gone. They are incapable of climbing up by the interior walls of the pitchers and are finally drowned, to their discomfiture, but probably to the benefit of the plant, hence they are called insectivorous, or insect-eating plants.

They are nearly all the most tropical of tropical plants, found in Borneo, Madagascar, Ceylon and pretty close to the equator. The pitchers hang on for months in perfect condition if not accidentally or purposely emptied of their fluid, which they never should be, or they will shrivel up.

Although plants requiring a very high temperature they are not at all difficult to grow providing you have heat and moisture. I have enumerated several of the finest and best known, but there are many hybrids of great beauty.

Propagation. They are not difficult to propagate by cuttings, which should be three or four eyes of the tip of a shoot, placed in sand and kept moist. The cuttings should be in a propagating case in a warm house and the sand should be 10 to 15 degrees warmer than the house, or about 80 to 85 degrees. May and June are good months to propagate and the cuttings will root in three or four weeks.

Rooted plants should be grown in hanging wooden baskets. Shade in the summer is necessary. Our summer nights are often too cool to do the nepenthes well and a gentle fire heat is essential the year round. The lowest night temperature in winter should not be less than 70 degrees. The baskets should be filled one-third their depth with clean crocks and then the roots of the nepenthes should be filled in with equal parts of fern roots and good sphagnum moss, rounding up the surface of the basket with good live sphagnum.

The daily spraying will be sufficient without water, and in summer spray them twice a day. What they want is an atmosphere fairly reeking with moisture. The more moist your atmosphere the more your pitcher plants will thrive.

The following all have grand pitchers: N. Dominiana, Mastersiana, Morganiae, Rafflesiana, Veitchii, Williamsii, madagascariensis. As the names of the above will denote, some of them are garden hybrids.

The lamented Mr. Court, who represented Messrs. Veitch, of London, and who made many trips to this country, was an enthusiast on these curious plants, and whoever saw the collection of nepenthes at Chelsea, as the writer did in 1885, could not fail to see that this wonderful collection of grotesque exotics were perfectly at home. One of the handsomest hybrids raised by Mr. Court bears his name. The pitchers on some of the largest

Otaheite Orange, in gilt basket, tied with ribbon.

are eight inches long by three inches in width.

OLEANDER (NERIUM).

There is a marked inclination among our patrons the past year or two to decorate their grounds, particularly where the grounds are confined to a city lot, with palms, sweet bays, tubs of hydrangeas and other plants, and the well known oleander may yet come into favor; in fact, we have of late had calls for large plants of it.

Our acquaintance with this fine shrub is too often an unpleasant one. Some worthy matron may possess an oleander too large for her window, and she enquires how much we will charge to store it for the winter. You are bound to charge about as much as the plant is worth, so the deal is off. Still, where you have a house entirely de-voted to the care of such winter boarders, you must take the oleander as well as other plants, only be sure you get enough for your space and labor. It is no more reasonable that we should take in a palm or sweet bay or an oleander for little recompense than that a livery stable should board a horse all winter for little or nothing.

With all their familiarity, oleanders are beautiful shrubs. We all hear so often about the hedges of them in Bermuda. In the cooler parts of Europe they are almost entirely a greenhouse plant. With us they are chiefly used for summer decoration outside, and our warm, bright summer suits them finely if well supplied with water.

They root easily from young growths in spring, and with occasional pinching and shifting on as required soon make large plants. It is with the care of large plants that we are most concerned, and to obtain a fine lot of flowers in the summer, and I might just mention that this summer of 1899 the oleanders have been unusually fine.

The flower comes on the matured wood of the spring growth or previous fall, so the ideal treatment would be to store them in October, after flowering, in a very cool house, or a light shed will do, but no frost must touch them. In early April prune back the growths that have borne flowers, and with more heat and more water encourage them to make their growth, which by June will be fairly matured, and they will then soon flower. During the winter months they will do with very little water unless kept in a warm greenhouse, when, naturally, they want more.

The correct name of our common oleander is Nerium Oleander, and several handsome varieties exist: Album plenum, double white; Henri Mares, pink, double; Madonna grandiflorum, creamy white, large and double; Professor Durand, pale yellow, free; Rose Double, bright rose; splendens, bright red, double and several others.

The oleander is pestered with mealy bug, and much more by a white scale. There is no excuse for the bug on a plant that will enjoy the hose as does the oleander. When you see the signs of scale, sponge the whole plant with kerosene emulsion.

ORANGE.

The writer's first experience in gardening, or that for which there was any pay, was in an old fashioned conservatory in the curious roof of which there was enough lead to make "sinkers" for all the fishermen of the great lakes. It was very dark at all times, and more than one winter can I remember that the old heating flues which ran beneath the white and spotless paths were never lighted. Such is, or was, the climate of the south coast of England. The frost never entered this house, for a venerable heliotrope grew against the south wall, a beautiful plant of Acacia pubescens flourished at the east end, a Phormium tenax grew strong and bushy in the northeast corner, close by a veteran Fuchsia fulgens; opposite them were two bushes of the tea tree, and not far off a beautiful tree of the Norfolk Island pine (Araucaria excelsa) that had to be sunk in the border to keep its top from the roof, and there were huge camellia trees that bore thousands of blossoms, the single red a more beautiful tree than any of them.

But the chief feature of this old house, that was torn down about forty years ago, was the large orange trees which were planted out in the borders. There were flowers or oranges in some degree of ripeness all the year round, and there were several varieties. Perhaps it was the cool, dark house that was accountable for the flavor and texture of these oranges, for I must say that inferior as most tropical fruit is when picked green and sent to us,

that the oranges we bought in the shops were much superior to those that ripened on those old trees. Quantity there was by the bushel, but the quality was not tempting, and the writer was at that age when anything good to eat was tempting. An accidental(?) shake of a tree would always bring a few of the big yellow fellows to the ground, but they suffered less from the omnivorous appetite of a 15-year-old than the peaches and nectarines in the same garden. Yet we hear travelers and residents of our orange-growing states declare that the ripe fruit, freshly picked, is far superior to those picked prematurely and sent to our northern markets. This little diversion on oranges is not what we are after, and we must cease.

Small dwarf oranges in pots have been grown for several years past, and are now seen in all the florists' stores at Christmas. A plant in an eight-inch pot and two feet high, well covered with fruit, is very attractive, and many people want one. We have not found them to hold their foliage as could be wished in a parlor or sitting-room, but the golden fruit hangs on. It is surprising to how many people the orange tree is yet a stranger. The majority of our people don't know whether they grow like a 'muskmelon or a chestnut.

The varieties of the orange are said to be almost as numerous as those of the apple, and the large, fine flavored kinds, such as the Navel, would not be precocious and free fruiting enough to make very small specimens in pots bearing two or three dozen fruits. The variety or species grown for this purpose is, I believe, the Otaheite, which flowers and fruits very young. As

might be expected, the fruit is small, but none the less ornamental on that account.

You had much better leave the growing of the plant to a specialist, who will or can supply you with small plants in pots and with fruit about ready to color or colored, from one foot to thirty inches high, and perhaps larger. I shall merely attempt to tell you how to produce another crop of fruit for the following winter on any that you may happen to have left over.

You can keep them anywhere in a cool house till the first of March, then cut them back a few inches and put into more heat. Keep them syringed and in the full light. They will soon make a good growth and in May will flower. Give air without a cold draft, and be careful not to let their handsome leaves burn. The fruit will soon set, and from that on they want a light, airy house, plenty of water and only shade enough to keep the leaves from burning. In September or October the fruit will begin to color, and from that on they can be kept in a temperature of 50 to 55 degrees.

The greatest enemy to oranges is the white scale, and when plants are badly infested with it, especially little plants, it is as well to destroy them, scale and all. If a larger plant in a tub that you value, cut it back in the spring and give the bark two or three spongings with kerosene emulsion.

Large oranges in tubs are used largely in some parts of Europe for ornamental gardening. We have not yet reached that, and I trust never will, for a large orange tree in a tub is a kind of white elephant to all concerned.

Calanthe Veitchii.

Cattleya Labiata.

ORCHIDS.

There is no class of plants at which the great majority of our commercial men look with greater apprehension than the orchids. To grow them successfully is something they may dream of but never achieve, so they think; but, fortunately, much of this mystery regarding their culture is rapidly passing away. Special houses are no longer deemed essential for the successful cultivation of orchids. It would be rash to say that orchids are among the easiest of plants to grow, because there is a wide difference between keeping them alive only and growing them to perfection, or as near perfection as we can with our artificial conditions. Yet it is the truth to say that no plant we grow will stand as much abuse or is more difficult to kill, providing the neglect is not too prolonged. A commercial firm whom I have every reason to believe thoroughly understand the most enlightened culture of orchids have adopted in their practice what may be called the board system of cultivation. For those growing large quantities for the cut blooms, the plan is doubtless admirable, and does not

conflict with any cultural directions that will follow.

In these introductory remarks a few words on the popularity and probable future popularity and profitableness of orchids will not be out of place. It is true that ten years ago, through the efforts of one American firm, there were many small collections disseminated throughout the country, and many of them were not the easiest species to grow, or even good commercial kinds. Disappointment occurred in hundreds of cases, and for several years you have heard less said of orchids, at any rate, less favorable mention. But another change is about us. Many of our enterprising commercial men realize that orchid flowers are going to be in demand, whether they grow them or not, and many of them are going into orchids in a businesslike way, and giving them a portion of their skill and ability, as they have for years given the rose, the carnation, or the violet. And to keep pace with this we now have firms, both at home and abroad, ready to supply us at moderate cost with the most desirable and valuable commercial species and varieties.

The writer cannot conceive that

there can be a doubt of the ever increasing admiration and fondness for these flowers, so beautiful, both in form and color, and so long lasting. Admiration they receive now by all, but there is neither supply nor demand as yet for the orchids to amount to much in the aggregate of our flower sales for the year. I am far from wishing to see the profit, or even liberal profit, of the present few orchid growers cut down, and believe that when the price of a cattleya flower is more in sympathy with the pocket of the average flower buyer the demand will so enormously increase that the immense quantities which will in a few years be sold will be a far better business than the relatively few high-priced flowers sold today. If any people under the sun like and crave for "a change," it is our own; flowers are no exception, and what a delightful change from the morning, noon and night everlasting Bridesmaid rose is a bunch of cattleyas or many other gorgeous orchids. In Covent Garden, the great flower market of London, there are possibly as many orchids sold as rosebuds; but that is not difficult to understand; their orchids are grand in quality and moderate in price, while their rosebuds are rubbish.

The genera of which cultural directions follow embrace all the orchids that are desirable or essential for the commercial man to handle. All can be grown easily and profitably, and the different genera, species and occasionally a variety, cover the entire season, giving you every form, color and shading of this gorgeous family, which may be called the birds of paradise of Flora's Kingdom. The student or specialist in orchids wishing to learn of every known species and variety should obtain the volume on orchids

written some years ago by Benj. S. Williams, London, Eng.

The "peat" so often mentioned in the following directions is not the same material which is found in many parts of Europe. That "peat" is the surface soil, where some of the ericas are or have been growing, and after the vegetable matter has been shaken out it is merely a lump of fibrous roots of no fertilizing benefit, but merely a mechanical medium. This quality of peat is seldom found here, but a very good substitute is found in the chopped-up fibrous roots of our strong growing native ferns, a good quality of which

is sold by several firms, and this is the "peat" referred to below.

I trust the would-be grower of orchids will dispel from his mind the idea that there is any secret or mystery in growing orchids. The cardinal qualities that will grow a house of roses will grow orchids—attention to the requirements of the plants, cleanliness, air, light, moisture, but above all, with orchids study the time and length of time the plants need resting. The latter is the most essential part of orchid culture.

The following cultural directions have been prepared and written by Mr. Wm. Hewson, whom I now have the honor to employ. He began his orchid experience with the fine collection at Goodwood, the grand home of the Duke of Richmond, afterwards being constantly associated with orchid culture in several places in the vicinity of London. After arriving in this country he was the practical cultivator of the wonderful collection of Mrs. Morgan, of New York, during the last three years of its existence. Since that time and always he has been an orchid enthusiast, and they have never been absent from his charge. What he says about them is plain and to the point, and can be understood by all, and I have proof, and with the utmost confidence say, that every word of his can be confidently relied upon and followed.   WM. SCOTT.

Best Orchids for Commercial Purposes.

All baskets or racks should be made of red cedar, or hardwood, and should be put together with copper wire or copper nails, to prevent rusting.

AERIDES.—This beautiful genus is a native of India and the Indian archipelago, and requires a rather high temperature. They can be successfully grown suspended from the roof of a palm house, where a temperature of 60 to 65 degrees can be maintained during the winter months. Their resting season is from about November to March, after which period the temperature can rise 10 or 15 degrees as the growing season advances. They can be grown in either pots or baskets, but I prefer the latter. Fill the pots or baskets two-thirds full of clean broken potsherds or charcoal; place your plant well up and finish off with a good top dressing of live, clean sphagnum moss. Care should be taken to keep the plants clean; remove all decayed matter from their roots and replace with fresh when occasion requires. Give a liberal supply of water during their growing season; in fact, they should never be allowed to become dry, or the leaves will shrivel. The white and brown scale are deadly enemies to this class of plants, and should be watched for, or the plants will soon become useless.

Aerides Fieldingii, a very free flowering species with bright, rose colored spikes, commonly called the fox-brush orchid. It generally blooms during

Mass of Cattleya Trianae, grown on wooden block.

June and July and lasts about three weeks in perfection.

Aerides crispum, another beautiful species, a free bloomer and of easy culture. This variety grows best in a basket suspended from the roof, blooms in summer, and the flowers have a very pleasing odor.

Aerides Lobbii, a dwarf growing species, does well in a basket, blooms during June and July, the spikes of pink flowers from 12 to 18 inches long and perfectly round. This is a grand variety.

Aerides odoratum majus, a grand old variety, very free bloomer, beautiful, aromatic odor, flowers in summer, lasting about two weeks in perfection; should find a place in every collection.

ANGRAECUM.—This peculiar genus requires the same treatment as aerides, only they all grow best in pots and require abundance of drainage and plenty of moisture during their growing season, which is about the same as that of the aerides. A little good fibrous peat can be used with the sphagnum for potting. They are mostly natives of Madagascar. The following I consider the best varieties for commercial purposes:

Angraecum eburneum, greenish-white flowers, very sweet and very large, strong spikes; blooms during the winter months.

Angraecum sesquipedale. This species I consider the best of the genus. It is a good grower and has large, peculiarly-formed flowers, with long white tails of ivory whiteness, and

Cattleya Mossiae.

very fragrant. I have seen these tails from 10 to 15 inches long. It blooms in winter.

Angraecum Ellisii, another fine species, with immense flower spikes of pure white color, lip a cinnamon brown; very sweet scented.

CALANTHE.—A terrestrial orchid, and many are also deciduous. They are best grown in pots, well drained, and the bulbs well elevated. Pot in a compost of good fibrous loam, some well rotted cow manure, a little good, sharp sand, and some broken charcoal, well mixed. Pot in March for flowering in December and January. They require a brisk heat and plenty of water in their growing season. An occasional watering with good liquid manure is very helpful to them. Place the plants in a cool house a few days before cutting the flowers for market, as this greatly adds to their strength and color. They should be rested in the same temperature as they were grown, but withhold water altogether until you wish to start them growing again. This variety is subject to thrip and should therefore be watched.

Calanthe Veitchii, a beautiful sort, with large, branching spikes of flowers of a fine rosy pink color.

Calanthe vestita rubro-oculata. This variety has flowers the same as the

House of Cattleya Trianae.

allowed to accumulate, will soon destroy the best of specimens.

Cattleya gigas, one of the finest species, from New Granada, has fine, bold spikes of beautifully marked flowers, pale rose and crimson, and yellow blotched throat. Blooms in April or May.

Cattleya labiata, one of the very best, from Brazil, with beautiful rose and crimson flowers, which come in November and December. This variety grows best in a pot.

Cattleya Mendelli, a beautiful species from South America, flowers in April or May. Color white and crimson; will do well in a basket, and on no account over-pot this variety.

Cattleya Mossiae. This fine, old species is perhaps the best known of this genus, and should be in every collection. It blooms in early spring and lasts a long time in perfection if kept cool and dry. It will do well on a block if room is limited, and, suspended among the palms, will grow finely.

Cattleya Trianae. This is one of the most extensively grown species of the genus. Flowering as it does during the autumn and winter months, it is a general favorite with all; can be grown on a block.

Cattleya Percivaliana is a fine winter flowering variety from South America, grows best in a basket or pot, profuse bloomer under proper treatment; should be in every collection.

Cattleya Bowringiana, a magnificent species, producing on one spike as many as twelve or fifteen blooms of rosk pink color, with crimson lip. It should be grown in a pot with plenty of room, as it is a very strong grower.

Cattleya crispa, a fine species, very free flowering, producing fine spikes of beautiful, pure white flowers, with crimson lip and throat. Blooms in July or August, and will grow well in a basket suspended from the roof.

COELOGYNE.—This genus has many species and varieties, though very few are of much value to the commercial florist. The most useful is the beautiful

Coelogyne cristata grandiflora, which produces its graceful racemes of white flowers with yellow blotches on throat in early spring. This is of comparatively easy culture. It likes abundance of water during its growing season, which lasts till the bulbs have matured, when water should be withheld until the flower spikes are well advanced; otherwise they will start growing again instead of blooming. This species grows best in pots or pans, giving the plants plenty of room and good drainage. Elevate the bulbs on a compost of good fibrous peat, broken charcoal, or potsherds about the size of hazel nuts, and sphagnum moss, and finish off with live sphagnum as a top dressing. Potting should be done as soon as the flowering season is over. This plant will do well in a night temperature of 50 to 55 degrees in winter.

Cattleyas Mounted in Various Ways.

preceding, only differing in color, which is white, with crimson eye.

Calanthe lutea, a beautiful variety, with fine spikes of white and lemon colored flowers.

CATTLEYA.—This genus is undoubtedly one of the best for commercial purposes, on account of its easy culture and the varied and extreme beauty of its flowers, which are produced at all times of the year and always find a ready sale in the large cities. Most of the species can be successfully grown where a temperature of 55 to 60 degrees can be maintained during winter. They can be grown in either pots or baskets, and many will do well on blocks of wood suspended from the roof, if the room is limited. All cattleyas like a strong light and should be grown as near the glass as possible, with but little shading and a

moderate supply of water, even in their growing season. By keeping them a little on the dry side, you insure stronger growth and better flowers. Have plenty of air and moisture around them and you will seldom if ever fail to be satisfied with the results. Pot in a well drained pot or basket in good, fibrous peat, with all the decayed vegetable matter removed, and some clean, live sphagnum moss. For blocks use a little peat at the back and fasten firmly with copper wire. Of course, plants grown in this way must be watched, that they do not suffer from lack of water, as they dry out much quicker than when in pots or baskets. The resting season of a cattleya commences as soon as they have finished their growth, when water must be withheld enough to just keep the plant from shriveling. The white scale is an enemy of the plants, and if

CYPRIPEDIUM.—This peculiarly interesting genus is of easy culture. They may be grown in either pots or pans, in equal parts of good, fibrous peat and live sphagnum; a little broken charcoal is beneficial, as it prevents the compost from becoming sour. You can feed liquid manure to the strong growing varieties and it will materially help them if they are well rooted. They like plenty of water during summer, their growing season, and being evergreen and having no bulbs to feed from, should never be allowed to suffer from lack of it. Do not overshade cypripediums, as they delight in a strong light. Most all varieties require a warm temperature. The following are the best for commercial purposes:

Cypripedium insigne is a cool house species, but can be grown in a warm house. It is a profuse bloomer if well cared for, flowers in winter, and lasts a long time in perfection. It is very beneficial to put it outside for three months in summer, slightly shaded and well watered.

Cypripedium Harrisianum, a fine hybrid, often flowering twice a year, is a fine bloomer and stronger grower than most cypripediums, therefore requires plenty of pot room and should be grown in a warm house.

Cypripedium Lawrenceanum, another species requiring a warm, moist atmosphere, is a good bloomer, with bold, straight stems and beautifully marked flower. Blooms in summer and autumn; do not over-pot it.

Cypripedium Spicerianum, which I consider the queen of the genus, is a very free grower and good bloomer, and is a great favorite in the cut-flower market. It requires a warm

Cattleya Percivaliana.

temperature, flowers in early spring, and lasts a long time.

Cypripedium villosum, a grand species from India; similar in color to insigne, but the flowers are much larger, and have the appearance of being varnished. This is a very useful sort, as it will thrive in either a cool or warm house, and should be in every collection. It is a very strong grower, requiring plenty of pot-room.

DENDROBIUM. — The members of this genus are almost numberless, and include some of the most beautiful, as well as the most useful, orchids for the cut-flower trade. They can be grown in pots or baskets, with plenty of drainage and a compost of good, fibrous peat and live sphagnum, with some broken charcoal or potsherds mixed with it. They require a warm temperature during their growing season, with plenty of water, but several species, such as Wardianum, nobile, Devonianum, etc., should be moved to a cool house as soon as they have stopped growing, and left there until their flower buds are well advanced, when they may go into a little warmer house to flower. If this treatment is followed up you will be seldom, if ever, disappointed in the results of your labors. Watch for the thrip on

Coelogyne Cristata.

Cypripedium Insigne.

but by following the above directions you can grow it just as well as Wardianum. It flowers in May or June, and they last about two weeks in perfection.

Dendrobium densiflorum is another erect-growing species from India, and grows best in a pot, but can be grown in a basket in good fibrous peat and but little sphagnum. It blooms in April or May, the large clusters of beautiful yellow flowers being in form like a bunch of grapes. This species requires a long rest after the bulbs are grown, but do not allow the plant to shrivel. The flowers last about a week in perfection.

LAELIA.—Of this genus only two species are useful to the commercial grower.

Laelia anceps. This can be well grown on a block of hard wood with a little fibrous peat fastened at the back of the plant, which should be firmly nxed on with copper wire. It can also be grown in a suspended basket. Use a compost of good, clean peat, charcoal, and live sphagnum moss, and keep well drained. This is a grand species, with long flower spikes, which last a month if kept in a cool house. Give plenty of water during the growing season, which is from about April to November. It is a free bloomer and blooms in January and February. It will grow well in a cattleya house, but can be grown considerably cooler.

these plants, as they soon destroy them if allowed to remain.

Dendrobium Wardianum, a beautiful species from Assam, is perhaps the best. It is a very strong grower and good bloomer if above instructions are followed, but be sure you do not overpot this species, as nothing is more injurious to it. It blooms in early spring and lasts a long time if kept cool and dry. It should be grown in a basket, suspended.

Dendrobium nobile is a well known old species from India, requiring the same treatment as Wardianum, but can, if necessity requires, be grown cooler and kept back, or forced into flower, as desired by the grower, at any time from December to May.

Dendrobium formosum giganteum, a beautiful variety, differs somewhat from the preceding, as it is evergreen and produces its beautiful, large flowers of pure white, with yellow blotched lip on the top of the stems, from two to five flowers on a spike. This variety needs but little rest and should certainly be grown in a basket and suspended in the warmest house. This is another sort that should never be over-potted, and must always be well drained.

Dendrobium Devonianum is a magnificent species, and is best grown in a basket. Give abundance of water in the growing season and freely syringe the foliage at least once a day in hot weather, to keep down the thrip, which is particularly partial to this sort. It is by many considered hard to grow,

Cypripedium Leucochilum Godseffianum.

Some Types of Cypripediums.

Laelia purpurata, a magnificent species from Brazil, in form resembles a cattleya, and requires about the same treatment. It can be grown in either pot or basket, has a grand spike of beautifully marked flowers, with crimson purple lip. Do not over-pot it and watch out for white scale. This species should be in every collection.

LYCASTE.—This genus is of easy culture and can be grown best in a cool or intermediate house. Pot in a compost of good, fibrous peat and a little sphagnum and broken charcoal. Give abundance of water during their growing season; in fact, this plant should never be allowed to become too

Freshly Imported Cattleyas.

dry at the roots, even during their season of rest. The growing season is from about April to October.

Lycaste Skinnerii, a native of Guatemala, is undoubtedly the best species, blooming freely, as it does, during the winter months, with fine, erect, beautifully marked flowers of white, rose colored, and crimson, anu they last a long time in perfection. Care should be taken to keep the flowers free from damp or they will soon become discolored or destroyed.

Lycaste cruenta is a very free flowering species from Guatemala, blooms about April, and has a very pleasing, aromatic odor. It requires the same treatment as the preceding.

ODONTOGLOSSUM.—This is a grand genus of orchids, probably the most interesting of all. They can all be grown in pots, with plenty of drainage and abundance of water during their growing season; in fact, they should never be allowed to become dry enough to allow the sphagnum to lose its beautiful, fresh green color, even in winter. They grow well potted in good fibrous peat, with a liberal top dressing of good, green sphagnum, which should be removed as soon as decayed and replaced by fresh; this sometimes has to be done twice a year. They delight in a cool, moist atmosphere, and plenty of air in summer, and in win-

ter, when possible. A northern aspect suits many of them, as they do not like the sun, and should in any case be shaded from its direct rays. A good syringing with a fine rose twice a day in summer and once a day in winter on all bright days is very beneficial to them. A temperature of 45 to 50 degrees in winter suits them admirably, with but few exceptions. They should on no account be over-potted, and must be always well drained. They all flower from the side of the bulb. Watch for slugs and snails, as they eat the tender flower spike very often. Cotton batting placed about the flower spike is a good preventive. They are

also subject to thrip if allowed to get dry.

Odontoglossum ᴀlexandrae (crispum), a most beautiful variety from Bogota, one of the best cool house orchids, has a very graceful spike of pure white flowers, blotched with irregular cinnamon spots. The plant blooms in fall and early winter.

Odontoglossum vexillarium (sometimes called Miltonia vexillarium). This grand species grows best in the cattleya house, but should have the direct rays of the sun kept from it. Elevate the plant well on the pot and use only the best fibrous peat and good, clean sphagnum, and plenty of drainage. This species comes from Brazil and blooms freely during summer and autumn under proper treatment. The flowers are large, rosy pink, and very distinct. They last a long time if kept free from damp.

Odontoglossum cirrhosum, a magnificent species, that is a native of Ecuador, and produces a very fine spike from 12 to 18 inches long of beautifully marked flowers, pure white, with heavy cinnamon spots. It grows best in a cool house and should surely be in every collection.

Odontoglossum citrosmum, a truly beautiful species that comes from Guatemala, and differs materially from the preceding. It is best grown in a basket, suspended in the cattleya house, as it produces long, drooping flower spikes of pure white ground. with almost invisible lavender spots; blooms in June or July.

Odontoglossum maculatum, a charming species that also comes from Guatemala, and produces its beautiful, erect spikes of yellow and crimsou flowers during the winter. Grow in a pot in the cool house.

Odontoglossum Phalaenopsis, one of the best of the genus if properly grown, and should be in every collection. It grows best in the cattleya house and should be grown in a pot well drained. This is a very distinct species, with very large, perfectly flat white and crimson flowers, which are produced during the autumn months.

Odontoglossum grande, a beautiful, free flowering species, that comes from Guatemala and is commonly known as the "Baby Orchid." It grows best in a pot, blooms in autumn and winter, the flowers lasting a very long time. It produces an upright, stiff stem, with from three to five large tiger-striped yellow and brown flowers. It is subject to thrip if allowed to become dry. Should be grown in the cool house.

Odontoglossum Rossii majus, a sweet little variety from Mexico. It grows best on a block, with a little fibrous peat and abundance of water. It is a very free bloomer, with short spikes of two or three beautifully marked crimson and white flowers. A very suitable variety for boutonnieres. It deserves a place in every collection.

ONCIDIUM.—This interesting genus is perhaps the most useful commercially of any for its gracefully delicate spikes of beautifully marked flowers, some of which can be had at all times of the year under proper cultivation. Most of them like the temperature of the cattleya house, but can be grown in cooler quarters if care is observed in watering. Oncidiums do not like much water on the foliage, but require plenty of moisture in the atmosphere as well as free ventilation. Many sorts grow well on blocks, with sphagnum moss or good, fibrous peat at the back of them, and firmly fastened with strong copper wire. All varieties delight to be suspended as near the glass as practicable, but must be shaded lightly. They like plenty of water at their roots in their growing season, and those grown in pots or baskets require an abundance of drainage. They can be grown in either peat or sphagnum, or both, but I prefer the latter for most sorts, with some broken charcoal. During their resting season water very carefully, but on no account allow them to suffer for want of it. Most species are subject to the white scale and should therefore be watched. Slugs are very partial to the young, tender flower spikes, and a small piece of cotton batting should be tied around them to save them from the depredations of these pests.

Oncidium ampliatum majus is, I think, a native of Guatemala, and produces its large, branching spikes of beautiful yellow flowers in spring, and continues blooming for at least six weeks if in robust health. It grows best in a pot or basket, but can be grown on a block if plenty of water is given.

Laelia Anceps.

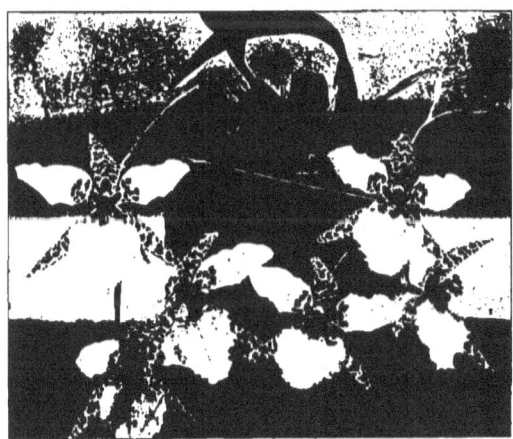

Odontoglossum Rossii Majus.

Oncidium incurvum, a pretty Mexican species, blooming very freely in winter, has long spikes of white and brown flowers. Grows best in a pot, with the same treatment as the above.

Oncidium crispum, a grand dwarf species from Brazil, grows best on a block with a little sphagnum or fibrous peat, loves moisture and does well in the cattleya house or any house maintaining a night temperature of 55 to 60 degrees; blooms generally in summer; has a large, branching spike of yellowish copper color; is very attractive and lasts about three or four weeks.

Oncidium reflexum, a fine old species from Mexico, produces numerous spikes of beautiful yellow flowers during autumn. It is a general favorite with both grower and purchaser and should be grown by all orchid growers.

Oncidium varicosum is a good species for all to grow, as it is a very free grower and good bloomer. Grows best in a flat pot or basket, in a warm house, suspended; has a fine spike of canary yellow flowers; very imposing in appearance; is a native of Brazil; blooms in summer and lasts a long time in perfection.

Oncidium varicosum Rogersii, one of the very best of the genus, similar to the above in habit and color, but

Phalaenopsis Schilleriana.

grows stronger and has much larger spikes; a very valuable variety for commercial purposes, both as a pot plant or cut flower. I have grown this beautiful plant myself with more than 100 blooms on a spike. It blooms in autumn and in early winter months and lasts a long time in perfection.

Oncidium tigrinum is another fine species from Mexico, with a large, branching spike of beautifully marked yellow and brown flowers, produced in winter; is a free bloomer and lasts a long time in perfection. Grows best in a pot.

Oncidium Cavendishianum is a beautiful species, having large, heavy, fleshy leaves, and is therefore best grown in a pot. It produces during winter enormous spikes of beautiful yellow flowers, and they last six to eight weeks in perfection. It is a native of Guatemala. Although when in good health it produces very large foliage, I do not think it needs a pot or pan in proportion to its size, as nothing is more injurious to it than being over-potted. It requires careful watering during the dull months of winter, which is its resting season.

PHALAENOPSIS.—There are many species of this genus, all beautiful, though many are not productive enough to warrant them a place in the commercial list. They all require a high temperature, not less than 65 degrees during winter, but 70 degrees is even better. They delight in light, heat, and moisture, and should be lightly sprayed once a day during hot weather; ventilate freely when it is possible, as they delight in pure air, but by no means place them in a draught. They grow best in perforated pots, or baskets, well drained with good, clean potsherds or broken charcoal, or both, with a liberal top dressing of good, live sphagnum,

which should be removed as soon as decay begins and replaced by fresh. As phalaenopsis delight in cleanliness, great care is necessary in potting this genus, particularly Schilleriana and amabilis, as they root freely and cling firmly to the pot or basket in which they are grown, and cannot be removed without the aid of a knife, and this is a very delicate operation, often resulting in serious injury to the plants. A good plan is to place the plant, pot and all, into larger size and fill up with charcoal and fresh sphagnum, and not disturb the roots at all. These plants should be suspended, if possible, as they love the light, but must be shaded from the direct sun, or the leaves will burn; and never allow them to suffer for want of water.

Phalaenopsis Schilleriana is a magnificent species from Manila, has large branching spikes during winter and spring of beautiful mauve flowers edged with white, with reddish brown spotted lip.

Phalaenopsis amabilis, a beautiful species also from Manila, is certainly the queen of this genus; blooms at all times of the year and lasts a long time in perfection. It has long, graceful spikes of pure white flowers, lip spot-

Orchids growing in hanging pots.

ted with pink. This is one of the best
for market purposes and requires the
same treatment as above.

Phalaenopsis grandiflora, a beautiful
species, that comes from Java and resembles amabilis in every way except
that the lip of the flower is marked
with lemon yellow instead of pink.
This plant grows well on a rack with
sphagnum moss at the back and is a
very prolific bloomer.

VANDA.—This beautiful genus requires a temperature of 60 to 65 degrees at night and delights in the
sun, remains very strong, and then a
light shading for an hour or two will
be sufficient. All the species will
grow in pots, well drained, and potted
in clean, fresh sphagnum and broken
charcoal, with plenty of moisture
about them, and lots of water at the
roots in summer, but be very careful
in winter, unless the pot is very full
of roots and growing freely. Give a
little air when possible in winter and
plenty in summer. Some species bloom
twice and even three times a year.
The flowers have a delightful odor and
last about a month if kept dry. All
vandas are subject to scale, and should
be kept free from these pests, or the
plant will soon be ruined.

Vanda caerulea, the beautiful blue
orchid, should be in every collection.

Group of Vanda Caerulea.

year, large spikes of beautiful white
flowers spotted with crimson. I have
seen this plant in bloom ten months
out of the year.

Vanda tricolor is similar to suavis,
of the same habit, and requires the
same treatment, only the flowers are
lemon yellow, with crimson spots,
purple and white lip, and last a very
long time. It also is a native of Java.

OTHONNA.

The species crassifolia is worthy of
notice. Because of its succulent, fleshy
leaves it is one of our very best basket plants. It withstands the heat and
drying-out process which our hanging
baskets undergo better than almost
any of the plants we use for that purpose.

It is most easily increased by cuttings at any time of the year. A
rather light, sandy soil suits it best,
and when its pendant growth is any
length you should find some place for
it on a shelf. Don't give it a cold,
damp place in the greenhouse, but
keep it warm and growing, and you
can multiply it indefinitely, as the
small pieces of the stem will root anywhere.

Vanda Suavis.

It is of easy culture and a very free
bloomer. A temperature of 55 degrees
at night suits it well, as the flowers
are a much better color than those
grown in a higher temperature. It is
a native of northern India and blooms
in autumn. Do not over-pot this plant
and suspend as near the glass as possible.

Vanda insignis, a grand old sort
from the Malayan Islands, blooms in
May or June. It has large spikes of
flowers of a magnificent combination
of colors, is of easy culture and a
very free bloomer.

Vanda suavis. One can hardly say
enough about this old favorite from
Java, blooming at all times of the

OXALIS.

A very large genus, of which a few are very familiar plants. O. rosea (floribunda) and O. lutea (yellow) are grown as pot plants and sold in the spring, and they make excellent basket plants, but not mixed with other plants. They do much better and have a finer effect when in a mass by themselves. An earthen basket or suspended pan is better for the oxalis than a wire basket, but either will do.

They divide readily, which is best done in winter when the plants are partly dormant. They dislike a wet, heavy soil, and need a good, light loam, well drained, and an airy, sunny exposure. In the fall they give them less water, and for December , January and February they could rest under a dry bench in a cool house with very little water. In March start them growing and divide if you wish.

They can also be raised from seed. There are a great many species, having yellow, white, pink and violet flowers, all greenhouse perennials, besides a few that are annuals. The two well known species mentioned are easy to grow and very free blooming.

PACKING FLOWERS.

The author might have called upon one whose business it is to daily, and perhaps all day, pack flowers, but since he received a letter from Chicago a year or so ago which acknowledged the receipt of a box of orchid flowers which conveyed the pleasant tidings, "The coelogyne flowers arrived in the most perfect order; they were finely packed," and as no one but myself had a hand in it, I feel competent not only to pack flowers, but to tell others how to do it.

This is an opportune time to repeat a short story of that great man, Horace Greeley, who embittered and shortened his days by accepting the nomination for president. In his young days he edited an agricultural paper somewhere in our state, and a delegation of western farmers called on him. After a pleasant chat in his office the leader of the party said: "Now, Mr. Greeley, we should like to see your farm." "H—l; farm! Gentlemen, you don't expect a man to write and farm too," was the forceful rejoinder. So it's not necessary for a man to be continually at the calling to be able to write about it. In fact, if he is too well posted on a specialty his brain is liable to be clouded.

In no part of the business (for this part is purely a business, unlike the cultivating, which is a profession) is there more need of good sense and judgment, which with constant practice makes an expert packer of flowers. In the first place, some men have a knack or gift of handling cut flowers different from others. Some men will take up a few dozen roses from the counter and move them or show them off to a customer as quickly but as gently as a mother handles a two-months-old baby, while I have often been annoyed to see others slap them

down as if they were a bundle of salt codfish. Every time the soft petals of a rose get a knock there is a bruise that does not show at once, but does in a few hours.

It is not the distance they travel; the quick ride in the express car can do but little harm; but they get jarred about many times before they are placed on the retailer's counter. The grower may handle them roughly; they get a bump at the local station, and another when thrown into the express car; another jar or two before they get into the express wagon to be delivered at the stores, and if they are going to the commission man their troubles have only begun.

There are, broadly, two rules to observe. Flowers should never be put into a box crowded so that they are actually squeezed, and, what is quite as bad, so loosely that they can shake or move about.

Roses should not be packed more than one layer deep. Their flowers should be sufficiently far from the end of the box that there is no possibility of their petals being jammed against the end. If they have any distance to go there should be a layer of tissue paper between every row of buds, and in warm weather, with varieties like American Beauty and Ulrich Brunner, every rose should be wrapped in tissue. The box should be long enough to take the stems at full length.

Small and tight buds may have another layer of buds on top, but with the choicest flowers one layer deep is enough. A great many buds will go into a shallow box because the flowers lie close behind each other. Some tissue paper over the lot and newspaper to keep them firmly in place, and then the lid. Flowers going by express, particularly where (as often there is) a change of cars on the road, should be packed so that no harm comes to them whether the box is standing on its side, bottom or upon end (which it frequently does).

Carnations don't bruise so much as roses, but their petals get crushed if crowded in and they have to remain hours in cellar or ice box before they get their perfect shape restored. What a change in the box suitable for carnations. Thirty years ago we thought a cigar box was handy to carry a few short-stemmed carnations in. A few years ago we had wooden boxes made, thirty inches long, and now we want a box five feet long, if it is to hold any quantity.

The best flowers of carnations should be laid in flat boxes, one row of flowers behind the others, as you do of roses, but they need no tissue paper between them. If you can give the flowers a few hours in a cool cellar before offering them for sale then you can lay them in the box in bunches of 25, but the less weight you have on the flowers the better for their petals.

Violets are easy to pack and are usually sent in bunches of 25 and 50, all tied by the grower ready to retail. They are often huddled into a box a

foot deep. That may do for some grades, but the finest should have a box some six or seven inches deep and the bunches placed one behind the other and each bunch wrapped in tissue paper.

Lily of the valley is easily handled, and if each bunch is wrapped you can pack quite closely, but let each bunch be reclining on the other and only one layer deep. It is weight that expressmen charge for and not space, so when supplied with suitable boxes it is useless to crowd and spoil flowers for the sake of another box.

Orchids are not packed every day, except by a few specialists, but laid on a bed of cotton batting, with the same material put between the flowers and sufficient covering to keep them from shaking, they travel all right. Cypripediums will, of course, travel with less care than the softer flowers of cattleya, odontoglossum and coelogyne, but with plenty of batting they travel well and two days' journey to them is the same as two hours.

The Lilums Harrisii and longiflorum are the most troublesome flowers to pack and have arrive without a grumble. If you let them rest on tissue paper their own weight will break their petals, and even if every flower was stuffed full of batting and every flower surrounded with it, there would be a great many damaged flowers. We have found the best plan is to get a box of sufficient depth and across it, say a foot from the bottom and the same from the end, fasten a strip of wood (an inch square will do). Then take half a dozen spikes of lilies and bunch them up with their flowers fitting in among each other and fasten that bunch on to the strip of wood a few inches behind the flowers. See that the flowers do not touch bottom, sides or any part of the box, or another bunch of flowers. The lily flowers will swing, but move all together, and not be bruising each other.

This principle we found a good plan when carrying lilies to town at Easter time. If you loaded up a hundred plants in the wagon and let them stand up singly, however mild and quiet the day, they would swing into each other and many would be broken; but if half a dozen are tied together and cannot swing into another bunch, they will travel perfectly.

In packing the cut stalks in a box you can put as many bunches as you choose, but never let one bunch touch another, or any chance to do so.

Bulbous stuff does not travel well when unexpanded. You should not attempt to pack them more than one layer deep, and lightly covered with tissue, but a great many can be put in a box, as they do not hurt in the least to be packed tightly together.

We do not have any more camellia or gardenia packing, and there is a vast army of young florists who perhaps never handled one. The slightest touch of your fingers on the petals of a camellia would leave a mark. You had to handle them from the under side of petals and in traveling each one had to lay on a bed of batting and be covered with a layer of the same. And the same care must be taken with gardenias or their petals will soon be a dirty yellow.

Eucharis flowers should also be packed in batting or their beautiful flowers are easily bruised.

I don't know that there is any special method for the other flowers we use. Common sense will suggest the right plan. As before stated, the main point is not to crush with over crowding, and don't leave room at ends, sides or top of box for any shaking or moving.

A few months in the autumn and again in the spring are the easiest and safest times to send flowers on any journey. The temperature is just right, no fear of frost and no need of ice, and during the cool days of October and November is when our chrysanthemums are mostly handled. Fine flowers of these, like the good roses and carnations, should be laid out in rows with tissue paper between their fine heads, and they are so heavy that one layer of them is always enough. In saying one layer it is always understood that when you commence with the first row of flowers, whatever they are, that you have a roll of tissue paper, or a roll of excelsior wrapped around with tissue paper, and that the first row of flowers rests against, which brings them up as high in the box as the last row put in, each succeeding row laying just behind the other, separated or not by a strip of tissue.

In the hot summer months there are not many flowers going long distances. When roses are sent a journey and the thermometer is 85 or 90 degrees, lumps of ice are distributed among the stems or placed in the bottom of the box; but if much is used it should be fastened so that it does not roll around. It is surprising how few flowers we get frozen when the weather is considered, but when going a journey by rail in the winter months always pack for zero weather. You can't tell how long they may be on the expressman's wagon, and there is where we get the trouble, if any.

There are other boxes besides pine now used for transporting flowers, but for very severe weather half-inch pine boxes are the best. Paper seems to be the best medium to resist the cold, a number of sheets inside and plenty more outside. Paper, if only common newspaper, which is so inexpensive, is excellent for the purpose. We all know, we ought to know, that a newspaper of a few thicknesses on our chest will in a cold time keep off the wintry blasts far better than the heaviest undershirt (you may as well have the undershirt, too). Paper is, although thin, airtight, and a number of layers will resist the coldest weather for a long time. So either in cold or hot weather plenty of it should be used, and it should be always dry. If wet it would be a conductor of cold.

The above remarks have been mostly suitable for shipping flowers some distance. The grower, and there are many such, whose houses are only a few miles in the country, who sees his boxes aboard the train, and Fritz, the express driver at the city end, knows them and shoves them on his wagon and soon delivers them, has not all this care and trouble. We know from experience that when we are quite sure our boxes will be carefully handled and promptly delivered, our carnations and roses and violets, mums or gladiolus or asters, can be just laid in the box, giving them lots of room, and they will arrive at our store in an hour or so just as they left the houses. But very different would it be had they to go into strangers' hands and journey 400 miles.

The cutting of flowers is hardly within the scope of this article, but here is an opportunity to say that our leading flowers should not be cut and at once packed. If you do, they are unfit for sale in the store for ten hours. A cool cellar is a great boon to a florist, where he can store his flowers a day or a night before shipping. I may differ with some, but if the cellar is moist as well as cool, none the worse; for roses I am sure it is better to be moist; for carnations, perhaps not.

Roses are cut several times a day when they are fit and should be in water a few hours before shipping. Once a day is enough to cut carnations, which should be always fully expanded. We prefer to cut (or as some say, "pull" them) in the morning and ship to town in the evening. Violets we like to pick towards evening and put their stems in water, but not in a cellar; under a rose or carnation bench is best; if kept on ice or in a very cool cellar they lose all their odor. Lily of the valley should also be cut and bunched and stood in water in the cool for twenty-four hours before using. The stems get charged with water and last longer and are stiffer. Chrysanthemums can be cut a day or several days ahead, just before they are fully developed. Here again my experience tells me that if the cellar is moist as well as cold it will keep the mums in fine order. Cut all bulbous flowers a day before you want to use them and then they won't wilt.

We are often sorely vexed at some miserable breakdown in the very last hours of the packing or care of flowers, and this is more than annoying. If your crop had failed at the start you could have perhaps replaced it, but carelessness or "thickheadedness" in the handling of flowers at the last mo-

Plants Prepared for Packing.

ment is heartbreaking. You have built the houses, watched and labored at the crops; perhaps through the curling smoke of a 10-cent domestic you have viewed your Flora Hill carnations or Marie Louise violets and through a hazy but pleasant daydream figured on the proceeds, penciling on the nearest plate or rafter so many thousand at so much per hundred, and all this is wrecked by some poor or careless handling at the last moment.

We are often called upon to send designs away by rail. There is only

store, when frozen, they would be useless.

PACKING PLANTS.

Among the large commercial houses of this country the packing of plants of every kind and at all seasons is reduced to a science and most admirably done; and still better, the purchaser has nothing to pay for their expeditious work and material. The Belgians are excellent packers, but we have to pay for their old boxes. The English are clumsy, old fashioned and antediluvian packers, but one

Then there are from eight to fifteen stout hazel stakes rammed in around the edge and brought to a point at the top, the whole enveloped by a Russian mat or mats which with a large sail needle is carefully sewed to the basket and stakes to prevent a cyclone from removing it. The whole when completed would make a most comfortable dog house or council chamber for a Lilliputian king and his cabinet. We must make one exception to these rather sweeping remarks. The English firms who send out orchids know how to pack them to perfection.

Good as our shipping firms are at packing, the general florist is not called upon to pack often enough to keep an expert for that branch of the business and sometimes the wrapping and boxing of plants is crudely done.

Small plants, such as small ferns or palms or asparagus, or the general run of bedding plants that are not wanted for immediate effect, are very easily handled. One plant, or in case they are from 2-inch pots, three or four plants, are wrapped lightly in paper (a tough but light and pliable quality of brown paper is best), a plant or bundle of plants is laid flat in the box with the roots against end of box. The next row is reversed so that the papers that protect the tops overlap each other and so you proceed till you have the bottom of the box covered. If you think the plants are heavy put in an inch or so of marsh hay or excelsior before you begin another layer, but if there is not much top to the plants, as in young carnations, then a sheet or two of brown paper is enough between the tiers of plants. Always fill the box, if not with plants, then with dry moss or papers, so that the plants cannot move. This way of packing small or medium sized plants where the bloom is not considered is entirely satisfactory with the lid of the box tightly nailed down.

In summer the sides and top of box can have spaces left between boards and in winter the box must not only be tightly made but well lined with several sheets of paper. This plan is quick, safe and inexpensive when the plants are going by express or freight and will be sure to arrive at their destination in a week or less, but it would never do to send plants this way in the hold of a vessel across the Atlantic, for they would rot.

Small plants that are wanted for immediate use in the spring, such as geraniums, coleus or cannas, should be stood up straight in a box, the ball and plant always wrapped, and you can generally squeeze in another plant on the ball of the lower plants, thus almost doubling your capacity, and doing no harm to the plants. These boxes, however mild the weather, should be covered lightly but strongly a few inches above the tops of the flowers or leaves, or the express charge on them will be just double, and the freight house will refuse them

Plants in Pots Prepared for Packing.

one way; they must be so fastened to the box, bottom and sides, by wire that they cannot move, and lightly covered with tissue paper and protected from frost. If any considerable amount and the distance is not too far, it is always more satisfactory to send a competent man with the flowers, to unpack and fix any little damage done in transit.

When receiving a box of flowers that you think are frozen, put the box without unpacking in a cool cellar, that the frost may come out very gradually. Many flowers are not much the worse for a degree or two of frost, but if suddenly unpacked in a warm

part of their packing is not obsolete and that is the charge for boxes, hampers and mats, which are always charged at full price. Strange that a people so great in horticulture are so old-fashioned in packing a few plants. Possibly it's because the English houses do not export so much as the Continental.

To this day when two dozen geraniums or calceolarias or a few bedding plants (if it was epacris or heath there would be more reason for it) is sent thirty miles to the Rev. Archdeacon Slowpay, D. D., The Frogs, Frogingham, Slopshire, they are sent in a large, round hamper that would hold five bushels of corn in the ear.

System of "slatted" packing, first layer.

altogether if unprotected. When the express people see that they are growing plants they won't dare not to handle them properly.

A lighter and better thing for sending these plants out in spring is a crate, which is much handier than a box. Make two frames, say 18 in. x2 ft. of 2x1 pine, strongly nailed; these are the ends and to the bottom and sides of these nail 6-in. boards, any length, and when packing is done two or three of them on top. Except for the bottom to carry the weight of plants half-inch stuff is plenty strong enough for sides and top.

Flowering plants, such as azaleas, can be sent away the same way, providing the weather is not cold. If it is, close packing is necessary, and then the ball or pot must be secured by strips so that if the box should get a turn on its side, which all closed boxes are liable to, the plants will still remain in position.

Palms and dracaenas of all kinds are easy to pack and very seldom can we make a complaint that any leaves are bruised or broken. If the weather is warm these plants can be safely sent by a fast freight line, which

saves the high charges of the express company, but whatever time of year it is the leaves should be brought up close to a stake, if stake is needed, and each leaf carefully tied in. Then they can be stood upright in boxes, with or without pots, and a frame work built around them. In cold weather or at least when there is danger of a hard frost, these plants should always go by express. The price of one palm may pay for the charge on the lot.

If only a few they can be laid in a box, well wrapped in paper, and any moving prevented by plenty of packing material, but when a considerable number they are better packed in the same way that we receive our azaleas, acacias, etc., so excellently packed, from Belgium, with this difference, that while the imported stuff have their roots wrapped around with moss and their tops entirely open and free, the palms should have their leaves well wrapped in paper, and all do for the roots, no need of any moss. The first plant is laid against the end of the box and when the row of plants is laid across the end, another row is laid at the other end with the tops overlapping. Then a stout strip of wood an inch square is nailed across the inside of the box and firmly against the ball of earth near the stem. Then some more packing material, paper, excelsior or dry moss, and another layer of plants, and another cross strip, till the box is full. No plant can move from its position if this is properly carried out and there is not the slightest crowding of the leaves.

The azaleas, which sometimes are twenty days from time of packing till they are potted with us, usually reach us in fine order, and so do palms, rhododendrons and other plants from Belgium. They wrap well in moss, which is tied on securely on the ball, but the heads of the hard wooded plants are left uncovered, and doubtless for the long journey it is right. Air they want, and for that reason in a large box of plants crossing the Atlantic several holes a few inches square are cut in the sides and top of box to let there be a circulation of air; without it the plants would lose their leaves. It is mighty important that these holes be covered with a piece of wire netting to keep out the ship rats. On one occasion this was not done with a box of azaleas we received and a ship rodent had made a state room of our box, and from the twigs and mince meat he had made of many of the plants he doubtless considered himself a first class saloon passenger. With our boxes of plants going by express a thousand miles there is no need of any air holes, in fact weather would not permit.

Whenever plants are going away, summer or winter, they should be watered, not a few minutes, but an hour or two before they are packed, and when wrapped in either paper or moss

they will remain several days quite moist. The material used for wrapping or packing should always be dry; the ball of the plant only should be wet.

Firms like Veitch, and Low, of London, take great pains in packing orchids. With cattleyas they put several small stakes around the edge of the pot and a stout one in the center, and every leaf and bulb is securely tied with cotton batting and raffia; a plant from J. Veitch & Son of Vanda Lowii 10 ft. high arriving in New York with scarcely the moss on the basket disturbed is pretty good evidence of the great care and pains that are used in packing these valuable plants.

Although our firms do not charge for boxes or packing, in some cases it would be quite proper were they to do so. The representative of a north of England orchid firm was assailed with the charge that the English firms charged too much for packing and we charged nothing. This was in Toronto in the Queens Hotel in 1891. He very naturally replied, not in

Finished for closing up.

System of upright packing, ready for "closing in."

be one to be decided by ourselves, and without any agreement must be left, like prices, to the discretion of the seller. The man who today advertised "cases and packing charged at cost," would get a severe blackeye, figuratively speaking.

PAEONIA.

We sometimes laugh at our old-fashioned friends for calling these handsome perennials "Pinies," but old-fashioned catalogues sometimes spell the name "Plony," and that comes pretty near it.

The cultivation of the herbaceous section is too well known to need any lengthy remarks. They should have a deep, rich soil; you cannot overdo it on either point. If planted for commercial use, four feet apart is as close as they should be placed. They will flourish for a number of years undisturbed, but every fall a good sprinkling of manure over the surface and forked or cultivated in the spring, will help them retain their vigor.

The flowers of the paeonia are in good demand every season and if you have plenty of room a few hundred plants will be quite profitable. The white and different shades of pink are the favorites. There are hundreds of varieties, and many beautiful ones that are called single, some being quite single and others having a small double center with an exterior row of large petals; these are very beautiful and can be called the anemone section.

The herbaceous paeonias are the hardiest of hardy plants. The best time to divide and transplant is to increase the stock is in October and November, or very early in the spring, as soon as the frost is out of the ground. A small section of root with an eye or bud will in three years make a large clump. When planting small pieces in the fall, be sure to get them well down in the soil; let the bud be

coarse horse trading Yorkshire, but in genteel English: "Yes, I know, but your folks put the charge on to the plants, don't you know?" Now this is the natural and reasonable supposition, but yet largely it is erroneous, and in the great majority of cases nothing is tacked on for compensation. Packing cases and boxes that answer the purpose cost us very little, far less than the same box would in England or on the Continent, but our labor, even if it is most expeditiously done, is higher than on the other side.

If you buy a good bill of palms or large ferns or any of those decorative plants that are easily packed, there is no need of any charge for packing, and if a man buys 100 geraniums of us in the spring, we are pleased enough to put them in a box and put a few slats over them. We get the 4-inch pots and that will about pay for packing. We would have to cart them off somewhere anyway.

But when you sell lilies or azaleas in full bloom, particularly the former, you ought to get more for them, for they take a heap of trouble and time to pack properly. Perhaps we will never make a specific charge for our packing, but there should be an understanding that to the man who sends his wagon and carts them away a lily is worth say 10 cents per bud and

flower, and when packed to travel 40 miles by rail it should be 12 cents per bud and flower. That is what we do every spring and it about pays for the extra labor of packing, and other plants in proportion where much tying and labor is needed.

This question will of course always

"Closed in."

with dark skins, a hot climate, crocodiles and poisonous insects, and the resident Caucasian among them would doubtless often sigh for his native maple, pine, oak or hickory, or a handful of his childhood's flowers, the primrose, heather, golden rod, or trillium.

A palm of medium size, say a kentia with a stem of three or four feet and perfect leaves, or a latania with a spread of ten feet and perfect, is much handsomer to me than the large but well kept specimens at Kew. Large specimens of the cocoanut palm, Phoenix dactylifera, Caryota urens, Latania borbonica, and others, we can remember as long as we can tops and marbles, but there are several of our most useful palms that were not then introduced.

As a small ornamental plant to adorn the living room, there is nothing, either in beauty or hardiness, that compares with the palm, and it is these qualities that make it so universally popular, and it is a popularity that there is not the slightest fear will ever recede. Years ago fine specimens were grown to be looked at, admired and discussed, and rarely seen in small, useful sizes. Now they are used everywhere and on all occasions. Besides the universal use of them to adorn the lawn and veranda in summer and the drawing room and parlor in winter, they are now seen at every social function, marriages and funerals, receptions, dances, orations and commencements, store openings, dog

Tree Paeonia Queen Elizabeth.

an inch below the surface, for the frosts will be sure to raise them up. Paeonias seed freely and if the seed is sown as soon as ripe and the little plants kept in a cold frame the following winter and planted out in the spring, they will flower the second year. For the commercial florist it is, however, much better to buy roots of both these and the tree section.

The Tree Paeonia, as its name implies, more nearly resembles a shrub and the flowers surpass in beauty those of the herbaceous section, but are not so useful to the florist. They make beautiful specimens for the lawn, either singly or in groups. They are largely used to force for conservatory decoration, and are a valuable addition to our Easter plants, though they can be forced as early as January. For forcing, good plants should be selected in the early spring and potted into good sized pots or tubs and grown the following summer; then they will force with ease and satisfaction the coming winter.

You cannot divide the tree paeonia at the root as you can those of the herbaceous section, they being grafted, an operation you had better leave to the specialist.

PALMS.

These are our chief ornaments in the conservatory of the wealthy, or the room or veranda of the more humble home. As fine ornamental plants they stand pre-eminently at the head. For many years they have been grown in hot-houses and conservatories, but it is only within thirty years that they became the plant for the million. In Europe hundreds of acres of glass is devoted to their culture and a very large area of glass in this country is

now occupied with the raising of hundreds of thousands of small palms for the commercial trade. The writer is one who has never seen the palms flourish in the tropics, but I have seen many species in the Botanic Garden of Kew, where you have to ascend a

Latania Borbonica.

spiral staircase to get a good view of these giants of the tropics.

Grand and noble they may be with their gigantic leaves and plumed heads towering up 80 or 100 feet high, and novel and majestic they must first appear to the traveler from the temperate zones, but they are associated

shows, and Midway plaisances; some of the performances in the latter resorts being peculiarly Oriental, the palm is a most appropriate adjunct to the tropical dance, etc.

Palms are widely distributed over the warmer parts of the globe, and the natives of these regions have found a use for their fruit. The Date Palm (Phoenix dactylifera) is the chief sustenance of millions. The milk and pulp of the cocoanut are a leading article of diet in all tropical countries. The leaves are used as thatch to cover huts, and the hard stem is utilized for building and in many other ways.

Many palms do well planted out in the mild states of our Union. We are continually told by tourists of the fine chamaerops and braheas that are seen in California, and that most splendid palm, Latania borbonica, thrives in the Channel Island, where only a few

It would be quite interesting if some statistician could trace the annual increase in the output of the palms for the past thirty years. In this country at least it would (please excuse the simile) be not unlike the career of the bicycle: At first rare, and, when seen, stared at by multitudes. Soon those that could afford them purchased one, then as prices became more popular the majority had one, or, for a variety, two or three. Then, when the best patterns or varieties came on the market and manufacturers and growers turned out so cheaply the best kinds, warranted not to break at the

er climate to contend with in winter, a matter of trifling consequence in a house or acre of palms, and surely with proper care and management we have the right summers. We never see such short, sturdy, finely developed kentias or latanias imported as those grown here by some of our own firms, but not by all. The latanias we see from Belgium are handsome in appearance, but drawn, long leaf stalks, and are only fit to put in a palm house and grow a year to accustom them to the treatment that we expect our palms to endure and come up smiling.

The general florist who buys his young palms from some of the home firms and wants them to retail or use at once, as do all storekeepers who have no greenhouse, and the very great majority of greenhouse men as well, will find out (if that is not already discovered) that there are palm growers and palm growers, and a vast difference there is in the quality of plants they send out. In very large establishments, where house after house is palms, they are manufactured quickly, and quality is entirely subservient to quantity. They are stood very close together, kept very warm summer and winter, altogether inadequate ventilation is given, and the shade is of the permanent kind, if not kept on all the year, then at least nine months of the twelve. The difference between these palms and those grown with plenty of room, abundance of fresh air, and shade only from the direct rays of the sun, is very marked. The former are run up with long leaf stalks, the growth is soft, and the color is a dull green. The properly grown plants, even if the temperature has been high, are quite different. They are shorter, stouter, giving the plant the appearance of having far more leaves; they are a bright shining green and are altogether more satisfactory to the purchaser, wherever you put them.

These remarks cover a good deal of the ground relative to the culture of most palms. For the commercial men they must be grown without excessive heat; this is particularly true of arecas. They must have had plenty of ventilation whenever it was possible, room to develop their handsome leaves, and not made soft by a heavy shade. I can only see one use for these unnaturally grown tall kentias or latanias; they make an effective appearance at a decoration, but are so soft that a few journeys to "society" soon deprives them of their beauty.

There is some difference of opinion about the advisability of standing palms in the broad sun. In the tropics, as most all of our commercial palms in a natural state rear their plumed crowns to the tropical suns, there can be little fear of their burning if their roots are in the proper condition, and I have proved time and again that if their roots are not too crowded and they are regularly supplied with water that the kentias, latanias, chamaerops and phoenix receive not the slightest

Kentia Belmoreana.

degrees of frost occurs. It is this ability to endure a low temperature (but only a limited number will stand a frost) that makes them of such great value to us as decorative plants, and again, being natives of some of the warmest parts of the globe, palms like the kentia will thrive under the great changes of temperature that frequently occur in a living room, hot to suffocation if baby is cold, and down to 40 degrees if John lets the furnace get low. This is not the way to grow them, but it is their nature to survive these changes and makes them our unequaled house plants.

forks or turn brown on the tips, our errand boy takes home to his washerwoman mother a Kentia Belmoreana mounted on a $20 "Rolling Ranger" paid for at one dollar per week, installment plan.

The raising of palms in this country, of the useful commercial kinds, is a large part of the business of a few of our largest firms. Formerly many thousands were imported, particularly kentias, but that is fast dropping off, for prodigious quantities are now grown here annually. Arecas are much better grown here, and so I think are all useful species. We may have a cold-

Areca Lutescens.

injury in the broad sun. If allowed to get dry in 10 or 12-inch pots, they will burn, and so will a geranium in a pot with its roots parched. The arecas, the most decorative of all palms, do not burn, but they lose the color so much that it is not well to put them out in the sun. They are better always under glass. The phoenix are the least susceptible to any harm from wind or rain; in fact, they are grand plants for a vase or center of a tropical bed.

Temperature.

All the palms we grow, either for sale or for decorative purposes, are natives of a warm climate, and although submitting for weeks to a lower temperature than they would ever be subject to in their native climate, yet that is not what they should be grown in. Men who raise thousands of young plants to sell to the trade must, to make it profitable, give them a good, high temperature, particularly in summer, although a slow grown palm is much better than one quickly grown. A good temperature for the florist who grows or keeps a stock of palms for sale would be 60 to 65 degrees at night, with a rise of 15 degrees in the day time during the dark days of winter, and in spring and summer 70 to 75 degrees at night and as warm as you like in the day time, providing you have plenty of air.

Large palms that you keep for decorations solely are better kept not higher than 55 degrees during winter. You don't want them to make young leaves

while you are using them, which would likely be injured by a chill in transit in cold weather.

Watering and Syringing.

This same old advice must be given with emphasis about drainage. A crock and piece of green moss is enough for plants in a 5 or 6-inch pot, but when in larger, and more especially when in very large pots or tubs and boxes, which they may remain in for four or five years, they should have two or three inches of drainage. If water passes quickly through the soil, whether the plant is in a 4 or 14-inch, then the drainage is all right. If it does not, and it is slow in disappearing from the surface, then it is all wrong. In spring and summer, when making leaves fast, they want copious watering, but usually when thoroughly watered, once a day is enough. In winter, with a lower temperature, darker days and slower growth, less water is needed. A gardener knows at a glance whether they are dry or not. Palms in winter want as regular watering as in summer, but with the difference that after a watering they may remain moist for two days, while in summer, with the pots full of roots, they want a watering twice a day.

Syringing is most essential to all palms. First it creates that moisture in the atmosphere so congenial to

Kentia Forsteriana.

their growth, and then again it cleans their foliage of insects, more especially that nuisance, the mealy bug. If the house is paved with stone or cement, you should syringe at least twice a day in summer, and frequently throw water about the paths and benches. If the floor is gravel or earth, there is always more or less moisture arising, but syringe every day, and when you do syringe, don't hold and direct your fine but strong stream upwards at the underside of the leaf. Constant syringing on such palms as

Phoenix Rupicola.

latanias, kentias and arecas is another reason why the soil should be in good condition to let the water pass through. In winter syringe occasionally in the morning, and when firing hard damp down the houses, but less moisture is needed in winter, as the plants are in less active growth.

Soil and Potting.

I have within a few years heard of several of our leading palms being planted out in spring on a bench in six inches of soil and grown there during the summer and lifted in the fall. You can doubtless with great heat and moisture produce a latania or a kentia much larger in the same space of time that you would be growing it in a pot, but would it be as serviceable a plant in the fall? Would you not have to lift it early and get it well established before you sent it out to the confid-

ing retailer? We don't believe it is a good plan and would not buy such plants if we were aware of it.

Producing a large, showy palm is not the only object. People who give three or four dollars for a 6-inch kentia or latania expect them to thrive in the house a few weeks at least, and the plaintive cry of "My palm is turning yellow" has robbed us of most of our hair, and we don't want to hear it. They must die sometime, it's true, when growing or existing in the house, but let them pass gradually away, fading away slowly, and then their demise will be taken by all hands as complacently as the departure of an elderly wealthy aunt.

Palms thrive in a small pot compared to the size of plant, and should not be given a large shift at once. Growers of large quantities shift on as the plants need it at any time of year, but the florist who keeps only a few hundred had better do his shifting in the months of March and April, when there is a constantly increasing temperature. Always pot firmly. Up to a 5 or 6-inch size this can be done by squeezing the soil with your fingers, but in large size, and particularly if the shift is small, a blunt stick will help very much to firm the soil. Some writers say that roots never should be cut. Perhaps there is no need of it, but I have seen the roots of latanias and old seaforthias chopped off without doing any harm.

Never pot too deep. The base of the stem from where the roots begin is

easily defined, and they should not be potted below that. Some species, kentia for one, raises the stem by its strong roots. When shifting, lower the plant to the base of stem, but not lower. It is never advisable to shift a plant, say from a 6 to an 8-inch, just before selling it to your customer; far better let it go in the smaller pot and tell them it will do very well in that pot till spring, but give it plenty of water.

Palms do not seem particular about soil, and the mica so often seen in the potting soil used about Philadelphia appears to agree with them very well. I would consider the ideal soil or compost for palms to be a rather stiff yellow loam sod, cut and laid up in summer, and between every foot of the sod a layer of two inches of cow manure. When this was thoroughly soaked, and after a month or so, cut it down and chop over, and in a few weeks give it another turn. By that time the manure will have about disappeared, and the compost will grow any palm. A good supply of this should be under cover during winter for early spring use. If you cannot make these preparations, get a fresh loam and add a sixth of well decayed manure. Bone meal is often used with palms, and if a quick growth is desired it can be added to the compost at the rate of one pound to a bushel.

Insects[1]

If a proper degree of moisture is maintained and syringing properly done, red spider and thrip is seldom seen. If thrip is very persistent, then vaporize with tobacco several successive nights. Mealy bug is sometimes very troublesome and more often when the plants are crowded. If not removed by ordinary syringing, then have the plants brought to some nearby place, where water runs off quickly, and by laying the plant down and turning it on all sides with a sharp, strong stream they can be washed clean off.

Scale is the worst enemy we have to contend with, and the common brown scale is much easier removed than the white. I mention these two, for that is sufficient here, because the remedy would be the same were there twenty species of these insects on our palms; and there are not only twenty, but perhaps twenty hundred species known to entomologists. It appears they do not multiply with anything like the rapidity of the aphides. That is a consolation. And they breed and lay a crop of eggs but once a year. So if the palms are thoroughly cleaned, say in August, you should see no more of them for another six months. It is often supposed that scale have not the power of locomotion, but when very young in the larval state they creep about till they find a comfortable spot, then insert their beak into the leaf or bark, and that is their residence for life. Entomologists say that the ants which feed on the excretion of the scales take the young insects

Livistona Rotundifolia.

stock over and above what has been
ordered, much to the detriment of the
stock as well as the senders.

"The florist who would have clean
stock must in the first place keep all
his own; plants perfectly free from
these pests, and whenever a new con-
signment of plants is received take
such measures with them as will insure their being thoroughly clean before introducing them among those already in his possession. As a preventive against introducing foreign-bred
scale or mealy bug into houses, we
would suggest the following method:
If the plants are not more than two
or three feet in height, have a suitable
sized vessel filled with luke-warm water, to which has been added fir tree
oil in the proportion of one-half pint
to ten gallons of water. As the plants
are unpacked and before they are potted dip them thoroughly overhead in
the mixture (excepting the ball, of
course), being sure to immerse the
plant right down to the neck. Plants
too large for this treatment may be
sponged or syringed thoroughly with
the same concoction. After this treatment pot them up, syringe with clear
water, giving them an isolated position—quarantining them, so to speak—
until one is satisfied that they are perfectly clean. If after a few days live
scales are still observed and the plants
are in too large numbers to go over
them by hand, take five gallons of

and plant them on different parts of
the leaves of palms and ferns. If this
is so, then we, should get rid of the
ants.

There are several means of removing the scales by washing with some
insecticide, and when you wash the
leaves, see that every part is thoroughly cleaned. You can see the large
scales, but the very small might elude
you. Sponge with warm water, to
which has been added two ounces of
whale oil soap in two gallons of water.

A solution of two ounces of kerosene
emulsion in five gallons of water.
Sponge.

Water to which has been added a
hundredth of its bulk of "Nikoteen."

A weak solution of fir tree oil is
also recommended by some.

You cannot with any effect syringe
these solutions on the plants. They
must be sponged; and remember that
the very young leaves will not endure
as strong a mixture as the matured
leaf, and the leaf stalks are uninjured
by a still stronger solution.

The following appeared in a recent
number of a horticultural journal, and
is, I think, worth insertion here. The
white scale we get from Europe on
imported plants is certainly a very bad
species, and although a free trader, I
would put a very high tariff on him:

"The sending out of palms and ferns
afflicted either with mealy bug or
scale is much to be deplored, but the
number of complaints that reach us
from time to time would indicate that
some houses continue to supply their
customers with a quantity of live

Latania Rubra.

11

luke-warm water, add one-half pint of fir tree oil and syringe again; or make up a less quantity and sponge them with it. By treating infested plants when they first arrive, it will be found that the pests can be combated much easier than if the work is deferred, while at the same time the danger of the insects spreading to other stock is greatly minimized."

Propagation.

Palms are always raised from seed. Of our commercial species the chamaerops and rhapis can be propagated by suckers, but all our leading palms grow easily from seed, which is now imported in large quantities, and it must be quite an industry, the gathering of the seed where the several species flourish. The seeds, which are large (the kentia as big as the common acorn, and the cocoanut will fill out a vest pocket) are sown in any light soil in flats or pans. A mixture of leaf mould, sand and loam in equal parts will do finely. Just cover the seeds, and place the pans over some heat. If the compost is at a temperature of 75 to 80 degrees, the seeds will germinate much quicker than at 60 degrees. Keep them moist but not saturated.

When they have made one or two

leaves at most, pot off singly in 2 or 2½-inch pots. Don't pot them too deep; just to the base of the young plant. Keep close and warm till they get started in their new surroundings. Young palms for the first few months take up little room, as they can stand close together, and I should have added that the seed can be sown very thickly, as the young growths go straight up and do not interfere with each other at all.

For the first year young palms will grow slowly if kept in a shaded house without fire heat during summer, for these houses get very dull and cool. The cool nights lower the temperature and the heavy shade prevents the sun from raising it in the day time. A hot-bed with the sash shaded will bring them along fast in the summer months, but I would prefer a little fire heat in the palm house every night in the year. Having a few palms and orchids that I wished to treat properly this summer I have never been a night without fire heat, and I am sure it pays. This is not forcing them because we also have the ventilators up. It is giving them only a genial heat and good circulation of air. Young palms that are expected to grow should have fire heat every night in the year and ventilation too.

Not as I have seen in some plant manufacturing establishments, fire heat with ventilators shut, 75 degrees outside and 110 degrees inside.

Shading.

In this place I might say what I should have done sooner, a few words about shading. I believe Mr. W. K. Harris tried French plate glass, and with clear glass the sun did not burn the palms. We are not likely to adopt that quality of glass, as it is too expensive. Ordinary window glass is out of our reach at present. Our double thick glass which is commonly used will burn our palms and some shade is necessary. I should really think that with those firms who make a specialty of palms by the tens of thousands that some portable or adjustable shading could be used; perhaps it is by some. We all know the great advantages of it. But if it can't be used then be careful and don't put on too heavy a coat of paint early in the season. A very thin coat of naphtha and white lead will do, and thicker can be added in May.

I often think we are very careless about leaving our summer shade on till late in the fall. If storms have not washed it off you will see frequently the glass very opaque till early November. Now, did you ever think how the first of November corresponded for strength of sun with the spring days? The sun on November first would be the same as it would February the 10th. Who would think of shading on the latter date? And then again the plants are better prepared to endure the sun's rays in autumn than in spring. So early in September brush or scrub off part of your shading, and by end of the month have it all off, particularly over your palms, and I can't think of anything that then needs shade unless it be orchids in bloom or your cutting bed.

Varieties.

To attempt to give a long list of palms is quite unnecessary. There are so many genera and species that even encyclopedias don't attempt to name them. The commercial kinds are rather limited and familiar to most of my readers, but how few these are when you consider the hundreds of species of this noble family, many of which are worthy a place in any collection. In mentioning some of the leading palms it is not easy to decide which to place first, for the graceful and finest decorative palm is not always the hardiest or best house plant, the latter a most important question with us. Nearly every florist has had some experience with a few palms and has decided for himself which suits him or his trade best.

The names I have used are those by which we familiarly know them, and it would be little use to call Latania borbonica "Livistona chinensis," for our customers know it as latania and they don't care about a lesson in long, crooked names. Call it the Chinese

Kentia Dumoineana.

Kentia Canterburyana.

fan palm and they would remember it. People who don't know Begonia Rex by name know it very well as the "beefsteak geranium." That must have originated in the packing house district of Chicago, but it's about as elegant as that invented by an ex-horse car driver, a young Irishman whom I set to moving some begonias, and in an hour or so he informed me he had "got through with the big-onions."

The leading commercial palms are Kentia Belmoreana and K. Forsteriana. These well known palms are deservedly the most popular of all. Quick growing, splendid plants for the house, beautiful either when one foot high or twenty feet. Belmoreana is dwarfer and more compact than Forsteriana and has graceful recurved leaves when well grown. This plant with light and room to spread is the very perfection of form. Forsteriana is more erect, but similar in all other respects, and makes a fine palm for large decorations. Both endure the extremes of temperature, but no frost, and all other unfavorable conditions better than any other palms, the phoenix alone excepted. Other species not so valuable commercially, but making fine specimens are, K. Baueri, K. Canterburyana, K. Lindenii, K.

McArthurii, K. Mooreana, K. Wendlandiana.

Areca lutescens. This magnificent palm is unrivalled as a decorative plant. It has bright, shining golden stems, with feathery and most graceful leaves. It grows quickly and soon makes plants of a fine decorative size. They are often planted three or four in a pot, but even without that the plant has the habit of sending outside shoots from base of stem and large plants are soon thick masses of foliage crowned with the most graceful of all as a house plant to the kentias. Other species are A. alba, A. rubra, A. sapida, A. Verschaffeltii. All fine, graceful palms.

Latania borbonica (Livistona chinensis). This palm had been in commerce many years, before the kentia and areca were known, and is familiar to all. Its broad, bright shining leaves suggest the use that is made of the leaf. It is the Chinese fan palm. It withstands heat or cold, even a few degrees of frost. It has always been a standard decorative plant as well as a favorite palm for the living room. Perfect specimens make fine objects in decorating, especially when placed in a vase or where the whole

outline and expanse of the plant can be seen.

There is a form of this with light yellow stems and leaves, a beautiful palm known as L. borbonica aurea.

Phoenix. These are not considered as fine decorative plants as the arecas and kentias, although as small specimens they are most beautiful. Yet they are the hardiest of all palms. They will thrive in a vase or jar or tropical bed in the broad sun without losing a particle of color, and as a house plant, among palms, they are unequalled. They also seem to bear the tying and untying and the crowding and wear and tear of a decoration better than any other palms we have ever handled. For any unfavorable situation that a palm can be expected to thrive at all recommend a phoenix. Some beautiful species are not common among us, but they should be. The principal species are:

P. rupicola. Wide spreading, weeping leaf stems, with finely divided leaves. A rapid grower, most graceful and most durable. A pair of these we have in mind have within the past six years been 500 times packed and unpacked and withstood heat and cold, gas and dust, and still stand today in the broad sun with their arching fronds perfect.

P. leonensis, or spinosa. Habit slightly stiffer than rupicola, very handsome, with dark shining color of leaf. This is a species we do not see often enough. As a small plant it is most ornamental.

P. dactylifera. The date palm. Not quite so graceful but strong, robust, dark shiny foliage; splendid for large decorations or for summer ornament in any position outside.

Other species of useful phoenix are P. pumila, P. canariensis, P. tenuis, P. farinifera.

Cocos Weddeliana. This little gem of a palm, for such it is, is now raised in immense quantities. It has when but six or eight inches high all the grace and beauty of a plant three feet high, and for that reason it is held in the highest esteem for the center of the small ferneries. When these dinner table decorations are returned with the ferns dried and dead the cocos still looks perfect. Larger specimens

make fine decorative plants and they thrive admirably in the dry air of a living room.

Livistona rotundifolia. This neat little palm could be called a miniature Latania borbonica. It makes a dwarf, rounded plant, most charming for its neatness. Small plants but eight or nine inches high have a great number of short, rounded leaves. This little palm makes a splendid table plant, and in many other positions in deco-

Phoenix Pumila.

rations it can be used with good effect.

The above palms include the principal species recommended to our patrons for conservatory or house culture and used in decorating. There may be other palms equalling them in beauty and grandeur (Pritchardia grandis is one of the most striking and noblest of palms), but these species have been selected and grown in such enormous quantities because they have the necessary qualities. They are easily and quickly raised, have a

fine decorative appearance and are not easily hurt by the vicissitudes of our treatment, and are all good house plants.

Other genera that are well known, handsome palms and not scarce, are:

Acanthophoenix crinita. Tall, spreading, handsome fronds. The stems are densely armed with black needle-shaped spines.

Astrocaryum. A genus from tropical South America. There are several species. The Muru-Muru palm is best known. They attain a height of forty feet. The leaves are dark green above and silvery white below. A. argenteum is described as one of the best silvery palms.

Carludovica. This is a useful genus. Several of the species are used for sub-tropical gardening. The fronds are erect and stiff and the plant has the appearance of a small latania. Two fine species are C. palmata and C. atrovirens.

Caryota. This is a fine, noble genus.

They would not add to our list of decorative palms, but should be in every collection. They have large, much divided fronds, the ends resembling a fish's tail. Two fine species easily procured are C. sobolifera and C. urens.

Ceroxylon niveum. Often called the Wax Palm. From the Andes. Handsome for sub-tropical gardening, and thrives in a cool greenhouse in winter.

Chamaerops. Low growing, compact palms. C. humilis is one of the very few palms found in Europe. It has short stems, with a much divided leaf, which is long, narrow and erect. The whole bush, as it appears, makes it splendid for a vase in a conspicuous place, or the very ideal plant when two or three feet high and as much through, for a tropical bed. C. macrocarpa is a very robust species, fine for any purpose where humilis is useful. C. excelsa is a grand, hardy palm.

Cocos nucifera is the cocoanut palm. It has fine fronds of a bright, glossy green, but would be useful only as an ornament to the palm house. Australis and flexuosa are two ornamental species. The handsome little Weddelliana has received notice.

Corypha australis. A low growing, compact, hardy palm. Makes a fine plant.

Euterpe. Tall growing, graceful palms. Would not be as useful as the kentias for decoration. E. edulis and E. montana are the best.

Geonoma. A very large genus of low growing hot house palms. All the species are handsome, but not to be recommended as house plants. The species gracilis has handsome slender fronds, resembling those of Cocos Weddelliana.

Martinezia. Medium growing palms, the segments of the leaf resembling those of the caryota or fish tail palms. Caryotaefolia and erosa are two of the most useful species.

Oreodoxa regia. From Cuba. Tall, rather slender stem, with large spreading fronds. Before the introduction of the kentias this palm was in great esteem. Useful in sheltered places for tropical gardening. O. oleracea is the cabbage palm of the West Indies, and there are several other species.

Phoenicophorium secbellarum or Stevensonia grandifolia. This handsome palm is from the island of Mauritius and should be always warm; it thrives in a moisture charged atmosphere. It would not be either a house or a decorative plant, but where there are the proper conditions for its growth it is one of the most handsome of all. H. Siebrecht & Son say of it: "It has grand dark green fluted foliage of immense size, exceedingly glossy, and dotted with many minute orange colored spangles. The stems also are of orange color and covered with long black spines. Justly considered one of the handsomest and most imposing of the whole race."

Pritchardia. This is a most imposing genus, but should always be kept in the palm house. The leaves are large and broad, fluted, and a deep green. The leaves of P. grandis when well grown are five feet across. They make but a short stem or trunk, but send out many of their remarkable leaves. P. grandis (or Licuala grandis) is the finest. P. pacifica. Dark green leaves, covered with a white down when young; a fine species. Several other species are in commerce.

Ptychosperma Alexandrae and P. Cunninghamiana. These are known as the Australian feather palms. Tall palms of rapid growth, with fine arching fronds. In general appearance they resemble the kentias, but they are coarser in growth and much softer, and will not endure the rough treatment that the kentia will, which for all commercial purposes is much superior. But for tall palm houses the ptychospermas soon make fine specimens. P. Cunninghamiana was for years known as Seaforthia elegans, and was twenty years ago our main decorative palm, but is entirely superseded by the kentias.

Rhapis. A useful genus of but a very few species. The plants spread and send up several straight, erect stems, large plants forming clumps, which can be divided, or the young plants taken off as they appear. The stems from near the ground are clothed with leaves, giving the plant a thick, bushy appearance. The rhapis are very hardy and useful for decorating, and can be used on the lawn or in

Areca Baueri.

the tropical garden in summer. Rhapis flabelliformis is the most useful. R. humilis is almost identical, but smaller.

Sabal. This is our native palmetto palm, which grows so abundantly in our southern states. When growing at its best it has a trunk of thirty to forty feet, and leaves six to eight feet long. There are several species, natives of Central and South America, but they are not of any special value to the commercial florist.

I have never mentioned the flower of the palm, that feature by which botanists classify them into genera, because we don't cultivate palms all our lives, and grow them to be large plants without ever seeing a palm in flower. Most species attain a great size and are many years old before they flower, but true flowers they do have, we know, for we eat the fruit of the phoenix (the date) and the seed of the cocos (the cocoanut), and the seed or nut of many others are edible.

In conclusion, let me give my opinion that the use of palms, great as it is at present, is yet to be largely increased. The supply of the useful kinds has barely kept up with the demand.

The return to the greenhouse of a scrubby palm to be doctored or recuperated is one of the disagreeable features of our business, and must be left entirely to the discretion of yourself. You don't like to offend, but you must be firm in this case. If a plant is in fair order and the customer wants you to keep it while they are away, that

Verschaffeltia Splendida.

is all right, if you charge for it by the month, as we do. But when a kentia or latania is brought home with two small leaves and a diseased center, write immediately to the owners and tell them that it would take four years to make a respectable looking plant of their palm, and the charge would be three times the cost of a healthy plant of the same size. By that plain but truthful and respectful information you will usually get a telephone order to

Cocos Weddeliana.

"do what you like with it," which means throw it away. If not, and you must attempt to make a plant of it, the least you can charge would be one dollar per square foot of bench room per annum that its spread of leaves occupied. But let us hope you will have very little of it, for the sight of a lot of scrubby, half dead palms is most depressing, and the occupation of janitor of a pesthouse would be preferred to their care.

PANDANUS.

For many years past some few species of pandanus have occupied quite a prominent place among decorative plants, and this is deservedly so from the fact that the members of this genus in general are not difficult to manage, and are also quite rapid growers under favorable conditions.

The well known P. Veitchii and P. utilis are two of our very best house plants. The late Peter Henderson on passing a plant of the P. utilis in the hall of his residence, remarked: "The best house plant I know of," and Mr. W. K. Harris observed to the writer a few years ago: "Yes, the best house plant there is, both of them if they get water once a month only." "You mean once a week, Mr. H." "No, I don't. I mean once a month."

We have noticed ourselves plants of utilis in rooms far away from the light of the windows doing well if kept very dry. When growing fast they want plenty of water, but if you have to winter them in a cool greenhouse, say below 60 degrees, then be very sparing of water during the dark months.

They are undoubtedly two of the most satisfactory plants we can sell our customers.

From the fact that the pandanus are natives of the tropics, a rather high temperature is required to secure the best results, a night temperature of 65 to 70 degrees being best adapted to their needs, and during the winter months little or no shading is needed, especially for the variegated species.

A good loam enriched with old manure forms a satisfactory soil, and as the plants make many coarse roots it is found best not to pot them too firmly, and during the summer to give an abundance of water. If grown in a moist atmosphere there is but little need for syringing overhead, and particularly during the winter an excess of water may lead to an attack of "spot," if coupled with an accidental low temperature at the same period.

Propagation is effected by means of cuttings of those species that sucker freely, and also by seeds. Where side shoots or suckers can be obtained there is but little difficulty in rooting them at any season, this operation being quickened (as in the case of a pine-apple) by keeping the cuttings rather on the side of dryness until they are calloused, and by giving them a fair amount of bottom heat.

Seeds should be planted in light soil, and placed in a warm house, and the seeds should preferably be set with the bottom end up, this being the end

from which the germs emerge. These seeds are somewhat peculiar, being closely set in a more or less globular mass that hangs down on a stout stem, while the individual seeds, or rather fruits, are compound, and often contain 8 or 10 germs, the latter being enclosed in cells of a tough, horny substance within the body of the fruit. Soaking of the seeds is sometimes resorted to prior to planting them, but I have not found any gain in rapidity of germination after soaking seeds of P. utilis for 48 hours in tepid water.

The most useful and most widely known species in cultivation at the present time are doubtless P. Veitchii and P. utilis, the first named being unquestionably among the best variegated plants for decorative purposes, while its endurance as a house plant depends largely on the conditions under which it has been grown, for soft and sappy specimens have an unfortunate habit of rotting off at times.

P. Veitchii has been in cultivation for the past thirty years, and has proved itself one of the most satisfactory introductions among foliage plants of the famous London firm whose name it bears.

The second species in importance in the trade is P. utilis, a species that has been in cultivation longer than the preceding, and is usually to be had in much greater quantities owing to the readiness with which seeds may be obtained and germinated. This species, like P. Veitchii, is native in some of the South Sea islands, notably Madagascar and the island of Bourbon, and on the latter island P. utilis is said to reach a height of 60 feet, forming a much branched tree.

The specific name of this pandanus, utilis, which signifies useful, seems to be especially applicable to the plant in Mauritius, where it is cultivated for its leaves, these being used in weaving the coarse matting from which sugarbags are made.

As a florist's plant P. utilis is most useful in small sizes, for example in pots of 4-inch to 8-inch sizes, there being but a limited demand for plants larger than these.

This species is a rapid grower, and requires generous treatment in regard to soil and watering, and gives but little trouble in its management, unless it may be in those cases where an outbreak of "spot" is developed. The latter trouble is caused by the burrowing of a minute insect in the tissues of the leaf, and its progress seems to be favored by overwatering. If plants become badly affected with this disease it is most profitable to throw them away at once, as they are likely to be permanently disfigured by it, but light attacks may be satisfactorily treated by keeping the plants somewhat drier and dosing them with sulphur.

P. candelabrum variegatum, perhaps more readily recognized under the name of P. Javanicus var., is another handsome variegated form, and a more recent introduction than P. Veitchii, having been introduced from Java in 1875. Our illustration indicates the very graceful habit of this plant, the leaves of which are narrow and pendulous, and grow to a length of 3 to 6 feet, the white variegation being very clear and sharply defined on the dark green ground color. Unfortunately this plant is very thoroughly armed, the leaves being edged with sharp spines, while the midrib possesses another line of spines which are turned the reverse way to those on the edges, thus making it almost impossible to handle the plant without getting caught.

P. candelabrum var. forms side growths freely even in a young state, and cuttings made from these growths root readily, but owing to its abundance of spines it has never become a very popular plant in the trade.

P. graminifolius is one of the small growing pandanus that has been found useful to a limited extent in the trade, being at its best in a 4-inch or 5-inch pot, and only reaching a height of 2 to 3 feet when fully developed. This species is of tufted habit, being much branched, and having dark green leaves about half an inch wide, not so stiff as those of most of the species of pandanus and armed with short whitish spines.

P. graminifolius is readily increased by means of cuttings, and in small plants may be considered among available stock for the centers of fern pans. The illustration has been prepared from a good photograph of this plant, and gives an excellent idea of its general character.

this species is lighter in color and slightly glaucous, a well grown plant forming a noble specimen.

P. heterocarpus is rather susceptible to overwatering during the winter, and in that case may develop "spot."

Pandanus Utilis.

tive of the Philippine Islands, from whence it was introduced about 1866.

P. reflexus is another notably handsome species, and though one of the oldest in cultivation is by no means common. This species produces very long and pendulous leaves, in a large specimen often growing 5 to 6 feet in length, dark green and shining and profusely armed with strong spines, those on the under side of the midrib being turned the opposite direction to those on the edges of the leaves, similarly to the arrangement of spines on P. candelabrum.

The leaves of P. reflexus are so much recurved that they frequently hide the pot in a well-grown plant, and really have a very graceful effect, as will be readily seen from our illustration, but owing to its ever-ready armor of spines this plant is a most unpleasant one to handle, and is consequently not likely to become a popular one.

P. Vandermeechii is a comparatively rare species that would probably be useful in the trade if grown in quantity, being of somewhat similar character to P. utilis, but stouter in growth and usually more upright. The leaves of P. Vandermeechii are broad and stiff, dark green and slightly glaucous, the edges of the leaves and also the

Pandanus Veitchii.

P. heterocarpus, also known as P. ornatus, is one of the handsomest of the green leaved pandanus, being a strong growing species with broad, dark green foliage, edged with whitish spines. The under side of the leaves of

but with a little caution in that particular there is no special difficulty in its culture. I have never seen this species produce suckers, and it seems probable that the only means of increase is from seeds. P. heterocarpus is a na-

spines being dark red, and the same color appearing to some extent about the base of the leaves.

This species forms a very effective specimen, but does not appear to produce any suckers, and propagation must therefore depend on seeds. P. Vandermeechii was introduced from the island of Bourbon, and is said to be peculiar to that island, though quite plentiful there.

Among novelties of the pandanus family that have been grown to some extent of late years are P. Baptistii

pointed leaves. It requires heat in winter and does not like the hot suns of summer, or anything like dryness. Warmth and moisture are conditions that suit it. It makes a very pretty basket plant for a shaded house in summer, either entirely filling the basket, or with other plants. Its variegation is very pretty.

Its cultivation is of the simplest kind as it roots from cuttings most easily, either in the sand or a few pieces put around the edge of a small pot in any ordinary soil. Excepting as a conser-

markings of the pansy he sees the faces of the German, French, English, Scotch, Irish, and Italian girl, and other nationalities which I forget. He failed to find one that reflected the bronzy features of our Pocahontas-like Indian maiden, the real American girl, although there is every shade of flower and girl from white to sooty black. His verses were too early for him to include the latest American beauties, the Filipino and the brown senorita of the Gem of the Antilles. As there are several types of our American girls he has taken a large pale blue to impersonate the Boston type, and a large ragged edged yellow with a black eye for Chicago.

Poets have attended to the pansy thousands of times, and the modern sentimental song writer says: "Only a pansy blossom, only a faded flower." I think this song has something in allusion to a lamented maternal parent. Now did you ever notice, good reader, that the youth who never or seldom works but who holds down a chair in some third class drinking place all day where a stray treat or two falls to his lot, and towards closing time a sufficient number of treats has excited his vocal powers and then with a squeak, or a rasp, with sloppy eyes and expression we are edified with a few verses, such as "We won't go home 'till morning," or something appropriate, but it is sure to be something about "dear mother." The gist of the song is sure to be how he loves and cherishes and works for mother, and admonishes all to do likewise. Nothing is said about father, but the motto of the house that this young man staggers home to is: "Do not worry father; mother's working."

The pansy has been cultivated in the gardens of Europe for ages. If its expressive features could speak it could tell you that its ancestors saw the dreadful deeds of the dark ages, the chivalry but barbarism of the feudal system, the oppression and torture of bigotry, the fight for liberty, the emancipation by education of the masses, and now at the close of this 19th century, in this "age of reason" and humanity, you see the humble but free citizen taking home his basket of pansies to make his little garden prettier and to please the children.

The cooler climate of northern Europe is much more favorable for pansies in the summer months than our hot and often dry summers. But I have seen beds of pansies here on the north side of buildings, with the seed pods picked off and an occasional good watering, look fine the entire summer. Whether they last longer than July or not there will always be a demand for them, not only in the cities, but the farmers and residents of our villages buy them for their door yards and there is where you often see them well taken care of. I have frequently heard Mrs. Buckwheat exclaim, "I guess, Mariah, you didn't wet them 'ere pansies last night. I see they be a drupen."

Pandanus Candelabrum Var. (Javanicus Var.)

and P. caricosus, but while both these species are attractive, neither is of much value commercially.

P. Baptistii is a rapid growing plant, the leaves of which are striped with yellowish variegation, and in some measure resembling the foliage of Phormium tenax var., but without the toughness of that plant.

P. caricosus is more dwarf in habit than the preceding, and has narrow green leaves that are but little armed with spines. It branches freely, and might be briefly described as a very strong P. graminifolius, though perhaps less useful than the latter for trade purposes.

PANICUM VARIEGATUM.

A very pretty free growing, creeping plant with white and pink striped

vatory basket plant, or for planting in borders among palms and ferns in a permanent border under glass, it has no special value to the florist.

There are several other species of panicum, ornamental, and useful to the private gardener.

PANSY (VIOLA TRICOLOR).

Next to the geranium perhaps the pansy is more universally known among rich and poor than any flower we grow. It is a favorite with all children. "My little boy wants some pansies," we hear continually every spring. And the old boy and girl must be made of queer stuff if they are not fascinated with the pretty faces of the "Heartsease." An M. D. of our city has written some very pretty verses in which he claims that in the varied

They are raised in very large quantities by some farmer-gardeners and sent to our cities in small baskets holding one dozen plants, and usually sold at the popular price of 25 cents per dozen.

For this purpose the seed is sown in beds out of doors the end of July. Kept watered they come along all right and make showy little plants. End of August or early September they are transplanted into beds four or five feet across and as long as you like, and the plants three or four inches apart. Usually with plenty of snow during our coldest months these strong plants (for they are strong plants in flower before winter comes) come through all right, and a warm rain or two and a few fine days in April and they are gay again and quickly start to grow, and are mostly sold in May.

Last winter was a scorcher, and when you get two weeks zero and below on bare ground it goes hard with these little plants; thousands perished. Some straw, very thinly laid between the plants will help a great deal. It will catch the fast driving, drifting snow that otherwise would fly along to join the other particles at the fence row. Hemlock boughs with their arching stems upwards is an excellent covering, it does not lie heavily on the plants. Whatever you use don't put it on early; there is never any harm done till middle of November.

Florists who have a demand for some good pansies by end of April,

Pandanus Reflexus.

Pandanus Graminifolius.

either for those who have the good sense to plant early or for vases in our cemeteries, should sow not later than middle of August. You can sow in cold-frame and shade the seed bed, but uncover as soon as well up or the little plants will be drawn.

Middle of September transplant into a cold-frame four or five inches apart, and after one good watering seldom anything more is needed till first of December, or even later if winter keeps off. Then cover with glazed sash, and on mild days in winter, which we do occasionally get, give ventilation. Be sure in March to give air on sunny days or your pansies will draw up and be useless. In fact on mild sunny days it is better to remove the sash, and as soon as frost is out of the ground remove the sash entirely.

The frosts of winter have usually heaved the plants out some so the first job in spring is to go over the beds and press them back. These plants will be large and give fine, perfect flowers, and you will get at least 50 cents a dozen for them and should get more. When Mr. Pumpkin brings in his wagonloads and sells at 25 cents a dozen, and every grocer handles them, you are out of it.

If you have forgotten to sow in the fall you can make a sowing in the greenhouse in flats in January or February, and by pricking out in other flats and giving them the coolest, lightest bench you have, and putting the flats into a cold-frame early in April, you will have plants to sell that for continuous summer blooming, if cared for, will be more satisfactory than either your own cold-frame or the farmer's field grown plants.

Pansy flowers are a favorite with many in the winter months. In some floral designs the blues and purples or white and yellow look very rich, and when grown for cut flowers you should sow in distinct varieties. For this purpose sow early in August and then select the strongest, healthiest seedlings and plant on the bench in September, giving them all the sun and air you can. They are often disappointing in not flowering. They must have a light house and need every ray of sun you can get between snow storms. Anxious as they are to flower when March comes, they don't want to send up their buds in the dead of winter. About 45 degrees at night will do, and 60 degrees in day time if the weather is bright, if cloudy, less, but unless you can give them a light house don't try it. The greenfly troubles them in winter, so smoke. Out of doors nothing troubles except the hot weather.

In Europe where they give the pansy great attention and select the finest flowers and name them Captain Dreyfus, Paul Kruger, Aguinaldo or Wm. J. Bryan, etc., they perpetuate these fine varieties by cuttings, which root easily from side shoots in a shaded cold-frame in September. Here I have never heard of that being done. We depend entirely on seedlings and they are certainly as, we often say in the vernacular, "good enough."

For large quantities the seed can be sown broadcast on a finely raked surface and the seed just covered and pressed slightly firm. With expensive seed in small quantities I prefer to sow in shallow drills two inches apart and scatter the seed thinly in the drills and then just cover. You can quickly make the drill by having a rod an inch square and pressing one angle of it into the ground.

The pansy is a cold blooded little plant of the northern temperate zone, and it likes water. And above all, to produce fine flowers and a good plant it takes an abundance of manure. A good friable loam is the thing, with the addition of a third of decayed cow manure, or if that is not to be had, plenty of old hotbed manure will do. If you try to grow them all summer don't be sprinkling every night but give them a soaking twice a week and be sure and pick off all withered flowers. It is not the flower that ex-

hausts the plant, it is the function of bearing seed.

There have been innumerable strains of pansies, and no two people fancy the same flower. A first class mixture suits the florist best, but be sure you get plenty of yellow and purple; they are always fancied, and a large flower will always be preferred. One of the best strains I ever grew came from Mr. James Fleming more than 25 years ago, when the firm was Peter Henderson and James Fleming. On inquiry I found that Mr. Fleming had been hunting over the markets of New York, selecting a fine flower here and there wherever he saw one, and had in that way obtained a fine strain, and that you can do yourself. The best of everything is either nature's or man's selection.

The Giant Trimardeau is a large, finely marked pansy, but not of great substance. Butterfly pansies are beautifully marked. Other well known strains are the Odier, very rich in color; Bugnot's Parisian strain, Belgian, German and English strains. Several of our own florists have selected the finest flowers from these and have now a strain that I prefer to any of them.

PELARGONIUM.

All the familiar plants we know as geraniums are pelargoniums, but they have been treated under the name by which they are so well known. Under Pelargonium we include only the show and fancy section, that which is strangely so often called Lady or Martha Washington. Possibly some of these pretty plants suffered with the cherry tree by that famous little hatchet.

In Europe the Show Pelargonium has long been a standard decorative plant, and considering the ease and short time it requires to grow, and their rich, handsome effect, they deserve all the popularity that is theirs. Magnificent plants for exhibition purposes were grown by several of the English firms, chief among which was the firm of Charles Turner, of Slough. Plants six or seven feet across, not over three feet high, and as perfect in outline as a well grown azalea, are a gorgeous sight and are surpassed in showy effectiveness only by an azalea. Millions are grown in 5 and 6-inch pots for the European markets and some are grown for our own, but not in such quantities.

Great as their beauty is, they have these defects or shortcomings compared to the semi-double geraniums. The pelargoniums are much more troubled with aphis; in damp weather in spring without fire heat they drop their petals, and their season of flowering is not continuous. Two, or at most three, months of spring and early summer is their period of flowering; after that the plant makes a strong growth without flower.

As a bedding or vase plant they are useless and to use them for such a purpose is a fraud on your customers. With all their lack of the ever-bloom-

ing qualities of the zonal geraniums, they are far superior as a decorative flowering plant and they are frequently seen in the windows of the dwelling house, growing and flowering as if they had found the very spot that suited them, and if not too warm the perfectly dry air of a living room is, I believe, most congenial to them.

Propagation.

End of August or early September is the best time for this country. The cuttings should be from plants that flowered the previous spring, and if the plants had been kept the previous two weeks rather dry so much the better. When you cut the plant down for cuttings don't be afraid; cut it down to within three inches of the pot. Don't look for eyes, as you would on a zonal; there will be any number of eyes break from the stems that you saw no signs of. Any part of the wood will root; the young, tender tops or the firmer parts. Make the cuttings with two eyes, one above and one below the sand. They will root in soil readily, as we do our geraniums, but I prefer to put them in sand, either in the bed or in flats. Keep only moderately moist, and after the first few days very little or no shade is needed.

In five or six weeks they will be ready to put into 2½-inch pots and should be grown on in a very light, airy house. From the time they start to grow in the small pots they should be encouraged by a light, warm, but well ventilated house, to grow as fast as possible. They will soon take a 4-inch, previous to which they should have had their top pinched out. This pinching, or stopping, after they have made about three or four eyes of growth above the cutting is enough. If a larger plant is wanted they can be pinched again in January or February, but they will be later in flower. I shall pause here to say that this fall treatment is the most important. We leave our zonal geraniums in 2-inch pots till after New Year's, and if they get hard and somewhat stunted no matter, but the show pelargoniums want the opposite treatment; grow them on as fast as you can without forcing in a moist heat.

I do not like to advocate anything so antiquated as a shelf, but nevertheless it is a fact that pelargoniums will make a better, stouter, more thrifty growth during winter on a shelf near the glass than on any bench I have ever seen them grown on. By January they will be stout plants with several side shoots, and before the end of the month should be shifted into their flowering pot, a 5 or 6-inch; no more is needed. During spring they will grow very fast.

In watering they are like the geraniums; during dark, cloudy, cold weather they need very little water, but in the bright and warmer days of spring they will take plenty. Avoid

wetting the leaves if the weather is damp and cool.

The soil should be a good coarse, turfy loam, with a fourth or fifth of decayed manure, and when they are in 5 or 6-inch pots, or larger, give them a crock and piece of moss for drainage, as they never want a wet, soggy soil. From a 4-inch to their flowering pot they should be always potted quite firmly; this is a matter of great importance.

Pelargoniums will thrive in a very cool house during winter. I would

Peperomia Saundersii (P. arifolia argyreia).

say that from middle of November to first of March 45 degrees at night was just what suited them, and 50 degrees at night by fire heat is enough at any time. The principal thing to avoid is dampness, and in May, when in bloom, if we get a cold, wet spell, especially if there is a shade on the house, you must drive out the dampness by fire heat or you will lose the blooms.

There is nothing troubles them but aphis, but unlike the common geraniums they are much troubled with it and must be constantly and regularly fumigated. Tobacco does not hurt them in the least, so there is no excuse for their being injured by green fly.

The old plants that were cut down in August or September should be kept in the full light but quite dry for two or three weeks; by that time they will have made a great many small shoots or breaks from the ripened wood. When the growth is

quite small, say in three weeks from time you cut them down, shake off all the soil, shorten back the long roots, and repot in a size smaller pot than they were growing in, and start growing with the same treatment as you give the young plants. These old plants need not be stopped or pinched at all, and if kept growing in a light, warm house, can be had in flower by April 1st. They can be used as one of our Easter plants, although there are many other plants that are preferred.

Pelargoniums can be rooted during winter most easily, but except where you are short of some variety there is no need of it, as you get plenty of stock when cutting down the plants in August.

There has been a great improvement in the pelargonium the past thirty years, and what is known as the Regal type, almost a semi-double with fringed petals, is very handsome, but not so easily grown and flowered as the older type.

It is difficult to find a list of varieties published in any of our florists' catalogues, showing that these plants have been supplanted in popular favor by many less worthy of a fine name and long description; and it is the great beauty and grand qualities of the zonal geraniums that have done this.

Of the Show flowers we recall: Crimson King, an early red; Gen. Taylor, same color, but brighter and an improvement; Desdemona, an

early free flowering white; Lord Clyde, scarlet, with maroon blotch; Retreat, rose, white center.

Of the semi-double flowers some of the best known are: Capt. Raikes, bright crimson; Dr. Masters, dark maroon; Maid of Kent, white, spotted rose; Queen Victoria, orange carmine, white edges; Madame Thibaut, white ground, richly marbled with rose, a very free and beautiful variety; Mrs. Sandiford is identical in habit, but a fine semi-double white.

The fancy pelargoniums have smaller leaves and smaller flowers, but borne in the greatest profusion. The plant has a neat, compact habit, and we have found them to be a grand window plant. They want a little higher temperature than the Show section. The best time to propagate them is in January or February from the young growths, when they root most easily and will make small flowering plants the same summer. They want less drying off when cutting back in August, and don't cut them as severely as the larger growing kinds. The Fancy section has a longer period of flowering. They are a most desirable plant and there is of late a returning taste for them.

There are innumerable varieties, but I am not acquainted with the newer ones except the grand variety Bridesmaid, which with many is called the Pansy Geranium; upper petals lavender, lower white. It is a most beautiful plant and we frequently see them in the windows of the village home flowering for months. Any of the Fancy flowers are fine and the few varieties of the other sections mentioned are merely what I remember; there are hundreds of varieties.

As a bedding plant the pelargonium is of no use, but as a market plant, to be sold to those whose gardening is confined to the window, it must again come into popular favor.

PEPEROMIA.

This is a very large genus containing hundreds of species. Those best known and most useful to the florist are P. maculosa, P. marmorata, P. pubifolia and P. Saundersii (often known as P. arifolia argyreia). They are from tropical South America, which stamps them as plants that like heat, but they endure a greenhouse temperature for weeks without any apparent harm. A pan of these beautiful little plants is very attractive and their fleshy, succulent leaves enable them to withstand the dry air of a living room better than the vast majority of our plants.

They need shade in the summer but none in the winter and should never be kept too wet. A lumpy loose soil with a mixture of broken charcoal, or even broken crocks, will suit them well, and a pan three or four inches deep is better for them than a deep pot. The best specimen of P. maculosa I ever saw was growing on a rockwork at the side of the path in a palm house where it received plenty of moisture but no superfluous water at the roots.

They are easily propagated in sand or sandy soil in a bottom heat of 75 degrees, either by the leaf, as you do Begonia Rex, or with an inch or so of the stem attached. Early spring is the best time to propagate.

The flowers of all are inconspicuous; it is the ornamental leaves that make the plant valuable. P. pubifolia is well adapted for a hanging basket. P. maculosa makes a fine subject for a pan, and the beautiful species illustrated herewith makes a compact plant of great beauty. All the species that are desirable for the commercial florist can be said to be of easy culture.

PERILLA NANKINENSIS.

This strong growing foliage plant is useful for sub-tropical flower gardening. It has very dark bronzy leaves and will grow fast in a lower temperature than the coleus, which makes it useful in cooler summers than ours.

It is raised easily from seed sown in March and grown on in 3-inch pots till bedding out time. Like our free growing coleus it should be pinched to make it spread.

PETUNIA.

These are very popular plants. In flower gardening they are one of the leading flowers. It appears that the garden varieties are raised from the species P. nyctaginiflora and P. violacea, a white and a violet species, but in the varieties now raised by selection and culture we have a great variety of color, both double and single flowers.

In large beds where there is much flower gardening to do and not a great facility for raising the plants, or where expense has to be studied, the petunia is one of our most serviceable plants, and for a flower bed the single is more effective than the double. We also find great use for them in veranda boxes and vases. We have seen the double white used as a cut flower, but that day is past.

Any fine double varieties that you wish to perpetuate must be raised from cuttings, and the plants seen in early spring in 4-inch pots are from cuttings, but for bedding it pays much better to raise them from seed. Obtain the best strain you possibly can. I have received seeds from a firm that were splendid, hardly two flowers identical in a thousand plants, and the next year from the same source they were nearly all that washed out purple that nobody wants.

Buy seed that is sold for double always. You will only get about 40 per cent. double flowers, and that will leave you plenty of single. There are some distinct strains that come true in form and color. Peter Henderson Co. advertise a strain called "Adonis," valuable for bedding, medium sized

flowers of a carmine color. The California strain of doubles is magnificent. The "Dwarf Inimitable" is also a fine single strain, of a cherry red color, with white throat. There are also many fine double varieties that are named, but the great majority of us depend on a good strain of seed, as they make a better bedding plant than those grown from cuttings, and every desirable color can be obtained. For most places a variety of color in the same bed is preferred when filled with petunias, and they should always be given a bed to themselves, as they would give no other plants a fair show.

When choice double varieties are kept over you should select the young, fresh growths and propagate in sand before a hard frost has touched them. When rooted they should be grown on a light bench in a temperature of 50 degrees. If not allowed to get stunted these plants will give you more cuttings, which root very easily in winter when there is heat in the propagating bench. By pinching once and potting into a 4-inch you can have nice plants in flower in early May. They need a small stake to support them. Many such plants are sold in our markets.

Seedlings are the cheapest and most satisfactory. The seed of the petunia is very small. Sow in early March on a well watered fine surface, and no covering of soil is needed. Just press the surface lightly with the bottom of a clean pot. We usually cover the seed pan or flat with a piece of damp cheese cloth till the seed begins to germinate, but it should be removed directly you see the seed starting. For a few days be careful not to let the minute seedlings get parched. Neither must you let them draw up with too much shade and heat.

As soon as the small seed leaves are developed they should be near the light, and 45 to 50 degrees at night will do very well. When large enough to handle we put six or seven around the edge of a 3-inch pot and two or three in the center. I like this better than putting them in flats. About end of April we give each plant a 2½-inch pot, and place on any light bench. There should be a full exposure to the sun and abundance of ventilation. They are often put into hotbeds, but I don't approve of that, as they make too rank a growth. In a cool, light house they grow fast enough and make strong, stout plants in fine condition for bedding out.

Aphis troubles petunias, so they should be fumigated with the many other plants that need it.

A good sifted loam with a third of old hotbed manure is what they like, and if you wish them to jump along quickly in May add a 6-inch pot of bone meal to every barrow load of soil. Although the parents of our petunias are from southern Brazil and the Argentine, it must be the high elevations, for they want a high temperature at no time and grow and flower

weeks after many of our bedding plants are killed.

PHLOX DRUMMONDII.

This is one of the very best of our summer annuals. There are now magnificent strains of distinct colors, and where large masses of brilliant color are desired there are few plants equal to this dwarf phlox. In very dry summers they go out of flower, so they should be within reach of the hose; and the dead flower heads should be picked off.

For culture see Aster. In making a flower bed put the plants five or six inches apart as soon as frosts are gone.

PHLOX (HERBACEOUS).

These have been included under herbaceous plants, but they are worthy of special mention, for they are among the best of our hardy border plants. These fine varieties are obtained from several species: P. suffruticosa, P. maculata and P. paniculata. They are not of great value as a cut flower, but you will never make a mistake in recommending them wherever a hardy border flower is wanted. New varieties are of course raised from seed.

The young shoots root freely in May, or as soon as you can get them after the plants start to grow, and can be grown in pots and planted out in September. They also divide with the greatest ease, either before they start to grow in spring, or in October and November. No plant is hardier. There are so many fine varieties that there is no excuse for growing poor ones.

PINKS.

We are often asked for the hardy garden pinks and are often unable to supply them. There is now a great variety of almost all shades of color, and their flowers are as large as our carnations were twenty years ago. They may not be all quite hardy, but our carnation is almost hardy, and these pinks with their spreading, free flowering habit, deserve more attention and more care than they get.

There are dozens of named varieties, but without going into them, we can grow a good assortment of colors and the hardy clove pink is a favorite with all. Her Majesty is a splendid white, and Abbottsford is an equally fine pink.

With our continuous blooming carnation they would not be of value to force, but are most useful to pick in the summer months. They can be propagated from cuttings, as you do carnations, and either kept in the flats in which they were rooted or potted off into 2-inch pots, but they must, when rooted, be kept in a very cool house or cold-frame during winter. Carnations root readily in sand in October, and so will the young growths of these pinks. Planted out in early spring they soon make bushy clumps. Our garden pinks are supposed to be the offspring of Dianthus plumarius.

POINSETTIA.

The showy Poinsettia pulcherrima is now botanically classed with the euphorbias, but is still far better known to the trade as poinsettia. It is a native of Mexico and that infers that at no time should it be subject to a low temperature. Since its introduction it has been a favorite in all collections of hot house plants, its brilliant scarlet bracts making it unequaled as a decorative plant in the very darkest days of winter. Of late years it has grown greatly in popular favor with our flower-buying patrons and as the lily is now known as the Easter flower, the poinsettia may and is known as the Christmas flower.

They are often used for decorations when cut with two or three feet of stem, but are more satisfactory in every way when it is possible to use them in pots. Although their fine leaves soon drop in a dry room, the showy bracts remain on for several weeks, always giving the purchaser good value, and as it is one of those plants which we never get returned "to keep for another season" it is satisfactory and profitable to grow, more so than the majority of plants we handle.

Old plants that have rested from January to April or May should be shaken out clean of any old soil, potted into 4, 5 or 6-inch pots as their size may require, the shoot or shoots shortened back only to the sound wood. Place in a warm, light house and syringe daily. In four or five weeks there will be a crop of cuttings. In taking off the cuttings leave one young eye at the old stem so that another break will give you another lot of cuttings. As most of your cuttings will go into the sand after you have discontinued firing, there will be no bottom heat; so the cuttings want shade and the sand must have a thorough soaking twice a day in warm weather. In about three weeks the cuttings will be rooted. Lift carefully from the sand and pot into 2½ or 3-inch pots. For the first few days, or till the young plants begin to make roots in the soil, keep shaded and moist by frequent syringing. When once they have got hold of the soil they want the fullest light, and in the warm months the greatest possible amount of fresh air.

The old plants that you are propagating from can after June 1st be plunged outside, and cuttings taken from outside growth make better plants than those grown inside. You can propagate at intervals till the middle of August, the last struck making fine dwarf plants. We seldom make use of the old plants, but shifted on in September and given plenty of heat and light they will give you a number of medium sized flowers.

The main object in the cultivation of the poinsettia is to obtain a stocky, sturdy plant, retaining all its fine foliage, as dwarf as possible, but crowned with a fine head of what the public call the bloom. Two shifts are enough; from the 2½ to a 4-inch, and from that to their flowering pot, a 6-inch or in later struck plants a 5-inch. Batches of cuttings can be taken off at intervals from May 1 to end of August, the very latest propagation often making most useful little plants.

The poinsettia is very unsightly without its large handsome leaves, and these are too often seen drooping and yellow or entirely absent at Christmas time just when the plant should be at its best. There are three causes for this: First, a low temperature (60 degrees at night is the lowest they should ever be); second, starvation at the roots, either through an impoverished soil or insufficient root room, and thirdly, as common a cause as any, their roots being disturbed after they begin to form their bracts. A very important point to remember is that they should have their last shift never later than the middle of October and two weeks earlier is better. They cannot endure having their roots disturbed in the least when near their flowering period.

The best soil for them is two-thirds of rather heavy turfy loam, with one-third of well rotted cow manure, and at the last shift add one pint of bone flour to one bushel of compost. They are very liable to be troubled with mealy bug, which infests their flower umbel proper, but if syringed daily as they should be they are easily kept down. Greenfly also attacks them if regular fumigation is neglected.

If very large bracts are desired, you can plant out in 6 inches of rich soil some thrifty young plants in August. In this way you can get bracts 20 to 24 inches across.

Plants unsold, or those you cut for the flower, should be stored away in January either in a warm shed or beneath a bench where not a drop of water will touch them, and allowed to rest perfectly dry till started again the following May.

There is a so-called white variety seen occasionally which is certainly not worth growing, and there is a variety called P. p. plenissima, or commonly called the double. It is with me about ten days later than the type, but it is very intense in color, stands travel and handling better and although not making such a wide stretch of bracts is most desirable in every way.

POTTING.

There is no chapter in this book that as this one. It is a treat. It is better than falling off a log. It is an ice-cream soda and a 15-cent cigar. It is more than equal to seeing the Highland fling danced for the three thousand eight hundred and fifty-sixth time.

There is a good display of egotism in it, because the writer thinks he knows how to pot, and he has seen a great many that did not and never seem to learn. Some will say: "There is a man who thinks nobody can do a thing right but himself." I beg your pardon; that is not so, for I have seen many young men who began to pot and shift plants when they were 15 years old and made experts at it, but when over 20 they seldom learn to perform this important operation properly, which must combine both speed and proficiency.

Our business is both mental and mechanical, and a good mingling of the two. It is the mental that sizes at a glance that a plant needs shifting and the size shift or pot it wants. It is the mechanical that expertly shifts the plant from the 3 to the 4-inch, because he has learned it, and it is not the slightest effort of the brain to do it right. It would be an effort to do it any other way.

It must be admitted that potting and shifting is the most important mechanical operation in our commercial houses, and any young man who is really a quick and good hand at it can always get a job, but how few there are when you want them. A Jaggs or a Baggs or a Raggs, if known to be an expert at this operation, would often get a favorable answer to his question, "Have ye got a job, sir?" instead of an evasive answer, even if he were known to have laudable loving for exploring all horticultural centers. We must put up with a slow gait sometimes, but I have suffered more than once by right down bad and careless potting; carelessness is not the word, it is right down stupidness, thick-headedness, with awkward handedness.

It is no good telling you how not to do it, but still I can convey some points by describing what I have often seen in the shape of potting, which causes itching of the skin and the mastication of a large lump of profanity that has to be swallowed instead of coloring the atmosphere.

You will see a man take hold of a cutting between his finger and thumb by the top of the shoot, and suspend it in the little pot, then fill up the pot heaping full and then begin to thumb all around on the surface. Then the same man or his class will take a plant that has come out of a 3-inch and after putting half an inch of soil in the bottom of a 4-inch, set the plant in with the old ball one inch down the new pot, then a big handful of soil is thrown on the top and the thumbing commences again with several revolutions of the pot and a few extra pressures of the thumb.

If you will knock out the 2-inch first described you will find that near the bottom, where the soil should be compact around the roots, it is loose, but firm on the surface, where you don't want it so. And if you will knock out the 4-inch you will find the first inch quite solid, but lower down where the roots are you will find spaces between the old ball and the pot, which I have learned to call, when exhibiting them to a workman, "mouse's nests," for I have found the cavities large enough to domicile a little rodent.

When potting see that your soil is in just the right consistency. It should never be too dry, and to be wet and sticky would be ruination. Some one, perhaps Mr. Henderson, described it admirably when he said it should be ·in such condition that you could squeeze up a handful and it would adhere in a lump, but when thrown on the bench it would crumble to pieces. That is just about the same condition so dear to the eye and heart of a farmer when plowing his clay loam in the spring, when it falls back from the plowshare in flaky particles.

In the old country, so called (this is the oldest, geologically, of some odd billions of years) we were taught to sprinkle the new pots before using them, and although it is disregarded in our hurry, it is, I am sure, an excellent plan to dip all new pots a moment or two. We are also taught in Europe to wash all pots before being used again. This is a good thing to do when you have the time, but we never seem to have the time, so we put them out of doors in summer when out of use. If you have a field and can spread them out the rains will do much to wash the outsides, but if the cows walk over them or children play ball with them it is somewhat expensive. Piled up in neat· rows with some boards for a foundation does us very well, for then they get thoroughly dry, and when wanted for use a coarse wad of cloth will give them what Nicholas Nickleby had to put up with the morning after his arrival at Dotheboy's Hall, "a dry rub." This dry rub will clean them inside near enough for most all of our common plants.

The very worst place for storing pots is under a wet bench, where they get so saturated that they must be in poor condition, for although the water we give our plants does not all go out through the porous pots, as somebody said it did, yet it is well to have as much of the porous quality as we can get. There is considerable humbug about porous pots, however, and we do not attach much importance to it because we see plants thriving in a green painted pine tub, which is no more porous than our neighbors' pie crust.

It is a great benefit to have our flower pots and pans all of one standard make, and, better still, to have one maker's make. The breakage of pots in the old days of hand made pots was terrific, and we should squeal awfully had we the same amount to lay out for good potting soil.

It is difficult to attempt to give any instructions on how to pot or shift a plant, but a few hints will suffice.

To begin with a rooted cutting. If the roots are small the pot can be filled to overflowing with soil and one dab of the forefinger makes a hole big enough to put in the plant; or if the roots are too long for that, hold the plant with the two first fingers and thumb and fill up with one handful of soil, then with the thumb and first finger of the left hand and first finger of the right hand run into the soil perpendicularly on three sides of the plant, you have well firmed the soil around the roots, where it ought to be firm, and as you pass the plant into a flat a rap will settle the soil and the first watering will do the rest.

You ought to learn to seize the plant with one hand and the pot with the other. A good hand at this light job with cuttings that are easy to handle, and has his pots and plants brought to him and carried away, ought to pot easily 500 an hour.

When it comes to shifting a 2-inch to a 3-inch, or a 3-inch to a 4-inch, you should hold the plant by the stem, letting your little finger rest a moment on the edge of the pot, fill the pot nearly a third full, and then lean the plant towards you and put in some soil, give the pot just one half turn and lean the plant again towards you and fill up the other side, and then squeeze the ball hard down; another rap, and the shift is done. Now, by this method you have gotten the soil solid all around the ball, firmer near the bottom, because you wedged the plant into the soil.

Up to 6-inch pots this method will do, with perhaps the addition of getting your fingers down the sides as a rammer. With all shifts of plants over 6-inch, especially with those that get a small shift, say 6 to 8 or 10 to 12, you cannot get the soil, which in these sizes should· never be sifted, down compact without the aid of a stick an inch or two wide and one-half or three-quarters inch thick. All hard-wooded plants, like azaleas, want to be firmly potted; and some of our soft-wooded plants, geraniums for instance, want hard potting. As a rule, plants are potted too loosely.

It would be a dirty job to be shifting plants within a few minutes of their being watered, but it would be far worse for the plant to shift it when it was quite dry, or in that condition that it needed watering, and the larger the plant the worse it would be, because the water would largely pass down through the new soil and the old ball would remain dry till the plant was thoroughly soaked, which all plants won't stand.

We are able to shift a plant from a 4 to a 6-inch or 6 to 8 with absolute safety at any time, because when properly done the plant does not lose a fiber, but many of our soft-wooded plants soon recover from a little disturbance of the roots and with many of our common plants you can always rub off half an inch of the surface of the old ball, which enables you to give them more new soil.

Many of the soft-wooded plants that make a stem, such as geraniums, fuchsias, heliotrope, etc., do not hurt any if the old ball is down an inch under the new soil, but in hard-wooded plants they should be kept very near the same height. This is particular in palms; they should never be potted below the base of the stems. Many palms will raise themselves several inches above the ground by the roots. Lower them down when shifting, but not below bottom of stem.

The best work of potting I ever kept the watch on was done by an expert at any greenhouse work. It was very common stuff; Centaurea gymnocarpa from 2-inch to 3-inch. He did not have to knock out his plants, but merely shifted them and did it well, and in just twenty-five minutes he had rattled off 500. That was too fast to last all day, but it was not day, it was night, by lamp light. For the first week or two after Easter we frequently have to put in some "bees," and during several evenings last spring, two men in three hours, with plenty of help, shifted 2,500 geraniums from 3 to 4-inch.

I have spoken of rapid potting, which most of our bedding plants must get or it would not pay, but the man who can pot well and fast can also slacken down his speed and pot carefully when occasion requires, and where care is needed it pays. He could not handle cyclamen or cinerarias, or above all herbaceous calceolarias as he could a geranium or a canna, or you would break and smash the leaves, but expertness and smartness will apply to all of them.

I have seen some men take hold of a dormant cattleya and hold it up and look at it and twist it around as if it were a new and unknown reptilian fossil, and then fuss with moss and crocks as long as it would take to visit the dentist and have a tooth out, and then from want of knowledge the poor plant pined and died; while I know another who fixes them up as fast as I would shift a cytisus, and this man makes them grow.

Don't think for a minute, young man, that you are an expert potter of plants unless a superior expert told you so and watched you. I have noticed some young men in very large establishments who were poor hands at potting because perhaps they never had a good lesson, or perhaps they were of that conceited build that they would not learn. I noticed in one place where a rapid potter had been at work on a lot of rose cuttings that were calloused but had lost their leaves, and quite a number were upside down. Perhaps some will do, but that in our common plants in springtime anything will do. It may do, but in the aggregate the difference in the result between the right and the wrong way will be considerable.

Just a word about a potting bench. It should always be of 2-inch plank, resting on cross-pieces not over two feet apart, so that it is solid, with no

Pyrimidal Flowering Chinese Primulas.

spring to it. And it should be high enough so that a man can work his hands conveniently without bending his back. It is the bending over that tires. You can't raise a low bench up to suit a tall workman, but you can raise the short workman up to suit the bench.

PRIMULA.

A very large genus of pretty dwarf stemless plants that are all from temperate climates or high elevations. Those of us who crossed the Atlantic will remember the fields and banks and hedge rows where the primrose covered the ground. The cowslip (P. officinalis) was not so common and was generally found in a colony in a pasture and the oxlip (P. elatior) was still less common.

Many primroses are hardy with us, but our severe winter, and often hot, dry summer, is not nearly so favorable to them as the more temperate parts of Europe. The polyanthus, similar to the cowslip except in color, is the leading flower in thousands of cottage gardens, and with it the old woman's story that if you plant a cowslip or common primrose upside down it will come red, double, etc. This strange phenomenon never occurred in the garden that you are visiting, but it did happen, because our Aunt Jane or old Bill Jones did it many times.

The polyanthus is sometimes seen doing very well here, and where it can be shaded, but not a wet soil, and protected in winter, it is a most charming hardy spring flower.

The old double white form of P. sinensis was once a most important plant with every florist. Its flowers were used in immense quantities for making designs, but we have gotten over that, and although we had no difficulty in cutting up the large plants with a sharp knife and making each section into a cutting which rooted slowly but surely, we no longer bother with that method of propagation. We have now

a double white equal to the old variety from seed and we have every shade, double and single, from pure white to crimson. The varieties of P. sinensis come true from seed and it is upon such we depend for our fall, winter and spring flowering plants, and they are now one of our most important plants.

Besides P. sinensis we have P. obconica and P. Forbesii, the "baby primrose." For some years we did not realize the great beauty and usefulness of P. obconica. It is a most charming and useful plant, and the baby primrose sells at sight. They are so profuse in bloom and have the great good quality that they are fine

window plants, and being easily raised can be sold at a very moderate price. Other species may be found very attractive for the private collection, but the three mentioned are the leading commercial plants, and all want about the same treatment.

Always obtain the best strain of seed. It takes time and tedious care to save primula seed, so don't begrudge paying for a good strain. The foliage as well as flowers of the P. sinensis are handsome. We have fern-leaved, parsley-leaved, curl-leaved, and in flowers most beautiful colors and markings. The flowers of obconica have been greatly improved of late and doubtless in both that and Forbesii great improvements will be made.

The primulas are the least troubled with any of our greenhouse pests of any cultivated plants. The principal thing to remember is that they do not like much heat. After they have left the seed pan they need a good open soil; two parts loam, one part sifted cow manure, and one part leaf-mold will do them finely, potted only moderately firm.

The leaves, or rather, leaf stems, break easily and here is where careful and skillful potting comes in. I frequently see people, when asked to "knock out those plants," take hold of the top of the plant as they would a cat's tail if they wanted to draw pussy from her retreat. Get the base of the plant in the fork between your fingers, and you can protect every leaf. I noticed some years ago that the English florist had small sticks pushed down on three sides of the stem of the

Primula Obconica.

primula just after shifting, to keep them from wobbling about, as they were potted what we would call "high." We never found any necessity for that, for they can be potted with care just right, sufficiently deep to hold them firmly upright, but not by any means to bury their crowns. This is particular; don't get them too low, but just so that they set firmly on the soil.

If you wish to have primroses by October you should sow in April, and if you wish to have them in spring you should sow again end of August. You can with care sow any time from March to November. We usually sow about first of May, which gives us flowering plants from November on to March, after which we think there are pots. I have found these little plants do finely on a shelf in a house that had a good shade. In another five or six weeks they will go into a 3-inch pot. If you don't have a cold-frame then give them a bench where it is shaded overhead, and they can get plenty of air. End of August or early September they should be shifted into their flowering pot. We sell most of them in 4-inch pots, and the great majority go as soon as one fine truss is developed, but to grow a fine plant they should have a 5-inch.

After the heat of summer is gone we try to keep them at about 50 degrees at night, but less won't hurt them in the least. And don't crowd them at any time; they must have full room for some large, healthy plants, but in this immediate neighborhood they are a failure. Thousands of dollars have been spent for their purchase and care, but in a few years they are gone. We have pulled up this spring the remains of rhododendrons and kalmias (and replaced with hardy deciduous shrubs) which the confiding owner had purchased from the agent, who showed him the gorgeous picture of a rhododendron warranted (till the bill was paid) to grow and blossom even more beautifully than the colored plate. So be careful, and unless you are sure that these plants thrive in your neighborhood don't sell them. There is any number of good, honest hardy shrubs.

It is said that the rhododendron, or

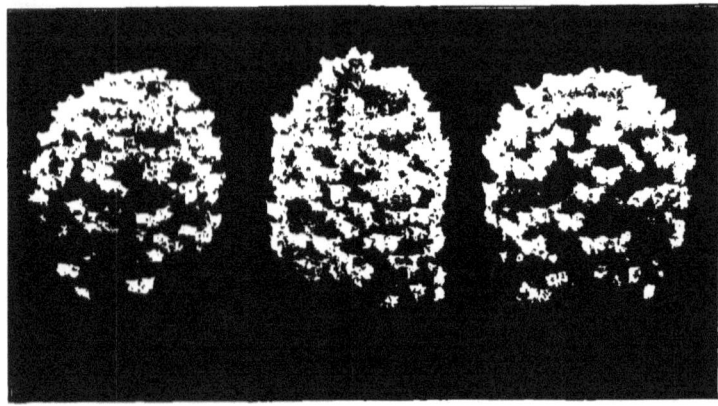

Specimen Greenhouse Rhododendrons.

many other plants, not better, but the people want a change, and for an Easter plant we do not prize them. It is in early winter that they are such favorites with everybody.

The cold-frame is an excellent place to summer over the primroses. With the glass shaded and the sash raised back and front, it is cool, and if you will not neglect them there is no place in the greenhouse where they can be grown so well. If the frame is in the shade of trees so much the better. It is coolness you want.

Sow on some light loam and leaf-mold that has been previously well watered. Just press in the seed and cover with more leaf-mold very lightly; when the seed is out of sight it is covering enough. Place a pane of glass over the flat or pan and don't let the soil get parched. When the little plants are up keep the pan in the coolest place you have.

In five or six weeks they can be potted singly in 2-inch pots, using clean the spread of their pretty leaves, or they are useless. They need little syringing, and none when in flower, but when growing during summer a fine sprinkling does them good. They wilt quickly when allowed to suffer for want of water and need plenty of water from seed pan to flowering. The soil should be always in that condition that it will take plenty of water. If you flower them as late as March or April their flowers will need shading.

RHODODENDRON.

Where these broad-leaved evergreen shrubs will flourish out of doors there is no hardy shrub that equals them for color and massive beauty. We have seen acres of them growing as freely as a welgelia or philadelphus, and in many parts of Great Britain they are planted for game covers, but that is on the other side of the Atlantic. In the vicinity of Boston they appear to do well, and nearer home I have seen any of the Ericaceae order, will not thrive where the soil is impregnated with lime. So there cannot be lime in some parts of the Alleghany mountains, for there the kalmias cover the mountain side. R. catawbiensis is widely distributed through our eastern states, and is quite hardy. There are other causes than the lime that make the rhododendron an undesirable plant for our northern states. It gets burnt with the bright suns of March when the leaves are frozen hard. The past winter has destroyed many.

It is as a forcing plant that we are chiefly interested, and strange to say, beautiful as they are when well flowered, they do not sell readily. They take up much room and we have several times declared we would leave them alone, but as the drummer pays his annual visit we relent and say, "Well, we will just try a few." And it is only a few you want in the commercial greenhouse; and the best time to have them is at Easter.

The rhododendrons that you see planted by the landscape gardener(especially if he is from a distance) and those we buy to force are varieties of R. ponticum. They are propagated from seed, by cuttings of the half-ripened wood, and by layers and by grafting. The latter method is the usual one to increase the fine named varieties. The business of propagating and growing the rhododendron is a specialty with those that have the suitable soil, such as the fine peat of Surrey, England, or the black peaty soil of Holland and Belgium.

If I attempted to grow on over summer any rhododendrons I would use two-thirds of turfy loam and one-third well rotted leaves. You could not, however, begin to grow them a season as cheaply as you can purchase fine young plants well set with buds that only need a few months' care, like our newly imported azaleas, with this difference, that you must expect to sell or give away all your rhododendrons, while your unsold azaleas are, with proper treatment, much better plants the second year.

When potting the newly imported plants see that the ball is not too dry. It is better to make sure by dipping it in a tub of water. Pack the soil firmly around the old ball and store them away in the coolest house or frame you have. At New Year's, bring them into more heat. We failed several years to get them into flower, thinking that like the azalea they would come along in a cool house. They won't do it; you must give them 60 to 65 degrees at night and syringe them daily; in fact it is heat and moisture that bring them out. They may not need three months to force them out, but it is well to be in time, and be sure to give the roots plenty of water, particularly when in flower. The flowers wilt easily in the sun if the roots are dry.

There are countless varieties, but some of the handsomest do not force well; so in ordering see that the varieties are suitable. Desirable forcing varieties are now largely grown for that purpose.

There are now beautiful hybrid rhododendrons, the offspring of several species, which make fine conservatory plants. They should be managed as we do azaleas, without the severe pruning. After flowering they make their growth and should be encouraged to grow by a good heat and moisture. When you see the buds set you can plunge them out of doors for the summer and remove to a cool house when you do the Indian azaleas.

RICHARDIA AFRICANA.

This plant is often called Arum lily, but with us is universally called the Calla lily. For many years it was a most important plant with us and to-day there are a number of people who prefer them to the true lilies. They are of the easiest growth, if you remember one important thing, and that

is that the calla comes from Northern Africa and does not want to be starved in a cool greenhouse.

There are several ways of growing them. To begin with, they propagate easily from offsets, which you can take off when repotting the plants in the fall. Some plant them out, but if they have much root room they grow too rampant and the flowers are too large to be useful.

In early May our houses are too crowded to keep the callas on the bench and they are taken outside and laid down where they can be covered in case of a sharp frost. The top withers away and for a few months the root is dry. In August we shake off all the soil and start them growing again in 5 or 6-inch pots, keeping them in a frame as long as there is no danger of frost, and in winter give them a light house where it is not less than 60 degrees at night. Although almost an aquatic the soil should be in such condition that water passes through it freely. For soil use three-fourths of coarse loam and one-fourth of decomposed cow manure. They want lots of syringing and fumigating, for thrip and red spider trouble the leaves.

If you want to raise some specimens that will require a 9 or 10-inch pot and hear three or four flowers at one time, select some of your strongest plants in May and plant them out two or three feet apart in a deep, rich soil, where you can water them copiously in dry times. They lift easily end of September and will make great plants.

The small offsets or bulblets that come off the corm in August can be potted in 2-inch pots and grown on, giving them a shift into a 5-inch and plunge out of doors, and if given plenty of water these plants will be in good flowering condition by October. Roots are now sent from California very cheaply.

Richardia albo-maculata has a small, greenish-white flower and a prettily spotted leaf, which we used to use in our veranda boxes. It rests in winter and the corm should be started growing in February. To increase your stock of this the corm can be cut in two or three pieces and started growing in February. Keep rather dry till leaf growth begins. In June plant them out and lift in fall and store in dry soil till time to start again.

There is a magnificent yellow calla; of its correct name I am not certain, but think it is R. Elliottiana. In size and form it is like the common calla, but the leaves are spotted and not so thick in texture. The flower is simply grand. I don't know when I have seen a flower that pleased me so much. Fancy a dozen or more of these flowers in a vase; what can be richer? It is not yet common or we would see and hear more of it, but every florist should obtain a stock of it.

A single corm was given to me two years ago by the late George Savage, of Rochester, with the advice to start it

in sand and give little water till growth began. This was good advice, for the following June it threw up a gorgeous bloom. They should be dormant in the soil during winter and shaken out and started in early spring. We divided this corm into four or five pieces with success, one of which flowered this spring. This is such a magnificent flower I cannot praise it too highly.

RICINUS (CASTOR BEAN).

Our warm summers suit this tropical plant well, and in very large beds or borders where a tropical effect is wanted it has a fine appearance. It is easily raised by sowing the seeds in March, either singly in small pots or in a flat and afterwards potted off singly in 3 or 4-inch pots.

There are now several varieties, those with the bronze colored leaves being very handsome. To get a good growth of the ricinus the soil of the bed should be deep and rich.

ROSES.

Volumes have been devoted to the rose. It is known as the Queen of Flowers. Whole books have dealt with merely the diseases of the rose. A great church dignitary of England gives all his leisure time to telling funny stories and studying his favorite love, the rose. In this country Mr. H. B. Ellwanger, of Rochester, has published a volume on the rose. And for centuries the literature of the rose has been pouring out in a steady stream.

The production of the plants and flowers has made a fortune for a few, a competency for hundreds and daily bread for thousands. There is no longer a sanguinary war between the roses of York and Lancaster in which thousands perished and a fair island was laid waste, but strange to say in one city, most famous for peace and brotherly love, there still exists a Duke of York whose pride it is not to exterminate his countryman who grows white roses, but to produce such grand red roses with stems of such a length as his Lordship the Earl of Lancaster never dreamed of.

The rose is not only Queen to all those who admire a beautiful flower— and they are low in the animal scale who do not—but is the most important by far in our commercial horticulture. If we happen not to be extensive growers then the commission man is for roses. Although I believe the orchids are bound to become great favorites with the wealthier flower buyers, yet they nor any other flowers can displace the rose as Queen of all of Flora's gifts. It is the perfection and grace of form, the beautiful leaves, the fine stem and the sweetness of the flower that places it pre-eminently above all other flowers.

In Europe the rose has been fostered by any number of rose societies, and we have a rose society here, an auxiliary of our national S. A. F. So far it has been a rose society only in name, but at Detroit it took a new lease of life and now bids fair to start off with the enthusiasm that belongs to the carnation society. It is sincerely wished that it may and if so what magnificent displays may we expect at its annual conventions and exhibitions?

Space forbids me to more than mention the literature of the rose. Among the books devoted to the rose may be mentioned Shirley Hibbard's "Rose Book for Amateurs," and "A Book About Roses," by Rev. Dean S. R. Hole. Both of these gentlemen are charming writers and ardent students of the rose. There you will find the history of the rose, almost from the dawn of our own history, as well as its present day beauties and associations. A far more edifying literature than campaign speeches, murders, shipwrecks, or the latest movements of the popular vaudeville actresses. Of American authors, besides Mr. Ellwanger's book, we have "Parsons on the Rose," by S. D. Parsons, a noted horticulturist; and "The Secrets of Rose Culture," by W. J. Hatton, a practical florist. One more foreign book is that by Wm. Paul, "The Rose

could have improved on that mysterious and ambiguous story of the Garden of Eden had I been the learned Israelite or syndicate of Israelites who by tradition handed down or scratched on tablets of stone or burnt clay the stories of their forefathers whose dreams included serpents, fig leaves, forbidden fruit and murder. Strange that these evil agencies surround us yet, and encompass a man most fatally if he steps far off the virtuous path. I hope I won't be considered presumptuous but I would have made Miss Innocent Eve tempt Mr. Frank Adam to present her with a moss rose bud. The roses were growing in Asia Minor, but no one knows what kind of fruit the forbidden species was. If Eve was a dark-skinned damsel we would say it was a watermelon. The moss rose bud would be far more poetical and has a meaning, for at 15 years of age we learned that a moss rose bud was an expression of true love, or at least the first true, but in poor Eve's case it would have been a case of force. It was first, last and only love. No flirting, no jealousies nor need of western divorce courts, where the sign hangs out: "Divorces granted while you wait."

Basket of Roses.

Garden." It is an expensive but magnificently illustrated volume, and Mr. Paul, as a raiser and cultivator is perhaps the foremost rosarian of the world.

The rose has been emblematic of no end of things and I will conclude my preliminary remarks by saying that I have thought many times that I

If you were to ask an American which was the most important class of roses he would probably say the Teas. If you asked an Englishman he would say undoubtedly that the so-called Hybrid Perpetual class was much the most important. The more temperate climate of Western Europe is very favorable to the rose, and in Great

Britain the Tea and Noisette roses are hardy out of doors. In our Northern States the Hybrid Perpetuals, while being quite entitled to be called hardy, are often injured by the severe winters, and the Tea and Noisette sections, unless most thoroughly protected, are entirely unfitted for our winters.

There is nothing that our people crave to have in their garden, let it be in the few acres of the millionaire or the small garden plot of the mechanic, so much as a rose, and in nothing is there so much disappointment. With our detached residences, both big and little, there is always some garden, and too frequently the attempt to grow roses in them is a failure. The soil is often worn out and there is not fresh air enough. The budded stock is purchased from the tree peddler, and in a few years there is a strong growth of the Manetti stock. "But the roses don't flower." The rose is long since dead and only the suckers of the Manetti exist.

I believe that where there is a good expanse of lawn and the soil is fresh and good the best results can be obtained by planting annually young plants of the Tea and Hybrid Tea varieties. Years ago where now stand buildings we used to plant out every May 3 or 4-inch pot plants of the old Bon Silene, Safrano, Isabella Sprunt and Duchess de Brabant, and from June on till middle of November we cut thousands of handsome buds, which I know would more than gratify any of our customers. For such is the love for and pride to produce roses that occasionally we have the busy business man call in during fall just to say that he "cut one fine rose this morning," and he is as proud of it as if it was a baby arrived during the wee sma' hours, the unearthly time at which Providence has ordained these interesting domestic events to usually occur.

This summer in an open field far removed from the refreshing influence of the hose and also the "madding crowd," on a piece of good light loam, we have had a row of Perle des Jardins, President Carnot and La France. They have flowered continually and will till 10 degrees of frost destroys their tender growth.

Before I enter on the two classes of roses that are the main objects of this article, as well as the plants of greatest importance to the florist, I want to say a word about the uses of some other classes that we occasionally have to supply.

The rose is spread over the entire northern temperate regions of the world, not so numerous in species in North America as in Asia and Europe. In this country they are found as far south as Mexico. Over 200 species of roses have been described, but there are probably 50 species well defined, and of varieties and hybrids of these many species there are thousands. The cultivator has done marvelous things with the rose, and some of our cultivated varieties are as far removed

View through a Range of Connected Rose Houses, with Raised Benches.

from the original type as any deviation from nature in the vegetable kingdom. Yet, a few of the original species are in cultivation and are most useful plants.

Noisette Roses.

These were much oftener seen in our northern greenhouses thirty years ago. Since the introduction of the beautiful Tea varieties little attention is paid to them, but in the private conservatory they are fine plants for pillars and rafters. They are useless to us outside but where they do not get more than 15 degrees of frost they must be grand plants, as they are in our southern states. A well known nurseryman, Mr. Smith, of Geneva, N. Y., who knows what a rose is, and does not talk wildly, as many tourists do, told me that he believed Northern Texas was the most favored locality on this continent for the rose, and that the Tea, Bourbon, and Noisette classes grew there to the greatest perfection.

The Noisette roses are easily propagated by cuttings from the half ripened wood at any time of year, either July or January. They should be always planted out in a well drained border, for you don't get their real beauty and worth till they are a few years old. After making a strong growth they should be rested by less water and less syringing, and before starting up again have the weak shoots cut off and the side shoots of the leading stems cut back to two or three eyes. Winter, of course, would be the natural time for them to rest, but by starting

into growth early in spring and resting in August and September you can get flowers during winter. Keeping these roses clean of aphis and red spider by syringing is the principal care.

Well known varieties of this class are Marechal Niel, the magnificent golden yellow rose; Solfaterre, a grand yellow; Gloire de Dijon, a beautiful creamy amber; and old La Marque, the old white rose that came in clusters with such luxuriant dark green foliage. Where these beautiful plants will do out of doors there are many fine varieties.

Moss Roses.

Everyone is fond of a Moss rose. There are now many fine varieties, and being hardy they will thrive wherever the Hybrid Perpetual class will do well. For propagation refer to the Hybrid Perpetuals.

Lord Penzance's Sweet Briars.

This is a new section, but they have proved themselves the past winter perfectly hardy. They are as sweet scented as the old English Sweet Briar and showy flowers. They are a great addition to our hardy flowering shrubs, and will doubtless be much planted. Like the H. P's, they can be propagated from the half ripened wood in sand, or from the matured wood in autumn and winter.

Rosa Rugosa.

Rosa Rugosa is a distinct species (from Japan) that is perfectly hardy. They have thick wrinkled or curly

foliage, very distinct, with large showy single flowers of white and pink, and are covered in the autumn with large conspicuous red fruit. Immense masses of these are now planted and they make splendid low plantations to the margins of taller shrubberies. Easily propagated from young or matured wood.

Hardy Climbing Roses.

While in the more temperate parts of our country the Noisette roses can be planted, we must confine ourselves to the hardy varieties. They are too well known to need any comment. They, propagate easily, and when planting them out they should be protected for the first few years or till they get a good start.

Some of the best of them are: Baltimore Belle, blush white; Bennett's Seedling, pure white; Gem of the Prairies, rosy carmine; Dundee Rambler, pure white; Allister Stella Gray, orange; and several others.

For this purpose too we have the magnificent Ramblers, of which the Crimson Rambler was the forerunner. There are now yellow, pink and white forms of it, and as hardy climbing roses they are unequalled. The hardy climbers have a fine burst of bloom in June, but do not flower again that season.

Wichuraiana Roses.

This is a very new and distinct strain, and produced by crossing the Wichuraiana with many of our cultivated roses, including some of the well known Teas. Some of them will take high rank as climbers, and some being creeping or low growing will be adapted for covering rock work and for cemetery use. Some have their flowers distributed along the stem, which gives them a handsome wreath-like appearance, and others flower in clusters like Crimson Rambler. Others have the fragrance of the Sweet Briar, so their pedigree is of various sources.

I cannot speak from experience, but some of them are said to be valuable plants for forcing in pots. Mr. W. A.

green character of the latter, and if they prove hardy and inherit the ever-blooming qualities of the Tea roses they must prove a great acquisition to our gardens.

Other Classes.

The Austrian Briar roses are a small class with bright yellow flowers, which cover the bush when in bloom. They don't last long but are very gay and beautiful, and the plant is perfectly hardy.

same treatment. Young plants set out in early May will continue to bloom till hard frost sets in. Some protection, should be given them in winter.

These can be propagated during winter if you have a few plants growing under glass, or in October you can take the cuttings from outside and root them in the propagating bed. Many of the Hermosa and Soupert type are forced in pots for spring sales. For this purpose plant out strong young plants in spring, and encourage them to grow till fall. Don't lift them till we have had some good sharp frosts. Then pot them and cut down to five or six good eyes and plunge in a cold-frame and be sure not to leave them without ventilation on a bright, sunny day or the buds may start, which would hurt them very much if a very cold spell again caught them before they were brought in. When you bring them in start slowly and increase the heat as flowering time approaches. Of the Soupert type there are varieties in white, pink and yellow.

We grew years ago a fine Bourbon rose called Appolina, a large pink flower, as good as many of the Hybrid Perpetuals, and a continuous bloomer. For the amateur this is a grand rose.

The Madame Plantier type are compact growing plants that come with a grand burst of bloom and are soon over, but not more so than most of our hardy shrubs, and as they are perfectly hardy they are splendid plants for a group, a hedge, or a single specimen.

Bedding Roses.

Where a bed or border of roses is wanted by our customers, and the situation gets light and air, and the soil is not a worn-out garden (if it is you must supply good fresh loam and manure) then I believe in and do recommend the Hybrid Tea and common Tea roses, knowing that they will give the greatest satisfaction. We know they will grow and bloom continuously weeks after our tender plants are killed by frost, and months after the green worm and aphis has ceased to bother the roses. I reason with our patrons that strong young plants in 4-inch pots cost little if any more than their geraniums and cannas, and if they get killed, which they expect, they have lost no more than they have in their ordinary bedding plants.

In this class we have a great variety. Not all the Teas are good for this purpose, but many are, and the Hybrid Teas are splendid, and with a slight protection they will come through the winter without any harm.

For a summer bed of roses you have many to choose from, and the following are good Hybrid Teas: La France, President Carnot, Kaiserin Augusta Victoria, Pierre Guillot, Mme. Schwaller, Crimson Bedder, Mme. Pernet-Ducher, Lady Mary Fitzwilliam, Countess of Pembroke, and others.

Among the Tea scented there is a still greater variety for this purpose.

Crimson Rambler Rose and Genista in a basket.

Manda, of South Orange, New Jersey, has sent out many fine varieties of these roses, among others: Universal Favorite, large double flower of a soft light pink; South Orange Perfection, blush changing to white; Manda's Triumph, a splendid climber, bearing large clusters of flowers. Those crossed with the Tea varieties have the ever-

There is a small class of roses that are truly monthly or continuous blooming and yet perfectly hardy. Hermosa is a good type of this class, which botanically may belong to several classes, but for our purpose we will treat them all as monthly. Agrippina is another, and the Polyantha rose, Clothilde Soupert requires the

Iron Frame Rose House with Solid Beds.

Those I have proved as most satisfactory for summer bedding are: Bon Silene, Isabella Sprunt, Safrano, Duchess de Brabant, Coquette de Lyon, Perle des Jardins, La Sylphide, Mme. Caroline Kuster, Marie Guillot, Souv. d'un Ami, Mme. Falcot, Mme. Welche, Goubault, Mme. Bravy, Mme. de Watteville, Sombreuil, and others. Some of the above are very old varieties, and you would not think of growing them during winter for cut flowers, but they are beautiful and free flowering out of doors. Our Queen of Queens, Catherine Mermet and its fine sports were not satisfactory bedded out in summer.

Hybrid Perpetuals.

These are the roses that are mostly planted to make a permanent bed. Many thousand of the budded stock are annually sold. Our department stores are now selling the imported stock at 10 plants for one dollar. There can't be a great margin for the de-

partment store or a great profit to the grower, but the popular price catches the man or woman who is looking for a bargain, and they are numerous. They get well dried out before they get into the purchaser's garden, and we haven't heard how they thrive. It is to be hoped they give one final "department" flower and then die, which the majority must.

Whenever you can get roses on their own roots do so. They will be far more satisfactory to your customers. But some of the finest sorts, the Baroness Rothschild type for one, do not grow well on their own roots, and of those you must rely on the budded plants. If you import the budded stock it should be unpacked and laid in trenches in a cold-frame during winter, and when filling your orders in the spring see that they are carefully planted and insist on their being cut down to within six inches of the ground.

If you handle but a few hundred

they can be potted when received in the fall, a pot that will just hold the roots is large enough, and after cutting down to a few strong eyes plunge them in a frame and cover with glass. Never let them get too warm. These plants will come along slowly in April and be well rooted by first of May, and if lots of ventilation has been given, or better still the sash removed, they must be satisfactory to your customers as you should not lose one. The department store price for them; you should get at least $6.00 per dozen.

If you have land of your own you should propagate during fall and winter all the Hybrid Perpetual roses that do well on their own roots. Small plants put out in May will be most satisfactory plants for your customers by the following spring, or even the first fall if they have had good soil, but it is safer to plant in the spring. Tell your customers about the Manetti stock, and teach them to distinguish between the suckers of the stock and the rose. But when on their own roots danger of that trouble is impossible.

The so-called tree roses are not to be recommended for our climate. They are called standard roses in Great Britain, and in that form countless thousands are grown. Here they look very charming the first season perhaps, and perhaps the next, but the third usually finishes them. They are budded on the wild briar. The briar stalks are collected from the hedgerows and thickets, and are sold to the nurseryman tied up in bundles like an English tourist transports his walking sticks; and there is little more apparent life about them than a bundle of golf sticks, yet they grow, and on a side shoot near the top the bud is inserted the following June or July and in another year they are sold. But don't buy them if you live north of Washington, D. C., unless you live in the Northern Pacific States, where many plants flourish that won't in our eastern states. The dwarf or bush roses are much better for us.

After a rose is well established there is not much use in strawing up the tops (you need to cut them quite severely every year if you want good flowers), but four or five inches of stable manure laid around the roots is a great help to them, and it need not be done till end of November.

Among the Hybrid Perpetual roses that do well on their own roots are:

Gen. Jacqueminot, crimson; Ulrich Brunner, deep pink; Mme. Laffay, red; Alfred Colomb, cherry red; Anna Alexieff, rose; Baron de Bonstettin, very dark crimson; Clio, blush; Countess of Oxford, carmine; Duke of Edinburgh, crimson maroon; John Hopper, bright rose; Mme. Gabriel Luizet, fine pink; Marshall P. Wilder, cherry rose; Mrs. Laxton, velvety red; President Thiers, large red; Roger Lambelin, crimson, edges of petals white; Sir Garnet Wolsley, bright red. There are many other fine varieties but the above list contains some splendid sorts.

Among the finest of those that do better when budded on the Manetti or Briar stocks are: Baroness Rothschild, a beautiful light pink; Captain Christy, flesh pink; Fisher Holmes, dark crimson; Mabel Morrison, fine white; Margaret Dickson, white with pale pink center; Marie Baumann, crimson; Magna Charta, dark pink, very fine; Paul Neyron, dark pink, immense size; Prince Camille de Rohan, crimson maroon. In this short list will be found some of the finest roses in cultivation.

Hybrid Perpetual roses can be propagated as follows, and this includes the hardy climbers or any of the deciduous kinds. When the current year's growth is about in that condition that the flower is fully developed it is called about half ripe. This is usually about middle of June. Prepare a frame in

which you have trod in eighteen inches or two feet of stable manure; in fact make a mild hotbed with the slope facing north. Put three inches of soil on the manure and on that two inches of sand, and insert your cuttings. Two eyes are enough, one above and one below the surface of the sand. Keep the sand moist and as cool as possible by shading, letting in only air enough to prevent too much moisture. By degrees they will endure more air, and in three or four weeks will be well rooted and can be soon potted into 2 1-2 or 3-inch pots and stood in a cold-frame, but they must be carefully watered and shaded till they get hold of the soil. These plants could be planted out the following October, but I would prefer to keep them plunged in a cold-frame and planted out the following April, when they will make fine plants.

Another plan is by using the dormant wood in the fall. Before very hard frost, say middle of November, cut off the well ripened growths of the previous summer and cut them into lengths of two or three eyes. Tie them in bunches of 25 or 50, and wrap some moist sphagnum around the ends, and store these bunches away in flats under a bench in a cool house. In two months the ends will be well calloused and then they can be placed in a few inches of sand that is a little warmer than the house, and 50 degrees for the house will do well. They will soon

House of Young American Beauty Roses.

House of American Beauty Roses in Full Bearing.

root and can be potted off and grown on to be planted out in April or May. Always remember that although these roses are hardy any growth that is made under glass is tender and will not stand a frost, so they should not go out till danger of frost is past. This is the simplest and surest way of propagating any of the deciduous roses.

Forcing Hybrid Perpetuals.

Since the American Beauty has been grown in such quantity there are much fewer of the H. P. roses grown for their flowers, but they are wanted in pots, and such sorts as Jacqueminot, Brunner, Magna Charta, Anna de Diesbach and Mme. Gabriel Luizet force well, and if properly prepared make fine pot plants, or their blooms can be cut. The fall importations of these roses are not satisfactory for this purpose. The long journey and the length of time is a poor prepara- tion for spring forcing, so strong plants with good stems should be ob- tained of our American nurserymen. The wood should be well ripened be- fore lifting and they should be potted as soon as possible and the stems cut down to three good eyes on each stem. The fewer shoots you have the finer they will be, and the more you have the poorer they will be. If the wood

of these roses has been well ripened, there is no good in letting hard frost touch them again, but they should be in a cold-frame till at least New Year's and then removed to a house where it is not over 40 degrees at night. They will endure nothing like forcing for the first six weeks after being brought in.

The idea is to begin as low as pos- sible with fire heat and slowly increase, which at flowering time, which may be the 1st to 15th of April, they will want 55 to 60 degrees at night. If you don't want them as early as April then leave them longer in the frame and they will come on all the better. It is useless to try and force these roses too fast because they have no working roots, but will make roots as top growth develops. If you want any of these roses as early as January you must use plants that are in quite a different condition. For those it is best to lift in the fall, or purchase, and pot and treat as you do those above described, only they should be left out till March and then brought in and started growing. They should be encouraged to make a strong healthy growth. Thin out the shoots to four or five of the strongest. By July they will have made some long stout shoots which should not have been cut off with the flowers; it would

be better to pinch off the flowers and let the strength go into wood.

In July they can be placed outside and plunged and mulched, but not over watered or the eyes may break and grow, and that is what you don't want. By end of August lay them on their sides so that they don't get the rain, and endeavor to dry them off, but not too rapidly or the wood will shrivel. Till the first of October the best place would be in a frame where you could cover them in case of rains. After the first frost or two there is no danger of their buds starting.

Now, these roses are in a fit state to be forced at any time and could if wanted be had in flower by the holi- days. They will not want any shifting, but as the growth starts and the roots are feeding they can be mulched and surfaced with loam and cow manure. The forcing of these plants is much easier than those lifted the same fall. The pots are full of roots ready to begin active growth directly the top starts. It is not advisable to start them too warm at first or you will get a weak growth, but they are much less liable to injury than the others.

I did not mention it, but of course when starting into heat you must again shorten back the shoots to two or three stout eyes. These roses are sometimes forced for several years.

The principal object is to get a good strong growth in the summer and ripen it in the fall. Over potting should be avoided, and with surfacing and liquid manure you can grow them for three or four years in the same pot. A good strong plant that started off well in the spring should need when lifted from the ground a 6-inch pot. Jacqueminot, Brunner and other Hybrid Perpetuals that are planted on a bench are put in four or five inches of soil in March or April. They should be good, strong plants when first benched. If budded plants, they should be cut down to a few eyes. If plants propagated that spring, they will need one stopping. They must be encouraged to make a strong growth that summer and in September be gradually dried off to ripen their growth. This is the most particular period of their time and they must not be dried off too quickly. Let in all

I intended to remark at the opening of these notes on the so-called Hybrid Perpetual roses that the term is highly misleading. They are not perpetual at all. Perhaps with a cool, wet summer you may get a few scattering flowers, and we usually do get an odd one here and there in September or October, but beautiful as is this most important class of roses in color, form and fragrance, it is all wrong to call them perpetual. So you see that a man who devotes nearly a year, and in case of solid beds, the whole year to one crop of flowers, must not only be sure of success but must realize a high price from his blooms or he is a loser. The American Beauty is a true Hybrid Perpetual, for with proper management it blooms from August till the following May; not profusely, or they would not command the high winter price they do; still they keep sending up flowering shoots. In an-

and put away in a cold-frame, but kept from very hard freezing. After New Year's they are brought in and slowly brought along. Until I tried this plan I had no idea that the Beauty was such a grand rose for the purpose. The year I alluded to we had several hundred plants for Easter that would average six open flowers and six buds, with stems twelve to fifteen inches long. Nothing sells like them, and we easily got $2.50 and $3.00 each for them. When first they break you would think they were going to be all blind, but they soon deceive you. Don't attempt to keep any unsold plants over; far better raise a new lot every year. The Crimson Rambler (and we are trying the Yellow, which will doubtless force as well) has become a standard Easter plant with all of us. You can obtain strong field grown plants in November, and if their shoots are six

Range of Short-span-to-the-South Rose Houses.

the cold air you can and if some frost is inside, so much the better. It is much better to ripen the wood by air and cold than by drying at the root.

The time of starting will depend on the time you want the flowers, and the earlier you want them the longer time you must give. Cut them close if you expect fine flowers. Mulch the bed and begin firing slowly, with plenty of syringing. If you get over the first few weeks without losing any plants, you are all right. The process from now on is plenty of water and syringing, with a gradual rise of temperature till flowering time.

These forcing hybrids are sometimes planted out in solid beds and forced year after year. It is precisely the same process. A growth in summer, a ripening in fall and pruning hack and starting with heat again at whatever time you want your crop.

other place I intend to say something about this wonderful variety as grown for cut flowers, but here I wish to say that although I have never seen it satisfactory when planted out of doors, it has been to me the most profitable of pot roses.

For this purpose we plant out a few hundred in a light house in four or five inches of soil as soon as our lilies are gone, in April. The best soil for that I ever raised were planted on April 1st, Easter being on March the 25th of that year. The flowers you get that summer and fall will pay you for bench room and labor far better than chrysanthemums. In November we dry them off some, having previously put in a lot of cuttings in the sand. The old plants are lifted and cut down to seven or eight inches of the pot. Not so short as we would the Hybrid Perpetuals, for the eyes near the base are not as good. They are then matured

or seven feet long shorten them back to three and four feet. They require a 7 or 8-inch pot. Pot them and keep very cool for the first month, but if Easter is early you want to begin early to start them growing. The success will all depend on starting slowly, but twelve to fourteen weeks is none too much to allow them in the houses. You can tie them in any shape, but the canes should not be allowed to run up straight. You will get a more even break if they are wound around a few stakes.

Another plan, entailing more time and labor but a surer way to get flowers in abundance and requiring less time in winter to force, is to pot some strong plants in April and put them in 7 or 8-inch pots and start growing in the coolest house you have. In fact, under a bench would do till they break; then give them a light bench and some long wires to support them, and by midsummer you will have five or six strong, long growths. Other growths should be rubbed off. If you have too many canes you will get a weaker growth. Put them out of doors in July and by end of August try and shorten up on water and the wood will ripen. As cold weather comes they will want little water and will lose their foliage.

These plants can be forced at any time, and although the canes are not quite as strong as the field grown ones, every eye gives us a cluster of bloom. After a few frosts we lay the plants down in a cold-frame and cover with boards, and a little hay or straw on the plants, where they can remain till you want to bring them in.

All the Ramblers we get are budded on the briar, hence their wonderful vigorous growth. And as long as we can buy of our nurserymen fine plants at such a low cost it would never pay us to bother about either budding them or propagating from cuttings.

Tea Roses.

This is far and away the most important section to the commercial florist. They are everything to him. They are used on all and every occasion and every day in the year. And what an improvement in them in 25 years! And the method of growing them has kept pace with the improved varieties. It is to the Frenchmen we are mostly indebted for the finest Tea Roses. Perhaps that will not always be so. Our American nurserymen and florists are doing a great deal in hybridizing and raising seedlings. Mr. E. G. Hill told me this summer that he had, I am afraid to say how many thousand, but I am sure it was 5,000. young seedlings of every conceivable cross. Surely we shall have some young Hoosiers that will startle the rose world. Let them come! We can stand several more shades.

Is it not remarkable that with the hundreds of fine Teas our demand seems filled with so limited a number of varieties? It is almost, or perhaps quite, correct to say that of all the millions of roses cut and sold, four varieties would cover 75 per cent of them, and one of them is not a Tea, the American Beauty. The remaining three are the two glorious sports of Catherine Mermet, Bridesmaid and the Bride, and the crimson Meteor. New varieties come and go, their advent heralded with shouts of praise and loud advertising, and their exit is a quiet retreat. They have answered two purposes: they have made money for the raiser and introducer and given us a little more experience. What a lot of experience we do get as we pass along.

A good place to begin with the Tea roses will be at the propagation. They root most easily anywhere from November till April, and both earlier and later, but slower and not so surely. We feel as much certainty that the rose cuttings will root as we do when we put in a batch of salvia. With the

sand at 65 degrees and the house from 50 to 55 degrees you cannot fail if you keep the sand moist. I never owned a north side propagating bench, and there is no need of it. Any bench will do if shade is supplied for the first few days.

Pot off as soon as the roots are started and shade again till the plants have started to grow, and then they want the full light, as they do every minute for the remainder of their existence.

The usual time to propagate, and the best time, is in January and February. Then you have time to get the young plants into a 3-inch pot for a couple of months before planting time. One author says the cutting should be of only one eye and another says it should be from only one flowering wood. I would much rather have the cutting of two eyes, one below and one above the surface of the sand, leaving a leaf or part of the leaf on the upper eye. If the wood is of any size, not too spindling and weak, it makes no difference to the future plant whether it is blind or flowering. That I have proved, and although I am by no means an extensive rose grower, the most vigorous young plants I ever grew were from cuttings of blind wood, and rather small and hard at that.

Large rose growers can't plant all their houses in a week, so they begin end of May and keep on till July. Those planted end of June should be in good bearing by middle of October, and many buds could have been cut before that if it were wise to let them flower, which it is not. On raised benches four inches of soil is considered ample, and some growers plant in three inches, allowing for future mulching to add another half or three-quarters of an inch. The rows on the bench fifteen inches apart and the plants one foot apart, is as close as you can plant them.

The bottom of the benches should be of 2x4 scantling, or not wider than 2x6, and between such board or scantling leave a space of three-fourths of an inch when building. When the boards swell with the wet soil they will only be half an inch apart. Perfect drainage is of the utmost importance. Unless the superfluous water passes freely through you will have no success. When the soil gets into that condition that the bed does not want water in a month there is something wrong, and most likely your rose leaves will be largely off by that time.

The soil of the bed should be quite firm, not beaten down as you would a mushroom bed, but good and solid. Plant very little below the surface, and firm the soil around the ball; unless the soil of the bed is very dry only water at the plant. In a few days, when the plants want it again, the whole bed can be watered.

If there is any excuse for shading it is just now in the hottest days, for the sake of the men who have to work in 120 degrees or more and the young plants that may have had their roots

FIELD-GROWN ..ROSES..

Two years old
On their own roots
Northern-grown
Bench-rooted
Full Assortment.
⎫
⎬
⎭
We are
Headquarters
for them.

JACKSON & PERKINS CO.
(Wholesale only)   NEWARK, NEW YORK.

very slightly disturbed by planting. If you shade let it be only a very temporary kind. A lump of clay dissolved in a pail of water and thrown on with a dipper will do very well. It will wash off at the first rain, and then you want it off.

Weeds grow apace in this tropical heat and it's a poor soil that won't grow weeds; they should be kept pulled, not only now but should never be seen. There is no harm in a scratching over of the surface for a month or so after planting, but later the surface should not be disturbed; hand weeding should do it all.

The young plants will grow fast, and there will be no trouble with mildew till the end of September, but from that time till steady firing begins is the most critical time, when we have slight frosts at night or a rainy cold day and night and the next week a warm sunny time with the thermometer at 80 degrees in the shade. Just such a time as I have described we have lately experienced, and it is 80 degrees at noon to-day and no wind to fill out the flapping sails.

From the time the roses are planted till frosts occur they can't possibly have too much ventilation. To digress a moment. We noticed in Philadelphia that they leave the end door open on a warm day in October, and we hear sometimes of side ventilation on roses. It may do in some localities but it will never do with us. Bottom or side ventilation or an open door for any length of time would be fatal because the draught would produce mildew; produce it to a certainty.

When the nights get down to 50 degrees outside you should have a little fire heat. Here is the advantage of steam, as you can let it in through one pipe; leave air on at night when this gentle fire heat is going. You don't want a high temperature but you want a dry, healthy atmosphere. All along about this time when using any artificial heat try to keep the house down to 55 degrees, and just about this time put a dab of liver of sulphur on the pipes.

There are times when from various causes you may not be able to fire till end of October, and have been without fire on chilly nights. By shutting up the rose houses tight on these nights you will notice in the morning the dewdrops in tiny beads on the edges of the pretty little leaves. If that continues for three or four nights you will have an attack of a fungus that is much worse than our common mildew. I have seen it take every young leaf off in a few days, and actually kill the young red growth. You can easily distinguish it from mildew for it shows on the young, tender leaves as distinct silver threads. A little fire and air would have effectually prevented this, but if you can't fire then leave on air. Far better have the house cool and dry, than cool, close and damp. I have learnt what this fungus will do years ago, and have not

Vase of Tea Roses.

forgotten it, for it touches our most sensitive organ, the pocket.

When steady firing commences the night temperature should be kept as near as possible to the right mark, as to which there is not much difference of opinion. Some growers like to keep higher than others. A reasonably low temperature means fewer buds and higher quality, and a higher temperature means more buds and poorer quality. From 54 to 58 degrees at night for all the ordinary Teas seems to be agreed upon, and I incline to the lowest mark, believing that quality is better than quantity. American Beauty should have 60 degrees. and the useful crimson Meteor should have from 65 to 68 degrees. Without a high temperature the Meteor is useless in the coldest months.

This fall at Mr. John H. Dunlop's, of Toronto, I saw some grand houses of roses ventilated by a thermostat which was controlled by water pressure. He was delighted with it, and if it works perfectly it must be the thing, for it never forgets. You can, of course, set them to any degree. I

will have more to say about ventilation in another chapter, but must say here, that it is one of the most important parts of rose growing. Seventy at day would be a good temperature; when any above that ventilation should be given, and where the ventilators are continuous and open at the ridge it is much safer given than with a ventilator here and there that lets the cold wind in.

There may be days when there is a cold, cutting wind, and the sun will raise the temperature of the house to 75 degrees, and it will be better to let it remain so than let in such a chilly blast. Again there may be dull, damp, mild days when it is better and proper to fire briskly and give air. An experienced gardener can tell directly whether a house is too chilly or too hot; whether the sashes are up too high or whether the atmosphere is too close. You ought to be a living, breathing thermostat, but if you were you could not divide yourself into twenty sections, and those gardening attributes are no more transmitted than the art of music or poetry or telling a story. So you must lay down a rule and your men must follow it to the best of their ability.

Young roses of all the kinds we grow very quickly throw up buds which you must pick off. As the plants grow along in August and September they will continue to form buds, and instead of picking the buds off as soon as they form let them grow somewhat larger. There is little weakening of the plant going on by forming petals (it is seed bearing that weakens), and then cut the bud off with two or three eyes of the growth; you will get a better break from the remaining eyes.

When cutting the fully developed buds after you are letting the plants flower you should cut back to three eyes. If very strong and the buds are numerous you may leave only two eyes, but three is better.

The neatest and best support for roses is a straight wire stake, one for each plant, and they are held in place at top by some lighter wire running over each row of plants three or four feet above the plants, and to which the upright wire stake is fastened by a string or a piece of fine wire.

One large grower I know, and a good one, runs stove pipe wire across the surface of the bench, or an inch above it, near the plant, and a similar wire five or six feet above the plant, and from the bottom wire to top one runs at each plant a strong but cheap string. This answers the purpose just as well, but the strings are thrown away every year and the bottom wire has to be removed, so it costs something, while the stout wire stake once bought will last indefinitely or till the end of the Philippine war.

I have said nothing yet about watering, and it is the hardest part to describe. To a gardener it should be only necessary to say, "water when they want it." Texture of soil and health and vigor of plant will make a difference. Sometimes you will have a big cut all in one week, especially is this true of the first and second cuttings. Be careful then not to over-water, for the plants have lost a great deal of their foliage and don't need so much. Let the beds get very slightly on the dry side and the water. Don't let the hose run on the beds in a hard stream. A coarse rose is a good thing; it will leave the surface of the bed in a more friable state, and you should only give water enough to wet through to the boards. A soaking that drenches the bed and runs out through the boards must carry with it lots of the fertilizing properties of the soil and manure.

In sunny weather the surface of the bed will often appear dry when an inch down it is abundantly moist. If we are strangers to the texture of soil we are watering, then sight is not an infallible guide, but with the addition of a touch you are dull indeed if you don't know when a plant or bed needs watering.

We syringe for two purposes. When using the word "syringing" it may

lead our brother craftsmen across the Atlantic to believe that we use a brass syringe. "Why, bless your dear heart, don't you know, old fellow," our boys would get so lazy with a hand syringe that they would never keep down the red spider, and fancy a man, or two men, syringing a house 600 feet long and 22 feet wide! They would have to begin on the 4th of July to get them syringed by Thanksgiving. The 3-4 or 1-2-inch hose will not only syringe them as well but much better, for you will do it thoroughly with that beautiful "upper-cut" so dear to a real gardener.

Syringing is done on bright mornings throughout the season, to produce a genial healthy moisture that is relished by the leaves, and it is also done to prevent the lodgment of red spider on the under side of the leaf (and the spider is ever ready to locate on fine leaves). If you are free of the spider then don't syringe on wet, damp days or very cold, stormy days; no harm at all in missing a day but when firing very hard, damp down the paths, under the benches, etc.

The greatest scourge to the rose grower is the mildew, the minute fungus that lays hold and soon covers every leaf. It cripples the petals, ruins the leaves and stunts the plants. A dose of it in winter is a calamity, but prevalent as it is our largest and best growers never fear it and seldom have give it a chance to get a start. Mildew is caused by any check to the vitality of the plant, which shrinks up the cellular tissue and renders the leaves susceptible to the resting spores, which must be ever floating around. Perfectly healthy leaves resist it, as do healthy lungs resist the germs of tuberculosis, while weak ones succumb, for consumption is contagious or infectious and not hereditary, as formerly supposed: only in certain families there is a predisposition, and in certain plants there is most truly a predisposition for mildew. Catherine Mermet is always ready on the slightest excuse to be host to this troublesome fungus, but as once said before in these pages, these things are all right as they are, and if there was no reward for watchfulness, care and brains, there would be nothing in it and the wise man would be no better than the fool man, which would be very annoying in this world, however great equality is to be carried out in the next.

A ventilator left open too late, a draught from an open door, ventilation forgotten till too late in the day, or a sudden drop at night from say 56 degrees, their usual temperature, to 46 degrees or less. Any of these causes will produce mildew, and all must be guarded against.

There are several ways of applying the best remedy, sulphur. Mix it with linseed oil and paint one steam or hot water pipe. Sulphide of potassium dissolved and mixed with clay can be painted on the pipe, but do not put too much on. Flour of sulphur thrown on the plants does not do much good, as it is not the sulphur itself but the fumes you want. Sulphur put in shallow pans or on bricks and placed where the sun will strike them will emit quite a little of the fumes. All of these can be used as preventives or as cures.

For aphis smoking is not advisable. I am certain I have seen its ill effects. Vaporizing, as described in chapter on insecticides, is best, and the plan of putting a hot (but not red hot) piece of iron into an iron vessel containing either the Rose Leaf extract, diluted ten to one, or the Nikoteen, reduced twenty to one, will do first rate. See that the dish or iron pan is deep enough so that the liquid does not boil over and waste when the iron is dropped into it.

Those whose water supply comes from river, lake or reservoir should have some means of warming it in winter and early spring. When steam is used this is easily done by letting the three-quarter or 1-inch water pipe run through a larger steam pipe, but when hot water is used there is no chance to do this, and it is better to have large barrels elevated in your shed that can be filled a day ahead, and when used the water is about the same temperature as your shed. Those who are away from the cities and towns have usually their water tanks under cover of their sheds with the means of warming the water with a steam or hot water pipe.

The water does not need to be warm, but when it comes out of our city mains it is little over freezing, and to water a rose bed with water at that temperature in January can't be good. If you can raise the water to 50 degrees that would be much better and high enough.

Soils of different textures grow good roses. Wm. Paul & Son, some years ago in an advertisement and description of their place, said: "At one nursery we have a clay suitable for the Hybrid Perpetuals, and at another a light loam suitable for the Tea Roses." Those were not just the words, but near enough. We have observed roses growing finely in many different kinds and textures of soil, but I must say that the tallest, strongest and most vigorous Brides and Mermets I have ever seen were in five inches of clay that needed a hammer to break it up, and that was at the end of December and under the care of a man who had never tried his hand at the business till that year.

It is useless to comment on the different soils that have grown good roses. What we want to know is which is the best when it can be had. Then I would prefer above all the top three, or perhaps four, inches of a rather heavy loam pasture. Not the pasture from an orchard that had been laid down forty years and was moss grown and the surface containing the deposit of rotten leaves, but a good fresh pasture that the cows had been

grazing on for a few years. If it's still more on the heavy side, no harm. The poorest soil of all would be a fiberless sand.

On asking one very large and successful rose grower what manure he used, he replied "any he could get," and a mixture of animal manures is more likely to supply what is needed for the rose than the use of one would be. But pure sheep manure must be used cautiously, and a proportion of one to twenty of soil is enough. Soil is often mixed haphazard, and a portion getting more manure or bone meal than another.

Pillar Rose.

A prudent grower cuts his soil in October or November and piles it up under an open shed, and a long shed it is. It is not put under the shed to keep the rain from it, but being dry it can be worked over earlier in the spring, and the men can work at it rain or shine. This is a valuable point. He has a frame made without bottom, with handles extending at both ends. The frame is nine feet long by three feet wide and one foot deep. That is just one cubic yard. As the soil is chopped down it is thrown into this box and when it is even full a certain portion of manure is thrown on top, and then a portion of bone dust, spreading manure and bone dust over

the surface. The frame is then lifted up and that lot is shoveled away into a pile. By this means there is no guess work, all parts of the bench have the same quality.

The quantity of manure (cow manure is most often used) is a matter of opinion. One-sixth the bulk of the soil is quite enough, and one peck of bone dust to one yard will be a good but safe allowance. Don't get the bone dust or meal too coarse, or it will be thrown out before you get the benefit of it. In placing the soil on the bench I have heard it asked, How do you keep the soil from running through the crack between the boards? There should always be coarse pieces enough of the soil to place over the spaces. If not, some well rotted stable manure will answer the purpose.

In shallow beds, such as all roses are mostly grown in, they want several mulchings. If they have grown fast and vigorous they will need the mulching all the more. If planted in June they can be mulched in August and again in October. It is better to mulch lightly and often. A good mulch would be well rotted cow manure, to which add one quart of bone meal to a bushel of the manure and one-third of loam, and put on only half an inch each time. About first of February mulch again and again in April. This last mulch will be not only for manuring the plants but will prevent their drying out so fast and can be a little heavier than the others.

I have had no experience with liquid manure except in applying it by watering can, which is too laborious a job for a rose or carnation house. Where it can be pumped through the pipes or run through by gravitation its application must be very beneficial, particularly when the bed is full of roots. Be sure not to overdo it in strength. A liquid made from animal manures would be the safest. Here is a chemical liquid, published some time ago and said to be excellent for roses, carnations or chrysanthemums. It is a formula published by Prof. Paul Wagner, of Darmstadt, and republished here by Prof. W. E. Britton. Quantities can of course be increased to any dimensions:

Phosphate of ammonia	oz.	1
Nitrate of soda	oz.	1¾
Nitrate of potash	oz.	1¾
Sulphate of ammonia	oz.	1¾
Water	gal.	50

Although the American Beauty is a widely different rose from the Tea section, yet its growing for winter flowers is the same, and I will say that in propagating it I have never found the slightest difficulty at any time from November to April, or even May. Choose wood that is medium in strength, and don't use either the green top or the hard base. When potting them off I have lost quite a number by their being left exposed to a bright sun. Be careful to shade and keep moist for a few days. Let there be always two eyes to the cutting.

House of Meteor Roses.

In growing them on into 3, or possibly 4-inch pots, give them all the light and air you can till planting time, as you do the Tea varieties. The Beauties want to flower early, but the buds should be picked off till end of August. From then till first of November you will get a good many nice buds with 18 to 30-inch stems, and the stems will break again and usually send up another flowering stem, but as soon as the dark weather sets in the break from a strong cut down shoot will be blind, or practically blind, for it may grow ten feet long before it flowers. So, after the first of November if you are looking for flowers at the holidays, when they are worth $1.50 each, you must let the flower fully expand and then cut it off at the neck and sacrifice it. You will notice that at the axil of the leaf just below the flower there is already a young growth. That growth will give a flower six weeks later, and you will be getting a dollar for your flower instead of twenty-five cents, or less.

American Beauties are very liable to be troubled with red spider, and should be thoroughly syringed, but never on damp, cloudy days or late in the day.

Some growers carry over for the second winter their beds of roses, both on benches and in solid beds. I have never seen a bed of this kind equal to a young well managed lot, but they occasionally do very well up to about February. When intended to

be grown on for a second winter they should have a little light shade in June, July and August, or they get so terribly exhausted. Plants in four or five inches of soil will not bear to be dried out but very slightly, and that better be done in July. All the pruning they need is just the blind and weak and worn out wood cut out. The young vigorous growth should be left untouched.

Those in solid beds, say a foot of soil, can be dried off considerably more and can also be much harder cut back. In a foot of strong, heavy loam we had a bed of old Safrano, Isabella Sprunt and Bon Silene years ago, and we used to let the bed get hard and cracked. About the first week in August we pruned them back to bare wood, gave them a heavy mulch of cow manure and started again, and I have never seen more roses to the square foot than those plants produced for several years.

The plan of running hot water or steam pipes through rubble stone with a foot of soil or less on top, is I believe abandoned. It is certainly nonsense to think that roses want bottom heat, and no pipes are run under a bench. Mr. Gasser, of Cleveland, who grows roses largely, is a strong advocate of a bench on, or a few inches above the surface, of the ground, on which he puts 2-inch drain tiles close together. I cannot see any advantage in this plan, excepting that it affords a most ex-

cellent drainage and would be a fine bottom to any solid bed.

Roses for summer blooming are not given the attention that they deserve. In June, July and August we frequently have a difficulty in getting large, clean flowers. Houses for this purpose should run north and south, because they would be the coolest. The beds should be well drained, solid beds affording plenty of head room, for these plants will be kept in the borders for several years and will be a considerable size before outgrowing their usefulness. You must begin in the early spring with planting and will cut a very paying crop the following summer and fall.

In October all possible ventilation should be given and less water and syringing. With a lower temperature growth will cease and in December and January and February if you just keep the house above the freezing point it is enough. A few degrees of frost will do no harm, but don't forget your water pipes if you let the frost in.

Early in March start them up again. As the wood is firm and ripe and the roots inactive these roses can be pruned hard when starting them in spring, and will bear a good heavy mulch of cow manure. Don't start with too much heat at once, but as the roots are undisturbed they will break immediately and can soon be given the usual rose house treatment.

As all the varieties you would grow for this purpose belong to the Tea or Hybrid Tea class you can make the season of rest still shorter and pick good flowers up to the middle of November, and merely lower the temperature down to 35 or 40 degrees till end of January, when you can lightly prune and start growing again.

For this purpose there is no finer white than the grand Kaiserin Augusta Victoria. Perle des Jardins is the best yellow and comes fine in the warm weather. President Carnot, the blush white and pink is splendid for the purpose, and for a red Meteor delights in the summer heat. Old La France will flower to perfection with this treatment.

In our largest cities the summer rose does not receive much attention, for society is largely absent. In our salubrious climate people stop here, and besides that roses are wanted every day in the year.

My readers will know more about the varieties of the Tea roses to grow than I can tell them, for they are familiar to all. The American Beauty stands first, if not in quantity most assuredly in high quality, and there is nothing in sight to depose it. Bride for white, and Bridesmaid for a clear pink, stand unrivalled, and their parent, C. Mermet, is still a most beautiful pink. Meteor is the standard red or crimson, but the beautiful Liberty is likely to depose it. If Liberty proves

to mention them may be misleading, as they have not yet been proved as all round worthy candidates to displace well known kinds. There will be no lack of advertising if they prove themselves desirable varieties.

Within the past two or three years there has been adopted by many rose growers a new method of propagating, viz.: grafting. The necessity for this is because some of our standard varieties, like Bride and Bridesmaid, are showing lack of vigor, and when grafted on the Manetti stock they grow much stronger and better. There is no doubt the stronger and more vigorous Manetti stock must induce a heavier growth to the rose. Unless you are in a large way of business you had better buy your grafted stock if you are not satisfied with the way your own stock grows. For a full and complete description of the operation of grafting refer to any of the trade papers containing Mr. Robert Craig's paper on that subject, read to the Omaha convention, or to a report of the society's meeting. You should be a member of the Society of American Florists; if not, you deserve to remain in the dark. Briefly the operation is this: The Manetti stocks are imported from Europe at a very low cost. In the fall they can be heeled in in a cold frame till winter. In January or February or later pot them in 2½-inch pots, and stand on any bench in about 50 degrees. As soon as you see root action

ing of the stem is where the sap flows, and there is where adhesion will first take place. Match the stock and scion as neatly as you can and then tie round the splice with raffia that has been made soft and pliable by wetting. Place the pots immediately in a frame on a bench where the pots can be plunged in a heat of 65 to 70 degrees, and the tops kept close by the glass covering. It is well to have partitions in the frame for each batch, so they can be aired when needed. In two weeks adhesion will have taken place and then some ventilation can be given, and in four or five weeks the plants can be removed to an ordinary bench. But be careful not to let too much sun or draught be upon them for another two or three weeks. For the first two weeks in the frame the air must be kept moist, but very little water will be needed at the roots. There is very little evaporation going on and the stock has been so mutilated that there is little for its roots to do.

Now this seems an elaborate performance compared to sticking cuttings in the bed, but it is not. Like all new jobs, it may be tedious at first, but when once familiar with the operation it is quite simple.

In conclusion I will say that in my humble opinion there would be no need of this more expensive method of renewing our rose stock if we were to treat our plants more rationally. I

Display of Tea Roses.

to be a good winter bloomer the fate of Meteor is sealed, for it is a far better flower, a true Jacqueminot color, bright and rich, and it does not have the bad fault of Meteor in winter. Perle des Jardins has no rival in yellow. Sunset, its sport, is a fine orange yellow.

The above will cover 90 per cent of all the roses grown for cut flowers, but many fine varieties find favor in some localities. Mme. Hoste, Mme. de Watteville, Belle Siebrecht, Mrs. J. Pierpont Morgan, Mme. C. Testout, Papa Gontier, Mrs. R. Garrett, and others, are grown. Several new varieties are coming out this winter, but

has commenced, and consequently sap rising, prepare for grafting. Choose such wood from the roses as you would for cuttings, good healthy shoots and about as firm as when the bud is developed. The graft (called scion) make three inches long, or a little less, with an eye and leaf on top. Cut the Manetti stock down to two inches of the pot and cut both stock and scion obliquely, so that they will about fit together. It is not likely that the scion will be as thick as the stock, which is not of any consequence, but it is of utmost importance that one side of stock and scion should fit exactly, for just below the bark or outer cover-

am well aware it is not a "new and original" idea with me, but I have thought of it very much of late and can recall a few instances where circumstances would lead me to believe that we are asking too much of our Tea roses. It can't be denied that we keep our stock of roses up to concert pitch the whole time, perhaps for seven or eight years, or until some new variety replaces an older one.

A cutting, as before said in these pages, is not a new individual; it is merely the perpetuation of the old, and without a natural rest it must get exhausted. The Tea rose is an evergreen, or nearly so, and a continuous

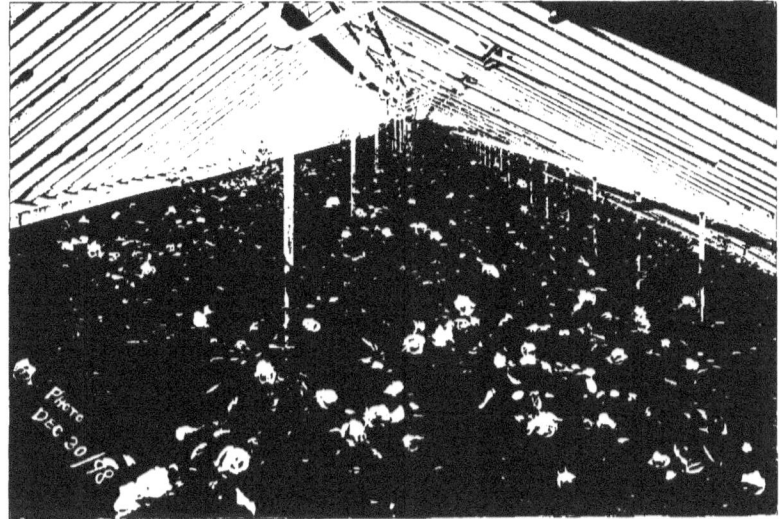

House of Tea Roses.

bloomer; or we make it so, but its parent or parents had a period of rest at some time of the year, that is sure. But we give none. Our cuttings are taken off when the plant is in most active growth, the cutting is grown along as quickly as possible and made into a vigorous young plant, and set out in June and forced along in growth and it continues to grow until propagating time again. Not a day of actual rest, and so the cycle revolves, but no rest for the roses. Now, the instances I remember was, first, a lot of young stock coming from a nursery firm in Pennsylvania who make a specialty of roses. They arrived in April, the cuttings had been strong shoots taken off the previous fall and the plants had been wintered a little if any above freezing. They were what we would say of a tramp, "hard looking citizens." Scrubby looking leaves. They were put into 3-inch pots and began to grow immediately, and when planted out in end of June grew most vigorously, far surpassing some much better looking plants that had been propagated that spring in the usual way. Those plants had had a winter's rest.

The other case was on my own place. Some plants left over from planting in July were knocking about the frames the following fall and winter, and in the spring stood under the wall of a shed, and occasionally when it rained stood with their pots full of

water; in fact, abused. Being short of fifty plants when planting in June or July we put in these "runts" and they simply started off and grew prodigiously, far outstripping the good looking young plants by their side.

I believe and feel sure that were we able to propagate in late spring or early fall and winter the plants in a very cold house, or in milder parts in a cold-frame, and bring them into slowly to planting time, we should not be obliged to have recourse to the fussy job of grafting.

One word as a final. When you want to buy don't send to the man who raises hundreds of thousands of young plants for sale. Send to the good grower of flowers who has a few thousand surplus of his own stock, and never study the price of two cents on a plant. It is the height of folly and extravagance to buy poor stock. One single bud will more than pay for the plant.

SALVIA.

A large genus of plants of which few are used by the florist. S. splendens is one of our showiest flowering plants. There are now several varieties or forms of it. It is used as a mass where brilliant colors are wanted. They are often rather late in flowering, especially in wet seasons, and should not be planted in too rich a soil or you will get a large growth with late flowering, so procure a strain

that grows compact and is early to flower.

Lifted before frost and potted they make showy plants for a month or two, and we often find their flowers useful.

They are easily raised from seed, and there is now a hybrid strain that contains various colors, and is said to be early and free flowering.

A few plants lifted, and cut back after New Year's, will give you an abundance of cuttings that will make fine plants for bedding out. The salvia is troubled with aphis and if in a warm, dry house and not syringed will soon become attacked by red spider. They should never be kept over 50 degrees. They grow so fast and strong that it is best to put off propagating till March.

S. patens we have not seen grown here, but in the gardens of Europe it is much used. It has very much the same habit as splendens, with erect spike and the flower is somewhat larger; the color is of the most beautiful blue of any flower that grows. Propagate by cuttings same as S. splendens.

Salvia officinalis, the variegated form of this, the common sage, is used in carpet and other flower garden designs. The coloring is not bright, but very pleasing. Lift a few plants when the flower garden is dismantled and in January shorten back the shoots. You will soon get any amount of cuttings that root most easily. And when in 2 or 2 1-2-inch pots there is no place to make nice little plants like the hotbed. It is almost or quite hardy.

SANTOLINA INCANA.

This almost hardy little herb is of great importance in the flower garden. It can be clipped and cut to any form or line. To design patterns in carpet bedding or as an edging it is invaluable. Its small, dense foliage has a grey or frosted appearance. Occasionally, when covered with snow, it comes through the winter unharmed, but such plants would not be useful for our flower gardening purposes. Lift some plants and pot, or put them in a flat in a few inches of soil. In February cut off two or three inches of the tops and they will send out numerous growths that root rapidly. This again is a plant that quickly

thawed in the spring they should be lifted and potted, when they will make their growth, the appearance of which is so useful in hanging baskets or veranda boxes.

Few plants will stand the hot sun, dryness and neglect so well as the sedums. For a border or rockery there is of course no need of cold-frame or pots. They can be divided and planted at once in their permanent position.

S. speciosum, rose pink, good for rockery, border or florist's use; S. Sieboldii, pink, very good 'basket plant; S. pulchellum, pink, dwarf, fine for borders; S. Rhodiola, pink, dwarf, fine for borders; S. ternatum, white, vases or baskets; S. kamtschaticum, yellow, very fine species for baskets or rockery; S. Maximowiczii, yellow, handsome, fine stems with greenish purple leaves.

There are many species, but the above can be relied on as some of the best.

in pairs, charging for boxes or baskets and using bell glasses belong to another continent and past age. But this is about seeds and not cuttings.

In the article on Asters I give in detail a method of sowing them or any other seeds of considerable size. We are asked repeatedly how deep to sow seeds. There is no rule, and out of doors in the garden you would cover much deeper than you would in the greenhouse. A very good rule would be to cover the seeds their own thickness, which would be with an aster seed just out of sight, and with a gloxinia so little that it would be impossible to measure it or apply it. Still, we are sure that a grain of wheat or oats will struggle to the surface when buried six inches, and a cabbage seed will send up its leaves to the light when covered an inch. And these depths are one hundred times the diameters of the seed.

However, we are not considering the seeds in the garden but how to raise

A Range of Connected Rose Houses.

makes a nice, compact and quick growth in a mild hotbed far better than on a greenhouse bench.

SEDUM.

These pretty little, hardy perennials are known to all. But a few of the species are useful to the florist, and they are not cultivated as much as they should be. Many of the species make good plants for the hardy border. Some are the finest of rock plants. And a few are valuable to the florist for vases and baskets.

They are of the easiest possible culture, thriving in any soil and needing little of it. They are propagated from seeds, or by pulling the plant to pieces and replanting in early spring, but for the florist's use are best propagated by cuttings in May. If wanted in quantity the cuttings can be put in the cold-frame in May in the ground, and when rooted remove the sash and leave the plants to grow all summer, protecting them with sash in winter. As soon as the ground is

SEED SOWING.

By sowing seed is the only method that we can get a new individual. A cutting or layer is only a division of the plant, and a graft and bud is not a new plant, it is still the perpetuation of the same individual with the help of another plant's vigor and strength. Still, cuttings are the only way absolutely that we can increase a hybrid or variety, and far more stock is increased by cuttings than by seeds.

I consider raising plants by seeds a far more delicate and particular undertaking than our usual method with the cuttings and propagating bed. And just let me say here that within thirty or forty years we have wonderfully simplified the cutting bed. There may be, and is occasionally, the need of a closed case or bell glass for propagating some of the hard wooded plants, but I can remember, and so can thousands of gardeners, when verbenas and petunias were put under a bell glass. Just fancy how we have progressed in this line. Selling carnation plants

them without failure under glass. The great Prof. Lindley in his "Introduction to Botany," says: "It is a well known seeds will not germinate in the light." What nonsense, for we have all seen many kinds of seeds grow in the light. The old seedsman's way of testing seeds was to wrap a piece of wet flannel round a bottle and sticking the seeds in the flannel and keeping the bottle full of hot water. Mustard seed will grow in the light and so will an acorn.

With seeds larger than those of the aster or verbena there is very little need of failure, and no need of covering them more than their depth because our seedlings are soon to be handled. But with begonias, calceolarias, gloxinias and other very minute seeds the operation is one of great care. Mr. Fred L. Atkins gives the correct method in an article on gloxinias in The Florist's Review, March 3, 1898, page 569, all of which is excellent.

The soil should be well baked or

scalded with boiling water to destroy the seeds or spores of any other vegetable growth. The pan or pot should be filled to within an inch of the fine soil with crocks and moss. The surface should be of sifted soil, which should be a soft loam and leaf-mould. The surface should be smooth and even, and to thoroughly wet this before sowing you should stand the pan in water. In a few moments the water will soak up to the surface. Then sow the seeds.

You are so liable to sow these seeds too thickly that great care must be exercised. The smallest pinch between your finger and thumb and a very slight movement of the same will with care drop the seeds equally distributed. Then the smallest quantity of clean sand distributed over the surface, not enough to hide the color of the soil but just a sprinkle. Then press lightly the surface with the bottom of a clean pot. Let the surface of the soil be an inch below the top of the pan.

Mr. Atkins recommends covering the surface with green moist moss and then over it a sheet of glass. We sometimes use a piece of wet cheese cloth instead of the moss, which can be dampened with the Scollay sprinkler, and as there is so little evaporation there will be little need of water, but the glass and moss, or cloth, should be removed once a day to see if they are dry in any spot.

Directly you notice the seeds germinating remove the covering and tilt up one side of the glass, and as the little plants get stronger remove the glass entirely. The Scollay sprinkler will water the surface while the plants are very young, and when stronger you can dip the pans in water and let it quietly run over the surface; that is better than a coarser sprinkling. When the seeds are well up, and by careful handling they should never be allowed to draw up, the seed pans should be given the fullest light, but never allowed to get parched by the sun.

However grown, plants may relish to be occasionally on the dry side and then soaked. Small seedlings, particularly at the critical time of germination, should be kept at a uniform moisture. Seed pans can be kept in a house 5 or 10 degrees warmer than you would grow the plants, but as soon as well up should be placed in the temperature most suited to the plant when growing.

All seedlings, with hardly an exception, should be transplanted into other pans or flats as soon as they can be handled; particularly is this the case with those that you have sown thickly. A sudden drying will often wilt and destroy many young seedlings, and forgetfulness to shade is often disastrous. At the same time it is most essential that the little plants should have the fullest light, for if you start off with a drawn, spindling plant you have seriously handicapped your future success.

Now, all the points related above

are easy to follow, but the great thing is to follow them faithfully. A watchmaker can throw down his tools and leave his watch for a week and return and take up his task with the loss only of time, but you can't leave a week or a day, or hardly an hour. It is in the care and watchfulness and everlasting attention and thoughtfulness that makes the gardener, far more than scientific action, either mental or physical.

Don't blame the seedsman always. I must at the cost of being thought egotistical say that for years I never blamed a seedsman when perhaps I had a reason. I blamed my own clumsiness and carelessness.

The man who has charge of the seeds should be given plenty of time, for he needs it.

SELAGINELLA.

Among the large number of species (over 300 in all) of the selaginellas there are comparatively few that are used in the trade, notwithstanding the fact that there are several of the species easily procurable and readily grown into very attractive pot plants. It is true that selaginellas in general prefer moisture and shade, and in consequence are somewhat tender in foliage, but this rule does not hold good in all cases, some of the species bearing exposure fully as well as many of the commercial species of ferns.

An example of this is found in S. Braunii, a Chinese species that has been long in cultivation, and that is frequently, though incorrectly labelled S. Willdenovi. The branches of this species are very tough and wiry, the leaves small and deep green in color, and it not only forms a very pretty plant in a 4 or 5-inch pot, but is also well adapted for growing into a large exhibition specimen, or to be used

among foliage plants in a veranda box, the branches of this plant often reaching a height of eighteen inches or more.

S. Martensii is another well-known and deserving species, the flat branchlets of which are quite effective among the plants in a table fernery. This species is very easy to increase by means of cuttings, these being potted up at once in light sandy soil without the preliminary treatment of the cutting bed, and only require to be kept moist and sheltered from too much sun and air until they take root. This species has also provided us with one of the best variegated forms found among the selaginellas, namely, S. Martensii var., the branchlets of which are variably marked with white. S. Martensii var. also roots readily

Selaginella Cuspidata.

from cuttings, it being necessary, however, to select well-variegated pieces in order to perpetuate the variegation. The freak of variegation is not confined to S. Martensii, for it also appears in the common S. Kraussiana var., and also in S. involvens, the latter being quite prolific in singular forms.

S. Kraussiana, also known as S. denticulata, is perhaps the most familiar example of this interesting family, and is one of the most useful plants we have for carpeting the surface of the soil beneath other plants, or for beautifying otherwise bare spaces beneath the benches of a conservatory.

S. cuspidata is another useful species, a plant of which is illustrated herewith. It will be readily noted that this illustration bears some resemblance to S. Emiliana, a variety that has been very largely grown for a few years past for filling table ferneries, and the explanation of this is found in the fact that S. Emiliana is simply a form of S. cuspidata. Cuttings of

13

this species soon take root in sand or sandy soil, and become compact, tufted little plants in a few months when grown in an ordinary fern house.

S. viticulosa illustrates another form of growth that we find in this diverse family, this species being better adapted for use as a pot plant than to be mingled in a fernery, its branchlets being large and standing up like the fronds of a fern. These branchlets are thrown up from creeping stems, and do not root readily, consequently the propagation of this plant usually depends upon division, or from spores. A good idea of this handsome species may be had from the accompanying photograph.

S. serpens is a singular member of this family that is quite common in gardens and forms a dense mat of closely rooting branchlets on the surface of the soil. The great peculiarity of this species is found in its changes of color during the day, the foliage being bright green in the morning, but gradually becomes much paler, as though bleached by the light, finally resuming its lively green hue at night.

Of the selaginellas that are especially valuable for private collections or for exhibition purposes a long list might easily be made, and prominent among them should be mentioned such beautiful species as S. Wallichii, S. Vogelii, S. Lyallii, S. Wildenovii, that very strong growing scandent species with the strong metallic tints on its foliage, a species that has been tossed about on the waves of nomenclature, being sometimes S. caesia arborea, again S. laevigata, and finally S. Wildenovii. Also S. haematodes, S. atroviridies, and S. rubricaulis, all of which are worthy of more extended cultivation, though not all are quite so easy to manage as the few we have specially referred to for commercial purposes.
W. H. T.

SHADING.

I have had occasion to mention shading many times in reference to plants that need it under glass. We are as yet without any portable shading that can be adjusted to our commercial greenhouses. The wooden slat shading applied to some private conservatories is out of the question for the commercial man, and if expense did not forbid, it is too dense.

Many of our plants that thrive in the broad sun will burn up under unshaded glass. This last July having occasion to remove the glass in a house to paint and reglaze, we left many plants standing on the benches fully exposed to sun and air. Among them I noticed Primula obconica and P. Forbesii and several kinds of flowering begonias. Before the glass was put on again, perhaps three weeks, the plants had made a great improvement in their growth, strong and robust. If the glass had been on without shading it would have been a different story.

We can at least use a light cloth on our frames over such plants as

cyclamen and others that are much the best in frames during summer. A stout pole a little longer than the width of the frame with cheese cloth tacked to it is easily and quickly unrolled or rolled up.

We frequently are tardy in putting on shading and then daub on a heavy coat. Put on a thin coat where needed and add another when the sun is stronger, and if you will go to the trouble of plunging many of our common plants in refuse hops or decayed leaves you will find their growth much better, and you can delay or dispense with shading entirely.

Supposing you have a house full of geraniums or cannas which, as soon as sold, say end of May or early June, will be filled with chrysanthemums. If you shade for these plants you must

Selaginella Viticulosa.

certainly brush it off again for the mums for they don't want and must not have any shade. Quite as important as putting it on early with such plants as palms and ferns is taking it off in good time. Begin end of August to remove the shade and by middle of October have it all off.

We are frequently asked what is the best material? We have tried many mixtures, and best of all like naphtha and white lead without any oil. We tried common coal oil instead of naphtha, but it is too greasy. Try the mixture before you settle on the thickness of it.

We have also tried applying it with a syringe, and are entirely opposed to it. It saves labor but you will use more material than will twice pay for the labor, and when put on with a long handled brush it is properly done. This mixture rubs off easily when dry and the hose makes a clean job of it.

SKIMMIA JAPONICA.

This is a greenhouse shrub from Japan and is very ornamental when

well supplied with its bright red berries. Its leaves are bright green, holly-like, and the plant has a fine, compact habit. Small plants not over one foot in height are of most use.

It can be raised easily from seed or cuttings in the usual way, made from the young growths in spring. Cut back the shoots slightly in February and give it a good light house and warmth and moisture. After flowering and the berries are set they can be plunged in a frame out of doors and removed to a cool greenhouse before frost.

S. oblata is said to be still more handsome and needs the same treatment.

Any good loam will grow them, and except when growing in the spring they thrive in a cool house.

SMILAX (MYRSIPHYLLUM ASPARAGOIDES).

This useful climber and twiner seems to have been grown here commercially long before its great usefulness was appreciated in Europe. Though the more graceful looking asparagus has superseded it in our decorations it is still a standard article with all commercial florists, and in funeral decorations there is no equal to it.

One author says it is propagated by "seeds, cuttings and divisions." I have never heard of its being rooted from cuttings, and to divide it would be absurd as it is so easily raised from seed.

Seed should be sown in flats and covered an eighth of an inch, in February. Good fresh soil is now always supplied. When two or three inches high pot off into 2-inch pots and keep in a temperature anywhere above 50 degrees. If you expect the best results from your newly planted bed you ought by middle of May to give these little plants another shift into a 3-inch. Getting strong plants to plant out in June will give you an extra crop over small, weak plants. And although you often see them standing under a bench in May and June that is not the way to produce well rooted, strong plants.

Make your Smilax bed in the center of the house on the ground with seven or eight feet of head room; and more is better. If the floor of the house is naturally dry you want no preparation, but make the bed seven or eight inches above the surface and confined with a brick or plank wall.

I have tried several kinds of soil. The worst smilax I ever grew was in a light sand, and the best was in a stiff loam, such a soil as roses like, with the addition of one-fourth of rotten cow manure. Plant at end of June or very early in July.

If you intend to renew the bed every year, which I strongly advocate, then plant ten inches between the rows and six or seven inches between the plants. Run a wire across the bed just behind the row of plants, and a corresponding wire near the roof, and at each plant run up a string of silkaline. It is invisible when cut and saves you much bother when using the smilax because there is no need of pulling it out.

Keep down weeds from the start and frequently teach the little growths that they are to climb up the strings. When once started they are no trouble, and when a crop is cut and a new growth is starting replace the strings at once. We are guilty of neglect and I have seen days of labor spent over a smilax bed that was allowed to grow without strings a few weeks and had to be unravelled and started up the strings much to the harm of the growths.

When growing fast smilax likes and must have an abundance of water and should be daily syringed to keep down red spider. It should be also fumigated, but not heavily or it will turn the tips of the leaves. Vaporizing with tobacco extract would avoid that, but with proper care we have no trouble with the smoke.

When a crop is fit to cut or your business demands that you cut it, begin at one end and clear it as you go. When the plant is denuded of its entire growth, as it is when you cut the strings, it does not want water till it begins to send up more growth. I have seen the roots rotted by a heavy watering just after cutting off the strings, and when the thick, fleshy roots rot they raise a bad smell, very similar to decayed Solanum tuberosum, alias potato.

When cutting the strings don't let a crude hand ruthlessly chop off all the growth. There may be several strong young shoots a foot or eighteen inches high that will quickly make another string.

By planting last of June you ought to get four crops before planting time again, and will if the temperature of the house is kept never less than 60

degrees at night throughout the winter, and if it is 65 degrees so much the better; contrary to what would be the case with most plants the warmer you grow it the harder it is providing it is matured when cut. Being naturally a twiner among trees it likes the shade, and is best shaded in summer and early spring.

I am sure it is wisest to plant every year. You get more strings; they are a more useful size, and easier managed. After the second crop is cut, about New Year's, the bed will be greatly benefited by a top dressing of an inch of loam and cow manure. Their strong asparagus-like crown of roots soon works to the surface and need this mulching. The smilax is a heavy feeder, so a strong soil, plenty of water when growing, and a good heat, suits it.

SOILS.

Although various soils have been often alluded to as most suitable for different plants I cannot impress on you too much the importance of being always well supplied with this most necessary article of our business. We too frequently are careless and often falsely economical in not buying a good pile of soil. Greenhouse establishments in or near cities, or where by its growth has surrounded them, have often a difficulty in getting a good supply, and it is too often a case of get what you can. I have learnt lately that when a teamster asks, "do you want twenty loads of good earth?" you had better investigate at once, and if it is good buy it; you don't know when you will get the next.

We pay out without a murmur thousands of dollars for fuel, but squirm a good deal over one-quarter the amount for soil and manure. And if by these words I have made you think seriously how important a matter is good soil I will have done you some good.

Those having five or six acres, or better, fifteen acres, can help themselves off their own place, and they should take care and husband their land or they will find that with broad acres they can soon use it up and have little in the right condition. No one nowadays thinks of using soil for roses or carnations or violets the second year, and these crops take a great deal of soil.

When an acre is what we call "skinned," three, four or five inches deep, it should be restored as soon as possible with the soil that comes out of the benches. Put as much back as you took away, and what you put back will be good soil, for while in use in the greenhouse you added animal manure, bone-meal and other fertilizers. You can grow a crop of potatoes on it the first summer, or use it for your planted out crops for a couple of years, or better still, after the potatoes lay it down to winter wheat and sow clover in the spring and in two years plow the clover under, and you have a grand field for your carnations.

I have proved within a few years,

what, not being a farmer I only knew by report, that a growth of a foot of clover plowed under is a wonderful agency in mellowing and fertilizing any land unless it be a black muck. Farmers consider red clover a foot high plowed in for wheat equal to an ordinary dressing of farm yard manure. Other pieces of your farm should be after a year's tillage laid down with timothy or red top, and in two or three years you have again a sod for your roses. Even in country villages you cannot always buy good soil. The thrifty farmer does not want to skin his land at any price, and the indigent farmer, who is sure to have a good sized mortgage on it, dare not or Mr. Mortgageholder will step in and forbid, and quite right he should. The majority of unthinking men are very glad to get the loan on their property but when interest comes due turn round and abuse the loaner for a Shylock.

There is often a very poor provision made for keeping soil over winter. Flower growers who have large places in the country don't feel this so much, but even they need a shed where the soil can be hauled under when it is dry and in good condition. In the fall it is a great help. If taken under cover in October and no rain or snow falls on it during winter it can be brought in even if frozen at any time, and when it thaws it will fall to pieces and be mellow and be usable in a short time, but if in the open and saturated with water when frozen and brought in in frozen chunks it will be days and perhaps weeks before it can be used. How long it takes in winter in our sheds to dry out.

The plant man uses the great bulk of his soil from March 1st to middle of April, and it is very seldom that even at the latter late date our outside soil heap is dry enough to handle, so you should either have a shed with a big supply, which can be got at during any weather, or else an ample supply stored in your potting sheds in fall, enough to last you till the first of May. We speak from experience and know what it is to be running round in April for a few loads of soil and offering as much for a load as would have purchased ten in September. I don't like soil under the benches if it can be helped.

Soil is much better mixed with manure several months before using than mixing on the potting bench just before potting. A good pile of soil (sod if possible) should be piled up in July or August with a layer of manure every six inches, about a fifth or sixth of its bulk, built up square, three or four feet high, and then thoroughly soaked. And in four or five weeks chopped down and thrown in a long ridge to shed the rain. If you have time another turn over will be all the better and in a dry time in October a good supply of this should be stored in your potting shed or some place under cover.

I make no pretense to any know-

ledge of the chemical ingredients of soil, and however desirable it would be that all gardeners did have that knowledge, it is not necessary to a practical acquaintance and use of soils. Soils all the world over have very much the same properties.

Broadly, they consist of two kinds, that made or deposited from vegetable matter, like peat or what you will find on the surface of clays a few inches of vegetable deposit which is the deposit of centuries of forest leaves; and the others, clays and sands or loams, is the grinding up of surface rocks which have been largely distributed and deposited during the glacial period.

Peat, such as you hear of in Europe, and especially in Ireland, is largely the growth of water mosses, perhaps the growth of thousands of years. The remains of the moss can be plainly seen near the surface, but a few feet down it is so decomposed that it is not discernible. The German peat moss imported largely to this country from Silesia for horse bedding is sphagnum, hardly old enough to call peat, for you can plainly see the remains of the moss in it. Jadoo is simply that with some chemical fertilizer injected into it.

Plants of the Heath family like this peat because their fine roots work easily in it and it retains moisture, but it is not always an infallible guide that nature can not be improved on, and because you find a plant struggling along in a certain soil in a state of nature is no proof that with a richer and better soil it will not improve.

There are extensive sphagnum bogs scattered over this country, and it is likely there are some that if drained would afford us the same excellent material that is found in Europe, and notably in Bagshot, Surrey, where the rhododendrons are cultivated by the hundreds of acres in such excellence and profusion.

The bulb fields of Holland are a black peat or muck. Perhaps that country and Belgium, called the low countries because most parts are many feet below the level of the sea, was fifty thousand years ago one vast moss bog, and most likely it was, for there are the remains of ancient primitive man who built his hut on stilts and lived on the shallow lakes and subsisted on crustacea, for there are the remains of his kitchen refuse. The Hollander and Belgian would not raise such crops were he not to saturate the soil with manure every third year. This peat is useful, and he uses the splendid azaleas, etc., that they grow that it suits them, but it is not indispensable and our most important plants can be grown without it.

Where our soil is sand or clay we do not avail ourselves of what we might, and that is leaf-mould. Hundreds of us see thousands of loads of leaves of maple, oak, and elm burnt up every autumn when if they were collected and mixed or covered with sufficient

earth or manure to keep them from blowing away they would be invaluable for many of our plants. Roses and carnations do not need them but all our hard wooded plants that like peat, and our begonias, fuchsias, ferns, in fact any of the soft wooded plants, would be benefited by their use. It is a tedious job raking them up, but in many of our streets and parks and cemeteries they are raked up for you. In the country you can always find in some hardwood forest places where the wind has laid up for years deposits of these leaves, and you should always have a good supply on hand.

When leaves are collected the same fall that they drop it will take two years before they are fit to use, and more than that, unless they get frequent turning. I would consider a heap of maple leaves well rotted by frequent turnings and to which had been added when first collected a third or fourth of their weight of cow manure, a regular heap of gold dust for adding to your loam for "cyclamen, or most any other plant.

Refuse hops turned frequently make a good substitute for leaf-mould, and I have even used it on carnation benches in the old days of La Purite and Edwardsii with the very best results.

We value the hotbeds not only for their use in raising plants cheaply and well in the spring but the "by-product," the old bed put up in a pile and the following spring and summer turned over and chopped down once or twice, makes the most useful ingredient for our potting soil. In fact, most bedding plants it is all you want added to your loam if you are minus that good pile that I first spoke of.

There are great growing qualities in clay soils, even in clay taken a foot below the surface, as we have often seen proved by rose growers, but it should, if necessity compels its use, be exposed a winter to the frosts, and when used must needs have considerable manure to make it mechanically right. Clay alone will go down too solid and be too retentive of moisture, and for our plants in pots would be not at all desirable.

The worst of all soils is a gritty sand, and you sometimes find this on the surface. Our cuttings grow in sand for a short while but soon show the need of something better. When sampling soil if it feels gritty to the hand don't have anything to do with it; it is mostly particles of sand whatever its appearance. If a soil feels smooth, or as it is technically called, "silky," you have the right stuff.

Sometimes we have to avail ourselves of soil that has been cultivated as a garden for years. If you know that it has been well supplied with manure it will grow most of your plants, for it is rich. But there is something about soil that has been cut a few months that is not equalled by any soil that has been tilled, however much manure has been used. The roots of the grass keep it open and in a good mechanical condition however firm you make it, and there may be something more; in decaying the roots and fibres may emit bacteria that are of great usefulness to the roots. As we depend on a bacteria to do our digesting, and possibly another one to do our thinking, it is quite likely that in the process of decomposition this vegetable matter generates or emits a valued species. Certain it is that a good fibrous loam is the sheet anchor of our soils. More important than any fine quality or mixture of soil is to have plenty of it available at all times.

Up to a 3-inch pot you have to sift through a half or three-quarter inch mesh, after that we never sift soils except for seeds. From a 3 to a 4-inch and upwards we only chop the soil. This is most important. Somebody, I forget who, cursed the sieve, and he was right. Use it as little as possible. Chop your soil or break it up with a digging fork, but don't sift it.

SOLANUM.

This grand genus (for a genus that gives us the potato must be grand) contains some species that are used as ornamental plants.

I wonder why the universally used tuber is called the Irish potato. Perhaps it is because its jacket comes off so easy when it's hot, or perhaps Sir Walter Raleigh first introduced it at Cork. If he had overlooked it John Smith would have taken it to Europe, and if Sir Walter had gone exclusively into the potato business on his return and not aspired to the hand of old Queen Elizabeth he might have saved his head. But his head was of little consequence to future generations, and we have the potato that has sustained life among thousands.

In some rural districts they have potatoes as a steady diet, mostly with salt, and for a change without salt. I once took supper with a rural florist and the solid edibles consisted solely of fried potatoes and a blessing. The latter lighter commodity came first, so its inappropriateness was not so apparent. And with pleasure we look back at the evening and hope we may never want for a fine dish of potatoes. A volume could be written on t'e many ways of cooking potatoes in this its native land, but at a cheap boarding house of our first experience we do not think there was so much variation in the method of cooking as in the varieties of grease used.

The Jerusalem cherry, S. Capsicastrum, is very ornamental when well grown. Select seeds from a compact growing plant, sow in February or March in a good heat and grow in 2-inch pots till frost is gone. Plant out on a light and rather poor soil. You don't want a vigorous growth, but want a dwarf, compact plant and plenty of flowers. If the fruit is set before you lift them, so much the better. They must have no frost. They come in finely for the holidays and will do in any greenhouse; when well berried

they are very attractive and sell well, and can be sold cheaply, as they have occupied room on the benches but a short time. Pinch them when first planting out and again if they are growing straggling.

STEPHANOTIS FLORIBUNDA.

This beautiful flower was once much used for the choicest bouquets and designs, but since the advent of the long-stemmed flowers there is not the same use for it. Its fine, pure white, waxy flowers of delicous fragrance commend it to all who have a warm house. It

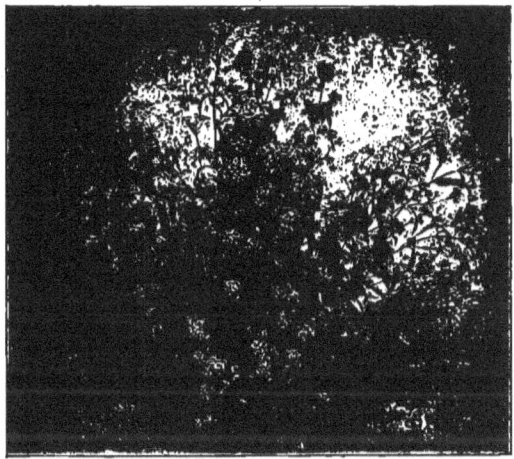

Bunch of Stevia.

is a true climber and should be planted out in a well drained border of coarse loam, but its roots are best confined so that they don't ramble too far. It is also grown in large pots and trained to a wire frame. Mealy bug is its worst enemy, but it will endure any amount of syringing.

A piece of the stem of the previous year's growth will root freely, but propagation is not of consequence; one or two plants is all you want. A plant I remember very well was trained along the roof of a small propagating house. It was in a 12-inch pot, but its roots had long ago passed through the pot into a bed of coal ashes, and every spring it bore hundreds of its lovely umbels of flowers.

That was an object lesson of the virtue of coal ashes; but it has been long known and frequently demonstrated in our houses that coal ashes will suit many plants. A neighbor of mine uses them entirely in place of sand for his propagating houses and succeeds quite equal to those using sand.

STEVIA.

The only species we grow and find profitable is what we know as serratifolia, or sweet stevia. It is an easily grown plant, but the flower is light and feathery, so that we value it highly at the holidays, and common as it may be we should miss it very much. After flowering cut down the plants to within six inches of the pots and stand them in some cool, light house. You will get a great many cuttings from a few plants. Propagate in February or March, and plant out end of

May. Any garden soil will do. They should be at least two feet apart. Stop them frequently till end of August.

Before any danger of frost lift and pot into 6 or 7-inch, but let the plants stand outside as long as you can. When you have to take them in give them the coolest (but light) bench you have. You want them at the holidays, and if kept light and very cool they will be robust and stout and give you fine spikes. Never let frost touch them, but they will thrive in a very low temperature.

STOCKS.

The Ten Week stocks are beautiful summer flowers, favorites with all. Their cultivation is very simple and for sowing seed and after care see Aster. They embrace many and varied colors, from crimson to purest white.

We grew for many years a pure white train of the Ten Week which made a handsome dwarf pot plant, as well as being useful for the flowers, but there is not now the same use for it.

Bed of Ten-Week Stocks.

The Intermediate and East Lothian Stock is much raised in Europe for winter blooming. Sow in August and September and as soon as the seed leaves are formed put into 2-inch and shift on and flower in 5-inch, and if wanted for spring use keep in cold-frame.

The Brompton Stock is the most handsome of all, and where it does not freeze more than 15 degrees in winter it is a grand flower. I have seen spikes of the Brompton that I am sure were more than a foot long and three inches in diameter, and in a cottage garden. They are a biennial, and if attempted here should be sown in August, wintered in a cold-frame and planted out in spring. In a more temperate climate they should be planted in the border in October.

STORE MANAGEMENT.

The evolution of the florist's store from its beginning, with most of us twenty-five years ago and with the oldest not more than forty years, is remarkable. It has kept pace with the enormous increase in the use of flowers and perhaps has been no little incentive to our patrons in the laudable luxury of the use of flowers.

We can all remember when the seedsman in many of our cities combined cut flowers and plants with his business. Now the line is as distinctly drawn between the seed store and the flower store as between a bank and a barber shop, although I have heard with surprise and regret that one of our most widely known New York wholesale and retail seed, bulb and requisite houses has recently opened

a cut flower department. This is to be regretted; it is a step towards the department store and is to be condemned, in our line particularly and on principle generally. We all remember exhibitions called florists' stores.

When the florist first essayed to rent a store and make it his exclusive business, the window decorations consisted in the main of straw baskets, a stuffed dove and some beautiful designs in wheat, all suggestive of the inevitable, but nothing to gladden the eye or heart. The gradual transition to the modern, first class store of today would be interesting to note were it any benefit, and what will be the appearance, appointments and tempting luxuries offered to the public by the florist of a future generation could we foresee the higher development of our business. From a basement or a narrow, cheap store the florist now demands the best stores in our very best streets.

Before I attempt to say what a high class retail store should be it is quite pertinent to mention a few things that it should not be. The florists and their clerks (or more properly shopmen) must have the reputation for good temper, civility and a most patient and obliging disposition, for the florist is asked more questions and more little favors than any other class of shopkeepers. If a lady faints in the street car she is carried into the florist's store. If a glass of water is wanted by a temperance man, if your neighbor wants to use the telephone, if a stranger wants to know where Mr. Tile, the hatter, is, or even when one lady will meet another, it is all at Mr.

Bud's, the florist, that they come in. A civil, polite answer should be given to all. Perhaps by discreet affability you have made a friend.

You store should never be known as a place where other florists congregate. If they have any business with you, let them do it quickly and get out. No loungers of any kind, friends of your own or of your employees, male or female, should be tolerated during business hours. Book agents, and what we are fearfully pestered with, advertising agents, should receive a civil but short answer. Drummers of all kinds should be put in a back room to wait your convenience, or if that is not agreeable to them then told to come around, if you need them, after business is over. Be sure and avoid having a group of three or four growers in the rear of your store discussing with animation the merits of the new carnations. If you are a grower yourself break up the meeting by leading them around the corner; it is cheaper and there they can argue with lubricated energy while you step back to attend to your business, for in these days of keen competition and all trying to excel, nothing but the closest attention to all departments of your business will bring even moderate success.

To be known as a reliable and prompt business man among your patrons is a blessing. To have the reputation of a good-natured, jolly fellow among your brother florists is a misfortune. You can be good, you can be jolly, even a philanthropist, but in self-defense and self-preservation subordinate the effervescence of your good nature till the appropriate occasions

View from the Front.

View from the Rear.
A Well Appointed Florist's Store.

arrive. Your lady customers notice loungers and it makes an unfavorable impression, deeper and more lasting than their pleasant features indicate.

Every wide-awake man will know what locality is best suited to his business in his own city. Where business men pass to and fro is the best of all locations, for with due respect to the gentler sex the men are our best customers. The ladies may be the inspiration by which they buy, but through the men come our best sales. They buy quicker, larger and want the best regardless of cost. The fashionable shopping district of our cities is the place for a florist's store, and I think I have seen some cities where with advantage a good store could be opened a long way from the business center of the city but in the residential part of the town.

Your store should be always clean, neat and attractive. Your window is the chief advertisement of your business and that should never be two days alike. Some men may have a large stock of flowers and place a large quantity in their window; yet they were put in, or rather jammed in, regardless of color or taste and were no attraction to the cultivated taste of the passer-by. You may not be able to have 360 varieties in one year, but you can always change it sufficiently so as to appear to the public fresh and new each day, and let there be some distinctive feature each day. A very first class florist in one of our large western cities who keeps six or seven young men in the store allots to each one in turn the duty of arranging the window display.

Some may say many flowers can be used up and wasted in these window

Corner in a Florist's Store in November.

decorations. There need be little waste if properly managed, for it is not the quantity but the taste displayed that makes an attractive window, and if it does cost something in sacrifice of flowers it is far cheaper than any other kind of advertising. On a recent winter visit to Philadelphia, in a fine window of the leading florist of Chestnut street the window decoration was a heavy branch of an elm tree, extend-

ing the whole width of the window and on it at intervals were tied sprays of Cattleya Trianae. Thousands were stopping to admire it. This is the idea, and whether it be orchids or only a vase of coreopsis it should be clean, neat, fresh, distinct and a gem if possible.

As in poetry so in flowers; it is not volubility that is highly appreciated, it is the clear cut gems that immortalize their authors. Longfellow's "Village Blacksmith" is worth a whole library of gush and slush which often passes for poetry.

The interior of your store should be also attractive. Where a rushing business is done there must be some little confusion, but the making up or boxing of flowers can be done in the rear and not at the counter where sales are made. The ice-box is a great feature of the present flower store. Next to the window it is the principal attraction and should not be in a remote corner but should be conspicuous to every one who enters the store. If a man enters the store to purchase a 5-cent carnation for his buttonhole he may be attracted by the beautiful flowers in the glass case, and if they have not tempted him sufficiently to affect his pocket they have made a favorable impression, and it is by a succession of favorable impressions followed by good and prompt service that fortunes are made, not by sudden leaps into popularity.

The salesmen, and sometimes they are women, should be as neat, clean and, if possible, as attractive as their surroundings. The young men should neither chew tobacco nor the girls gum, eat onions, drink beer or anything stronger during business hours.

A Florist's Store at Easter.

The ability or genius to make a sales-man is a gift with birth. Ability can be greatly improved by study and ex-perience and an earnest endeavor to reach the ideal, but a thoroughly ac-complished salesman is as much a genius as a great painter or sculptor.

I am by no means one of those who believe that genius is the steady ap-plication and industry devoted to a certain object. Such is the definition by some modern philosopher (Carlyle, I think) of genius. My humble opin-ion is that genius is inherited from an ancestor or ancestors, immediate or re-mote, and improved and glorified by the chance of environment. So if you have not the gifts that make a good salesman seek other departments of the business. If a man has no faculty behind the counter he may be a good decorator, or in the packing and dis-patch of orders he may show great ex-ecutive ability.

A little book was handed me many years ago by my brother. Its title was, "How to Make Money and How to Keep It." As the book came from a fine public library I devoured it with eagerness, confident I had struck a jewel. The first part of the book was devoted to advice in the various mer-

Two Views in a Florist's Store.

cantile walks of life and every chap-ter finished off strongly and impressed on the reader "to be polite." Over and over again was the simple instruc-tion, "Be polite." The latter part of the book could be summed up in a few words, which are simply this: After you have acquired a competence in some pursuit you understand, don't go into a business or enterprise you do not understand.

Undoubtedly politeness is a great factor to success, and cannot possibly be out of place with every class of your customers. The quantity and quality of the affability shown your customers is pure tact, and too much suavity in-discreetly applied is as bad as none at all. This is the part of the salesman's ability that is a natural gift and so business, often our most liberal buyers, wants no superfluous chat of any kind. Neither does the aristocratic lady who

forgets her grandfather carried a hod. The motherly matron may want to tell you about her sick husband or her injured limb caused by the runaway of her team. For her you have an at-tentive ear and sympathy, and so you should for the worthy but poor people who want some flowers for a bereave-ment. To accommodate them with their wants to match their purse is tact. We can no more have all pleas-ant people to purchase our goods than we can expect all church members to be virtuous people. We must adapt ourselves to our customers' tempera-ment as far as possible without losing self-respect. This is not hypocrisy, it is fitting ourselves to the require-ments of our business.

All articles should be just what they are represented or promised. A bunch of roses that will fall to pieces when taken from the box, violets that have been twenty-four hours in the ice-box, or carnations about to close their pet-als in slumber, will be very disappoint-ing and leave with your patron an impression that takes a lot of good be-havior to efface.

There are too many retailers that have only one price, and supposedly only one quality of flowers. If you are only going to keep one quality then it should be the best, and some very high class stores may find it unprofitable to do otherwise, but the great major-ity of florists have, and want to have, several grades of flowers in the lead-ing articles. Take carnations, for in-stance, we have been too much on the one price system. "What do you charge for your carnations?" "Fifty cents a dozen," or some price, according to season, is the same old answer. It should be more in this style: "These are $1.50 per dozen, these $1.00, these 75 cents, and we have some not so fine

worth 50 cents." The same with roses
and violets and all other flowers. It is
the same with all other businesses,
and why not with ours, where quality
varies so greatly?   *

The most important feature in our
business next to quality of goods and
polite attention to customers, is
promptness. Many an elderly man is
worrying to get his orders off promptly on the time promised and agreed for
their delivery, while his shopmen are
lolling around with the serene manner
and thought that the old man need not
fret himself, the wedding is not till 7
o'clock, or the party till 3 p. m., or the
funeral till tomorrow. When these
events occur is no business of yours;
you have promised the order at a certain hour and you should never fail to
keep your promise. There may be several reasons why the order was wanted
at a certain hour, of which you were
entirely unaware. No part of the business is more important than promptness, and in no part do I notice a
greater inclination to ignore it. A
reputation for a late and disappointing
delivery is a deplorable handicap to
success.

Finally the three great requisites to
success are to keep and supply a good
article, be prompt and deliver all orders how, when and where you promised, and treat your customers with
polite deference and respect. If you
are asked for an article which you do

one grown by the commercial florist.
The young shoots root readily in an
ordinary propagating bed. They grow
quickly and if given much root room
will not flower for a long time. They
are hardly of consequence enough to

flowers. And what can be more truly
springlike, for these you cannot have
any day in the year as we do now have
many of our other flowers. Early
April is as soon as sweet peas are seen
in any quantity, and they are then a
luxury, but middle to end of June they
are everybody's flower, and as long
as they last are favorites with all. We
have seen cool, moist summers when
the peas lasted till we cut off by frost, but
usually our hot, dry August winds
them up.

For forcing under glass they can be
sown in early September. If you de-
vote a whole bench to them the rows
ought to run north and south and be
2 feet 6 inches apart. Sow thinly and
support with chicken netting. My experience is that in a solid, deep bed
under glass they grow too strong and
do not flower freely, so I would rather
give them six inches of soil, rather
heavy and firm, with little if any manure. The first bed we tried under
glass in a fine, light house was a failure because the roots had too much
room and too good a soil.

We sow a few seeds by the iron supports in our carnation houses on the
north side of a middle bench. They

SWEET PEAS.

Of late years the greatly improved
varieties and beautiful colors of the
sweet peas have brought them up to
be one of our most important spring

Two Views of a Store Interior.

not have, procure it if possible to
oblige, but never promise what you are
afraid you cannot supply. You will
never seriously offend a customer by
declining an order, but you will have
given great offense by promising and
not fulfilling.

SWAINSONA GALEGIFOLIA.

There are red, pink and white forms
of this plant and the latter is the only

occupy bench room, but where you
have a chance to plant them out in a
box or confined space at the end of a
house the flowers will be at times very
useful.

Pot very firmly in some good, coarse
sod. They can be thinned out and cut
back in the spring. A carnation house
temperature will suit them very well.
I know of no use that we can make of
them as small plants.

Interior and Exterior Views of a New York Store.

take up little room till February and as they grow the light is growing stronger every day. They certainly do impair the growth of one or two carnation plants, but you will get ten times the money from these sweet peas that you would from the plant or two of carnations. Two or three

rows. It will help keep the ground moist and be of the greatest benefit when you water. Unless we get a rainy season you must water. Give the ground not only close to the plants but all the surface a thorough soaking twice a week if you want your crop to last. Another important thing to observe is to

days is of great importance in the sweet pea market in spring.

Within a few years the varieties of sweet peas have become very numerous, and many of them of great beauty. Mr. Eckford has been largely instrumental in this. Mr. Eckford first became an enthusiast on the verbena and later turned his attention to sweet peas. Mr. E. has probably never heard of the writer, but when I was 10 years old I knew him, when he first went to be head gardener to Dr. Martin, of Purbrook, Hants, England. Dr. Martin was one of the pioneers of dentistry, who charged $10 to look in your mouth, $10 more to pull a tooth, and $50 more for a new one. But as he spent his leisure time and money in gardening his extravagant charges were most commendable.

Some of the finest sweet peas are as follows: Mrs. J. Chamberlain, white striped rose; Lovely, beautiful pink; America, white striped red; Stanley, deep maroon; Ramona, pale pink; Maid of Honor, white tipped lilac; Golden Gleam, primrose yellow; Mars, bright crimson; Countess of Radnor Improved, fine lavender; Royal Rose, very fine rose; Lady Penzance, orange tinted carmine; Blanche Ferry, extra, white and pink; Blanche Burpee, best white; Catherine Tracy, daybreak

strings are run up by the side of the post for the peas to climb on, and an occasional tie is needed to keep them within bounds. Two strong plants are plenty at each post, but sow enough seed so that you can thin out. If not convenient to sow the seed on the bed then sow in 3-inch pots and later transplant. They do not make much growth in the dark days of winter, and 50 degrees is about as high as they should be kept in winter.

For outside they should be the very first thing sown in the spring, the moment the ground is dry enough to plow or spade, or better still, it can be dug up rough in the fall, and will need no digging in the spring. Draw trenches three or four inches broad and the same in depth, three feet apart, sow thinly and cover with an inch of soil. If you think it's going to be dry pour some water on top of the seed before you cover in with earth; it will hasten the growth. At the first hoeing you can let the earth be drawn in a little higher around the stems, but if the trench is somewhat below the level all the better for future waterings.

The soil for peas out of doors should be deep and rich. There is nothing equal to brush to support them, which should always be placed with a line of it on each side, when the growth is only two or three inches high, not waiting till the peas are up a foot and have fallen over to one side. We don't suffer with drought usually up to flowering time, but a short while before you begin to pick you should spread 2 or 3 inches of stable litter entirely over the ground between the

Some New York Stores at Christmas.

pick all the flowers. If they escape you they will quickly go to seed and then your plant gets exhausted.

Some growers sow in October and by this means I have seen flowers picked ten days earlier than those sown on the same ground in April. You must judge for yourself the best week to sow, according to the weather. You don't want them to make any growth above the ground, just sprouting near the surface is enough, but sow four inches deep. For this purpose choose a rather high part of your ground where surface water will not lie. Ten

pink; Little Dorrit, fine pink; Aurora, striped orange and white; Her Majesty, rose and carmine; Gray Friar, white clouded with lilac; Emily Henderson, a standard white; King of the Blues, a handsome purplish blue.

Perhaps many of these fine varieties will soon be superseded. It would be inadvisable to grow too many kinds under glass, and less will do. If limited to five kinds I would say the best for forcing are: Emily Henderson, white; Blanche Ferry, pink and white; Countess of Radnor, lavender; Golden Gleam, yellow; Catherine Tracy, light pink.

Some New York Stores at Christmas.

SYSTEM.

This is a plant that wants cultivating in a good many smaller establishments, and its introduction into some large ones would not be amiss.

I think it is a great advantage to a gardener when he has been educated where neatness and cleanliness were strictly enforced, even if it were a private garden. The worst cases of disorder we see are where a man has left the shoemaker's bench or the machine shop or the office, and we have even known where they have left the pulpit for the pulpit's good and made horribly bad florists. When a young man is wavering between the church and the greenhouse always take to the church.

There is less dirt and more spirituality about the church, and you would not be always thinking about what you might have been if you became a florist. While looking for your salary in the church will always prevent your pining after the greenhouse.

I must admit though that there are instances in this country of young men total strangers to the business who have entered it and made a marked success of it, setting us all a bright example by their systematic management and orderly and business-like methods. Their places are models of neatness. But they are the great exception and those I refer to are bright, intelligent men whom nature blessed

with brains, and they would shine in any business.

If order is the first law of nature, it ought most assuredly to be carried into the greenhouse, for ours are most perishable goods and disorder is not only unsightly but a great pecuniary loss. These remarks are not intended for the bright, well trained greenhouse man, for he knows the value of order and system, but there are hundreds who keep their places in a dirty muddle from one year's end to the other. I have no patience with the man who lets his place get fearfully untidy and dirty and then has a grand clean up. People will form an impression of your place as they usually see it and perhaps won't see it just after you have had the great house cleaning.

Untidiness is not accident or press of business, it is pure carelessness. Fifty dead or cut down plants standing on the edge of the path is too much for you to carry back to the shed at one time, but if the workman who put the first one or half dozen there had carried them back and dumped them and put the pots away there would have been none there. Untidiness does not arise from want of time, not in the least; it is solely the habit of not putting things in their right places at the right time. Some men don't know the difference between a heap of old soil that is sure to come in handy for some purpose and a heap composed of broken glass, wood, old plants and dead cats. It's all alike to them, and is thrown out with the indifference that you see the refuse of the tenement house go out of the back window.

How much time is lost in the mislaying of tools, or worse still, loaning them. Neither borrow nor loan tools unless it be something like a steam roller that you are not warranted in buying. Borrow nor loan no tools. They are far worse in the country at borrowing than in the cities; and they don't say, "Could I have the loan of your post auger?" but "I come up for that post auger I saw you use t'other day." Another sample of waste of time is when Jack says, "Where's the monkey wrench, Bill?" Bill says, "I guess you'll find it in the stoke hole. Bob was fixin' the boiler yesterday." And so it goes.

Keep your tools where they belong. Keep your flats piled up neatly. Let your sash be in use or properly stood up against a wall or fence. Let your compost piles be neat and in order. Have a proper place for your watering cans. And above all have your pots always in their sizes in neat rows, not under a bench in many different sizes all mixed up. Some men like to buy pots before they have half used up what they already have.

Here is a sample where disorder comes in. The driver from a store or the delivery man brings home an azalea out of bloom and two or three other flowering plants that are past, or perhaps a flat half full of geraniums that were not used at the flower gardening job. He jumps off the wagon, slings the flat and its contents on the ground by the shed wall, and then asks for another job. The next man that wants a flat in a hurry throws out the plants and runs off on his errand. A pot or two is broken, or the plants are run over, all because the driver did not take a minute's time to dump the useless plant and put the others in the shed where they would be attended to.

All that may be a trifle, but a lot of such performances creates great confusion. You can do your work quicker, better, and feel more comfortable and happy all around when things are in order. And depend upon it orderly places are the prosperous ones.

In the greenhouse among the plants is still more need of system and order. The old-fashioned way of years ago of having a bench all mixed up with fifty species of plants like a fourth class botanic garden is played out. We knew greenhouses, some not so long ago, that always looked alike the year round. A cactus and sanchezia and Begonia Rex and Hoya carnosa beautifully (?) arranged. A show house is all right, where a few of the brightest and best of all you have should be shown off, and that should be changed as often as possible. Let your show house undergo a transformation scene very frequently, as your store window does daily.

In other houses everything should be in blocks. They are better cared for in every way and look better; it is the only way. Stand over your plants frequently, and it is much easier to throw your leaves and rubbish into a bushel basket than it is to throw them on the path and then have to sweep them up.

We frequently have hot words in the spring with the men when picking out plants or filling orders. If a hundred geraniums are wanted of one kind take them as they come. If two or three

are not quite good enough or not in flower don't leave them standing out alone to dry out; bunch them up with the lot. Your precious time will not be missed, for it will only take a second and will be better for the plants, better in appearance, and much better for the man who waters. And so with all your plants.

Views in Two Stores.

Stand all rows of plants straight across the bench, and never crowd for want of room, nor spread them out for appearance sake. There is a right distance for the plants and they should have it, neither more nor less.

I cannot mention all the details of

running a greenhouse, but do let it be clean, neat and orderly, and it will cover many other deficiencies. Never scruple or sigh at having to throw away any plants that you see there is no sale for. If you made a mistake the quickest way to recover is to out with them. The ability to discard useless stock is only second to the ability to grow good plants.

Having everything in at the right time it is wanted is one of the greatest accomplishments of a good florist, and next is having your stock well balanced, not propagating or growing twice as much as you can dispose of of any article. You have your past experience to guide you and should know the probable demand for the next. You can't grow everything and what you don't succeed with, buy if you must have it. The man who tries to grow everything he is asked for will never succeed.

You must never be bothered with the best of meaning people who bring you seeds or plants for you to grow because they are curiosities, and Gen. Candleef sent the seeds to her from Cuba, or Lieut. Floater brought them from Manila. The plants of the whole world are pretty well known now and they will be nothing desirable for you. Tell the kind person that you are afraid they would not get attention among your men, who only have a knowledge of common commercial plants, but you are sure Mr. Private Gardener, your neighbor, or the Bot-

anic Gardens would be delighted with them.

Division of labor is a great thing. The operations in a greenhouse are very diverse. Put men at what they can do well and quickly. And there is no labor, either in potting, watering,

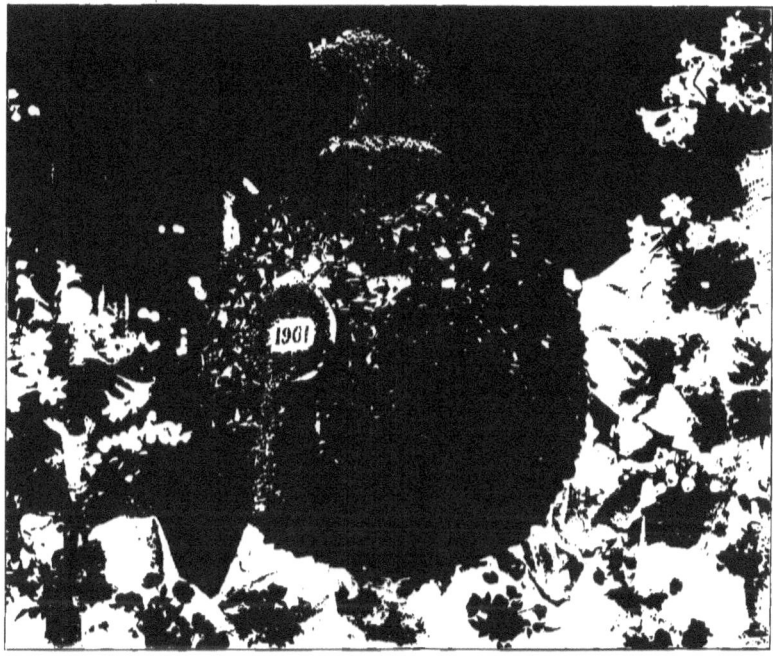

Window Display Symbolizing the Pan-American Exposition.

tying or setting over plants, but what should be done quickly and with a rush. When men get accustomed to work quickly at these light jobs it is no effort to keep it up and it must be done quickly or it won't pay. When you set a man to turn over fifty loads of earth don't expect big shovels and quick work all the time. Have mercy; you shoveled once yourself and may again.

THUNBERGIA ALATA.

There are few prettier basket plants than the above, and its variety T. aurantiaca. Their flower resembles a miniature convolvulus. They are annuals and easily raised from seed sown in March. Being true climbers they are most suitable for our hanging baskets.

Sow the seed, which is quite large, in light soil and keep in good heat. When well up pot into 2½-inch pots; why I say 2½-inch is to give them room to grow, for if stunted early they soon get infested with red spider, in fact they are very badly addicted to it, and that is their chief defect.

When put into a basket they grow quickly and soon wind up the wires or hang over the sides. They should not be at a lower temperature than 60 degrees at any time, and are not suited for a basket in a windy situation.

TORENIA.

These pretty plants are grown for conservatory decoration, T. Fournierii being one of the prettiest species, but would not be a florist's flower. T. asiatica is often used with us as a bedding plant, being a fine plant for an edging. Its blue and violet flowers are very pretty and a change from the prevalent reds of our flower gardens.

It can also be carried over winter by putting in cuttings in August and further propagated during winter and spring. Any good ordinary soil will grow it. Fumigate, for it is troubled with greenfly and it requires a high temperature at all times. In the

flower garden it should have a rich soil, and it thrives well in partial shade.

TROPAEOLUM (NASTURTIUM).

This useful genus is very familiar to all. The tall nasturtium is one of the best plants for covering fences or walls when given some strings or brush to climb on. The dwarf nasturtium is used as a bedding plant and in mixed borders its round, compact clumps have a fine appearance. They are always treated as annuals and although growing most freely in our summers they will not endure the slightest frost.

The dwarf varieties of the nasturtium are not always a success as a bedding plant because they are planted in too rich a soil and the leaves hide the flowers. Plant in rather poor soil in the full sun, and you will have better results. The double forms of the nasturtium were formerly used as a bedding plant, but we have many better plants for the purpose. A dark scarlet variety of the tall form is often grown in an 8 or 10-inch pot and trained up a rafter where it will give many flowers in any greenhouse where the temperature is not under 50 degrees.

Both the tall and dwarf forms are too easily raised from seed for us to think of them as bedding plants, but as a plant for our veranda boxes they are of consequence, their fine, bright green leaves and showy flowers being always liked by our patrons and soon filling up and making a fine show. We never remember having any left when trade was over by middle of June.

Obtain the best strain you can of the tall growing kinds, and sow middle of March. As soon as they have formed their seed leaves pot into 2½-inch and keep them in a temperature of 50 degrees. They will grow very fast and in any soil. If grown on the bench they will quickly become unmanageable, so we put them on a hanging shelf where they will get air and light and occasionally short of water, which does not hurt them at all, but induces them to flower. Their roots when put into the basket or vase have not much room to spread and they flower freely.

There are many named varieties of the tall growing nasturtiums, but we find a good mixture answers every purpose. In the dwarf or Tom Thumb strain for bedding you can buy any variety true to color and some of the foliage of these is very distinct.

Varieties of T. Lobbianum grow as finely as the common nasturtium. The foliage is somewhat smaller, but they flower in great profusion.

TUBEROSE (POLIANTHES TUBEROSA).

We can remember in another country when, if asked to deliver a dozen tuberose bulbs to a customer, they were as much trouble to procure as it would be now to get a young kangaroo from Tasmania. And we can also remember when they were used here with us to such an extent that the people utterly tired of them, or fashion said so. Twenty-five years ago they were a flower of the first importance. But how have the mighty fallen! To put in cheap cut flowers is about all you can do with them. Nevertheless it is a beautiful sweet flower.

The bulbs are now offered so cheaply that the cost is of no consideration if you have the room to grow them. The raising of bulbs is done by planting the young offshoots in the spring in good, rich land and in favorable seasons they will make a flowering bulb by the following fall. But that better be left to those who have a suitable soil, a genial climate and cheap help, although as far north as Ohio good bulbs are raised.

Tuberose bulbs should never be sent by rail during a cold spell. A slight frost will destroy them and a low temperature for a few days will much injure them. When unpacked keep them in flats in a shed which is never below 50 degrees. We pull off all offshoots and scrape off all signs of any side growth and cut square off the hard root growth below the bulb. Fill some flats, such flats as we use for tulips, with a mixture of sand and loam, about half and half, and plant the bulbs about two inches apart, putting bottom of bulb an inch into the soil. If kept moist with the flats placed on or just over some hot water pipes growth will soon begin and in two or three weeks we pot them into 4-inch and place them in a mild hot-bed. This gives us good, strong plants by starting them in March to sell at bedding time.

For your own use you can start them still later in the same way. Where you have good light, warm soil you can plant them out, but they come cleaner and finer when grown in pots under glass, and you have usually plenty of bench room in the summer months. They make many roots and when growing want lots of water.

The spikes are now sold very cheaply, but you should always raise a thousand or more, for you can raise them very cheaply and although there is or was a foolish prejudice against them they are a sweet and most beautiful flower and will come very useful on many occasions.

VALLOTA PURPUREA.

This is generally called amaryllis, but is botanically a genus of its own, and one of the most beautiful of its class. Having seen some plants of these very recently grown in 8-in. pots with nine to twelve spikes and thirty flowers, under the care of a matron who had nothing but a cottage window, it seems worthy of some notice. It flowers during summer.

Three bulbs in an 8-inch pot will make a fine display when they are well established. Dry bulbs can be bought in the spring, but it should be treated as an evergreen bulb, and during winter they should be kept cool with less water, but not dust dry or be disturbed. Plant the bulbs four inches below the surface. They may not flower the first year, but will in a year or two get well established, and in June or July send up a number of spikes with their handsome red and pink flowers.

V. purpurea is the species, and V. p. eximia is a grand variety. To grow them well they should be given a cool but light bench in winter and be kept moderately dry. In May when they begin to grow give them plenty of water. Drain the pot when starting new bulbs, and use good fibrous loam with a fourth of decayed manure. 𝒶

A Florist's Uniformed Driver and Messengers.

A Corner in a Florist's Store.

VASES.

The florist adjacent to or in a town or city and who does a general retail business will have many vases to fill, and if his establishment is near a leading cemetery it will be one of the principal features of his trade. I know several who consider it their most important business.

Filling vases for cemeteries in some cities is at a price very close to any profitable margin, and if one or two set the price low the rest have to follow, for few people will pay more than their neighbor does. In some cemeteries the florist agrees to fill and water the vase for the season, and although the price charged for the watering, $2.00 to $2.50, for watering a vase from June 1st to the time frost kills the plants, does not seem much to charge it is by far the most profitable part of the business if you have two or three hundred of them.

I know some florists who have almost a "corner" on certain cemeteries, and there they charge a good price for filling, including a coat of paint. We are so situated we cannot do that. We charge 50 cents for one coat of paint and 75 cents for two coats.

Our best cemeteries are now kept in the most perfect shape, walks, drives and grass kept as trim as in the private grounds of the wealthy, and with shade trees scattered here and there in judicious groupings, the pleasant surroundings marred only by the over-use of monuments and statuary which in their glaring whiteness dispel at once any comfortable or cheerful feeling that might otherwise be associated with a cemetery. And the innumerable white iron vases only still further add to the cold dismalness of the scene. Why should it be so?

Some day a better and more advanced idea of our final resting place will be shown by subduing the ostentatious display of wealth and marble. Graves will be leveled and a small marker will denote the spot where the departed lies, and the whole cemetery will be a beautiful garden with its necessary features reduced to inconspicuousness. Monuments are not by their size and cost the slightest indication of the worth or genius of the person gone before. The most commonplace man lies at the foot of an imposing column, while the remains of a President of the United States rests near a humble stone. But this lavish display is good in one way, it distributes wealth and the greatest good a wealthy man can do with his money is to spend it. Work is the best of all charities. We can help some by telling our customers to have their iron vases painted dark green or drab; a few are, but not enough.

Most of our vases, whether for the grounds or cemeteries, are iron, stone, or rustic wood work. The stone vases are usually large, are costly but much superior to any in appearance. I have never noticed any difference in the health of the plants in either of these

styles. Sometimes the handsome, massive stone vases are left without any outlet for the water to escape; always see to that if you are consulted. If a long dry spell occurs they do very well, but if we get a week's rain in July the consequence is disastrous.

The wooden vases, or baskets as they should be called, are lined with green moss, before the soil is filled in. Plants always do well in them but as the drainage is most perfect they take an awful lot of water in August and September to keep them green.

Plants do excellently in iron vases. The great majority of the iron vases are now what is called of the reservoir pattern. There is an iron basin which holds three inches of water immediately below the roots separated from the earth by the casting but connected with the water in the center by a funnel of two inches in diameter which dips into the water and which we fill with sphagnum. The inventor meant it to be filled with a sponge so that the soil would be always soaking up the water by capillary attraction. This also works well in dry seasons but in wet times when the reservoir is always full the soil gets saturated and the plants die, and we frequently have to lift off the top of the vase and empty out the reservoir. This is a case of sub-watering to excess. I prefer the vases without reservoir. They look all right on theory but in practice are often more harm than good.

When the frosts have killed the plants in the vases we empty them. The wooden baskets are stored in our sheds. The tops of the iron vases are turned upside down and the soil taken out of the stone vases, or as is often done with the large vases we fill them with some neat evergreens for the winter; the Chinese arbor vitae and retinospora are good for the purpose. We make no charge for emptying the vases. They are mostly steady customers and if they are not we do it for our satisfaction, for what would look worse than withered plants where all else was neat and trim. It is no longer as it was when Gray wrote:

Perhaps in this neglected spot is laid
Some heart once pregnant with celestial fire;
Hands that the rod of empire might
have swayed,
Or waked to ecstasy the living lyre.

All now is neat and cared for. Even rural cemeteries are now well kept. Before I leave the precincts of what should be a most pleasant and beautiful spot, and as far as care goes is, I must say that the abolishing of fences and the care and control of the whole grounds by the cemetery authorities, who treat all alike and study general appearance and not individual, is a vast improvement over those cemeteries where the lot owners pay some outside party for its care. It is the whole locality or section that should be pleasing and beautiful, not one lot scrupulously cared for and the next one neglected. The man or woman who would delight in their lot being mowed and clipped and decorated and contented to see their neighbor's in weeds would be narrow minded indeed.

There are various ways of filling vases, but where there are thousands in one cemetery and perhaps two or three hundred on one "section" alone, there must be a good deal of sameness. Some few have one palm alone. Many are filled with one color of geraniums with or without any drooping plant for an edge. A few are filled with cannas or caladiums. Some contain a mass of one variety of coleus with a distinct edge, but more than half of the whole are filled with a variety of plants with some drooping plants to hang over the edge. If in a windy place the so-called "vines" or droopers have a hard time of it, and are little ornament.

Nearly everyone wants his or her vase to look just perfection the day it is put out and expect it to continue to keep looking so till October, the unreasonableness of which we have to strive with and do our best to please. Watering is not the only thing a vase wants in summer. Much can be done and must be done by keeping off withered flowers, yellow leaves and pinching out the stronger growing plants, of which the coleus is the worst to crowd out the rest. Cleaning the vases, as we call it, should be attended to at least once a week.

In palms or that style of plant, a Chamaerops humilis, any of the phoenix or Dracaena indivisa can be used in the broad sun. It is impossible to give water enough to keep the latanias or kentias from burning, but if in the shade of trees then any of the handsome palms can be used. Any of the foliage plants such as coleus, achyranthes or acalypha have a good appearance if nicely pinched and in order.

It is undeniable that the geranium is unequaled as a vase plant if flower and color is wanted, but they should be in the full sun. The varieties should be not only good bloomers but strong, vigorous kinds that will keep their foliage as well as flower. The single, for this purpose, are of little use. Of those we have tried for the purpose the best are Prokop Daubeck, a very robust, large, double red; there is hardly a variety as good; Ernest Lauth, fine for the purpose; Alphonse Ricard, orange scarlet; S. A. Nutt, crimson; Tower Eiffel, bright scarlet; Emile de Gerardin, pink, but now superseded by F. Perkins, a pink unequaled; Beaute Poitevine, salmon; La Favorite, double white. The silver leaved Mountain of Snow is most useful as an edge, and so is the compact Mme. Sallerol. Sometimes the geranium vases have only one of the variegated geraniums for an edging, and sometimes some drooper, but when the latter only one kind should be used. Vinca, glechoma or the ivy geranium are very suitable. A favorite vase with hundreds is pink geraniums with the pink ivy leaf for an edging.

The mixed vases are in the majority and are the least profitable to the florist and the least satisfactory. In the center we use a small phoenix or a dwarf canna, but nearly all ask and expect us to use a Dracaena indivisa. This wonderfully useful plant not only thrives under the worst kind of treatment but actually improves every day till fall, and near the end of summer is the redeeming feature of many a vase. When using mixed plants there is quite a variety. Dwarf flowering cannas; Grevillea robusta, which gives a light, feathery effect; all the geraniums mentioned; coleus, in great variety; three kinds of achyranthes, Begonia Vernon, and some other flowering kinds; Abutilon Souv, de Bonn (and we think Savitzii will be a great addition to our vase plants), anthericum, Centaurea gymnocarpa, aspidistra; fuchsias, but these should only be used in partial shade, and Black Prince and old speciosa are the two best for the purpose; variegated euonymus; and perhaps a few more can be added to the list. The coarse monster Caladium esculentum should not be used with other plants, for it entirely exhausts the soil.

For droopers we have a variety to choose from. The weaker kinds get crushed out, but look pretty for the first month. We use first the variegated and green trailing vincas. We consider this the most important of all our vase droopers. Several varieties of the ivy geranium, English ivy, gramanthea (a small creeping succulent), glechoma (variegated), the so-called German ivy (senecio), lysimachia, double sweet alyssum, lobelia, nasturtium, Abutilon vexillarium, lopospermum, Solanum jasminoides, Pilogyne suavis, nierembergia, petunias, Kenilworth ivy, etc.

The prettiest vase in our cemetery this entire summer is a vase of tuberous-rooted begonias. It is grand, but it is in the shade of trees. Where this is the case it makes a splendid plant. Asparagus Sprengeri is yet a little expensive; when as cheap as smilax seed we believe this asparagus will be one of our finest drooping vase plants, and particularly for our veranda boxes. In a warmer section of the country the crotons make splendid vase plants. Do not put in plants that are showy, but that you know will quickly go out of flower and flower no more that season; such plants as our Show pelargoniums and pyrethrums.

As the soil you use is to support as many plants in a 2-foot vase as would properly fill a 6-foot flower bed, you must use the richest soil. In addition to one-third of rotten manure added to your loam, add a 5-inch pot of bone flour to every barrow-load. Keep the plants pretty well up on the surface, but see that the soil is firmly packed around every plant. We find workmen very guilty of neglecting that part of it, and we find when three or four hundred vases have to be filled in a week that there has to be some system about it.

First a list is given the boss of the gang, of the names of the owners which reads like this: "Mrs. Particular, one iron vase. Fill good mixed, only light colored geraniums." Or "Mrs. Usual, one iron vase. All pink geraniums and pink ivy leaf." And every vase has the name of owner attached. With a man to place the plants in, another to fill in solid, another to moss and water and another to keep the supply of plants on hand, a great many vases can be filled in a day.

I had almost forgotten the important item of moss. We cover the surface of the soil, or at least four inches all around from the edge, with green wood moss. We used to load up wagons and drive to the country with plants and soil, but find a much better plan is to bring home the top or bowl of the vase, fill it and return it the same or next day. People ask you to get their vase started in the greenhouse. We should want a circus tent to hold them all, and they are none the better for getting the tender growth of the greenhouse. Fill them up and away with them.

Decoration Day, or about that time, is the only week of the year that we are truly miserable, but with all the hurry and vexation we survive, or have up to date.

VENTILATION.

Ventilation is primarily afforded to keep down temperature when the sun's rays have heated up the houses, but to give and afford a free circulation of fresh air to the plants is quite as much a reason for ventilation. Our large glass of the present day quickly runs up the temperature with the sun shining, and if ventilation is not faithfully attended to at the proper time great harm is done, and in the case of roses months of hard and faithful labor can be ruined.

The necessity and benefit of ventilation is too well known to need any lengthy remarks. It is the mental side of the business. It wants watching like the water gauge of a steam engine, but more scientific. It is the same sort of science that is brought into use by Mary Murphy when she knows the potatoes are just done, and cooking is a science. You can lay down rules that this or that house should be ventilated when the thermometer registers a certain degree, but to that should be added some knowledge and judgment. In rose growing it is perhaps the most particular of all work connected with them, and if a man has charge of three or four houses it will almost keep him busy in the spring and fall months running from one to the other regulating the ventilation.

A man should be able to tell without even looking at the thermometer whether the sashes are too much or not enough open. The thermometer is of course an infallible guide and authority, but there are times when even a few degrees higher is of less injury to the plant than a keen, cutting draught of air. Often the sashes are opened six inches when two inches would be plenty. There is one good rule and that is to begin ventilating

A Rustic Vase.

early and take it off early. Too many are yet guilty of waiting till perhaps 10 o'clock on a bright morning and then opening up wide; first subjecting the plants to an enervating heat and then giving them a sudden chill. By shutting up early in the afternoon you have utilized the sun heat and saved coal, and sun heat is always better for the plants than fire heat. There are thousands of houses throughout the country that are sadly inadequate in ventilation, and in such houses roses, carnations and all our flowering plants will draw up weak.

What we are most concerned about is not the mistakes that have been made, but to prevent any more. In houses that are attached it is obvious that side ventilation can only be given on the two exterior walls, and in any rose house we would not have any ventilation in the side wall or glass, even if it cost nothing. In plant houses or in carnation houses side ventilation is perhaps desirable, but I think not at all necessary if ample ventilation is given at the ridge.

In equal span carnation houses we have in addition to the ordinary ventilating sash on the south side a large sash about 5x3 hinged on the north side, 8 feet between sash. We have no ventilating gear attached, but after settled warm weather, or when there is no longer danger of weather that would hurt carnations, we raise these sash eight or nine inches. on blocks of wood, and then tie them securely down, leaving them so till first of Oc-

tober. Believing that if ample ventilation is provided on one side of the ridge is enough, and we do believe it from experience and observation of other people's houses and crops, then it is useless to discuss the matter further.

Ventilation should be provided the whole length of a house. If it is wanted all in one place in the roof then it is wanted the entire length, and it must be better to give three inches all along than six inches only in spots. And this will apply not only to a rose house but any greenhouse for whatsoever use intended. Though you may need but one inch of ventilation throughout the whole month of January, in June our climate demands the utmost you can give. It takes no more glass to have continuous ventilation, no more in cost of apparatus except a few arms, and only a few dollars more in extra ventilators.

In the long-span-to-the-south the ventilation is always on the south side of the ridge, and the same in equal span houses whose ridge runs east and west. In the short-span-to-the-south the ventilation is on the north side of the ridge. In houses where the ridge runs north and south, always equal span, the ventilation should be on the east side. You can open them earlier and our prevailing winds are from the west. We are often able to give an inch of air at the ridge when cold outside without feeling any draught whereas if the ventilators were hinged at the ridge and opened two feet down the sash we should feel a draught. And

If it is good for one house or one kind of plants it certainly is for all. So that is the way to hang your ventilators; let them all open at the ridge.

While you are having sash made have them large enough. If the house is from 19 to 23 ft. wide the ventilators should be from 30 to 36 inches deep and continuous. The length of each section should be not over 5 ft. or the sash will be too heavy to lift easily, but there is not nearly so much weight to lift when they open at the ridge as when hinged at the ridge. The ventilator man will tell you how many machines you need.

No one would think in this day of ventilating without the use of one of the machines which do their work so admirably. They will pay for themselves easily in labor saving in one year, and without them I can't see how you could manage. Yet some struggle on without them. It is not the labor saving alone, it is the plants that suffer when the sash are moved by ropes or rods or sticks. To raise or lower a lot of sash by those crude methods is quite a chore and too often if you are busy and you think actual necessity does not compel, you are too apt to say, "It's pretty warm, but I guess it won't hurt." You are shirking the job, but how easy to say, "Jim, put on a crack of air," and Jim turns the handle and up goes a hundred feet of sash in a moment, and only fun to do it. There are several good appliances. I have five different makes, and like best the "Challenge" ventilator.

VERANDA BOXES.

This style of ornamental gardening is very much in vogue in some cities. In none I think more than the fine residence city of Buffalo. They are an evolution from the more humble window box which I noticed was very much in use in humble dwellings of European cities, where the yellow Calceolaria aurea floribunda was one of the most useful and gaudy plants, and with the blue lobelia made a most striking show. The calceolaria is useless here.

Veranda boxes are not suitable in connection with a brown stone castle, and they don't have anything as common as a veranda, but in many of our beautiful homes where part or the front or side of the house is a veranda they are most appropriate. They are seldom on the top of the rail, but usually on the level of the floor of the veranda, and the tops of the plants reach up to the rail.

If asked to furnish the box you should be able to do it and have some planing mill man of your acquaintance know how to put them together. Have them made of cypress and well painted to suit the color or the wood of the veranda. A very good size is 6 inches deep, 9 inches wide at top and 8 inches at bottom, all inside measure. We fill many larger, but they should not be smaller for plants to do well. Holes are bored in the bottom to afford drainage. If they are made in sections of 6 feet they are easy to handle and can be taken to the greenhouse to fill, but if very large we cart the soil and plants to the lawn. Such a box as I have given the size for is worth to mak) of cypress and painted 75 cents per lineal foot and you should get the same price per foot for filling it. Like the vases a good appearance is.expected from the very start.

If in the afternoon sun the same plants are used as those mentioned for vases, but more cannas can be used in the back of the box, and don't use too many coleus or they will smother the geraniums. The drooping vines will be the chief beauty of these boxes and it matters not how common they are if they grow freely. The pilogyne and lophospermum are two splendid droopers for this purpose. Mignonette and lemon verbena can be used for their sweet odor.

If the boxes get only the morning sun, or very little at all, the geraniums will not flower, but you can use several plants that you could not in the sunny bleak exposures of the cemetery. Begonia Rex looks well. Fuchsias will thrive and flower if not too crowded, and small plants of latania and kentia, and better for fine effect than all is the beautiful nephrolepis, both the Boston form and tuberosa. Nothing is equal to these ferns and if kept watered they stand the sun finely.

Veranda boxes are nearly always satisfactory. They are more or less sheltered and get plenty of water. Instruct your patrons that the soil being crowded with roots they want a good soaking every evening and tell them that when the coachman or they themselves handle the hose not to stand and let drive at them as if they were putting out a fire, but let the hose run in on the soil till they are well wet.

VERBENA.

The garden variety of these well known plants are probably hybrids. They have been decidedly deposed from their former popularity by the carpet and sub-tropical bedding, but of late we see many more verbena beds, and few plants can be prettier. The varieties we get from seed are now so good that little attention is paid to named sorts and the trouble of keeping them over winter is dispensed with.

If you wish to propagate fine varieties they should be shortened back about the first of September and kept watered. By the end of the month there will be plenty of nice, fresh cuttings, and only a quick, tender growth should be used. Put the cuttings in the propagating house, or what is as good, in flats with some soil in bottom and sand on surface. Keep the flats in a cold frame and keep moist and shaded from the sun. They will take a copious watering every day.

Verbenas will stand quite a frost, but it is not well to let the cuttings freeze. When rooted they can be kept in a cool but light house and be kept in the flats till after New Year's, when they can be potted off into 2½-inch pots and kept in a temperature of 50 degrees. You will soon get plenty of cuttings which root very freely, and before spring you can have a large stock. Plants propagated from cuttings want to flower early and those propagated in February and March will want at least one pinching.

Seed is now used by most florists for their stock of verbenas. It has the advantage of producing good, healthy plants free of all disease, and when planted out they are sure to do well and make a most satisfactory flower bed. Sow the seed in February, and pot into 2-inch pots as.soon as up an inch. You can usually get a cutting from an early sowing if you wish. If not just pinch out the tip of the plant. A temperature of 45 to 50 degrees will answer these seedlings, but they should be given full light.

There is no place equal to a mild hot bed for the verbenas, so about the middle of April plunge the small pots in a few inches of soil in a mild bed. They will grow very fast and quickly get rooted in the soil of the bed which will delay their flowering, particularly the seedlings, and for that reason they should be lifted, the roots rubbed off and put back in the same spot. That will check their growth and induce them to flower. Most of our customers want to see the colors, so it is important to get them into flower.

Verbenas are much troubled with green fly, and they should be perfectly clean when they go into the hot-bed. If affected with the rust so troublesome to the verbena when we grew named varieties, throw them away; it is much cheaper to buy clean stock.

Verbena venosa is a true species and always raised from seed. It can be sown in February and grown along in flats. Its beautiful and abundant blue flowers make a fine bed either alone or in combination with a silver leaf geranium.

Verbenas can be planted out early in May. A slight frost will do them no harm, but our customers seldom look for them till end of May.

VINCA.

The trailing V. major, and its variegated form, is one of our most useful trailing or drooping plants. The long drooping growths seldom flower, but the short, erect growths do. The flower is, however, of little consequence. Plant out a sufficient stock of young plants in the spring. They make a great growth in any good soil.

Put in cuttings in September. The cuttings should not be made of the hardest part of the stems, and should always be of two eyes, as we depend on growths from the bottom eye. We like the propagating bed for these cuttings. They root rather slowly, but surely. Keep in 3-inch pots till January in any cool house and then shift into 3-inch. As they grow they will need the edge of the bench, or the edge of a rose or carnation bench, so that their long growths can hang down.

Some growers lift up the plants from the field in October and stand on the edge of the benches. They make fine decorative plants for some occasions, as their numerous growths will be several feet long. In February they divide the large plants and pot into 3 or 4-inch pots.

The young growths are troubled with green fly. Any soil and any cool house will grow them, and they need little light till they begin to make their growth in early spring. Use good rich soil when shifting from 2 to 3-inch, as you want them to grow fast.

Vinca minor, often strangely called myrtle by our people, is perfectly hardy. Where grass won't grow in shady city lots it covers the ground finely. It can be divided and planted either in spring or fall and will quickly cover the ground.

Vinca rosea is a very different plant and requires a warm house in winter. It makes a pretty greenhouse plant, but its chief use with us is in the flower garden, where it makes a very pretty bed, and a change from the high colored geraniums. It can be easily raised from seed sown in January and grown on in a light, warm house, and needs an occasional pinching to make the plants bushy.

Plants can also be lifted and after New Year's cut back, when you will get young growths which root freely. Don't plant out till frost is surely past.

VIOLET.

The violets we grow are varieties of V. odorata. There is ever an increasing love of the violet, and it seems that the past three or four years the quantity grown and sold is enormous. Violets are rather a precarious crop here; if you fail you fail entirely. In milder climates where only the protection of a cold-frame is needed there is not so much fear of failure. South of Baltimore violets are grown in cold-frames and covered with mats in cold weather. That would not do for us, although with careful attention you can have a lot in the cold-frames that will give you flowers sometimes till Christmas, and again in April, and for later they are better than those grown all winter inside.

Fine crops of violets have been grown by several methods. And many yet adhere to the plan of planting out

Bed of Vinca Rosea.

the young stock in May and lifting in September, and planting in six inches of soil on a bench. If you are successful that way keep on. I, however, have seen many failures that way, and believe in and practice a method that is I think more natural to the plant, and by which method I have for several seasons now been entirely successful. Without mentioning the methods of other people or what I don't practice I will at once give my plan and experience.

I have repeatedly tried both the runners and division of the old plant, and have decidedly the best results with the runners, cut off in February and put in the sand as we do other cuttings. As we use no bottom heat for them flats with two inches of sand will do just as well. When well rooted we pot into 2½-inch pots and keep for a few weeks in a carnation house temperature, and give them the full light. By middle to end of April we put them into a cold-frame and by middle of May remove the sash entirely. There they will grow stout and strong. Early in June we plant them about ten inches apart on the benches.

I will stop here to say that a violet house should be equal span, running north and south, with solid beds. The walls need not be over 2 feet high and the paths can be dug out 1 foot, which leaves the surface of the beds at a convenient height to work; 19 feet is a good width, with two side benches, two paths and a 6-foot 6-in. middle bed. Although the plants in the middle of the center bench are ten feet from the glass they are just as

good as those on the side bench that are only two feet from the glass. The pipes are hung on the side walls a foot above the plants; no heat descends to cause red spider. Three 2-inch hot water pipes on each side will heat this house very nicely. A small house will do as well, but it is much cheaper to build the larger house than two small ones.

The beds being solid, we remove the top six inches of soil and fork in some bone dust another six inches deep, then put on our new soil. A rather heavy loam suits them best, but not at all stiff. Violets don't like fresh animal manure and if the compost is put up the fall previous it will be to advantage. It need not be turfy soil such as you would look for in rose growing. We have used the top five inches of a clover sod and found it excellent. When piling it up add an eighth of well rotted cow manure, and when chopping over in spring for use add half a peck of bone flour to every cubic yard. Make the bed only moderately firm.

For two seasons we removed the glass entirely. This you can do if your roof is sash, or better still, butted glass, but on building a larger house we rather begrudged the labor and removed only every third run of glass. As the sun moves, or rather we do, the same plants do not get the sun for very long and when it rains those immediately below get the benefit of the rain, but that is easily regulated in watering. The remainder of the glass is shaded. This plan gives a perfect circulation of air and keeps the house

cool. If I could not remove the glass then I would have a continuous foot of ventilation in both side walls.

The violets soon begin to grow and need plenty of water during all times. Up to New Year's you should keep the runners cut off. Not the stout little off shoots that are near the original crown, let them remain, but the real runners that make a growth of three or four inches. During summer and at all times violets must be kept scrupulously clean. There is work about them and so there is about anything that there is an honest dollar in. You must go over them repeatedly and clean off imperfect flowers, yellow leaves, etc.

During July, August and September the violets must be frequently syringed to keep down red spider. Don't sprinkle them just to make them moist, but let them have a sharp, fine stream with the hose every two or three days, and remember the spider is on the underside of the leaf. If you let red spider get a foothold in August you will have a great job to get rid of them by October, when too much syringing would not be good, but syringing in the hot months is beneficial. If your violets are clean of spider by end of September there is little fear of your being troubled with them after that. During winter they do not want any syringing, but want plenty of water at the roots, which can be given copiously without wetting the leaves. We put our glass in towards end of September. Top ventilation is then plenty.

Firing should be put off till there is

danger of the houses going below 40 degrees at night, but a little fire with the ventilators open will do good in a wet, cool time. By fire heat we like to keep the houses about 40 to 42 degrees at night and 55 degrees in day time. If sun heat goes up to 60 or 65 degrees no harm is done. Green fly does not trouble the violets in summer but appears often in September or October. For that we vaporize with tobacco extract, being careful not to make it too strong.

End of October we clean the beds carefully, sprinkle on some bone flour and stir it into the soil, and then put on half an inch of rotten leaves or very rotten manure.

The chief trouble with the violet is the spot, which is probably a mould or fungus, and has been proved to be spread by syringing. I know of nothing else but picking off the affected leaf the moment you see it. It appears first as a little black speck and then radiates out, killing the tissue. Some application of sulphur or Bordeaux mixture might destroy it, but either will destroy every leaf of the violet. We have tried the Bordeaux mixture and had a most convincing experiment. We do not consider the spot at all dangerous if you keep your foliage dry and maintain a genial dry atmosphere, and destroy the leaves whenever you discover it.

The violet is subject to a small green slug which appears in the autumn. Perhaps this small half-inch long worm is the larva of some beetle. It riddles the leaves sadly. I have never been troubled with it, but have frequently seen it, and saw it destroyed by an application of flour and paris green dusted thoroughly among the leaves.

What we most dread is what we call "curled leaf," when the young leaves curl and wrinkle up. An authority informs me that it is caused by a minute fly that punctures the leaf and lays an egg that destroys the tissue. We have seen the fly. Tobacco in any form has no effect on it. As a preventive we have used the hydrocyanic acid gas, and it had nothing but the very best results on violets. And it destroys all kinds of aphis or anything that has lungs.

A little experience with this deadly gas very recently may be of interest. We generated the gas to kill the black fly on chrysanthemums, but brought into the house a plant each of Adiantums cuneatum and Farleyense, both of which had young, tender fronds. After the operation we found that a few of the very tips of the chrysanthemums were touched, mostly near where the jars stood, but the ferns the next day or since have not shown the slightest effects from it. The formula for this gas is in article on Fungicides and Insecticides.

We are often asked for pots of violets, and it is quite an Easter plant. They would not last long in a living room, however well established, and we cannot grow a plant so satisfactorily as by lifting a few of the best budded a week or ten days before they are wanted.

There are several varieties of this sweet flower, but we cannot find one to suit the public, or so satisfactory to grow and flower, as Marie Louise, the beautiful blue with more or less white eye; the better grown the less eye. Farquhar is no improvement. The old Neapolitan is a beautiful violet and is still grown by some, but its color is not liked by the many. You don't want many white violets; about a tenth of your stock. All of the above want the same treatment.

The strong growing single flowered California can be grown in the same way, or it does very well planted out and lifted in September. They sell very well, but not equal to the double. The California does not want its runners cut off after November, as from the runners you soon get flowers. A few plants should always be grown for their leaves, which are always in abundance, and fine, small green galax violet; it is better than robbing our plants of their leaves.

WATERING.

No subject connected with horticulture is more difficult to handle than this. You cannot give any specific directions; you can only give general ideas. Watering occupies much of the labor of a florist and its proper execution is of the greatest importance. Plants in the ground are assisted occasionally by artificial watering, but with our entirely artificial way of growing them on benches and in pots and tubs they are entirely dependent on our attendance to their most important element, water.

I remarked some years ago that good waterers, like poets, are born not made. Here again is the most truly mental part of our business. The mechanical application is considerable, but not near as important as the knowledge and judgment required to know just when to water. A gentleman at the Canadian Horticultural convention, lately assembled at Ottawa, expressed his admiration for the exclusive use of the watering pot in the European gardens.

The writer has had a good deal of practice with the watering can, both here and in Great Britain, and has not the slightest veneration for the watering pot or its use. We don't believe that the production of fine plants has anything to do with the use of them and believe the hose has many advantages and no disadvantages that we can see. It is simply a matter of who is handling it. The hose in the hands of a careless man may be dan-

House of Violets.

gerous to the plants from over watering, while if the same man had to carry water in cans he would be probably too lazy and the plants would suffer for want of water. The watering can is laborious, slow, and expensive. The hose is one-tenth the labor; no excuse for scrimping the plants, the water can be applied at any degree of speed, and the hose can be used as a syringe to perfection.

You can soak a carnation bed in the month of May in one-twentieth of the time you could with a can. You can run a stream among violets in November without wetting their leaves far better than you can with a watering pot. You can water a bench of geraniums in the month of May with pleasure and do it thoroughly. You can with a very slow stream look over all your palms at any season. You can water a 7-foot bench of lilies perfectly when they are standing pretty close together, which you could hardly do at all with a watering pot. You can with a fine rose attached moisten the most particular orchid, or water a propagating bed, or even a flat of seeds if you know how to handle the hose. In fact, you can do anything and everything with a hose connected with watering or syringing plants, and to go back to the old watering pot would be as bad as a Manitoba wheat farmer discarding the gang plow and adopting the peculiar method described by Dean Swift's Gulliver who dropped on a race of people who plowed their land by burying in their fields acorns and then drove the pigs in which hunting with their noses for the acorns, disturbed the soil. And the handling of 4-gallon watering cans at a tender age used to produce a corn on our palms.

It is merely the science of handling the hose. A man to be a first class hand at watering in plant houses should have perfect sight. We had a man for several years who in other respects was a zealous worker, but would miss plants here and there and leave plants that were very dry without a drop of water. When he left us he donned spectacles. He was very short sighted and had always been so but did not want us to know it.

We have read in a very good little volume on floriculture that a man watered a house in a very few minutes by spraying the whole lot. We don't of course believe in any such work. Pouring a stream of water over a mixed lot of plants would be absurd. The houses that contain only one kind of plants are much more simple to water than a house or bench containing several, or perhaps twenty, but as we have all plants standing in blocks, each sort by themselves, it is yet simple to distinguish whether this batch wants it or whether it would be better left till to-morrow.

We don't all have whole houses or benches of one plant. Just now, October, a very particular month for watering, you may have on a bench a few ericas, next azaleas, next some Harrisii lilies, next pot chrysanthe-

mums, next acacias, next cyclamen, next some flowering geraniums. Some may want water and some are much better left to the following morning, and if your hose is running slowly how easy to pass on to the next batch. Some men have to be told repeatedly that they do not get through watering any faster by letting such a strong steam run, and do not do the work so well. Whatever judgment is required about quantity for a bench, there is very little about watering plants in pots. If they want watering they want it, and that means that the space between the soil and rim of pot is filled with water; that is a watering, and that is what we tell our customers when they ask the question, "How much water shall I give it?"

Now, if the stream is moderately slow the water you pour on will remain and fill up, but if a strong stream it will dash off onto the bench and leave the plant deficient of water. In April and May and the summer months a less experienced hand can water many things for there is less danger of overwatering, and if the benches and paths receive a lot of overflow no harm is done, for you want to damp down as it is, when evaporation is great.

It is quite different in October and November when there is little fire heat and superfluous moisture would be injurious. As you pass along with the hose you water the flowering geranium without any syringing, and you come to 500 achyranthes that want not only watering but a good syringing too. The cinerarias won't want syringing but the cytisus will. And there you have with your hose and your forefinger in watering can and syringe in one.

After middle of May watering in plant houses can be done in the afternoon. In fall, winter and early spring it should be done in the morning. Perhaps it is the color of the soil, perhaps it is instinct or long practice that enables us to see at a glance when a plant or batch of plants needs water. A practiced hand will know that the plants along the back of the bench where the heat of the pipes may be coming up, or the front row where the sun and air gets more play at them, may want water while the rest do not. So he will run his hose along those rows and say to himself if he is thinking of his business and not of his best girl, "Tomorrow the whole lot will take it."

The quantity of water that a plant in pot needs, as before said, is not a question; it wants water or it does not. It never wants a little. With a bench of carnations or roses it is different. I believe except in hot weather in spring that no more should be given a bench than will go thoroughly to the bottom, and no more, but be sure you give it enough to do that. This is not so easy to determine, but practice and observation will ere one or two waterings will soon teach you about how much will be proper, and it should be applied softly, either with a rose attach-

ed to the hose, which is quickly unscrewed when you want to begin to syringe, or with a piece of flattened tin attached to hose, off which it passes in a gentle stream.

Some authors say a plant should be allowed to get rather on the dry side and then be given water. Plants going to partial or entire rest in the fall will of course want to be allowed to get more and more often dry, but it is not so with our roses, carnations, violets, or our lilies or cyclamen or geraniums, or any plants that are growing fast, especially in spring.

Have you ever noticed that a batch of plants, let it be fuchsias or geraniums or roses in pots, or anything else that is growing fast, that are plunged to their rims in refuse hops, ashes or tanbark, will far outstrip a batch of the same sort with the pots bare. There is no evaporation from the sides of the plunged pot and consequently a more uniform moisture, and that is the sole reason. This is very marked and a good lesson for us. Letting plants whose roots are active get repeatedly on the dry side day after day will tell on them and stunt their growth compared with those that are kept at a more uniform moisture. This may be of no detriment to our bedding geraniums or coleus or cannas, but it is to the plants that we want to make a fine growth or produce fine flowers.

Some may say, look at the plants in the field. "My carnations have not had a drop of water or rain in six weeks, but they are growing." They are under entirely different conditions. We hoe the surface, or ought to. Evaporation from the ground is continually going on, and the looser we keep the surface the faster will be evaporation, and the more evaporation from the surface the more moisture rises to the surface from the depths of the ground to nourish the roots. This is called

RUBBER HOSE

For Florists, Seedsmen, Nurserymen, Gardeners, Etc.

Zinnias.

capillary attraction. Hence it follows that the deeper we have plowed or dug, or the more we have broken up the subsoil, the better will be the law of capillary attraction benefit the plant. So there is a more uniform moisture at the root than you think, even in the dryest time.

All this benefit is of course cut off entirely in cultivating in pots and on bench.

Have you ever noticed where a drain or sewer was laid four feet deep in a stiff clay the grass for years over the drain will be green in the dryest time, because by the disturbance and breaking up of the soil capillary attraction is helped?

The sub-watering experiments on our benches is yet too new for me to enter into, and our trade papers have given full accounts of the methods. Something practical may be yet evolved by our learned professors.

In conclusion you should keep one man watering one house. He may water half a dozen, but if it is the same man and he is a gardener he will remember the condition that he left the plants on the previous day,

and will know just about what will want it the next. A good, intelligent, faithful waterer is as valuable a man as you have on your place.

ZINNIA.

The annual zinnias are the only ones in which the florist is interested. With selection and culture, they are now among the handsomest of our annuals for the border, and in certain places a whole bed of them, in many shades, is very striking.

They are very easy to grow and need only the ordinary treatment given many other annuals, except that no frost must ever touch them while in a cold-frame. Sow from the middle to the end of March, and when an inch high transplant into flats two inches apart. By the middle of April a cold-frame is the right place for them. Plant in beds or borders after there is no danger of frost.

They are strong, rampant growers, and should have plenty of room; eighteen inches to two feet apart is close enough. They should have a well tilled piece of ground and will then

stand our hot, and often dry, summers better than most of our summer flowering plants.

While the zinnia well deserves a place in the flower garden, it is the most unpopular of all flowers for even the cheapest sort of a bouquet. The poorest purchaser does not want them at any price. We have noticed this so often that we never cut them, however short of cheap flowers we may be. This proves that there is an unconscious taste for the artistic, even among the most lowly. The zinnia is so absolutely regular in form, stiff and formal, one flower being exactly like another, that the eye rebels against it. In a bunch of roses, carnations, or almost any other flower, no two are precisely alike, but the zinnias look as though they all came out of one mould. Then again, the stem is so rigid that while it is all right on the plant, it detracts from the flower when cut.

Grow zinnias to make your border gay, but don't offer the cut flowers to your customers. We raise quantities every year and sell the young plants from the flats at 25 cents per dozen.

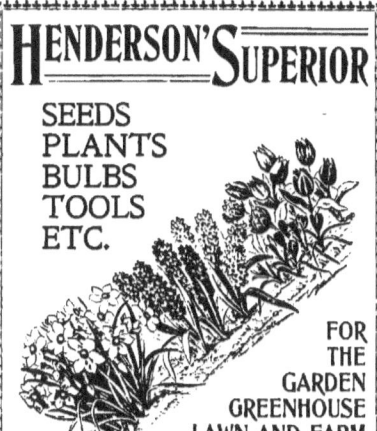

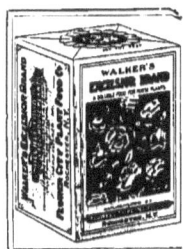
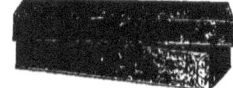

THOS. W. WEATHERED'S SONS,

ESTABLISHED 1859.

Horticultural Architects and Builders

....AND MANUFACTURERS OF....

GREENHOUSE HEATING AND VENTILATING APPARATUS.

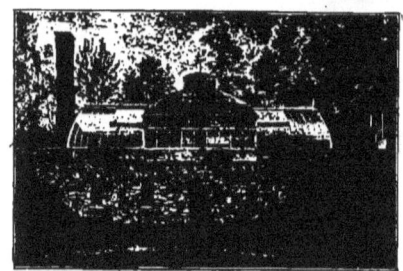

Winners of the Highest Award....

AT THE WORLD'S FAIR;
THE DEAN GOLD MEDAL, MADISON SQUARE GARDEN, FOR BEST AMATEUR GREENHOUSE;
CERTIFICATE OF MERIT, SOCIETY AMERICAN FLORISTS, and the
SILVER MEDAL FOR 1898 of the N. Y. FLORISTS' CLUB.

REPORT OF JUDGES:

Model of Iron Frame Greenhouse combining many good qualities, and the Committee consider same worthy of special mention. Points awarded:

Utility	30
Simplicity	25
Desirability	20
Cheapness	15
	90

(Signed) JOHN N. MAY, Chairman,
JULIUS ROEHRS,
LAWRENCE HAFNER, } Judges.
A. S. BURNS,

CONSERVATORIES, GREENHOUSES, Etc., erected complete of our patent Iron Frame Construction, or of Wood and Iron combined, or of Wood alone. Hot-Bed Sash, Frames, etc.

Self=Feeding Hot Water Boilers....

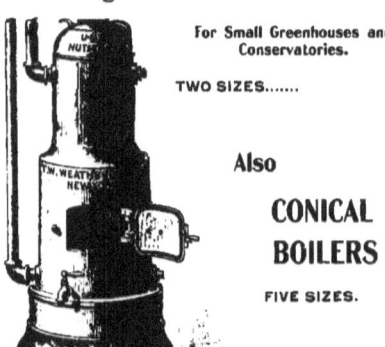

For Small Greenhouses and Conservatories.

TWO SIZES.......

Also

CONICAL

BOILERS

FIVE SIZES.

THE WEATHERED

PATENT IMPROVED SECTIONAL BOILER

1899 MODEL,

For Water or Steam Heating

ABSOLUTELY SECTIONAL IN EVERY PART.

SECTIONAL VIEW.

A Few Points Claimed for this Boiler:

Simplicity of construction.
Sectional headers.
Sectional ash-pit.
Maximum vertical circulation.
Minimum friction.
Direct or indirect draft.
Smoke-box on front or back.
Rapidity of water circulation.
Easily cleaned in every part.
Grates on level with fire-door opening.
Greatest amount of boiler surface exposed to radiant heat.
Heating surfaces so arranged in fire-box that the hot gases must strike every part before entering combustion chamber.

Send four cents for catalogue, Greenhouse Construction or Greenhouse Heating.

THOS. W. WEATHERED'S SONS, FACTORY, 196 to 240 Orient Ave., Jersey City, N. J. OFFICE, 46 and 48 Marion St. (New Elm St.), New York.